UNDERSTANDING
CONTEMPORARY IRELAND

Edited by
Brendan Bartley and Rob Kitchin

Pluto  Press
LONDON • DUBLIN • ANN ARBOR, MI

First published 2007 by Pluto Press
345 Archway Road, London N6 5AA
and 839 Greene Street, Ann Arbor, MI 48106

Distributed in the Republic of Ireland and Northern Ireland by
Gill & Macmillan Distribution, Hume Avenue, Park West, Dublin 12, Ireland.
Phone +353 1 500 9500. Fax +353 1 500 9599. E-Mail: sales@gillmacmillan.ie

www.plutobooks.com

British Library Cataloguing in Publication Data
A catalogue record for this book is available from the British Library

Hardback
ISBN-13   978 0 7453 2595 8
ISBN-10   0 7453 2595 5

Paperback
ISBN-13   978 0 7453 2594 1
ISBN-10   0 7453 2594 7

Library of Congress Cataloging in Publication Data applied for

10 9 8 7 6 5 4 3 2 1

Designed and produced for Pluto Press by
Chase Publishing Services Ltd, Fortescue, Sidmouth, EX10 9QG, England
Typeset from disk by Stanford DTP Services, Northampton, England
Printed and bound in India

Dedicated to John Driscoll and Tim O'Connor

Acknowledgements

We would like to thank all the contributors to this volume for writing an interesting set of chapters that followed our brief; Aine Smith, Mary O'Brien, Tara Wynne and Martin Charlton for producing some of the maps and data; and Emma Murphy for help with some editorial tasks. The Department of Environment, Heritage and Local Government generously supported the production of this work through a publication grant. We also thank Jong Kim, Masterplan Associates, Town Planning and Development Consultants, <www.masterplan.ie> for additional financial support.

Figures 1.4, 1.5, 3.1, 3.2, 4.1, 4.2, 5.3, 6.1, 9.2, 9.4, 9.5, 13.1, 18.1, 18.2, 18.3, 19.1, 19.3, and 20.1 are reproduced by kind permission of Ordnance Survey, © Ordnance Survey Ireland/Government of Ireland, Copyright Permit No. MP005706.

Contents

LIST OF FIGURES

LIST OF TABLES

1

Ireland in the Twenty-first Century

Rob Kitchin and Brendan Bartley

By any standards, the Republic of Ireland (henceforth Ireland) is a country that has undergone enormous transformations since the start of the 1990s. Economically, socially, culturally, politically, environmentally, there have been profound changes to the Irish landscape and everyday life. Concurrently, Ireland's position on the world stage has been elevated. Ireland is no longer a poor nation on the periphery of Europe characterised by a weak economy and high emigration. Ireland is a country with a booming economy that is the envy of many nations. Economic growth over the last decade has been double or more that of its European neighbours, and wealth levels in terms of average income are amongst the highest of any developed nation. A sustained growth in population, fuelled by return migration, immigrants seeking work, and natural increase, has meant that in 2004 the population exceeded 4 million for the first time since 1871 (CSO 2004a). Irish culture has a high cache globally – Irish music, literature, fashion, art, dance, and pubs have become global phenomena (think U2, Enya, Seamus Heaney, John Connolly, John Rocha, Waterford Crystal, Riverdance, and so on). Huge strides forward have been made in addressing the so-called 'Irish problem' – 'the Troubles' of Northern Ireland, first with a cease-fire in 1994, followed by the Good Friday Agreement in 1998 and the peace process in general. As a result of these changes, being Irish has gained cultural capital (in Bourdieu's, 1984, terms), as evidenced by the resurgence in diasporic identity and the popularity of St Patrick's Day events in numerous countries (some 2 million people were reported to have either taken part in, or watched, the New York parade in 2006; O'Driscoll, 2006).

It is little wonder then that Ireland's success story has become the focus of attention for economic analysts and social commentators from around the world. Ireland demonstrates that radical transformation on a number of fronts is possible in a relatively short space of time. Negative features such as a stagnant economy, a relatively moribund social order, and political conflict have been tackled and transformed into virtuous trends in ways that were beyond comprehension in the 1980s. Ireland has thus become a place that other countries want to emulate, particularly those of Eastern Europe, which have experienced similar situations in their past and whose social, economic and political situation at present is similar to pre-Celtic Tiger Ireland. It also holds lessons for other developed nations (for example, it is possible to ask what the economically depressed areas of the north-eastern United States can learn from the Irish strategy and experience). These countries even send their students, policy makers and government officials to Ireland to identify lessons that might help them to re-energise their economies and tackle issues of social development. As strange as it may sound to many Irish people who have witnessed the recent changes and are familiar with on-going problems in Irish society, other countries proclaim that they 'want to be the next Ireland' (for example, Hungary).

This book examines Ireland in the twenty-first century. It sets out to document the various ways that Ireland has changed over the past 15 years or so (while still placing that within the context of longer-term, historical development), the key drivers shaping change, and how government, policy makers and workers on the ground have managed the transformations occurring through specific policies and interventions. In particular, it provides a *spatial* analysis that recognises that Ireland is not a homogenous country, and that there are significant variations in the patterns and processes of phenomena and the ways in which policy interventions are scaled. For example, the situation with regard to housing, transport, tourism, and industry, to take a selection of issues, is markedly different in urban and rural areas, and varies dramatically between different parts of the country (contrast for example the differences between the Atlantic seaboard and the Dublin Metropolitan Region). Interventions take place on different scales – local, county, regional, national – driven by policy itself formulated and implemented on varying scales including the international (European Union, United Nations, etc.). In short, the contributors highlight the various ways in which geography matters for what is occurring in Ireland, but also for understanding the ongoing transformations of the country. Undertaking this kind of analysis is important because it is often overlooked by social scientists who instead focus on undertaking more traditional, aspatial, social and economic investigations. In taking space seriously, the contributors provide a platform for us to think about Ireland differently, in a fundamental, applied, and policy-oriented sense. In doing so, they provide fresh insight into Ireland in the twenty-first century.

In this introductory chapter, we provide a broad overview and explanation of some of the changes that have taken place, and examine their consequences. In the first section we provide a brief picture of Ireland in the 1980s as a benchmark for understanding and evaluating the transformation of Ireland in the 1990s and early 2000s. In the following section we outline six key trends and phenomena that underpin the changes that have occurred, and detail what some of their key effects have been. In the penultimate section we explore some problems by-passed or even exacerbated by these trends, before drawing some conclusions.

IRELAND IN THE 1980s

Like the rest of the developed world, Ireland was seriously affected by the global recession of the late 1970s and early 1980s. The economic growth of the early to mid-1970s ground to a halt in the aftermath of the 1970s world oil crisis and could not be redeemed by government efforts to prime renewed development through tax reductions and an increase in public spending. In fact, increased public spending became a liability so that by the early 1980s the country was on the brink of bankruptcy and acknowledged to be spending beyond its means. This led to further emergency measures including a series of cutbacks in services together with tax increases to cover public finance deficits. Ferriter (2004) reports that at one point the foreign debt was equivalent to €7,620 for every income tax payer and that income tax payments were barely covering the interest due. The situation was exacerbated by interest rate increases. Between 1980 and 1983 interest rates were above 15 per cent, and at times over 20 per cent, before falling to 5 per cent by 1985, and the Irish pound struggled against other currencies (Kelly, 2003). At the same time, between 1979 and 1985 unemployment rose from 7.8 per cent to 18.2 per cent, with 26 per cent of people 'living below a poverty threshold set at 40 per cent of average income in the EU', the EU average being 16 per cent of people (Ferriter, 2004: 670–1). By 1987, Irish GDP was 63 per cent of the EU average making it the second poorest country in the EU behind Portugal (Breathnach, 1998).

As a result of economic instability and the attendant social hardships, the 1980s was a time of political instability and tension and conflict between state, employers and unions. There were three general elections between June 1981 and November 1982 with successive governments faltering under their spending ambitions and proposed tax reforms, and the fact that their policies were often underpinned by short-term political visions aimed at appeasing the electorate rather than tackling spiralling debt and rising inflation. The minor parties and independent candidates gained the balance of power hampering the ability of any single party to rule by fiat; backbenchers constantly threatened to revolt, and the opposition parties opposed almost anything the ruling parties tried to achieve. As a result, policies were often compromised by trying to pull in different directions simultaneously, making it difficult to achieve a coherent overall policy with associated long-term strategy or appropriate remedial interventions.

In addition, social conservatism dominated civic life and the social agenda, with the result that Ireland remained relatively conservative in its social attitudes in comparison to its European neighbours. The bans on contraception, divorce, abortion and homosexuality, all made or reconfirmed as illegal in the 1937 constitution, remained in place at the start of the 1980s. Contraception became legal to buy for over 18s in 1985. A divorce referendum was lost in 1986 (though won in 1995), and abortion referenda were lost in 1983 and 1992. The legal status of homosexuality was challenged in the High and Supreme Courts at the start of the 1980s, but rejected in both cases, although it was eventually over-ruled by the European Court of Human Rights in 1988 and decriminalised in 1993 (Hug, 1999). The Catholic Church continued to play a pivotal role in welfare and education, providing many social services through its various charities and associations, and running the majority of schools.

Both the dire economic situation and the stifling social conditions led to widespread emigration during the 1980s. Crucially this emigration included large numbers of young, well-educated people seeking a better life overseas. For example, Ferriter (2004) reports that 36 per cent of students earning a degree in 1988 emigrated, with NESC (1991) documenting that some 70 per cent of all emigrants were under the age of 25. Over the period 1981–85, the net out-migration was on average 15,000 people each year, rising to 35,000 per year over the period 1986–89.[1] Net out-migration was over 40,000 people in both 1988 and 1989 (with 61,000 and 71,000 respectively leaving, whilst 19,000 and 27,000 returned), totalling some 2 per cent of overall population.

At the same time, the political conflict in Northern Ireland continued to cast a shadow over Ireland and its relations with its main economic market, the UK. The Troubles continued throughout the 1980s claiming the lives of 890 people between 1980 and 1989 (McKittrick et al., 1999). The intransigence of all sides, plus the presence and strength of paramilitary groups, countered by the RUC and British Army, made the prospect of peace seem unlikely in the short term.

The combination of a struggling economy, stifling social order, widespread emigration, and a political conflict on its doorstep that was seemingly fought in its name (but with very mixed support in Ireland), provided few clues as to the transformation that was to occur in the following decade. Ireland was very much seen as a small, poor, peripheral country of low international importance, and relatively poor future prospects beyond small-to-medium-size indigenous companies, foreign direct investment in low-skill manufacturing, and EU subsidies. Given the volatile and disastrous situation of the previous few years, the prospects for slow, or even steady and stable growth did not look promising, let alone the success story of the Celtic Tiger era. Indeed, in 1988 *The Economist* concluded that Ireland looked to be heading for catastrophe due to its spending on public services that the country was too poor to maintain (*The Economist*, 2004).

THE GREAT TRANSFORMATION

From the early 1990s through to the time of writing, Ireland has been transformed from the poor, peripheral nation of the 1980s to a largely prosperous, confident, multicultural, globally embedded nation. In this section we chart six broad sets of factors – social partnership and the planning regime, foreign direct investment, the European Union, the peace process, secularisation and social change, and population change and increased mobility – that have led to, but also at the same time are outcomes of, the transformation of economy and society.

Social Partnership and the Planning Regime

Although sometimes overlooked in the analysis of the Celtic Tiger in favour of economic and educational explanations, the start of the social partnership movement and the reorientation of the planning system in the mid-to-late 1980s provided a platform that was conducive to economic growth and stability. As Larragy and Bartley note in Chapter 14, the social partnership movement arose out of the political and economic turmoil of the early-to-mid 1980s.

In an effort to curb industrial unrest and garner political support for harsh spending cuts, the government, through the Programme for National Recovery (PNR), offered social partners (employer, trade union and farmer organisations) a set plan of pay growth over the coming years, with the promise of wage increases if conditions improved. By making the social partners part of the political process, rather than being in opposition to it, negotiated settlement was achieved, thus providing labour stability and removing the threat of strikes. The social partnership process has proved highly successful, operating ever since, widening to include community and voluntary partners, and providing long-term, stable employer–employee relations. Importantly, in the early 1990s the social partnership model was broadened to include local development initiatives through the creation of local and area-based partnership companies designed to drive local economic change. They included rural programmes such as LEADER started in 1991 and County/City Enterprise Boards (CEBs) set up in 1993. Designed to be flexible, proactive, market-responsive and user-oriented, local development partnerships were able to cut through red-tape to drive change. In effect, they provided a new third way – a middle route between the perceived inertia of the public sector and the dangerous strivings of the market. They have proven to be important sources of indigenous economic development.

At approximately the same time, the approach to planning started to be transformed with a move in 1986 to designate certain zones for regeneration using tax emption and public–private partnerships as a mechanism to encourage and drive development. In a change of focus from wide-scale, regional-level, spatial planning policies, the new approach targeted very select, flagship sites that would seek to attract specific industries, notably those of the service sector. As a result, planning became more pragmatic, flexible and results-oriented, focusing on areas that were perceived to have the highest potential for success. This change in approach provided the planning conditions conducive to encouraging inward investment, gentrification, and speculative property development. For example, the first urban development corporation, the Custom House Docks Development Authority (CHDDA) was a public–private partnership charged with regenerating a central Dublin site (see Chapter 2). The development provided the location for the International Financial Services Centre (IFSC) that subsequently attracted significant numbers of banking and financial companies to Ireland. The Industrial Development Agency (IDA) was similarly charged with encouraging inward investment by skilled, manufacturing companies to selected, ready-made and serviced sites, accompanied by grants and other incentives. Planning thus became more responsive to creating the environmental and spatial conditions necessary to attract inward investment.

Foreign Direct Investment

Since shifting away from the protectionist policy operating until the late 1950s, Ireland has sought foreign direct investment (FDI) into its economy. The State's aim was to take advantage of the increasingly mobile and global nature of businesses as they sought to maximise their profits by locating elements of their production in cheaper places and by opening up new markets. Foreign direct investment is highly attractive because not only does it create direct employment within these companies, but they provide markets to indigenous companies, stimulating domestic industrial growth. Breathnach (1998) argues that in the Irish case for every 100 jobs created by FDI, 125 jobs have been created elsewhere in the Irish economy. The business taxes raised from industrial activity by both foreign-owned and indigenous companies flow into the exchequer and the wages that employees earn are spent locally, further supporting local businesses. Moreover, FDI helps to build international networks and linkages that in turn help to plug indigenous businesses into the global economy and attract export income. In other words, FDI is seen as a vital ingredient to sustain a growing economy.

In the main, up until the late 1980s Ireland attracted US-owned, low-skill, export-oriented manufacturing plants. They located in Ireland to take advantage of low-cost and educated labour, government subsidies, and access to European markets. The key question facing Irish policy makers and government in the 1980s was how to make Ireland an attractive place to locate high-skill, high-value FDI in both manufacturing and services given that every country was keen to attract multinational companies. On the negative side, given Ireland's political and economic troubles, the economy as viewed from outside Ireland did not inspire confidence. Success breeds success and companies are more likely to locate where they can see others doing well. Moreover, the country was perceived as being peripheral with poor intercontinental links as compared to other countries. On the positive side, Ireland had a ready supply of young, relatively cheap, highly educated and skilled labour, who spoke English, plus a huge reserve of relatively untapped female labour that would sustain employment growth. The 1991 census reported that 44 per cent of the population was under the age of 25, the highest proportion in the European Union (Ferriter, 2004). In addition, Ireland was a member of the European Union giving access to these markets with reduced tariffs. The Irish government and Industrial Development Agency (IDA) set about adding to these positive factors by creating a set of additional incentives. As noted in the previous subsection this included a shift to entrepreneurial planning to create the necessary infrastructure, but also included economic measures such as providing a favourable corporate tax rate, offering grant subsidies for the building of facilities, providing necessary resources and infrastructures, and reducing bureaucracy and red-tape.

Corporate tax in Ireland, combining capital gains, income and corporation profits tax, is very favourable to FDI. A 10 per cent tax rate for manufacturing was introduced in 1981. This was increased and extended to a rate of 12.5 per cent for all corporate trading profits in the mid-1990s. Tax rates in other competitor European countries are much higher giving Ireland a significant competitive advantage in attracting inward investors.[2] While the exchequer takes less tax from each company, it gains through inward investment as well as job and wealth creation elsewhere in the economy. In short, it benefits from the 'momentum effect' – 12.5 per cent of a large stock of declared profits yields a much higher tax return than 30 or more per cent of a small profit base. In addition, low personal income tax rates (one of the lowest in Europe[3]) have been attractive in recruiting and retaining skilled labour.

These policies, plus the energetic work of the IDA, reaped rewards leading a number of companies to locate high-skilled manufacturing plants (see Chapter 9) and low-skilled service work (see Chapter 10) in Ireland. The priority from the mid to late 1990s was to use FDI successes to leverage an upscaling of activities by companies already in Ireland, and to attract higher-skilled service jobs. So, in the case of high-skilled manufacturing and low-skilled service companies, they were encouraged to locate their financial and business services, research and development, and marketing functions in Ireland, with their base of operation becoming the headquarters for European operations. The secret here has been to hook in companies, demonstrate the benefits of locating in Ireland, and then to reel in other parts of their business. It has been a highly successful strategy. Ireland's corporate tax, repatriation of profits policy, and tax exemptions on certain patents, have helped enormously, with other overseas profits being routed through Ireland using internal company cross-border accounting (transfer pricing) to maximise profits.[4] The effect has been to save companies millions of dollars in tax revenue as recent stories in the US media have highlighted in relation to Microsoft and Google (Simpson, 2005). As a result, Ireland is reported as being the world's most profitable country for US corporations, with $26.4 billion worth of profit made in 2002.[5] So, while labour is now relatively expensive given its skilled nature and the cost of living in Ireland, savings elsewhere offset these costs. In addition to Microsoft and Google, other major multinationals employing significant numbers of staff include Dell, IBM, Hewlett-Packard, Intel, Pfizer, Wyeth, Xerox, eBay, Oracle, Apple, and others. They are accompanied by hundreds of other smaller foreign direct investments, particularly in services.

The success in attracting significant amounts of foreign direct investment has created and sustained the Celtic Tiger economy. FDI accounted for almost half of Ireland's GDP by the end of the 1990s (OECD, 2001a: 56). From 1994 onwards Ireland has been the fastest growing and highest performing economy in Europe with year-on-year GDP growth often double or more that of its European neighbours (see Figure 1.1). In 2003, the OECD estimated that in terms of GDP per capita, based on Purchasing Power Parities, Ireland was ranked 4th in the world, with GDP per capita estimated at US$ 33,200, with only the US, Norway and Luxembourg ranking higher (ESRI, 2005). Accompanying the boom has been a growth in labour force size and participation rates, and a fall in unemployment. Numbers of persons at work were relatively stable between 1970 and 1991, varying by little more than 100,000 workers (the lowest number being in 1971 at 1.049m workers, the highest in 1990 at 1.165m workers). Between 1992 and 2004 the number of workers increased by 755,000 from 1.165m to 1.920m (Department of Finance, 2005). At the end of 2005 it was estimated that total employment was 1.99m workers (AIB Global Treasury Economic Group, 2005). Unemployment dropped from 15 per cent in 1993 to stabilise at around 4 per cent from 2000 to 2004 (see Figure 1.2).

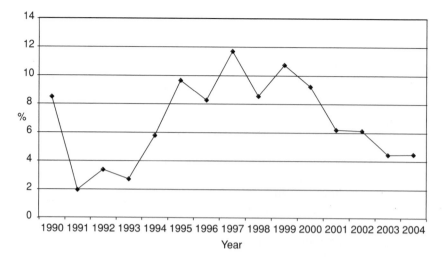

Figure 1.1   Real GDP growth in Ireland, 1990–2004.

Source: OECD (2005)

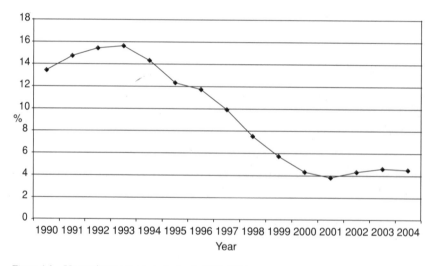

Figure 1.2   Unemployment rate in Ireland, 1990–2004

Source: OECD (2005)

To help sustain the growth in the economy and meet the demand for employees, women were recruited into the workforce. Ferriter (2004) reports that only 5 per cent of married women were employed in 1966 (in large part because of a marriage bar that precluded married women from working except in some sectors such as nursing), but by the close of the twentieth century 40 per cent were working, while 48 per cent of all women were classified as at work in 1997. In addition, Ireland turned to foreign workers to help meet the labour demand, predominantly in relation to low-skilled service work, agriculture and construction, but also in relation to skilled work in the health, education and service sector (see Chapter 17). In 2005, it was estimated that 8 per cent of the workforce (c. 160,000 people) were non-nationals (AIB Global Treasury Economic Group, 2005). As the economy grows, it will become increasingly reliant on such workers to fill vacancies, resulting in Ireland becoming more multicultural.

Some analysts suggest that the Celtic Tiger period came to an end in 2001/02 when Ireland's economy was affected by a global economic downturn following the bursting of the dot.com bubble and the 9/11 attacks in the US, and more locally by the effects of foot and mouth disease on Irish tourism. However, the Irish economy is still growing steadily at rates above most of its European neighbours, driven especially by the boom in the construction sector, suggesting that the Tiger economy is still operating, even if its roar is not so loud.

The European Union (EU) and EMU

Ireland is typically depicted in EU reports as a satisfied and committed member of the European Union (Eurobarometer, 2003). There are understandable reasons for this. The impressive economic growth experienced in Ireland owes much to its membership of the evolving European 'mega-region'. Ireland's entry in 1973 into what was then referred to as the European Economic Community (EEC) was viewed in Ireland as an opportunity to expand Irish markets and reduce the country's over-reliance on trade with Britain. In due course, both of these aspirations were achieved. Trade with other EU states expanded, particularly after the 'Single Market' was created by the Maastricht Treaty in 1992. This treaty effectively eliminated trade barriers between all member states and thereby established a consolidated economic union in Europe which impacted on Ireland in a number of ways. Firstly, it amplified and diversified Ireland's trade linkages to the extent that Ireland now regularly heads various league tables of globalised or 'open economies' based on the degree of export orientation and extent of trade with other countries. Although Britain continued to be Ireland's largest trading partner, by the end of the 1990s other European countries accounted for two thirds of Irish exports (OECD, 2001b). Secondly, it enabled Ireland to become a key gateway for US trade with the EU. The reluctance of Britain to commit fully to the EU project meant that Ireland became even more attractive to American FDI which rose from a little over a third of all foreign investment to account for almost four-fifths of the total by the end of the 1990s (OECD, 1999b). Ireland provided not just a doorway but also a reliable inside route to European markets for US companies with the added bonus of having English as a main language. In turn, American investment has helped to drive the widening of Irish trade linkages which have contributed to Ireland's prosperity and balance of payment surpluses. However, it is important to point out that American FDI is less monolithic now than it was in the late 1990s, and that FDI into Ireland by other (including EU) states, and out of Ireland by thriving indigenous companies (such as Smurfit and Kerry Group) constitute a significant and growing dimension of Ireland's increasingly international trading profile.

The third area of EU impact on Ireland has been in relation to its receipt of financial transfers from EU funds. The benefits accruing to Ireland from EU funding were ratcheted up following the reform in the late 1980s of the EU Structural Funds which targeted support at those poorer parts of the EU that needed structural adjustment support to prepare for and adapt to the 'Single Market'.[6] Ironically, this support continued to be forthcoming in Ireland long after the Irish 'economic miracle' had become embedded. Table 1.1 provides an indicative account of EU contributions to and from Ireland for selected years. It shows that Ireland's net receipts peaked in absolute terms at €2,527.9m in 1997, a period when the Celtic Tiger was moving at full tilt. The fact that this highest level of EU net contribution to Ireland accounted for a decreased proportion of the country's GDP at 3.8 per cent compared to the figures for the previous ten years reflects the increased level of national prosperity in that period. In fact, only six years earlier the net receipt surplus was of the same magnitude (€2,352.8m) but made up 6.2 per cent of the country's GDP. Thus, successive Irish National Development Plans (NDPs) between 1989 and 2006 have been allocated €14.33bn in EU Structural/Cohesion funding contributions (or Community Support Framework) bringing the total figure for transfers since accession in 1973 to about €25.4bn (Bennett and Collins, 2003).

Table 1.1   Ireland's receipts from/payments to EU budget

Year	Receipts from EU budget €m	Payments to EU budget €m	Net receipts €m	% of GDP
1973	47.1	5.7	41.4	1.2
1977	346.5	28.1	318.5	4.4
1983	924.0	234.5	689.5	3.6
1987	1397.1	324.0	1073.1	4.0
1993	2850.9	575.8	2275.1	5.3
1997	3179.9	652.0	2527.9	3.8
2003	2611.6	1190.4	1421.2	1.1
2005*	2395.0	1398.0	997.0	0.6

* Department of Finance estimates

Source: Department of Finance (2005), *Budgetary and Economic Statistics* Table 10.

The NDP is the multi-annual spending programme that underpins national development policy in Ireland. Successive NDPs in Ireland (covering the periods 1989–93; 1994–99; 2000–06) have adapted to EU Cohesion (Regional) Policy and incorporate the Community Support Framework (CSF) for EU Structural and Cohesion Funds. In effect, the NDP sets out total programme spending comprising Structural/Cohesion Funds together with the balance, referred to as Co-financed Investment, required to complete the Community Support Framework. If the first NDP was seen by cynics as a ploy to satisfy EU funding criteria and maximise potential funding, NDPs have recently been seen in a more benign light. The adoption of the programmed, multi-annual spending approach deployed in the NDP is now viewed as evidence of a move to a more systematic and strategic (long-term and integrative) approach to investment based on a more sustainable and enlightened view of resource planning and usage. This positive perception is attributed to the influence of EU policy leveraged by EU funding.

Some commentators have argued that EU financial support was also an important 'bridging' element of the Irish economic success story by contributing to the new institutional environment that emerged in Ireland in the 1990s (Callanan, 2003a; Keogan, 2003). Early funding transfers to Ireland from Europe focused predominantly on compensation for the agricultural sector through the Common Agricultural Policy (CAP). However, a gradual rolling back of funding for agriculture has resulted in new reforms of the CAP that will see a transfer of funding from agriculture to rural development (which is much wider in scope than agricultural activities) in line with the EU's evolving cohesion policy (see Chapter 11). Taken together with the reorientation of the Structural Funds that started in the late 1980s a lead emphasis is now placed on more competitive economic sectors. A new relationship is being created between agricultural and rural, whilst new partnerships are being constructed for rural and urban, built on a broader range of relationships and linkages than applied in the 'agriculture era'. Thus, the main thrust of EU policy and funding has moved towards facilitating leading edge commercial activities and enhancing the competitiveness of all territories including the already strong core urban regions. The evolution of this approach witnessed a move towards fostering a more desirable milieu for innovation and competitiveness throughout the 1990s. It culminated in the adoption of the Lisbon and Gothenburg Agendas which shape the thinking of most governments in Europe.[7] In Ireland, the funding by Europe of local development agencies – including LEADER, area partnership companies and city/county enterprise boards – pump-primed the economic experimentation and local innovation that stimulated the emergence of a more responsive and entrepreneurial governance milieu (see Chapter 13).

The EU also sought to strategically reformulate the roles of its territories so that they could collectively contribute to the creation of a more globally competitive Union. The European Spatial Development Perspective (ESDP) was agreed by the Member States of the European Union, in co-operation with the Commission in May 1999. It endorsed the view that good spatial planning can promote competitiveness and simultaneously address problems of regional disparities. The main aim of the ESDP was to maintain the individual characteristics of the various countries within the EU while simultaneously increasing integration between the member states, socially and economically with the protection of the environment as a core element.

The ESDP places much emphasis on the importance of co-operation between different tiers of government, from local to regional through to community level. In particular, dynamic cities are viewed as the motors of wider, regional economic development in an increasingly competitive global environment. Many of the principles of the ESDP have been incorporated into key Irish strategy documents including the NDP 2000–06 and the Irish National Spatial Strategy (NSS) 2002[8] (Egeraat et al., 2006) (see also Chapters 2 and 3). Thus, key EU principles of social and economic cohesion are stitched into the territorial frameworks provided by the ESDP and NSS. As such, they find expression in the envisaged scenarios of a competitive Europe and Ireland comprised, at their respective scales, of integrated networks of regional territories linked together by a poly-centric (i.e., clustered) city region system which is sustainable, balanced and fair to all.

Another 'bridging' view suggests that EU funding also provided critical support to public sector spending (for training, welfare and infrastructure) that would not otherwise have been available because of the low taxation thresholds and yields applied during the early stages of the Celtic Tiger (Sweeney, 1999). Indeed, as late as the mid-1990s, about 8 per cent of the Irish government's spending budget was provided by EU funding sources (Collins, 2001: 153). While Ireland has been a major net beneficiary of EU financial assistance since its accession to Europe, the period of extensive direct EU financial transfers to Ireland is drawing to a close and the country will soon become a net contributor to the EU budget. The decision by the Irish government to divide the country up into two major regions – comprised of a wealthy region (South East) and a lagging region (Borders, Midlands and West) – for the 2000–06 NDP was undoubtedly the last successful attempt to squeeze significant Structural resources from the EU (see Chapter 3). Ireland's remarkable economic performance over the past two NDPs has seen it converge with and surpass the EU average per capita income so that it no longer merits priority assistance (Objective 1 status).

Ireland faced its most difficult dilemma in relation to EU membership during the mid-1990s when it chose to adopt a common EU currency (the euro) and financial protocols under the aegis of Economic and Monetary Union (EMU) which came into effect in 2002. While this decision was expected to yield political and economic stability in the form of low inflation and interest rates allied to the benefits of reduced money exchange costs and a boost in economic trade with EU member states, anxieties were aired about the likely outcomes, not the least of which was the concern expressed about the surrender of key financial controls (including the setting of interest rates) to the new European Central Bank (ECB). Another major worry centred on the absence from the EMU of the UK (including Northern Ireland) and the negative implications that a devalued sterling would have for the competitiveness of Irish trade with Britain and trading relations across the EMU/non-EMU border with Northern Ireland. To date, none of these concerns have translated into insurmountable problems for Ireland. The low interest rates set by the ECB have not undermined the Irish economy whilst depreciation of the euro relative to the pound sterling has provided Ireland with a currency advantage in its trading relations with Britain. In relation to Northern Ireland, the challenge of a border with two currencies persists but the EU has provided direct assistance with this dilemma by allocating additional funding for border area development. This has benefited both jurisdictions on the island of Ireland and, unlike the

Structural/Cohesion Funds, is likely to continue well into the future under the INTERREG programmes.

The Peace Process

The peace process in Northern Ireland started in earnest in 1993 with discussions between the SDLP (Social Democratic and Labour Party) and Sinn Féin parties, and between Sinn Féin and the British government. These discussions led to The Downing Street Declaration in December of 1993. In the summer of 1994, the IRA declared a cease-fire and between 1995 and 1997 further political negotiations took place between the British and Irish governments and the political parties in the North, aided by the interventions of Bill Clinton and the US senator, George Mitchell. Despite the IRA breaking the cease-fire between February 1996 and July 1997, the peace process was given a legislative framework by the signing of the Good Friday Agreement in April 1998. This agreement was popularly endorsed after an all-island referendum and established the basis for sustained co-operation between Northern Ireland and the Republic of Ireland. Strand II of the Good Friday Agreement led to the establishment of the North South Ministerial Council (NSMC) in December 1999, and created an institutional framework for fostering co-operation.

The role of the NSMC is to 'bring together those with executive responsibilities in Northern Ireland and the Irish Government to develop consultation, co-operation and action within the island of Ireland – including through implementation on an all-island and cross-border basis – on matters of mutual interest and within the competence of each Administration, North and South'.[9] Through the NSMC the Northern Ireland Administration and Irish Government agreed to hold collaborative discussions with respect to twelve sectors: agriculture; education; environment; food safety and health; Foyle, Carlingford and Irish Lights Commission; health; inland waterways; language (Irish and Ulster-Scots); special EU programmes; tourism; trade and business development; transport. In addition, six of these issues were formalised through the creation of North/South bodies: Waterways Ireland; Food Safety Promotion Board; Trade and Business Development Body (Inter*Trade*Ireland); Special European Union Programmes Body (SEUPB; responsible for administering EU funding to Northern Ireland and the Border Region); The Language Body/An Foras Teanga/North-South Body o Leid (consisting of two agencies, i.e, Foras na Gaeilge and Tha Boord o Ulster-Scotch);[10] and the Foyle, Carlingford and Irish Lights Commission.[11]

While the peace process, the NSMC and the various cross-border bodies and initiatives have made an enormous difference to the political, social and economic situation in Northern Ireland and the border counties (see Chapter 16 and next subsection), the situation is far from being resolved, with on-going political tensions and some setbacks that have delayed progress such as the suspension of the Northern Ireland Assembly in October 2002. The peace process and North/South co-operation are therefore on-going issues that will attract attention and diplomacy for years to come. That said, the peace process is acknowledged to have had a number of effects on the socio-economic landscape, not least by helping to foster the Celtic Tiger economy in the South by creating political stability across the island and thus a favourable environment for investment. It has also stimulated the beginnings of a more coherent, all-island economy and enhanced cooperation between interests North and South.

Secularisation and Social Change

As already noted, in the 1980s Ireland was still quite socially conservative in comparison to its European neighbours. Catholic ethos and ethics built up over the previous century continued to dominate social attitudes and norms. However, the 1990s saw a secular transformation as people increasingly questioned the role of the Church and abandoned aspects of its social doctrine (although not necessarily their faith). People started to live more secular lives and church attendance rates plummeted from around 90 per cent of people attending Mass at least once a week in 1973 to 48 per cent in 2001.[12] The move to secularisation was given added impetus by scandals concerning child abuse, which rocked the Church as enquiries were set up to investigate such occurrences, e.g., the Ferns Report (Department of Health and Children, 2005). This was aided by a series of human rights and equality legislation that challenged social attitudes and protected the rights of disadvantaged and discriminated groups (e.g., decriminalisation of homosexuality), employment practices (e.g., job sharing for working mothers), and reforms in attitudes and legislation concerning families (e.g., legalisation on divorce). The latter has led to a growth in non-traditional families (e.g., non-married couples living together, single-parent families (14 per cent of all families in 2002)), reduced family sizes, and dual-income households. Moreover, more women are having children in their 30s rather than 20s, a possible consequence of establishing their careers before starting a family; and 30 per cent of babies in 2000 were born to unmarried mothers (up from 15 per cent in 1991; ESRI, HIPE and NPRS, 2004). As noted below, these changes have been added to by the large number of return migrants importing social and political values from abroad and immigrants bringing their cultures to Ireland. The result has been the development of a more socially plural and liberal society, one almost unrecognisable to immigrants who left in the 1980s.

Perhaps one of the clearest indications of widespread social change is the changing patterns of wealth, consumption and lifestyle (see Chapter 21). The standard of living in Ireland has increased dramatically over the past 15 years and has run ahead of population growth. While there are still very real problems concerning poverty (see next subsection and Chapter 19), there has been a huge shift in people from the lower to upper social classes. As a result, 200,000 people have moved from the poorest social classes to the middle classes between 1996 and 2002, with the poorest social class contracting by 29 per cent (Walsh, 2005). Following this trend, Ireland has quickly become a consumer society due to increasing wage levels and disposable income. An American-style mall seems to have been opened in every town in Ireland that has a population above 10,000 people. Brand name shops from countries across the world increasingly dominate the shopping landscape, and people wearing designer label clothes are a common sight. There has been a massive growth in the restaurant trade, Irish people are taking more foreign-based and domestic tourist trips than ever before and are spending more on them (see Chapter 12). Perhaps a good indication of spending power is the fact that between 1991 and 2002 the proportion of households with at least one car increased from 59.5 per cent to 78.3 per cent. Households with two or more cars increased from 87,174 to 478,660, and the overall number of cars in the state increased from 445,226 to 1,601,619 (Walsh et al., 2005). A large number of these cars are luxury models and SUVs that are expensive to buy and run (between 1990 and 2006 there was a threefold increase in cars with engines larger than 1900cc; Reid, 2006). This growth far outstrips population growth and has occurred in a country where car prices are the highest in Europe.

Population Change and Increased Mobility

The overall growth in the economy and the spatial unevenness of this growth has led to widescale population change and widening daily mobility patterns. Between 1996 and 2006, the overall population of the state increased by 16.8 per cent to 4.23m. Since 2002, natural population increase and in-migration have pushed the figure over the 4 million mark (Figure 1.3 shows long-term population change using cartograms). Population change has been influenced by three key processes: general demographic variation, large-scale internal migration, and net in-migration consisting of large-scale return migration and new migrants. Between 1996 and 2002, births exceeded deaths by almost 140,000 (Walsh, 2005) leading to a strong natural increase in population. This is despite the fact that the Total Period Fertility Rate (TPFR) – the average number of children per woman of child-bearing age – fell to 1.98, a figure below the rate required for long-term replacement (Walsh, 2005). As detailed below, there was a strong rural to urban flow of migrants, meaning that there was a decline in population in some rural areas, with strong growth in urban areas. Emigration fell steadily during the 1990s (though it did not fall below 21,000 per year prior to 2004, averaging over 31,000 per year over the period 1990–2003[13]), and it was not until 1996 that increasing immigration started the present period of sustained net in-migration. In-migration, including both return migrants (approximately 50 per cent of all in-migrants) and immigrants, accounted for a net growth of 163,000 persons between 1996 and 2002 (there were 356,000 people – 9.2 per cent of the population – born outside the state, resident in Ireland in 2002). Since 2002, net in-migration has continued to grow, especially with the influx of workers and their families from the EU accession countries. Between May 2004 and May 2006 over 200,000 PPSNs (Personal Public Service Numbers) were issued to workers from accession states (O'Brien, 2006). While some of these workers only came for short periods before returning, the numbers do not take account of additional family members or those that are working illegally (see Chapter 17).

Migration and net growth through immigration have led to profound changes as to where people are now living, with the spatial pattern being highly uneven. While many parts of the country, including many rural areas, are feeling the strain of trying to cope with the rising demand for housing and associated

1841   1861   1881

1901   1926   1946

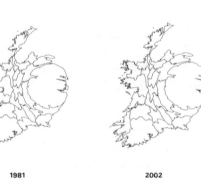

1961   1981   2002

Figure 1.3   Cartograms of population change in Ireland, 1841–2002

Source: Martin Charlton, National Centre for Geocomputation

services and infrastructures, the greatest demand is concentrated in the cities and their hinterlands. Walsh et al. (2005) report that the Gateway cities, identified in the National Spatial Strategy (Athlone/Tullamore/Mullingar, Cork, Dublin, Dundalk, Galway, Letterkenny, Limerick/Shannon, Sligo and Waterford; DoEHLG, 2002), and their catchment areas included 73 per cent of total population in 2002 and accounted for 83 per cent of population increase between 1996 and 2002. A large proportion of this growth is located in the commuter catchment areas as house price increases push housing development further away from city centres. This effect is especially pronounced around Dublin but also the other principal cities (see Figure 1.4). For example, the counties surrounding Dublin all experienced very large population growth over the period 1996–2002 – Fingal (43 per cent), Meath (48.2 per cent), Kildare (37.8 per cent) and Wicklow (23 per cent). Counties a little further out also

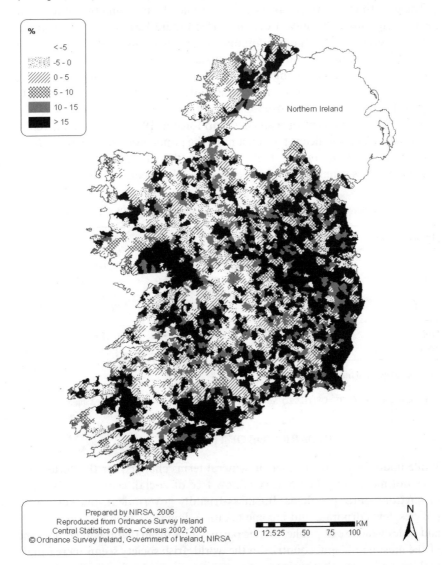

Figure 1.4 Population change in Ireland, 1996–2002

Sources: Central Statistics Office, 2006; Ordnance Survey Ireland

experienced large growth such as Louth (20.3 per cent), Laois (20.8 per cent), Carlow (21.3 per cent) and Westmeath (25.4 per cent). Cork County increased by 23.3 per cent, Galway County by 20.8 per cent and Limerick County by 16.2 per cent. In contrast, a number of inner-city EDs (electoral divisions) have experienced population decline (e.g., Cork City declined by 8,044 people, minus 6.3 per cent), as well as some rural areas in the West, Northwest and Southwest (often countered by growth in medium-size towns in these areas indicating local rural to urban migration).

The growth in catchment areas is also revealed by mapping the numbers of people commuting significant distances (see Figure 1.5). Table 1.2 illustrates that the average distance people commute increased significantly between 1991 and 2002. Given that people are living further away from their place of work, on average they are becoming more mobile. And given that most people are travelling by car, congestion is increasing and road infrastructure straining to cope with demand (by 2002 over 55 per cent of workers drove to work by car compared to 39 per cent of a smaller workforce in 1991; Walsh et al., 2005). The result is that significant proportions of the population are spending a large part of their day commuting. Not surprisingly this raises questions about the environmental sustainability of patterns of development.

Table 1.2   Numbers of workers travelling different distances to work, 1981–2002

Distance (miles)	1981	%	1991	%	2002	%
0	167,617	14.8	197,650	17.4	73,094	4.5
1–4	422,654	37.4	408,013	35.9	571,457	35.5
5–9	188,667	16.7	197,192	17.3	302,105	18.8
10–14	78,489	6.9	87,473	7.7	176,499	11.0
15+	76,049	6.7	93,227	8.2	282,026*	17.5
Not stated	196,868	17.4	153,902	13.5	205,700	12.8
Total	1,130,344		1,137,457		1,610,881	

* includes 93,087 who travel more than 30 miles

Sources: Walsh et al., (2005); CSO (2002), Volume 9, Travel to Work, School and College, Table 5

THE DARK SIDE OF THE CELTIC TIGER

While undoubtedly Ireland has in general terms changed for the better, this does not mean that the country is now free of social, economic, political or environmental problems. Business-friendly government, market-driven policies, low corporate and income taxation, low state spending on services, and widespread use of public–private partnerships mean that Ireland is now one of the most neo-liberal countries in the world. Irish society seems increasingly built around generating business, encouraging private development, sustaining the economy, minimising state spending and responsibilities, and promoting individualism (albeit alongside a responsible civic engagement). As a result,

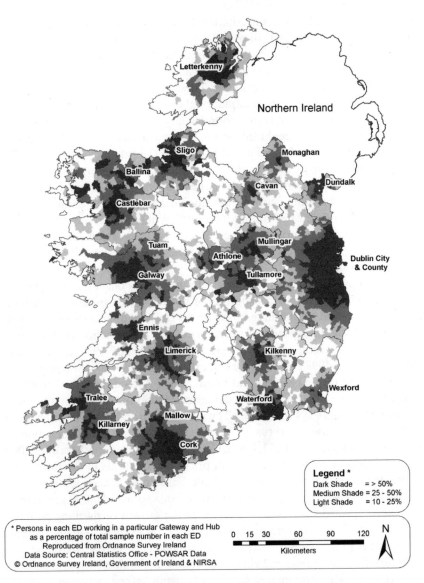

Figure 1.5   Travel to work patterns 2002: gateway and hub catchment areas

Sources: Central Statistics Office, Census SAPS file, 2002; Ordnance Survey Ireland

many of the issues that faced Irish society in the 1980s remain and in fact have become exacerbated by the transformations that have been occurring. In this section we examine, in brief, a few illustrative examples, some of which are covered in more depth in the rest of the book. As such, by no means are the issues we discuss exhaustive.

Ireland may have economically outperformed other developed nations, but inward investment, the growth of the economy and new wealth are highly uneven and unequal across the country. Most inward investment has flowed into Ireland's four principal cities, and especially Dublin. For example, Walsh et al. (2005) report that Dublin and its hinterland had a workforce of 730,000 in 2002 (or 44.6 per cent of the total) and accounted for just under half of all growth (49.4 per cent) in the workforce. These cities have acted as growth poles because they are attractive to multinational companies, which have functional requirements that are most readily found in large urban centres; for example, a large labour pool to source skilled labour, access to a wide variety of specialised business services (e.g., financial and legal) and the presence of major infra-structure facilities (e.g., high-grade telecommunications, international travel). Multinational companies also want to be near to a variety of cultural attractions (e.g., theatres, shopping centres), amongst other things, to enable them to satisfy and retain educated and mobile staff. Where multinationals locate in major urban centres, a gravity attraction process tends to come into play with indigenous companies then tending to locate nearby, especially if they too require skilled labour.

The result is to entice people to move to them, thus placing severe pressure on the housing market due to a shortfall of housing stock. In turn, the demand for housing has led to spiralling house prices and vast quantities of new build (see Chapter 18). The growth of house prices has been phenomenal, rising at rates often well exceeding 10 per cent per year from the mid-1990s to the time of writing (between 1998 and 1999, for several months, year-on-year comparisons exceeded 30 per cent; O'Rourke and Thom, 2000). According to the Permanent TSB/ESRI house price index[14] the average price paid nationally for a house in February 2006 was €284,096 (€378,822 within Dublin and €245,925 outside), an 11.1 per cent increase on February 2005 prices. The average price paid nationally by a first time buyer was €253,459, a 13.5 per cent increase on February 2005. All indications are that this growth in prices will continue in the foreseeable future. This growth is mirrored in new-build housing. In the late 1980s less than 20,000 houses were built per year, rising in 2005 to over 80,000 per annum. This steep upward trend is also reflected in the growth of dwelling planning permissions, which rose from 9,156 in 1992 to 27,512 in 2004.[15] Unable to afford house prices in the cities themselves, large numbers of people are flocking to the more affordable towns and villages surrounding the cities. These places have also grown rapidly through new build, and existing infrastructure and services have come under pressure given increased demand.

A drive through rural Ireland, past the endless 'ribbon-developments' of new housing, can give the impression that, like the cities, the rural economy is thriving. It is true that there is new wealth in the countryside, but this is new and often mobile wealth. New-build housing is predominantly the accommodation of commuters who are unable to afford to live nearer to their place of work or who seek a certain lifestyle. In other cases, it constitutes second homes for those that have prospered and have disposable income to invest. As Chapters 6 and 11 reveal, the rural economy, especially agriculture, is struggling in many parts of the country. In particular, farming is becoming difficult to sustain given global competition vis-à-vis production and pricing and the pressures from supermarket chains reduce profit-margins. Irish farming has become over-dependent on subsidies and grants from the State and European Union, and many farmers have diversified into other economic sectors such as tourism (e.g., opening bed and breakfasts), moved to employ cheaper immigrant labour, and taken to selling land for sites, in an effort to make ends meet. A large number have lost this battle, with a 17 per cent decline in farms from 170,600 to 141,500 between 1991 and 2000 (see Chapter 11). While many small, rural towns could support relatively large services industries, and the IDA has been keen to encourage businesses to locate near to them, to date most inward investment has concentrated near to the larger centres of population. The rural economy then is, in many ways, in difficulties, especially when compared to the economy as a whole.

Rural areas are not the only places to experience relative disadvantage. There is a marked difference in people's access to the new wealth being generated. So much so, that the wealth gap between rich and poor has widened significantly over the past 15 years (despite the upward movement from lower to middle classes described earlier). In 1998, the United Nations' *Human Development Report* indicated that Ireland had the highest levels of income-based social polarisation within the European Union; that the number of children living in poverty had increased twofold since 1971, and that the gap between the economic status of men and women was worse than in any other OECD country. Although annual social spending in Ireland increased in absolute terms while the Tiger boom was under way, rising from €5.85bn in 1993 to €12.1bn in 2002, it nevertheless declined as a proportion of national income thereby contributing to increased relative poverty (Department of Social and Family Affairs, 2003) (see also Chapter 21). Whilst in part the result of wage differentials, these social divisions have been exacerbated by rising costs of living, especially in relation to house prices. Given the structuring of the labour market, the continued economic boom and growth in house prices and other commodities, there is nothing to suggest that this situation has improved. If anything it has worsened. And of course, as Chapter 19 illustrates, this wealth gap has a spatial pattern, with certain areas having high concentrations of relative poverty, and others relative wealth. This varies by scale, so that some regions such as the Northwest are relatively poor compared to others such as the Dublin Metropolitan Region. Within regions, some towns have prospered relative to others, and within towns there are marked differences between neighbourhoods. As a consequence there are some places that the Celtic Tiger seems to have by-passed – places with high deprivation, unemployment, crime rates, drug taking and so on. Others, such as Ballymun in north Dublin, have had makeovers through public–private partnerships that provide designated proportions of social and affordable housing, with the balance for private sale.

Such public–private schemes are being used not only to replace obsolete social housing stock, but also in other major infrastructural projects such as road building and constructing public buildings such as schools and hospitals. They are being used to spread payments over time and mean the state has sold and mortgaged many of its assets to private interests. This is, in part, because of the scale of investment needed to (a) replace aged infrastructure that the state, due to its relative poverty and taxation strategies, had been unable to maintain and expand, and (b) build new infrastructure to cope with extra demand (arising from the increased population numbers as well as more disposable income being spent on infrastructure-hungry items such as cars). Despite the huge hikes in investment, Ireland continues to experience massive infrastructural deficits in relation both to transport and other public infrastructure. As a result, there are regular news reports about traffic congestion and gridlock on the roads, over-crowded trains and buses, patients lying on trolleys in hospital corridors, and school classes being housed in semi-permanent prefab buildings.

For the past few years, a number of reports and the newspapers have all detailed the pressures being placed on various health and welfare services as they try to modernise and cope with population change. Welfare provision is an instructive example of this. Despite the large increase in government revenues, the welfare system is still over-reliant on voluntary and charity organisations, and the role played by family care givers. In some sectors such as intellectual disability, estimates by organisations such as NAMHI (National Association for People with an Intellectual Disability in Ireland) suggest that over 80 per cent of social services delivered are provided by non-state agencies, and family care givers provide the services that these organisations and the State do not deliver. The services that are provided are highly uneven across the country – depending on where voluntary and charity agencies are located, with a disproportionate number in the principal cities, especially Dublin (Power, 2005). There is minimal co-ordination across services and many people fall between the gaps. Similar problems arise in relation to education for disabled children, which is also spatially uneven with regards to services and access (Kitchin and Mulcahy, 1999). The shift to dual-income households (where two partners pursue employment careers, often due to the need to service high mortgages) has revealed serious issues around childcare provision, and similar stories can be found in relation to care for older people and other aspects of welfare provision.

The evidence provided by some of the contributors to this book (see especially Chapters 2 and 5, and also Chapters 18 and 19) suggests that a process of reurbanisation (regeneration and gentrification) is occurring in Irish cities and towns alongside the counter-urbanisation (suburbanisation and commuterisation) trends in the Irish landscape. This is contributing to the creation of accessibility-rich and accessibility-poor spaces. The renewed town centres are increasingly occupied by either immigrants or young elites. At the same time, the physical footprint and commuter zones of urban areas have expanded enormously so that easy accessibility to central or other parts of the spread out towns is only available to those with private transport. The poor who live in outlying rural locations or in the extensive suburbs at the edge of towns are increasingly isolated as the quality of public transport diminishes (due to congestion and viability difficulties associated with sprawling urban forms). In terms of access to the services and facilities distributed throughout the urban areas, the poor have a much more limited range of choices available to them than the wealthier car-borne population.

Further, despite widespread economic and social change, Travellers (Ireland's indigenous nomadic population) continue to be one of the most marginalised groups in Irish society. Small in number (0.6 per cent of the Irish population), Travellers fare badly on every indicator of disadvantage including unemployment, illiteracy, poverty, health status, access to decision making, and political representation. During the 1990s several processes were enacted to address Traveller racism and issues of disadvantage and discrimination. For example, the Prohibition of Incitement to Hatred Act (1991), the Equal Employment Act (1998), and the Equal Status Act (2000) all gave legal protection to Travellers. This was accompanied by the Traveller Accommodation Act (1998) that offered rights for managed nomadism and required each local authority, in consultation with Travellers and the general public, to prepare and adopt a five year Traveller Accommodation Programme by 31 March 2000. However, by 2002 only 111 of a recommended 2,200 Traveller-specific accommodation units had been provided (*Irish Times*, 9 March 2002), and poor relations between Travellers and the State led to new legislation that aimed to force Travellers to change their lifestyle and become settled (see Crowley and Kitchin, 2006). This included an amendment to the Criminal Justice (Public Order) Act 1994 which further strengthened the powers of local authorities and the Gardai to evict Travellers from public spaces; an amendment to Section 32 of the Traveller Accommodation Act that made trespass a criminal rather than a civil offence; and the introduction of the Housing (Miscellaneous Provisions) Act, 2002, which criminalised camping on private and public property, gave the Gardai new powers of arrest, allowed property to be confiscated and disposed of, and trespassers to be jailed for a month or fined €3,000. As a result, the general stand-off between Travellers, the State and general public has little altered despite the intentions expressed in the 1990s.

The acceptance of new immigrants has also run into a few problems, most notably in relation to refugees and asylum seekers. Throughout the late 1990s and early 2000s a moral panic started to develop around certain immigrant groups, especially Nigerian, other African, and Romanian immigrants who were seen as undesirable and moving to Ireland (and by default into Europe) in large numbers to exploit holes in immigration legislation. In June 2004, a citizenship referendum was held to determine whether the children of immigrants born in Ireland should be automatically entitled to Irish citizenship as then defined in the constitution (see Chapter 17). The electorate voted by a margin of four to one for a change in the definition of Irish citizenship. As a consequence, the right to citizenship by birth was removed from the constitution, and Irish citizenship is now primarily defined by blood ties. There appears to be a number of troubling paradoxes concerning this decision, especially given the experiences and rights of previous generations of Irish immigrants in other countries (see Crowley et al., 2006).

In Northern Ireland, sectarian divisions, violence and political stalemate are all everyday realities despite the peace process. In fact, Northern Irish society is, in many ways, becoming more polarised politically and spatially. For example, patterns of voting have shifted from the more centrist parties of the Social and Democratic Labour Party (SDLP) and Ulster Unionists (UU) to the more staunchly republican and unionist parties of Sinn Féin (SF) and the Democratic Unionist Party (DUP), and many people are choosing to live in communities that reflect their religious and political views, rather than in mixed communities. It is a surprise to many that there have been more peace walls built post- rather than pre-cease-fire, and tension between communities remains in place in some locales (notably in North and West Belfast) and still flares up into cross-community violence, especially fuelled by deep-seated notions of territoriality. An example of this was the dispute in 2001 and 2002 over the Holy Cross School in Ardoyne where Catholic schoolgirls had to walk through a unionist area to get to school (due to changes in patterns of population and the erection of a peace wall along Alliance Avenue). Parade routes and the right to march as part of a cultural tradition are also deeply contested in many areas. This is not to say that life in Northern Ireland has not changed significantly for the better since the 1994 cease-fires, but rather to note that the situation still has on-going problems that will likely continue for some time.

It is important to note that these problems are not simply being ignored by the Irish government, policy makers and citizens. Although the main thrust of Irish policy since the late 1950s has been towards promoting economic growth, substantial efforts to address other issues such as social equality and environmental sustainability have moved to the forefront of policy formulation and action in recent years. While some issues do not seem to gain serious attention, others have been the focus of numerous policy analyses and formulation, although this policy might not be implemented. Two examples may help to illustrate this. Firstly, there has been a concerted effort to sustain the peace process and promote cross-border co-operation, despite successive setbacks due to political fallout and stalemate in the North. Secondly, and in contrast, the National Spatial Strategy (NSS), put together by numerous government officials and consultants, and designed to promote sustainable development and prosperity in all parts of Ireland, has seemingly had little impact to date on policy. Even the government's much criticised decentralisation plan largely ignored the NSS. Of course, it takes time to implement policies and a lead-in (or trickle-down) time is necessary for policies such as the NSS, which was introduced in late 2002, to be translated into practice at other scales. Regional Planning Guidelines (RPGs) to give effect to the NSS were adopted by the Regional Authorities in 2004, so the next step for implementation is for local authorities to incorporate the logic of the NSS and RPGs into the strategies of their development plans. Thus, it is the policies and actions of the next generation of local authority development plans that provide the key to effective implementation of the NSS.

In many ways, the challenge for policy makers and implementers has been to try and work out how to address outstanding and problematic issues whilst not implementing interventions that might slow the economy and bring the good times to an end – no easy task. In such a situation the danger is always that the government does as little as possible in order minimise any threat to the status quo, and the present government has certainly been accused of such a strategy. That said, the good times have not yet come to an end, despite the problems outlined and predictions by analysts that they must come to a close at some point.

IRELAND IN THE NEW CENTURY

In the last 15 years or so Ireland has certainly come a long way. The transformations that have occurred since the dark days of the 1980s are truly staggering, and were certainly in excess of any of the predictions of economists and social and political commentators of the day. From the nadir of a deep economic depression it seemed that the most the country could hope for was slow but steady growth. Nobody predicted that between 1987 and 2003 Ireland's economy would move from being 63 per cent of the EU average to 136 per cent, that the influential role of the Church would simultaneously collapse, that a relative peace would be instigated in Northern Ireland, and so on. So, what can other countries, indeed the Irish themselves, learn from the transformations that have occurred, and where is the future of Ireland heading? These are questions we leave until the concluding chapter. First we invite you to read the contributions to the volume.

Before doing that, however, it is important to note a couple of limitations in the book's coverage. First, the book has been designed to provide an analysis of a broad range of topical and important issues concerning everyday life in Ireland, but it is by no means a comprehensive analysis. We have had to be selective in choosing issues to be discussed and have had to limit the depth of analysis provided. To do anything otherwise would have meant undertaking a much bigger project. Our aim was always to provide a broad, spatial analysis of Ireland backed up by strong empirical evidence, and the chapters deliver this. Saying this, all of the authors refer in passing to other issues and the references at the end of the book will guide the reader to relevant texts for further reading. Second, the authors' discussion is largely concentrated on the Republic of Ireland, although there are a couple of chapters that focus predominantly on issues in Northern Ireland, and others that make reference and comparison to the North. We are aware that these chapters only provide a partial picture of a very complex social and political picture, but we have included them because they illustrate the profound differences in governance and social issues in the North, and some of the on-going challenges policy makers face in thinking about cross-border and all-island planning as regards infrastructure, the economy, and social development (something that is rapidly moving up the political agenda as a priority area of policy). There is a plethora of books that focus exclusively on Northern Ireland and we recommend you consult these texts for fuller accounts of the situation there.

While the chapters can be read independently of each other, to provide an organisation logic and structure we have divided the book into four parts: (I) planning and development, (II) the economy, (III) the political landscape, (IV) population and social issues. Each section contains four or more chapters that focus on specific issues. Each chapter provides a relatively broad overview of trends and policies, with specific points and arguments illustrated using example material. Individually they provide detailed introductions to specific aspects of Ireland and the transformations since the late 1980s, collectively they allow the creation of a fuller picture of Ireland at the start of the twenty-first century and a sense of how Ireland might progress in the future.

Part I
Planning and Development

Introduction

Planning and development are key aspects of economic and social progress. They provide the regulatory and policy context for change. The chapters in this section provide an overview of the planning system, the strategies employed to try and stimulate and manage development, and their effects upon different aspects of the economy and society across contexts and scales. What the chapters highlight is that since the 1960s a whole series of policies and new legislation have been formulated and implemented that have had varying degrees of success in improving the economy and society. Some policy was poorly conceived, some poorly implemented, some had effects that were not anticipated, and some worked to great effect. In general, policy was determined at a national level in response to pressure from actors on the European, regional and local scales. The strategies employed to implement policy and attain objectives were charged to different parties, usually national agencies and regional and local authorities, but also other sectoral and private interests.

While the overall governmental aim of strategic planning and development is to ensure that all sections of economy and society, and all parts of the country, grow and develop, with the exception of initiatives such as the National Development Plan and National Spatial Strategy, planning and development in Ireland largely focuses on particular areas (e.g., urban or rural) or sectors (e.g., transport or utilities). This can cause tensions and contradictions between policies aiming to achieve different ends. For example, the *industrial* policy of developing Dublin to compete economically on the global scale seems to run counter to *regional* policy that stresses balanced regional development and argues for the transfer of services and industries away from Dublin to other areas of the country. Balancing the needs of different sections of society, and different parts of the country, is then a difficult task. It means assessing the benefits and costs to different parties, for example weighing up national benefit vis-à-vis local cost.

In the opening chapter in the section, Brendan Bartley provides an historical overview of planning in Ireland, charting three distinct phases. Focusing on the latter he highlights the adoption of an entrepreneurial form of planning in the mid-1980s, which targeted specific areas for investment and development, and was instrumental in creating the planning conditions necessary for the Celtic

Tiger economy. For example, the first urban development corporation – a public–private partnership – the Custom House Docks Development Authority (CHDDA), was charged with developing a key site in central Dublin for the International Financial Services Centre (IFSC) that subsequently attracted significant banking and financial company investment in Ireland. Bartley notes that the evolution of successive National Development Plans and their recent convergence with the National Spatial Strategy, 2002, constitute a move away from an ad hoc piecemeal approach to development towards a more coherent planning-led approach. This blending together of spatial planning and long-term funding programmes involves a major rationalisation of Ireland's customised entrepreneurial approach. It seeks to secure more integrated and balanced development across a range of scales and to provide a strategic framework for managing future, large-scale development of industry, housing and infrastructure.

Complementing this account, Jim Walsh details policies and strategies designed to promote development within and between regions, albeit often working in tandem with national policies. Given the population and economic dominance of Dublin and the mid-East region, together with the spatial variance in other aspects of Irish economy and society, there are a number of regional disparities in wealth generation and quality of life within Ireland. These disparities have a number of important implications for the viability and sustainability of regional economies. As a result, there is a long history of policies designed to pursue balanced regional development. In recent years, these policies have had to try and cope with a Celtic Tiger economy that selectively promotes development in some places, notably the principal cities and their hinterlands, and a rural economy that is increasingly becoming less sustainable.

Des McCafferty identifies imbalances associated with the destinations of inward investment, which are in large measure a consequence of the nature of the urban system. Many industries require substantial pools of skilled labour, and these can be principally found in the cities. Ireland's urban system is characterised by a dominant city (Dublin), with four other principal cities with populations over 35,000 (Cork, Limerick, Galway, and Waterford). Other towns are growing rapidly, but often as commuter towns for the principal cities, placing considerable strain on local services and transport infrastructure. Inevitably, inward investment is attracted to already large and growing places, and increasing urbanisation has accelerated the shift from a predominantly rural population to an urban society. McCafferty provides an interesting comparison to Northern Ireland, which has a similar urban system within which Belfast dominates.

Andrew MacLaran and Sinéad Kelly provide a detailed picture of the policies and processes at play within cities, focusing in particular on property development and the supply of business space and residential units in Dublin. They outline the various ways that property development has been both a stimulus and an outcome of economic growth, especially over the last 15 years. In this period there has been a significant growth of both office developments for service industries and residential units for the new city workers. To save costs, offices have been developed extensively around the city, not just in the city centre. In contrast, many new dwellings have been built in the city centre whilst other central residential areas have been significantly gentrified. Given the demand for these desirable units, property prices have spiralled to such an extent that many local people can no longer afford to live in this area. As a result, there has been a growth of the suburbs and commuter towns transforming a relatively compact city into a sprawling, multinodal city and in the process adding enormously to city congestion. Resolving these issues, while sustaining economic growth, poses significant challenges to policy, problems that they argue have so far been neglected.

In contrast, John McDonagh provides an examination of rural development in Ireland from the early 1970s to the present, concentrating on the period from the 1990s to the time of writing. Given the historical importance of the rural economy and rural way of life in Ireland, allied to the rural nature of many parliamentary constituencies, rural issues have received much attention recently. The focus of this attention has largely been on how to reinvigorate and maintain a rural economy that is in decline. As McDonagh notes, there are no easy solutions to this problem, and indeed it represents a significant challenge to government. He provides an overview of the policies being implemented, often driven by European directives and plans, and provides two case studies of specific initiatives, the LEADER programme and the REPS scheme.

Transportation infrastructure is one of the most important sectoral issues associated with social and economic development. It provides the stabilising character or structural glue that enables much development to occur and also constitutes the connective sinews that unify otherwise disparate places. James Killen details the state and capacity of various forms of transport in Ireland – road, rail, air and shipping. He notes that transport infrastructure and the various services they support (e.g., passenger travel by car or bus, or freight) have long been under-developed. He points out that despite enormous increases in investment in recent years, the latest transformation of the economy, together with major population changes, has placed enormous pressures on the various transport systems. To address the infrastructure deficit the government has turned to public–private partnerships to co-fund and build new systems such as the Luas (a light rail network) and to expand the motorway system. Killen suggests that these developments are often piecemeal and tend to serve specific communities rather than general need. He predicts that existing problems of road traffic congestion and overcrowding on public transport will continue until there is comprehensively planned and systematic development across the various infrastructures. This will require a co-ordinated, integrated transport policy for the country as a whole that recognises the needs of specific locales, including rural areas and cities.

The final chapter in the section, by Michael R. Murray and Brendan Murtagh, focuses on spatial planning in Northern Ireland. Although the system they describe has had little effect to date on planning and development strategies in the Republic, despite there being some similarities in structures, procedures and priorities, there is growing pressure for an alignment of planning policy that will maximise cooperation and aid the development of an all-island economy. Their chapter then highlights present thinking in the North, and comparison with the other chapters in the section provides a means to envisage how planning and development might develop on an all-island basis, with for example an alignment of spatial strategies. As many policy analysts and politicians, North and South, are realising and arguing, such an alignment will be important for sustaining the economy in the South, stimulating the economy in the North, and promoting peace and reconciliation. Judging by the proliferation of significant initiatives in this area – including the PEACE programme, the formation of North/South bodies such as the North South Ministerial Council and Inter*Trade*Ireland, and recent announcements by administrations in both jurisdictions concerning infrastructure spending – cross-border co-operation will be a significant part of future development plans.

In combination, the chapters provide an insight into the role of planning and development in shaping Ireland's economy and society. More particularly, they highlight how spatial strategies and policies operating on different scales have shaped the landscape of the Celtic Tiger. While the economy has been highly significant in providing the platform for change, planning and development controls have provided the regulatory context and structure for inward investment and associated changes in transforming Ireland's landscapes through processes such as urbanisation, urban renewal, rural development, property growth and construction of new infrastructure.

2
Planning in Ireland

Brendan Bartley

The way planning is structured and implemented varies from country to country and the context provided by the legal and political systems of each country influences the exact nature of planning as it is experienced in each setting. In the Irish case two main organisations presently have primary responsibility for planning within central government: the Department of the Environment, Heritage and Local Government (DoEHLG) and An Bord Pleanála (the Planning Appeals Board). As the main overseer of the planning system in Ireland, DoEHLG is responsible for the framing of planning legislation as well as the preparation and issue of policy formulation and guidance. Ireland is unique among European countries in that it has an independent, third party planning appeals system which is operated by An Bord Pleanála. The appeals board provides an arbitration forum in which any decision made by a planning authority on a planning application can be reviewed at the request of the applicant or another interested party. In 1993, decision making on major environmental matters was transferred to a new organisation, the Environmental Protection Agency, thereby restricting planning to consideration of land-use issues (Bartley and Waddington, 2000). At the local level, all tiers of local government – county councils, city councils, borough councils and town councils – are recognised as planning authorities except those town councils which are former town commissioners. The present physical planning system in Ireland is, accordingly, run by 88 local planning authorities: 29 county councils, 5 county borough corporations, 5 borough corporations and 49 town councils. The Minister for the DoEHLG is responsible for planning legislation (Grist, 2003). The contemporary planning system in Ireland has three main functions:

- making development plans;
- deciding on planning permissions through the assessment of planning applications (unless exempted development applies), including appeals against planning decisions;
- planning enforcement.

This system has developed through three phases of macro-economic strategy and associated physical planning (see Table 2.1): the preindustrial, minimal planning stage; the industrial modernisation phase; and the entrepreneurial phase.

This chapter outlines the political and economic background against which the modern form of compulsory planning was introduced in Ireland and traces the subsequent evolution of the Irish planning system. It concludes with brief comments on some of the problems associated with the planning system and offers some observations on likely future trajectories of planning in Ireland.

Table 2.1   Policy phases and related trends in Ireland

Policy	Phase 1 1922 to 1960	Phase 2 1960 to 1986	Phase 3 1986 to present
Economic policy	Economic isolationism; sustainable indigenous development	Industrialisation and integration into world economy; strategy to attract inward investment	Post-industrial strategy to attract only high-growth, high-tech industries and services
Governance	Centre populist party dominance of central government; weak local government	Centre populist party dominance of central government and emergence of coalition governments; weak local government	Coalition governments and proliferation of partnerships; relaxation of central government controls over local government
Urban planning	Minimal (ad hoc); main focus on housing provision	Local government urban planning introduced but authoritarian control maintained by central government	Adaptive entrepreneurialism; targeted regeneration (four models evolution) and flexible planning
Landscape	Rural/agricultural landscape and society; compact cities and towns	Urbanisation: low density suburbanisation model and inner-city decline	Urban reassertion and revitalisation; polymorphic inner-city renewal with suburbanisation and commuterisation

Source: Bartley and Treadwell-Shine, 2003

PLANNING FOR THE MODERNISATION OF IRELAND

The first stage of planning in Ireland was the *preindustrial, minimal planning phase*, which stretched from national independence in 1921 to the late 1950s. In economic terms, Ireland was not an industrialised (or urbanised) country when it embarked on its first steps as an independent state. Early initiatives to modernise the country involved the establishment of peat and hydro-electric power plants by the Free State government as a means of stimulating and supporting native industrial development. This early emphasis on facilitating the emergence of a modern manufacturing and business sector was undermined in the 1930s by Fianna Fail Taoiseach, Eamonn DeValera's 'Dancing at the Cross-roads' speech, which described his vision of Ireland as a self-sustaining nation supported by small-scale industry and traditional values. These Sinn Féin principles envisaged a country capable of both governing itself and providing for its own economic needs. In planning terms this led to a planning regime that was characterized by laissez-faire policy and political clientelism (Bartley and Waddington, 2001).

Given government policy, up until the 1960s Ireland continued to be a predominantly rural society with an agricultural base and very high rates of emigration. However, a major shift occurred in macro-economic policy and settlement strategy during the Lemass-Whittaker era of the late 1950s and early 1960s when the country embarked on a clear policy of achieving industrial growth through attracting multinational companies to establish in Ireland. The aim was to open Irish markets to inward, international foreign investment with a view to creating significant growth in industrial employment. These new, growth-oriented economic policies attempted to stem the haemorrhage of Irish emigration by dropping Ireland's prevailing protectionist trade policies. It was against this backdrop of new open-trade economic policies in the early 1960s that the Irish government accepted expert advice from the World Bank and United Nations about the need to introduce a new physical (land use) planning system (Bartley, 1999). Modernisation was equated with industrialisation and it was considered that Ireland could emulate more prosperous modernised societies by following their industrialisation paths on a planned basis. Thus, in order to deal with the anticipated pressures of economic development, increasing population and urbanisation, the Irish government introduced the Local Government (Planning and Development) Act 1963 to create a modern planning system in which planning to facilitate and regulate change would be obligatory throughout the country. The Act provided for the orderly planning and development of the country on a local government basis with local authorities also designated as *planning authorities*. Importantly, this second stage of planning emphasised the managerial approach that forms the bedrock of the current Irish planning system (Bannon, 1989).

Planning was thus envisaged as having a major role to play in smoothing the way for the emergence of the new geographies, or spatial patterns, required by the modernisation of the Irish economy and society. It would manage these transformations by making appropriate Development Plans and harnessing (or regulating) land use change through development control policies so that future change would be 'rationalised' and undesirable change restricted where necessary. In this way, the desired gains of industrialisation could be secured as quickly and effectively as possible whilst potentially negative consequences would be anticipated and avoided. Planning was also expected to manage the potential conflicts that could arise in the course of these transformations through accountable ('democratic') procedures which would allow for public involvement at all stages of plan making and implementation.

The new Irish planning system shared many similarities with the post-war British system. This seemed to make good sense at the time in view of the shared experiences of the two countries – the structure of the Irish legal system and the political-administrative machinery of local authorities were inherited

evaluate.

from Britain. However, Irish planning did not completely mimic its British counterpart. At the time the Irish legislation was being introduced, British planning was undergoing a major upheaval because it was perceived to be undemocratic. Confidence in the 'managerial' (scientific decision-making) aspect of planning was undermined by reports of problems being experienced in the British New Towns. Accordingly, the right of unelected technocrats to make decisions about where people should live and work was widely criticised. The absence of sufficient opportunities for involvement of the public in matters that affected them was perceived widely as a 'democratic deficit' and this applied most acutely to the unelected New Town Corporations (Bartley and Waddington, 2001).

The Irish legislation did not allow for the creation of such new-town companies. Instead, the political nature of planning was emphasised and, in an attempt to reinforce and widen the democratic remit of planning, the new Irish planning system allocated all of the new planning functions to the local authorities and provided channels for consultation at all stages of the planning process. The 'technical' and 'managerial' aspects of planning in Ireland were subordinated to the 'political' aspects. Local authorities were designated as planning authorities but also charged with the responsibility of facilitating, initiating and pursuing appropriate development in accordance with the new pro-development, macro-economic policy of the period. They would do this using the tools of development plan zoning and development control policies. The Irish legislation also explicitly linked planning with development. Development was viewed as the processes of innovation and activities designed to increase resources or wealth; industrialisation was envisaged as the means of achieving development, whilst planning was seen as the means of managing the process through the allocation and use of resources. Essentially, the planning system would be organised around a development plan made by elected members of a local authority and implemented by the manager and his/her staff who decided upon and enforced individual planning applications.

Accordingly, when the new planning legislation was introduced in 1963 local authorities throughout the country were assigned the responsibility of devising and implementing spatial development plans for their areas of jurisdiction. Scope existed at this time for executive agencies other than local authorities to be given the role of overseeing the preparation and implementation of development plans by using, for example, semi-state bodies. However, this did not happen and state land use planning in Ireland thus became a purely local government function. To reflect this, local authorities were also given the formal title of 'planning authorities'. The planning code created by the founding legislation came into operation in October 1964 and required each planning authority to make a development plan within three years, and thereafter review it every five years (Grist, 2003).

The government also defined nine planning regions for the country in 1964. Chapter 3 explores the role and contribution of regional planning in detail, but for present purposes it should be noted that the regional planning authorities were commissioned to prepare regional scale strategy plans to assist the newly established planning authorities with their new tasks, including the preparation of the statutory local plans. International planning consultants subsequently produced advisory plans for Dublin City and the Dublin Region designed to spatially articulate national economic policy and provide the physical basis for the local plans of the Dublin planning authorities. A similar strategy was prepared for the Limerick-Shannon region, and a separate regional planning framework, the Buchanan Report published in 1968, was prepared for the seven remaining regions covering the rest of the country. It was envisaged that the regional plans would foster complementarity and co-operation between neighbouring planning authorities and provide a means to achieve co-ordination of their activities and avoid unnecessary waste or duplication of resources (Bannon, 1989).

It was also considered important that the regions outside Dublin should foster local growth and divert pressure from the capital. Ironically, although Ireland had not experienced industrial revolution on the scale of Britain, it mirrored the British situation in one sense – it had a dominant metropolis that continued to grow by drawing people and resources away from other urban centres. Balanced planning was viewed as the key to ensuring that the gap between Dublin and the rest of the country would not intensify in an industrialised Ireland. Without proper planning, Ireland might recapitulate the problems experienced in the UK due to the divergence between an expanding London and the declining northern regions. It was feared in Ireland that a concentration of people and investment in Dublin could produce similar congestion and decline problems in Ireland. The Buchanan Report had advised that balanced regional and national development could best be achieved by promoting the industrialisation and demographic growth of a limited number of urban growth centres across the country as potential counter-magnets to Dublin. However, the recommendations of the Buchanan Report were not implemented. Dublin continued to grow and the regional plan prepared for the metropolitan region allowed it to grow in a manner that many critics argued was both unbalanced and unsustainable (Bartley and Treadwell-Shine, 1999a).

The regional frameworks proved to be unsuccessful (see Chapter 3). Reliance was placed almost entirely on the private sector to develop all aspects of settlement apart from necessary infrastructural development and social housing. During the 1970s and the early 1980s land use planning became almost exclusively concerned with settlement and housing as the economy flagged following the world oil crisis of 1973. During this period, planning presided over rapid and extensive provision of public and private residential accommodation as settlement policies persisted with suburban housing estates as the appropriate response to continuing urbanisation trends. Most of the new housing estates were constructed as low-rise, low-density (six to ten dwellings per acre) developments with three- or four-bedroomed, two-storied, semi-detached houses as the architectural norm. However, the extensive housing provision was not matched by adequate accompanying commercial, retail or social facilities. The local authorities took the blame for many of the problems that arose due to funding shortfalls and the absence of integrated development.

Without a statutory regional level of government to promote a more holistic urban policy, and in the absence of co-ordinated central government direction on some kind of cohesive urban policy, local authorities could do little to challenge the resulting 'planning drift', or to change prevailing trends. In the absence of central government commitment to redress matters, attempts by the local authorities to address the emerging problems were hampered and the decentralisation trends in the main urban centres including Dublin continued as a 'default policy' until the mid-1980s. The consequential decline of city centre and inner city areas associated with these trends generated debates about the prospect of American-style empty centre (the so-called 'doughnut' type) cities emerging in Ireland (Pringle et al., 1999). Decentralisation provoked a huge outcry and reaction from many quarters. Central government took the baton from local government and ushered in planning policy phase three (the entrepreneurial or urban renewal phase) (Bartley and Treadwell-Shine, 2003).

ENTREPRENEURIAL PLANNING

The third and current phase of economic and physical planning policy, the entrepreneurial planning period, coincides with the latest pressures of globalisation and trends of intensified competition between places. In Ireland it effectively got under way in 1986 when blighted urban zones were officially designated by central government for renewal and provided with tax exemption status in order to attract investment into targeted redevelopment projects in these areas. In the post-industrial era, success is based on attracting investment and jobs for knowledge and service products rather than traditional manufacturing plants. These post-industrial, 'weightless' businesses need to be located in high-quality office complexes and business parks. In order to attract such businesses many national governments and their municipal centres have adopted adventurous entrepreneurial practices and regeneration policies designed to modernise and 're-image' their major urban centres with a view to boosting their competitive advantage and obtaining pivotal positions in the emerging new urban order (Hall and Hubbard, 1998; Oatley, 1998). Ireland was no exception and from the mid-1980s Irish cities, including Dublin, have experimented with new 'flagship' projects and new implementation arrangements in the race to attract such investment and 'avoid being left behind' by national and international competitors.

While globalisation was a key catalyst, the political situation helped shape the Irish approach. After the turbulence of the early 1980s and the advent of minority and coalition governments, the Irish governments adopted a new business-friendly, partnership macro-economic strategy which has underpinned all subsequent national development programmes – the so-called National Partnership Agreements (see Chapter 13). Local authorities have been encouraged to become more entrepreneurial while planning has also become pragmatic and results-oriented. Urban planning has evolved from a concern with integrated comprehensive planning for all areas within the planning authority's area of control to an approach based on planning for fewer, selected areas based on highest potential for success and (where feasible) most need. The new approach favours renewal over new-town development and places a strong emphasis on achieving renaissance through targeted urban regeneration. This changing approach to piecemeal development has moved from an initial concern with securing property-led economic objectives through a traditional style of planning to broad partnership schemes which seek to achieve a wider mix of economic and social objectives for targeted areas on a project-by-project basis (Bartley and Borscheid, 2003).

Also, the quest for urban renaissance was no longer viewed as a matter for governments or their subordinate agencies alone. Instead, it was seen as a collaborative effort involving new and flexible political, administrative and participatory arrangements employing a range of options such as single objective regeneration agencies like Urban Development Corporations (UDCs), public–private partnerships and, more recently, tripartite public–private–community partnerships.

This process can be seen at work in Ireland through the case study of Dublin, which illustrates the evolution from a trend planning approach up to the mid-1980s to the emergence, after 1986, of a vision-led, entrepreneurial model designed to facilitate urban renaissance and enhance the international competitiveness of the city. A similar logic is discernible in other Irish cities.

In Dublin, the local authority was sidelined as central government sought to emulate a similar experiment in London Docklands by establishing an independent, single task organisation for the purpose of rejuvenating the Dublin Docklands at Custom House Quay. Thus, in 1986 the transition to post-industrial planning commenced when Ireland's first UDC, the Custom House Docks Development Authority (CHDDA), was established under the Urban Renewal legislation. The docklands project became the proto-typical first model of urban regeneration (Mark I) for Dublin. As an independent organisation with its own planning powers, the CHDDA was given responsibility for the largest urban renewal project in Ireland. Its remit was to secure the regeneration of the redundant Custom House Docks Area (CHDA) in the north-east inner city of Dublin, fronting onto the River Liffey. It could enter into partnership with private companies in order to achieve its objectives and was boosted in 1987 by the decision of the Department of the Taoiseach to designate the CHDA as the site for an International Financial Services Centre (IFSC) (Bartley and Treadwell-Shine, 2003).

By the mid-1990s, the CHDDA had successfully achieved the physical and economic regeneration of the CHDA in partnership with a private property development consortium. The direction of development in the CHDA and in the IFSC, with its emphasis on entrepreneurial approaches, set the stage for new and competing models of urban regeneration into the 1990s. The collapse of the international property and equities markets at the end of the 1980s, together with criticisms about democratic and community deficits associated with the Docklands project (due to the exclusion of local government from the project and the lack of regeneration benefits accruing to local residents), led to changes in urban regeneration policy in Dublin in the 1990s. Four stages or models, starting with the UDC approach, can be identified in these evolving changes (Bartley, 2000; Bartley and Treadwell-Shine, 2003).

If the first model of urban regeneration is the independent UDC approach, as represented by the CHDDA, the second urban regeneration model (Mark II) is exemplified by the Temple Bar regeneration project. Financial centres and office complexes went out of favour and heritage-related tourism projects quickly became the prevailing fashion in urban renewal for most 'competitive cities' – Temple Bar is a typical example of the new fashion which emerged at that time. This second model still required an independent agency (Temple Bar Properties) to manage the project. Private sector businesses were invited to participate in the regeneration process in partnership with Temple Bar Properties. However, Dublin City Council retained planning control and worked in conjunction with Temple Bar Properties to develop a framework plan for the site. The local authority was back in the picture as a constituent player, although not in the leading role.

The third urban regeneration model (Mark III), brought about under the new Urban Renewal Schemes Act, 1994 is typified by the HARP and Ballymun urban regeneration projects (DELG, 1994; Dublin Corporation, 1994). Here, the local authority took the lead in choosing which sites were designated for regeneration, and retained planning control over these sites. This model allowed for considerable involvement by local community representatives and others interested in the development of the area. In this model the local authority led the potential public–private sector partnerships but the community and other elements of 'civil society' were drawn into the partnership arrangements.

A review of the first decade of the Urban Renewal Schemes was commissioned by central government in 1996. The findings of the report by the Management Consultancy firm KPMG echoed the results of a similar study carried out by the same firm in the UK for the British government. The Irish report recommended that future urban regeneration schemes should be based on a 'social partnership' model similar to the Mark III model, which was considered to have a more 'democratic' emphasis than its predecessors (KPMG et al., 1996). When the CHDDA's ten-year term of office expired, it was succeeded in 1997 by the Dublin Docklands Development Authority (DDDA) which was required by government to embrace the Mark IV (partnership) model (DDDA, 1997). Subsequently, the KPMG Model IV approach was given wide endorsement by central government in 1998 when the Integrated Area Plan (IAP) approach to area regeneration was introduced and applied throughout the country. In this model, local government or another management agency could be responsible for the designation and planning for each IAP. In order to obtain designated status as a regeneration zone from central government, IAPs had to demonstrate clear development potential, social needs and other credentials in competition with other potential IAPs. In effect, this competition for selection favoured applicants who could express creative 'visions' for the total regeneration of the area and show a commitment to local participation through partnerships in the ensuing planning and development process (Bartley and Treadwell-Shine, 2003).

The IAPs were a clear embodiment of the 'adaptive entrepreneurial' approach that evolved in Dublin after the inception of the CHDDA. IAPs had, in many respects, moved to the opposite end of the spectrum from the first independent UDC urban regeneration model, as represented by the CHDDA. As Table 2.2 demonstrates, each of the subsequent models of urban regeneration incorporated progressive moves towards new partnership strategies, with increased local government and local community involvement apparent in each case. Planning had also become more targeted and fragmented as flexible, piecemeal approaches were employed in pursuit of urban regeneration 'visions'.

Table 2.2 Four models of urban regeneration in Dublin

Model	Mark I	Mark II	Mark III	Mark IV
Representative project (inception)	CHDA UDC (1986)	Temple Bar (1991)	HARP site (1995)	Integrated Area Plans (IAPs) (1998)
Changing governance/planning procedures	Local authorities by-passed by independent executive agency (UDC) which produces master plan for designated area	Local authority included in negotiated framework plan by dominant UDC	Local authority leads project and prepares planning scheme for site; local authority also retains planning control over site	Central government selects IAPs via competitive bidding contest; local authority, UDC or other agencies can lead project
Partnership	Public–private partnership (PPP) only	Public–private partnership (PPP); some formal co-operation between UDC and local authority	Early tripartite partnership approaches. Liaison between local authorities, community, private sector	Intensified and more diverse partnership approaches (including tripartite stakeholder partnerships between state agencies, communities, businesses, etc.)
Social housing component	None	Minimal	Significant housing dimension – mixed tenures	Major focus on social benefits including local housing needs

Source: Bartley and Treadwell-Shine, 2003

Thus, in recent times, Irish policy makers and shakers have pursued an 'adaptive entrepreneurial' approach to urban development. This approach is an unusual hybrid of (a) American-style economic policies – promoting competition through the availability of a cheap and flexible labour force, and (b) EU emphasis on social partnership and social policy initiatives designed to secure social inclusion and common basic welfare standards (Bartley and Treadwell Shine, 1999a). This 'adaptive entrepreneurial' approach seems to avoid the worst excesses of American-style 'boosterism' approaches to achieving economic growth, by addressing aspects of social polarisation and poverty while at the same time promoting entrepreneurial practices (Bartley and Treadwell-Shine, 1999b).

Local authorities have also squeezed themselves back into the equation as active entrepreneurial agents – ironically with a strong emphasis on development that is often at the expense of planning. Clearly, Irish local authorities were not successful in their initially assigned role as combined planning and development agency. Indeed, most local authorities in Ireland now have separate development departments, which operate alongside and often in conflict with the department that discharges planning functions. However, this may have been largely attributable to the limitations placed on them by their subordination to central government in Ireland's highly centralised government system. Unlike most European countries, Ireland's regional government and planning is extremely weak. Like Britain, Ireland has a dual political system comprised of two statutory levels of government – local and central. The local/central divide in Ireland involves a high degree of political and administrative centralisation. Despite the allocation of planning functions to local authorities in the mid-1960s, central government retained control over the allocation of resources and, therefore, over economic promotion and development in Ireland. In short, the dual political nature of Irish government meant that the proactive 'development' powers of the planning authorities were severely restricted. Moreover, the blatant abuses of planning powers that became the focus of subsequent Tribunals of Inquiry into corruption in the planning system reinforced the view that central control needed to be exercised over unreliable local authorities (Grist, 2003).

CRITICISMS OF ENTREPRENEURIAL PLANNING

The current central government sponsored approach of fragmented planning is subject to growing criticism (McGuirk, 2000; McGuirk and MacLaran, 2001; Bartley and Treadwell-Shine, 2003). Obviously, the urban regeneration model and competitive IAPs have the potential to become a useful tool in the armoury of urban planning. However, critics of this 'multiple mini-visions' approach to development do not view it as an alternative to wider, comprehensive planning strategies. As the infrastructural and housing crises in Ireland illustrate, piecemeal urban regeneration does not compensate for the absence of comprehensive housing and settlement policies. Despite the apparent successes of the various urban regeneration models, critics argue that more effective and strategic planning, linked to coherent policies, are still essential to viable and sustainable development (McGuirk and MacLaran, 2001; Bartley and Treadwel-Shine, 2003).

One result of the 'planning drift' and 'entrepreneurial planning' that has shaped the transformation of the metropolitan area over the past four decades has been the creation of cities and towns with accessibility-rich and accessibility-poor spaces. The success of national economic policy in securing economic growth in Ireland since the 1960s brought major changes to the geography and social life of the country's major urban centres. The prevailing 'planning drift' settlement strategy transformed the main urban centres from small, compact, high-density urban realms into sprawling decentralised areas with declining inner districts. In short, and to put it crudely, many urban centres transformed very quickly from European-type urban centres designed for maximum accessibility and low vehicular mobility to an American-type urban sprawl model where private car ownership and mobility became essential for access to work opportunities and services (Breathnach, 1998; Williams and Shiels, 2000). Social divisions were quick to emerge, especially along the lines of residential tenure. Whilst house owners in private residential estates were mainly lower-middle-class, marginal differences in house values were accentuated to create a status hierarchy of residential areas. Social housing was residualised at the bottom of this hierarchy as the least respectable tenure even though the quality of public housing often exceeded that of private housing. The poorer local authority estates quickly became stigmatised as areas that usually had the most limited local amenities for young families with children (Bartley and Saris, 1999; Pringle et al., 1999; Breathnach, 2002b).

There is now evidence of a process of *reurbanisation* (gentrification) taking place alongside the *counter-urbanisation* (suburbanisation and commuterisation) trends in Dublin and other major urban centres – and this may be attributable to the new entrepreneurial planning policy measures designed to reinvigorate town centre areas. However, the renewed urban centres are increasingly the preserve of immigrant groups and young elites who have helped to gentrify it, while the rest of the spread-out urban area is readily accessible only to those with private transport. The poor who live in rural areas and at the urban edge are increasingly isolated due to inadequate public transport provision. In terms of access to the services and facilities they have a much more limited range of choices available to them than the wealthier car-borne population. They are, in effect, physically and socially marginalised (Nolan, 1998; Pringle et al., 1999).

RESPONDING TO THE CRITICISMS: THE NEXT PHASE OF PLANNING

Recent calls for balanced national and regional development through a comprehensive and integrated approach to planning, have resulted in concerted efforts to address the criticisms. Arising out of commitments in the Fianna-Fail/Progressive Democrat government programme and a review of policy by the National Economic and Social Council (NESC, 1997) a comprehensive review of planning legislation was initiated by the DoEHLG in 1997. The objective of the review was to ensure that the planning system of the twenty-first century would be strategic in approach and imbued with an ethos of sustainable development, and would deliver a performance of the highest quality. A new planning code containing many new initiatives was introduced by the Planning and Development Act 2000 which consolidated all of the existing planning legislation and most of the environmental impact assessment law.

The National Spatial Strategy (NSS) has the stated aim of achieving a better balance of social, economic and physical development across Ireland, supported by more co-ordinated and effective planning (Department of the Environment and Local Government, 2002). In order to drive development in the regions, the NSS proposes that areas of sufficient scale and critical mass will be built up through a network of urban gateways and hubs that will link Ireland more effectively into the new 'hot-spots' supported by territorial strategy devised for Europe by the European Spatial Development Perspective (European Commission, 1999). The NSS draws upon the ESDP concepts of poly-centric development (networked connections between urban centres) and the creation of new relationships between urban and rural areas to capitalise upon the potential of all regions to contribute to the development of Ireland in a sustainable and balanced way.

The DoEHLG is currently furthering implementation of the NSS through working with regional and local authorities in the application of regional planning guidelines to facilitate the roll-out of the NSS at regional level. Regional Planning Guidelines were finalised for each of the regions during 2004. Moreover, to ensure the relevant policies are being reflected in new County Development Plans, as well as overseeing the initial preparation of Regional Planning Guidelines, the DoEHLG monitors the preparation of County, City and Local Area Development Plans, to ensure that they are consistent with the objectives of the National Spatial Strategy. Development plan guidelines are currently being prepared by the DoEHLG to assist this process. In early 2005, the Department also issued Best Practice Guidance on transposing the policy objectives contained in the Regional Planning Guidelines into Development Plans (DoEHLG, 2005b).

The NSS has been criticised for ignoring or failing to deliver on its objectives (the Government decentralisation programme for civil service being a case in point). However, this is probably unfair. A time delay is inevitable in a democratic regime that provides for multi-scaled planning based on multiple levels of governance and consultation. Local authority plans in Ireland need time to catch up with the NSS and the subsequently prepared Regional Planning Guidelines devised to give effect to the NSS at regional level. It takes time to devise plans across a range of spatial scales and there will inevitably be consequential time delays associated with the filtering process from national through regional to local levels. This applies particularly to the local plans, which have statutory time frames for adoption and review. While it is envisaged that at a later stage the filtering process will occur simultaneously at all levels (up, down and across) it is understandable that delays and other time discrepancy problems will occur in the start-up stage. Moreover, the NSS was only published in late 2002 in fulfilment of a government commitment in the most recent National Development Plan (NDP) 2000–06. The NDP is the strategic funding strategy prepared by the government in conjunction with the EU Community Support Framework (CSF). The introduction of the NSS has obvious immediate implications for planning and development; it is in effect a prelude to the planning and funding required for the period commencing after 2006, when it is likely to become the key funding allocation guidance tool for the next NDP, covering the period 2007–13. This realignment will introduce a new disciplinary environment and incentive for planning authorities and is likely to lead to more delivery on the aims of the NSS.

CONCLUSIONS

New strategies for spatial planning and regional development must reflect the transition to the entrepreneurial phase – a relaunch of the strategies of the modernisation era is not sufficient to address the issues that confront society and the environment in the twenty-first century. A much better understanding is needed of how to merge the possibilities for new flexible geographies offered by the networked society and economy with more established perspectives. For a variety of reasons there is a dearth of geographical and spatial planning research in Ireland on the dynamics of contemporary economic and social adjustment that could inform policy making and application (Clinch, 2004). This lack of information for evidence-based policy formulation and decision making needs to be addressed urgently. The latest planning period suggests that much effort will be exerted to articulate a national spatial strategy combined with a stronger commitment to regional planning and development. There are several research issues to be addressed in this context. New empirical research is urgently required in relation to recent patterns of territorial organisation for numerous economic and social activities, including the possibilities associated with new technologies and emerging business location priorities. Another set of issues requiring further research concerns how to effectively manage the transition from government to governance which is already well under way in many other countries and which is regarded as a central component of spatial planning and development. While some progress has been made in relation to governance at central and local levels, there remain major challenges at the regional level and scope for better integration of multi-level governance to achieve more effective vertical and horizontal functional relationships (see Chapter 13). There are, therefore, many challenges facing Irish planning and practice in the new century.

3
Regional Development

James A. Walsh

Since the mid-1990s there has emerged a renewed interest in regional development and associated policies and strategies in Ireland by government and development agencies. This culminated in the publication of a National Spatial Strategy in 2002 guided by an approach that represents a break with traditional approaches to regional planning. This approach combined political pragmatism with the capacity of professional policy advisors to incorporate key European ideas and concepts about spatial planning into new frameworks, emphasising spatial relations and development based on local potential, as distinct from relying primarily on inter-regional investment and income transfer strategies. This chapter commences with a brief review of the background to the current phase of regional development in Ireland. This is followed by an overview of recent trends in key indicators, before proceeding to a discussion of current policies and strategies.

REGIONAL DEVELOPMENT POLICIES
AND STRATEGIES UP TO THE LATE 1990s

The history of engagement by government with the issue of uneven regional development in Ireland originates with the Undeveloped Areas Act of 1952 and can be broadly subdivided into three phases over the past 50 years (Gillmor, 1985; Boylan, 2005). The first phase, which lasted until the late 1960s, was mainly characterised by an association between development, industrialisation and urbanisation. For Ireland, given the very weak indigenous manufacturing base and also the imbalances in the urban system, this meant a strong orientation of industrial policy towards the attraction of inward investment and a strong preference among influential policy advisors for an urban-oriented strategy which was most explicitly expressed in the proposals for a regional development strategy contained in the Buchanan Report published in 1968. However, this first phase also highlighted a tension, which has persisted, between the objectives for national economic growth and other objectives in relation to the regional and rural dimensions of development, which included social and political concerns as well as the narrower economic goals.

The sound theoretical underpinnings of the growth-centre strategy which was adopted by many governments across Europe in the 1960s, and which was advocated by Buchanan and other commentators in Ireland, did not find sufficient political support and was quickly abandoned by the government in 1969. The perceived risks to the 'efficiency' of national development policies from an explicit proactive approach to championing the regional 'equity' dimension via growth centres, along with the anticipated political difficulties of promoting an urban-led approach to an electorate comprising a very large rural component, resulted in a move towards a regional strategy that became heavily reliant on the dispersal of inward investment in manufacturing, coupled with a restriction on supports for the capital city.

The second phase was the period from the early 1970s to the late 1990s. Government statements in 1969 and 1972 on regional policy (NESC, 1975) effectively identified the regional industrial strategy of the Industrial Development Agency (IDA) as the main instrument for achieving the goals of regional development. The IDA plans, which were characterised by detailed target settings for 48 town groupings throughout the State, were implemented between 1973 and 1982 with considerable success when measured by the levels of new manufacturing employment in regions with limited prior experience of industrialisation (Breathnach, 1982; Gillmor, 1985). The 1970s was also a time of considerable expansion and improvements in farm incomes during the period of transition to full Common Agricultural Policy (CAP) guaranteed prices (Walsh, 1986). The redistribution of employment in manufacturing along with the new prosperity in the more commercially oriented farming regions resulted in a major demographic turn-around, where net in-migration, coupled with a high birth rate, resulted in a population increase of 465,200 (15.6 per cent) between 1971 and 1981. Most importantly the demographic change was experienced throughout most of the State (Horner et al., 1987). However, throughout this period there emerged significant weaknesses in the government strategy for regional development. The effects of industrial restructuring in Dublin and old industrial centres were largely ignored; elsewhere there was an over-emphasis on inward investment without sufficient support for indigenous firms, and there was a policy vacuum in relation to the emerging services sector (Walsh, 1989).

Throughout the 1980s a combination of factors led to the demise of regional policy and a retreat from the strategies implemented during the 1970s (Breathnach, 1982). Following the establishment of the European Regional Development Fund in 1975 the government chose to consider all of the Republic of Ireland as a single region, which diverted attention away from internal imbalances. A major review of industrial policy published in 1982 was highly critical of many features of the inward investment model promoted in the 1970s, upon which much of the regional strategy was dependent (NESC, 1982). This resulted in a White Paper on Industrial Policy in 1984 which included a major revision of the role of industry in promoting regional development.

The strategy of specific job targets for groups of towns that was characteristic of the 1970s was to be replaced with a policy of supporting industry where it could make greatest progress. The White Paper also recommended a more targeted approach to supporting firms in a small number of expanding high-technology sectors which also had significant implications for the location of new companies, with the larger urban centres more likely to benefit most. The shift in the focus of industrial policy was further supported by the National Economic and Social Council in 1985 when it recommended that in future the designation of areas for industrial support should be based on criteria related to the potential rather than the needs of regions (NESC, 1985). This was the beginning of a return to a more urban-focused regional development strategy which at this stage was more cognisant of the emerging threats from the proposed Single European Market (to be in place by January 1993) than the domestic fears of politicians which had resulted in the rejection of the Buchanan growth-centre strategy.

In addition to the reorientation of industrial policy, the general stagnation of the Irish economy in the 1980s resulted in a policy environment where a significant reduction in the volume of inward investment greatly diminished the capacity of the IDA to influence the location of new investments, especially towards the weaker regions. Widespread losses in manufacturing employment, a faltering agricultural sector, a weak producer services sector, and increasing unemployment, all combined to bring about a return to high levels of net emigration from both rural and urban areas (Walsh, 1991).

The foundations for a new era of economic development were laid in the mid-to-late 1980s which resulted in unprecedented rates of economic growth in the 1990s. The reasons for the so called 'Celtic Tiger miracle' are varied and interrelated in a complex manner. They include the adoption of a new approach to negotiated governance, macro-economic stabilisation measures, the social dividends from a late demographic transition, and also the accumulated benefits of investment in education, new orientations in policies for manufacturing and internationally traded services, the role of the European Union in the provision of additional financial supports (especially the Structural and Cohesion Funds) and also in opening up new trading opportunities following the establishment of the Internal Market (Breathnach, 1998, Walsh, 2000). Collectively all of these factors contributed to a renewal of confidence among key decision makers in relation to the global foreign investment strategies of multinational corporations which resulted in a very major expansion in the volume, and also an improvement in the quality, of new investments attracted to Ireland. Most commentators are agreed that it is this sector which has become the principal driver of the economic transformation since the early 1990s.

The transition to the Celtic Tiger era was not immediately accompanied by a revival of interest in regional planning or spatial development strategies. Rather a number of factors combined in the early 1990s which led to a new approach. In order to satisfy the EU partnership criterion in relation to the Structural Fund it became necessary to establish eight regional authorities in January 1994. While their roles are extremely limited, the initiative did provide fora for promoting debate on regional issues. Later, in response to the fact that some of the regional authority areas (which are treated as NUTS 3 level regions by the

EU statistics agency Eurostat) had exceeded the threshold level of per capita GDP for Structural Fund eligibility, the government established two regional assemblies to administer regional development programmes in two new NUTS 2 level regions (see Figure 3.1).

The external pressures emanating from the EU were matched with pressures emerging from both the urban and rural parts of Ireland (Walsh, 2000). On the one hand, the very rapid economic expansion which was disproportionately concentrated in the Greater Dublin area resulted in several problems including

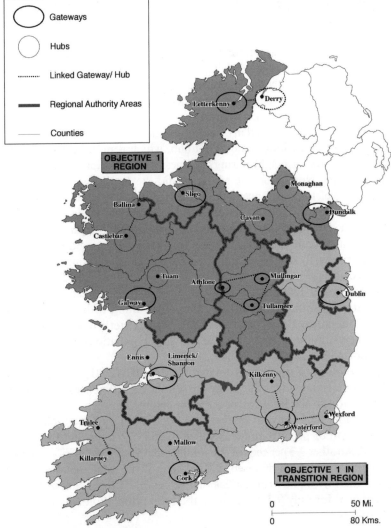

Source: Based on Map 2, The National Spatial Strategy, 2002

Figure 3.1 Gateways and hubs as defined by the National Spatial Strategy 2002

Source: NSS (2002); Ordnance Survey Ireland

excessive levels of congestion, escalating house prices, and the emergence of large numbers of car-driving, long-distance commuters. Such unsustainable trends contributed to increasing demands for a regional policy that would help to alleviate the new problems of the Greater Dublin area. On the other hand, spokespersons for the weaker regions drew attention to the uneven geographical spread of opportunities in the new economy. Before considering the policy responses that were initiated in the late 1990s it is necessary to review the regional trends in key economic and social indicators over recent years.

PATTERNS AND TRENDS IN REGIONAL DEVELOPMENT

Demographic Trends

The period since 1991 is characterised by the highest rates of population increase since the 1970s. Growth post-1991 has been truly exceptional. However, the underlying demographic dynamics and the resultant patterns are very different from those of the 1970s with net migration being fuelled by substantial numbers of immigrants, including return migrants.

The population has increased in all counties since 1996 with particularly high rates of increase in the hinterland of Dublin, which is no longer confined to the contiguous parts of neighbouring counties; rather it extends to encompass large parts of the Northeast, the Midland and the Southeast (CSO, 2003a). The emergence of long distance commuting (CSO, 2003b; Walsh et al., 2005; see Chapter 1) and the related residential developments, often in previously small compact settlements, has significant implications with regard to achieving balanced sustainable development. Improvements in the demographic structure of counties primarily due to an influx of long-distance migrants should not be construed as a positive indicator of more regionally balanced development. Beyond the Greater Dublin area significant population gains have also been experienced in the hinterlands of the other cities along with the catchments of some of the larger towns such as Tralee, Sligo, Leterkenny and Kilkenny. However, there are also extensive rural areas where population decline continues to be the norm (Haase and Pratschke, 2005).

Using a typology of rural areas devised by McHugh (2001; and see Chapter 6 in this volume) it is evident that there are significant differences between area types in relation to the levels of population change between 1991 and 2002. Over the period, 86.5 per cent of the total population increase took place in either the urban or peri-urban areas which include 72.7 per cent of the total population. Another 3.3 per cent of the total increase occurred in mostly coastal high amenity areas which represent 8.4 per cent of the total area. By contrast the predominantly weaker rural areas that represent 51.6 per cent of the total area accounted for only 0.5 per cent of the total population gain (Commins et al., 2005).

Employment and Unemployment

Most of the data available on the numbers of persons in employment relate to the place of residence of those who are enumerated. Taking account, therefore, of the deconcentration of population and also the impacts of a very large expansion in the numbers of females at work, it is not surprising that there have been widespread gains in the numbers at work in each region (see Table 3.1). While in absolute terms the largest gain has been in the Mid East region, the effects of long distance commuting are evident in the data for both the Midland and Border (mostly residents of Louth) regions. However, there are pronounced urban–rural differentials which are particularly evident in relation to the educational qualifications of those at work, a factor that is of considerable importance in relation to future patterns of regional development (Commins et al., 2005). There are also important sectoral differences (see Table 3.2) which impact on the productivity components of each region's per capita GDP. For example, approximately 10 per cent of the workforce in the Border and West regions are engaged in low-productivity agriculture. While a similar percentage are employed in the sector in the Southeast the productivity levels are higher. Of particular concern for many rural areas are the high levels of reliance on employment in either agriculture, manufacturing or the building and construction sectors.

Table 3.1 Employment and unemployment by region

Region	% change in employment 2000–05	% share of employment 2005	% unemployment rate 2005
Dublin	8.7	29.8	4.2
Mideast	22.1	11.3	2.7
Southeast	17.7	10.4	5.6
Southwest	14.9	14.4	4.2
Midwest	12.7	8.5	4.7
West	21.3	9.7	3.7
Border	20.5	10.3	4.9
Midland	24.1	5.7	4.0
Ireland	15.4	100.0	4.2

Source: CSO (2005)

Table 3.2 Percentage of total employment by sector in each region, 2005

Region	Agriculture	Manufacturing	Construction	Services
Dublin	0.4	10.7	9.2	79.8
Mideast	5.2	16.7	14.5	63.7
Southeast	9.8	17.9	15.4	56.8
Southwest	7.4	16.5	13.5	62.6
Midwest	8.4	20.3	11.0	60.4
West	9.6	15.6	14.9	59.8
Border	10.3	17.2	13.8	58.7
Midland	7.3	16.8	15.0	60.9
Ireland	5.9	15.2	12.6	66.3

Source: CSO (2005)

Data relating to place of work in the manufacturing and internationally traded services sectors point towards increasing levels of concentration in the major urban centres. Between 1995 and 2004 almost two-thirds (63 per cent) of the increase in the numbers at work in manufacturing and internationally traded service companies occurred in Dublin and neighbouring parts of the adjoining counties. There were also significant gains in Cork and Galway. Unemployment rates have declined considerably compared to levels in the early 1990s. As might be expected the lowest rate (2.7 per cent) is found in Mid East region which has the youngest and most highly educated labour force. By contrast, the rates remain comparatively high in traditionally weaker rural areas, especially in the Northwest. The highest regional rate in 2005 was in the Southeast (5.6 per cent), reflecting the failure to diversify the regional economy which continues to be disproportionately reliant on traditional labour intensive, low-value-added industries.

Regional Output and Income Trends

Data compiled by the Central Statistics Office on estimates of regional gross value added (GVA) per capita (this is similar to the concept of per capita GDP used in international comparisons) reveal significant differences between regions and furthermore a trend of increasing divergence between regions since the early 1990s, in contrast to the trend in earlier decades (O'Leary, 2001). For example, the per capita GVA in the Border Midland West (BMW) NUTS 2 region was only 74.9 per cent of the State average, while the index for the remaining NUTS 2 region (Southern and Eastern) was 109.1 giving a differential of 34.2 percentage points compared with 27 in 1991. By 2002 the comparable indices were 69.1 and 111.1 resulting in a gap of 42.0 percentage points. Thus between 1991 and 2002 the BMW regional share of the total GVA declined from 21.6 per cent to 18.3 per cent. The Midland NUTS 3 level region has persistently had the lowest index, which was only 63.2 per cent of the State average in 2002. The combined Dublin and Mid East region index has recently been surpassed by the Southwest at 131.3 mainly due to the value assigned to some pharmaceutical products produced in Cork. Differentials in sectoral productivity levels are the principal source of variation between regions in per capita GVA (Boyle et al., 1999).

Gross value added per capita is not a measure of personal income. It includes company profits that are not part of the income of Irish residents, which is particularly important in Ireland due to the role of multinational corporations in the economy. Caution is also required when comparing per capita GVA levels across regions because distortions may be introduced by inter-regional commuting and state income transfers. This is especially relevant in relation to Dublin and the Mid East regions, and more recently there is evidence that these factors also impact on Border and Midland region estimates.

A separate series of data on household incomes are compiled by the CSO on an annual basis for each region and county. Comparisons of per capita personal disposable income levels reveal greater consistency over time and a much smaller inter-regional gap. For example, in 2002 the average per capita disposable income in Dublin had an index of 113.4 (Ireland = 100) compared with 89.4 in the Border region giving an inter-regional gap of 24 percentage points. The comparable gap in 1991 was similar at 24.8.

Focusing specifically on poor households, a research team from the Economic and Social Research Institute has found that there are significant inter-regional and intra-regional variations in the distributions of a number of poverty related indices (Watson et al., 2005). Significantly, they emphasise that structural rather than spatial factors are the main influences on the distributions. Finally, Haase and Pratschke (2005) have used small-area census variables to systematically assess the spatial patterns of socio-economic disadvantage in Ireland. Combining measures for three dimensions of disadvantage they found that between 1991 and 2002 there was a general decline in the absolute levels of disadvantage throughout most of the country but the relative positions of districts changed very little (see Chapter 19). Significant urban–rural differentials persist with populations in the most rural areas most likely to be socio-economically disadvantaged.

RECENT POLICY INITIATIVES FOR REGIONAL DEVELOPMENT

The need to develop a new government policy and strategy emerged in response to both external (mostly EU) and internal pressures. The trends described in the previous section are associated with a phase during which economic growth rates were much higher than anticipated and for which there was no overall spatial framework, nor were there appropriate administrative structures in place to ensure co-ordination and integration of government policies and strategies.

The National Development Plan 2000–06 (NDP) published in November 1999 included as a key goal the objective of fostering balanced regional development. The government's objective for regional policy as set out in the NDP is a complex one requiring a reconciliation of potentially conflicting aims:

…to achieve more balanced regional development in order to reduce the disparities between and within the two Regions and to develop the potential of both to contribute to the greatest possible extent to the continuing prosperity of the country. Policy to secure such development must be advanced in parallel with policies to ensure that this development is sustainable with full regard to the quality of life, social cohesion, and conservation of the environment and the natural and cultural heritage. (para 3.19, p. 43)

In order to make progress in relation to this objective the NDP included a commitment by the government to prepare a strategy for spatial development. The preparation of the National Spatial Strategy (NSS) between Spring 2000 and Autumn 2002 involved extensive consultation and a major research programme (Walsh, 2004).

A number of key concepts emerged during the preparation of the NSS (DoELG, 2001). A central objective is to promote *balanced regional development* (BRD) while at the same time maintaining the competitiveness of the economy, improving the quality of life of all persons, and ensuring that the development model is sustainable. An approach based on potential rather than on needs was adopted. This was consistent with the approach advocated more than 15 years earlier in 1985 by the NESC and repeated in its Strategy Report published in 1999.

Potential is defined as the capacity which an area possesses for development arising from its endowment of natural resources, population, labour, economic and social capital and location relative to markets. Different areas have differing types and levels of potential. *Critical mass* is an important concept in optimising local and regional potential. It has been defined as the size, concentration and characteristics of populations that enable a range of services and facilities to be supported and which, in turn, can attract and support higher levels of economic activity. The transformation that has occurred in Dublin since the early 1990s illustrates the importance of critical mass. Dublin's success has been assisted by its population size and structure, levels of education, the availability of educational resources, the mix and clustering of different types of labour pools in niche sectors, transport links to other regions and countries, and informal networks of people and enterprise that provide the scale or critical mass to support rapid economic progress.

The same level of critical mass cannot be achieved everywhere. Concentration of resources to achieve stronger centres and thereby the development of related areas is a crucial dynamic in bringing about more balanced regional development. This inevitably involves difficult choices about how and where to concentrate efforts.

Maintaining an on-going dynamic of development is crucially dependent on the capacity to promote and sustain a high level of innovation within regions. Research on regional innovation systems points to the importance of supportive institutional structures to nurture innovative milieu (Morgan and Nauwelaers, 1999). There is a very strong emphasis on communication structures to facilitate both formal and informal knowledge exchanges, and also on maximising the potential of local resources. Much of the international experience also suggests that local labour markets need to be large enough to cope with relatively high levels of staff turnover. These requirements support the emphasis placed on the approach to BRD in the NSS.

Against the background analysis summarised above, the NSS recommends a strategy for spatial development based on gateways and hubs plus a supporting infrastructure network and a requirement that all relevant public sector policies comply with the spatial framework of the NSS. It recognises explicitly the vital national role of Dublin as an international gateway in the future and it also recognises the possibilities for increased co-operation between Dublin and Belfast (Walsh, 2005a).

The NDP in 1999 had already identified Cork, Limerick/Shannon, Galway and Waterford as additional gateways. The NSS envisages closer links being developed between these centres through improvement of transport infrastructure and measures to foster co-operation that will lead to a much greater level of critical mass in the context of a poly-centric network. The achievement of this objective will be a major challenge, for which there are few international precedents (McCafferty, 2002).

As none of the gateways identified in the NDP (with the exception of Galway) are located in the BMW region the NSS proposes four additional gateways: (1) Dundalk in the Northeast and centrally located between Dublin and Belfast; (2) Sligo as the principal town between Galway and the new gateway for the Northwest based on (3) Letterkenny linked with Derry in Northern Ireland, and (4) in response to the weak regional urban system in the Midlands the NSS proposes that over the long term the towns of Athlone, Tullamore and Mullingar should be more closely linked in order to establish a local poly-centric gateway. The system of gateways will be supported by another tier of hub towns that are each linked to a gateway. While in most cases the hubs are strategically chosen single centres there are two instances where duocentric hubs are proposed: Tralee-Killarney in the Southwest and Castlebar-Ballina in the West (Figure 3.1). The principal characteristics of gateways and hubs are summarised in Table 3.3.

The gateways and hubs are the foci of functional regions. Using travel-to-work data compiled from the 2002 census of population Walsh et al. (2005) have identified the hinterland of each gateway and hub (see Figure 1.5). In 2002 the gateway hinterlands included 73 per cent of the total population and they accounted for 83 per cent of the total population increase between 1996 and 2002. The comparable figures for the hub towns are 10 per cent of the total population in 2002 and 8 per cent of the inter-censal increase. Thus while the majority of the population are within commuting distance of the proposed centres there is nevertheless a substantial proportion (17% = c.666,000) who live beyond the prioritised hinterlands. This represents a significant challenge for the areas and populations concerned.

A further issue of concern might be where future population growth is likely to occur. Regional population projections prepared by the CSO (2005) suggest that the total population may increase from 3.917 million in 2002 to 5.070 million in 2021. Walsh (2005) has argued that some adjustment of the population targets for the larger gateways may be necessary in order to avoid a further increase in the concentration of the population in Dublin and the surrounding counties.

The gateways and hubs are complemented by specific roles for smaller urban centres and also by general guidelines in relation to housing in the countryside. In order to promote balanced regional development, the settlement strategy will be supported by a national transport framework that will include (a) strategic radial corridors linking each of the gateways to Dublin, (b) strategic linking corridors to improve interaction between the major centres and (c) international sea and air access points (Figure 3.2). The linking corridors are vitally important to altering the current pattern of movements between centres. The proposals include a western corridor from Derry to Limerick and Cork; a southern corridor linking the seaports and airports in the Southeast, Southwest and Midwest; and a central spine linking the proposed Midland gateway to Dundalk, Waterford and Rosslare.

Table 3.3   Characteristics of gateways and hubs

Gateway	Hub
A large urban population (100,000 or more) set in a large urban and rural hinterland	A significant urban population in the range of 20,000 to 40,000 with an associated rural hinterland
Wide range of primary and secondary education facilities and national or regional tertiary-level centres of learning	Primary and secondary education facilities with the option of tertiary-level or outreach facilities
Large clusters of national/international scale enterprises, including those involved in advanced sectors	A mix of local, medium-sized and larger businesses serving local, regional and national/ international markets
A focal point in transportation and communications terms: (a) on the national roads and rail networks; (b) within 1 hour of an airport either with international access or linking to one such access; (c) adequate, reliable, cost effective and efficient access to port facilities; (d) effective, competitive broadband access	An important local node in transportation and communications terms: (a) on the national road and rail or bus networks; (b) with access to a national or regional airport; (c) having adequate, reliable, cost-effective and efficient access to port facilities; (d) effective and competitive broadband access
Integrated public transport with facilities for pedestrians and cyclists	Effective local transport system with facilities for pedestrians and cyclists
Regional hospital/specialised care	Local and/or regional hospital
City-level range of theatres, arts and sports centres and public spaces/parks; cultural and entertainment quarters	Wide range of amenities, sporting and cultural facilities including public spaces and parks
City-scale water and waste management services	Effective water services and waste management arrangements
Integrated land-use and transport planning frameworks	Strategies for physical, social and economic development
Phased zoning and servicing of land banks in anticipation of needs associated with growth	Phased zoning and servicing of land banks in anticipation of needs associated with growth
Strategic Development Zones	Industrial and local business parks

Source: National Spatial Strategy 2002, p. 40

Since the publication of the NSS in December 2002 Regional Planning Guidelines (RPGs) have been adopted by each regional authority which provide regional-level frameworks for promoting the NSS objectives. The RPGs also provide the frameworks for future county Development Plans which must always take account of the medium-term strategies for economic, social and cultural development prepared by each city/county development board in 2002. Thus there is now in place for the first time an integrated hierarchical framework to promote an integrated and co-ordinated approach to development which aspires to be sustainable in respect of its economic, social and environmental dimensions. This, rather belatedly, represents a fundamental broadening of

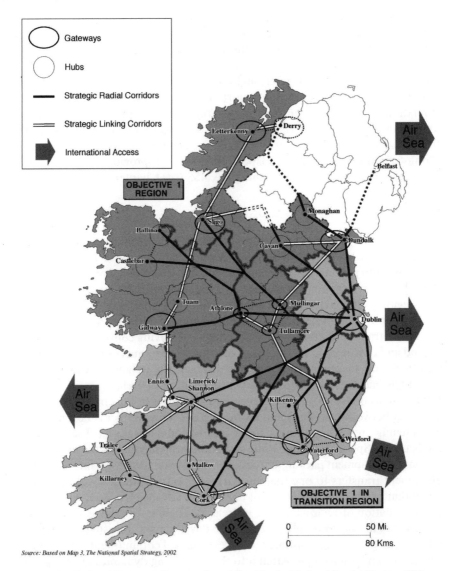

Source: Based on Map 3, The National Spatial Strategy, 2002

Figure 3.2 National Transport Framework as defined by the National Spatial Strategy 2002

Source: NSS (2002); Ordnance Survey Ireland

the approach to regional development that extends the objectives beyond the narrower focus on regional economic growth rates.

In addition, there has been progress on other fronts. Detailed long-term land use and transportation studies have been completed for Cork and Galway and others are under way. An assessment of the challenges and potential associated with developing the Atlantic Corridor linking each of the major gateways outside Dublin has been completed by the Department of Environment, Heritage and Local Government (2006). The Atlantic Corridor project is a long-term strategic approach to supporting a poly-centric network that will serve as the principal alternative to an East Coast Corridor linking Dublin and Belfast. The DoEHLG and Forfás (the national policy and advisory board for enterprise, trade, science, technology and innovation) jointly commissioned a study to identify investment priorities for the gateways in the context of the next National Development Plan. The report, drawing on international experience in relation to successful centres and also on local consultations, identifies a comprehensive list of supports that are vital to successful implementation of the NSS (Fitzpatrick Associates et al., 2005). The government has also published a long term transport plan, Transport 21, which will provide funding for the key transport proposals underpinning the NSS (see Chapter 7).

CONCLUSIONS

This chapter has provided an overview of the history of policies and strategies for regional development in Ireland. After several years of neglect a new commitment to regional development has evolved. The experience since the early 1990s has shown that in the absence of a national spatial strategy significant inter-regional and intra-regional imbalances are likely to occur. More generally the development process is likely to become unsustainable. A fundamental issue is the trade-off between on the one hand, achieving convergence between Ireland and core regions of the EU in relation to economic indicators, and on the other hand, increasing inter-regional divergence in Ireland. The Dublin city region has had a pivotal role in the transformation of Ireland since the early 1990s, but, as in many other late developing countries in Europe, there may be a conflict between European and national goals. This conflict is best resolved by attaching greater significance to the international role, as has been done in the National Spatial Strategy, while simultaneously modifying the underlying regional development paradigm from one which relies heavily on inter-regional investment transfers to one that supports efforts to optimise local potential. From that perspective, a significant conceptual advance has been achieved in the formulation of regional policy in Ireland. There is, of course, much more to be achieved, most notably in relation to developing a consistent implementation strategy with appropriate resources, political commitment, training for key actors, and on-going research into the underlying dynamics of the spatial aspects of economic and social development in a state that is uniquely open and, therefore, in constant need of being vigilant about its position (location) in the international space economy. The transition to a new regional development paradigm has been very slow and was mostly a reaction to deepening regional, environmental and social issues. Going forward, a more proactive long-term strategic approach is required, which poses a particular challenge to a political system more sensitive to shorter-term goals.

4

Urban Systems

Des McCafferty

In the popular imagination, Ireland has long existed as a rural, agrarian society, and much of the symbolism, imagery and mythology of the country has reflected its strong rural heritage. The reality, however, is that significantly more people live in urban than in rural areas. This is true not just of Northern Ireland, where modern urbanisation dates from the nineteenth century, but also of the Republic of Ireland, where the decline of employment in agriculture, the restructuring of manufacturing, the growth of the services sector and recent immigration have fuelled a shift in population from rural to urban areas. This chapter considers the changing form of urbanisation, as expressed in the urban systems of the island. It looks at some of the key structural aspects of those urban systems, and the challenges that they pose for public policy formation, especially in the realm of territorial development. The emphasis will be mainly on the Republic of Ireland, though important contrasts and similarities with Northern Ireland will be noted throughout. The chapter begins with a brief consideration of the concept of an urban system, and its application in Ireland. It then proceeds to examine recent (post-1981) trends in the distribution of population across the settlement systems of both Ireland and Northern Ireland. This is followed first by an analysis of the size distribution of urban centres, and then by a consideration of their spatial distribution, noting the changes that have resulted from the regionally differentiated pattern of urban growth. The chapter concludes with a review of some policy and planning issues arising from recent developments.

URBAN SYSTEMS IN IRELAND

The key idea behind the urban system concept is that, to understand the individual city or town, it is necessary to study it within the context of its links to other places, in particular other urban centres. These relationships, which may be expressed through flows of materials, goods, services, information, or people, affect not just the kinds of work done in towns and cities, but also their social character and, arguably, the political outlook of their inhabitants. Together the set of urban places and the functional relationships between them constitute the urban system. Urban systems can be identified on various geographical scales, ranging from the regional to the international and global. Because of the pre-eminence of the territorial state as regulator of production and exchange throughout the modern era, urban systems have been defined most often at national level. However, in recent years much attention has been devoted to the development of a European urban system, given meaning by the deepening of European integration in the context of the EU, and of a global urban system, brought into existence by the process of neo-liberal globalisation (Sassen, 1994; Knox and Taylor, 1995). Much of the renewed impetus for urban systems research derives from analyses of these transnational systems.

Reflecting the historical importance of the state in the development of urban systems, two different systems have traditionally been identified in Ireland, north and south of the border respectively. However, while the separate development of these systems was strongly influenced by political partition in 1920, the process had begun earlier (Harrison and Anderson, 1980; Pringle, 1980). Nineteenth-century industrialisation imparted to the towns of East Ulster a different functional role from that of towns elsewhere in Ireland, which continued to be mainly engaged in service provision to their rural hinterlands. The dominance of this rural service role in the South, in a context of declining population, resulted in a weakly articulated, inchoate urban system. The policy shift from protectionism to free trade in the late 1950s boosted Southern Irish industrialisation, but it was still not until 1971 that more than 50 per cent of the population was enumerated in 'aggregate town areas'. Urbanisation has therefore taken place in a context where the economy has developed into one of the most open in the world. In a comparatively short time, the external dependency involved in the colonial relationship with Britain has been replaced with that entailed in the process of globalisation. As a result, Irish towns and cities have had little opportunity to develop the kind and intensity of interlinkages that define a well integrated, national urban system. Instead, urban change and development have been largely affected by forces and processes operating beyond the national level, a condition that, as Taylor (2004) points out, does not fit well with traditional urban systems analysis.

Notwithstanding these reservations about the strength of urban integration in Ireland, consideration of the set of urban places is still worthwhile for several reasons. First, the study of the urban system affords valuable insights into what Bourne (2002) refers to as 'the macro-geography of the urbanisation process', allowing us to gain an overview of how that process is crystallising at various nodes in the national territory. Second, and related to this, there is the increasingly important role of the urban system as mediator of regional development in Ireland. As the service sector expands, in part through the growth of internationally traded services, and as the manufacturing base is increasingly restructured towards high technology/high-value-added activities, production and employment are becoming increasingly concentrated in urban areas. In this context, the development prospects of regions depend very heavily on their urban structures. This was recognised as long ago as the Buchanan report on regional development (Buchanan, 1968); it was reaffirmed by the NESC report on population distribution and economic development (NESC,

1997), and it is fundamental to the National Spatial Strategy (DoELG, 2002).

URBANISATION AND THE URBAN SYSTEMS

The outcome of recent urbanisation in Ireland in terms of the urban system can be ascertained from an examination of population change by size category of settlement, for the period from 1981 to 2002. The population data used here refer to built-up urban areas, as defined for census purposes. This definition extends beyond administrative boundaries (where these exist) to incorporate the urban 'environs' or suburbs. All settlements over 1,500 in population are included initially, and they are divided, fairly arbitrarily, into six size categories as illustrated in Table 4.1. The largest of these size categories contains just a single centre, the continuously built-up Greater Dublin area. For discussion purposes, these categories will be referred to as Dublin, the other cities, large, medium and small towns, and (borrowing a term from Northern Ireland usage) 'intermediate settlements'.

Table 4.1   Population change by town size category, 1981–2002, Republic of Ireland

Size category	Absolute change	% change	Share of urban growth	Change in urban share
200,000+ *	89,499	9.78	21.33	−4.75
35,000–200,000 **	79,327	25.86	18.91	0.52
10,000–35,000	239,274	93.14	57.04	7.84
5,000–10,000	−13,301	−5.38	−3.17	−2.89
3,000–5,000	−753	−0.75	−0.18	−0.97
1,500–3,000	25,451	28.76	6.07	0.26
Aggregate town areas	419,497	21.91	100.00	0.00

* Dublin, ** Cork, Galway, Limerick, Waterford

Source: CSO (2002)

The population of the state increased by 474,000, or 13 per cent between 1981 and 2002, with 89 per cent of the increase (419,000) taking place in the aggregate town areas, which grew in population by 1 per cent per annum. Significant differences are evident in the distribution of population growth across size categories, and the general pattern is one of strongest growth in the larger towns and the cities (see Table 4.1). The size category that has shown both the largest absolute gain and the highest rate of growth over the last 20 years is that ranging from 10,000 to 35,000 population. This category almost doubled in population, with an increase of 240,000, or 57 per cent of the total urban increase in the period. As a result, its share of the urban population increased by almost 8 percentage points, from 13 per cent in 1981 to 21 per cent in 2002. The cities other than Dublin also experienced a relatively high rate of growth, and as a result increased their share of urban population, as did the intermediate settlements (population 1,500 to 3,000). All other settlement categories declined in terms of their percentage share. Dublin's population expanded by almost 90,000 persons over the period as a whole, but its growth rate was below that of the aggregate town areas (and indeed the national average), so that its share of urban population decreased by almost 5 percentage points, from 48 to 43 per cent. Population decreased in both absolute and relative terms in the medium and small town categories.

The population trends described above are in part due to changes in the number of centres in each size category: as settlements grow (or decline) they can pass from one category to the next. For example, the strong population growth of the large towns category is in part due to the expansion of medium-sized towns to the point where they exceeded the 10,000 population threshold. In fact the number of large towns (10,000–35,000) increased from 16 to 28 over the 21 year period, and the number of medium settlements (5,000–10,000) from 40 to 53, the latter a reflection of population growth in rural villages. In contrast, the number of settlements in the two largest size categories remained static. To allow for changes in the number of settlements per size class, we can focus on the *average* size of centres in each category, and on the change in these averages over the period (see Table 4.2). This reveals an increase of over 10 per cent in the average size of centres in the large town category, a similar rate of growth to that of Dublin. The highest growth in average size – 26 per cent – occurred in the cities other than Dublin.[1] By contrast with the cities and large towns, towns with populations between 5,000 and 10,000 showed very little growth in average size of centre, and the average size of intermediate settlements actually declined.

Table 4.2   Trends in the number and average size of centres, 1981–2002

Size category	No. of centres 1981	No. of centres 2002	Change in average size 1981–2002
200,000 +	1	1	9.78
35,000–200,000	4	4	25.86
10,000–35,000	16	28	10.37
5,000–10,000	35	33	0.35
3,000–5,000	27	25	7.19
1,500–3,000	40	53	−2.83

Source: CSO 2002

Clearly, population growth in Ireland since 1981 has been strongly focused on the cities and larger towns in the middle of the size range. This trend also prevailed in the 1970s (Cawley, 1991) and indeed has been identified as far back as the 1950s (NESC, 1997). The strength of the trend suggests that, within the context of on-going urbanisation, there has been a degree of deconcentration of urban population away from the capital city. While there appears to be evidence here of 'polarisation reversal', with the Republic entering the 'intermediate city stage' in the model of differential urbanisation developed by Geyer and Kontuly (1993), both these concepts carry connotations of spatial decentralisation (Geyer, 1995) which, it will be argued below, are not supported by empirical data.

Some insights into the nature of recent urbanisation north of the border can be obtained from data published in connection with the Northern Ireland Regional Development Strategy introduced in 2001. These data are not directly comparable with those for the Republic of Ireland, with, for example the Belfast Metropolitan area (BMA) much more widely bounded than the Greater Dublin area, so that it incorporates both open countryside and large 'free-standing' towns such as Bangor and Carrickfergus. These form part of the functional region of Belfast, but are not part of the continuous built-up area. Bearing in mind this difference, the data indicate some similarity with trends in the Republic in the case of the large centres of population (10,000+), which grew strongly throughout the period and marginally increased their share of population (see Table 4.3). However, what is more striking is the inverse relationship between size of settlement and both absolute and relative population growth. Thus, between 1981 and 1998 small towns and villages increased in population by 59,000 (23 per cent), as compared to an increase of just 14,000 persons (2 per cent) in the BMA. As a result, the distribution of population shifted away from Belfast towards the smaller centres. This shift was even more pronounced in the earlier part of the period. Most (58 per cent) of the growth in the smaller settlements occurred in the 1980s, but the Belfast region lost more than 3 per cent of its population, a trend that was led mainly by a sharp decrease in the population of the city itself. While the BMA recovered in the 1990s to record the largest absolute population gain (+33,273), much of this growth took place in the small towns and villages within the region (Department for Regional Development, 2001b).

Table 4.3   Population change by town size category, 1981–1998, Northern Ireland

Category	Absolute change	% change	Share of urban growth	Change in urban share
Belfast Metropolitan Area	14,057	2.44	11.40	-3.49
Towns over 10,000	50,439	14.13	40.91	1.02
Small towns and villages	58,782	23.14	47.68	2.47
All nucleated settlements	123,278	10.38	100.00	0.00

Source: Department for Regional Development (2001b)

These data suggest that, compared with the South, urbanisation in the North has been associated with an even greater degree of population deconcentration within the urban system. This finding is consistent with an analysis for the period 1971–86 by Poole (1991), who found evidence of a degree of counter-urbanisation, particularly in the eastern part of Northern Ireland and in the early 1980s.[2]

POPULATION CONCENTRATION AND
THE SIZE DISTRIBUTION OF CENTRES

Apart from the problem of comparability between the Republic and Northern Ireland, the analysis so far suffers from the limitation that the trends identified depend on the way that the size categories are defined: obviously, the use of different size categories may alter the results. To overcome this limitation, we can 'unpack' our categories and examine trends in population concentration taking account of the actual sizes of centres. By treating each urban centre as an individual observation, we can measure concentration using a number of well established approaches. One (indirect) approach derives measures of concentration from formal models of the size distribution of urban centres. Amongst the best known of these is the inverse-power or general rank-size model, which relates the sizes of centres to their relative position (or rank) within the urban system, the largest place being ranked 1, the second largest ranked 2, and so on. The model can be stated as:

$$P_r = kr^{-q}$$

where P_r is the estimated population of the centre of rank r, and k and q are empirically determined parameters. Calibration of this model for a particular urban system entails finding the values of k and q that give the best 'fit' between the modelled and actual populations. The more interesting value is q, the slope parameter. This determines how sharply the modelled population decreases with increasing rank, so that it can conveniently be used as a measure of population concentration within the urban system: higher values of q indicate greater concentration, lower values a more even distribution. This approach has been followed, for example, in a recent study of the Chinese urban system (Song and Zhang, 2002). One advantage of using the slope parameter as a measure of concentration is that a value of unity ($q = 1$) characterises a well known type of urban size distribution – that which follows the restrictive rank-size rule or Zipf model – and therefore provides a convenient reference point for assessing population concentration.

The main disadvantage of using the rank-size parameter in an Irish context is that the overall fit of the model tends not to be very good, largely because of the rather unbalanced size distribution arising from the dominance of Dublin and Belfast in their respective urban systems. For this reason, a second (direct) measure of concentration will also be employed. This is the well known Gini coefficient which is widely used to measure inequality or unevenness in distributions such as those of income, employment or population. The value of the coefficient ranges between 0 and 1, with 0 indicating a perfectly uniform distribution, and 1 a completely concentrated pattern.[3]

Before deriving these measures for the Irish urban systems, we need to define two things: the boundaries of the urban areas, and the set of centres that make up the urban systems. Urban areas will again be defined as built-up areas in the Republic. For Northern Ireland the nearest equivalent for which data are conveniently available is the 'settlement', defined mainly on the basis of the statutory development limits for urban centres, but also taking into account the identity of settlements. In the case of Belfast this unit (Belfast Urban Area), with a population in 2001 of 276,459, considerably under-represents the built-up area. For this reason two other definitions are also used: (1) the Belfast Metropolitan Urban Area (or BMUA, population of 579,554); and (2) an adjusted definition of the BMUA (population of 483,418) which excludes those settlements which do not form part of the contiguous urban area.[4] These different definitions result in different numbers of centres in the system (see Table 4.4). Because settlement populations are only available for 2001, analysis of the Northern Ireland urban system is for that year only.

Table 4.4 Measures of population concentration within the urban systems

Area	No. of centres	q value	Gini coefficient
Republic of Ireland			
1981	56	1.77	.767
1986	57	1.72	.755
1991	57	1.70	.744
1996	57	1.69	.736
2002	66	1.62	.715
Northern Ireland			
2001[a]	38	1.02	.582
2001[b]	30	1.75	.715
2001[c]	33	1.51	.670

Note: Belfast defined as: (a) Belfast Urban Area; (b) Belfast Metropolitan Urban Area; and (c) Belfast Metropolitan Urban Area adjusted (see text).

In order to define the urban system we need to establish a cut-off population level above which settlements can be regarded as urban in character. While there is no universal agreement on this, nevertheless there has been some convergence in recent usage. Thus, while it is recognised that different cut-offs are suitable for different purposes, a 'default' urban threshold of 4,500 population has recently been suggested for Northern Ireland (Northern Ireland Statistics and Research Agency, 2005). In the Republic, recent practice has been to set the threshold slightly higher, at 5,000 population (e.g., Brady Shipman Martin, 2000). Hall (1999) argues that, in Europe and elsewhere, centres below this population threshold have lost services through competition and mobility to larger centres of population, and as a result have ceased to perform any significant role as central places. Some Irish evidence of this comes from Hourihan and Lyons (1995) who argue that 5,000 population is an important threshold that must be reached for a town to diversify its service base. Also in Ireland, Commins and McDonagh (2000) suggest that places under 5,000 population are finding it increasingly difficult to generate or attract new manufacturing enterprises. In the remainder of the chapter this cut-off will be used to define both urban systems.

The concentration measures indicate a number of findings (see Table 4.4). First, the degree of population concentration is greater for the urban system of the Republic than for all definitions of the Northern Ireland urban system except that using the BMUA, which undoubtedly over-states the relative size of Belfast compared to that of Dublin within their respective systems. Second, for both systems the degree of concentration is considerably greater than would be expected according to the restrictive rank-size rule. This reflects the fact that both Belfast and Dublin are archetypal primate cities, which dominate their respective urban systems and have population sizes that are several times greater than the second ranked cities of Derry and Cork respectively. It has been suggested by a number of authors that, in so far as a rank-size distribution is the outcome of system-wide processes, conformity to it is an indication of higher levels of integration within the system (Taylor, 2004). Such an interpretation is consistent with the opening remarks offered here about the comparatively low level of integration of the urban system in the South in particular. Third, bearing out the findings from the earlier analysis, the trend in the Republic has been towards a deconcentration of population in the last two decades, as is indicated by the steady decline of both the q parameter and the Gini coefficient. In other words, the primacy of Dublin has decreased somewhat, due to the strong growth performance of the other cities and the large towns in the middle of the size distribution. An analysis of the Northern Ireland urban system for earlier years would almost certainly point in a similar direction, i.e., to a decreasing primacy of Belfast.

However, two caveats need to be entered here. First, the rate of decrease in concentration in the Republic is very slow. At the rate observed over the period, it would require another 115 years for the urban size distribution to correspond to the strict rank-size rule! Second, the wide divergence between the concentration measures for alternative definitions of Belfast demonstrates how sensitive the results are to the way that the largest urban centre is bounded, and reminds us that this analysis takes no account of spatial aspects of the urban system. Similarly, a number of the towns exhibiting strong growth form the hinterland of Dublin. It is to these that we turn in the next section.

THE SPATIAL EXPRESSION OF THE URBAN SYSTEMS

Whatever may be said about trends in the size distribution of urban centres, their spatial distribution in Ireland remains highly uneven. There are two main components to this uneven geography: first, and reflecting its history of industrialisation-based urbanisation, there is a greater density of urban centres in Northern Ireland; and second, there is a pronounced east–west, or, perhaps more accurately, core–periphery differential both north and south of the border (see Figure 4.1). In Northern Ireland, the main contrast is between the Belfast region and the Southwestern part of the province. In the Republic of Ireland, the divide runs along a line from the Shannon Estuary to the Carlingford peninsula, which broadly corresponds to the boundary between Horner's 'more-favoured south and east' and 'less-favoured north and west' regions, as defined in terms of land quality, historical settlement patterns, rural population density, and the capital intensity of agriculture (Horner, 2000).

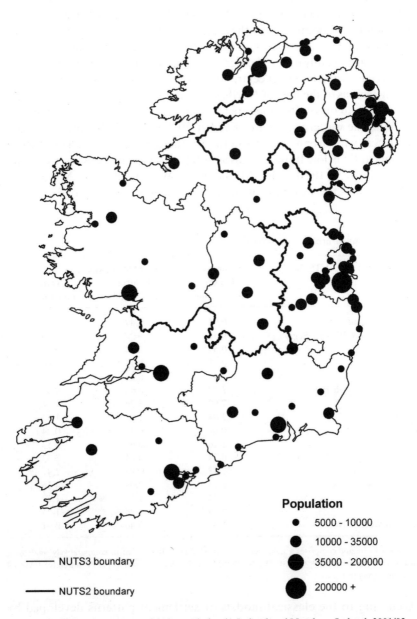

Figure 4.1   Urban centres over 5,000 population in Ireland and Northern Ireland, 2001/02

Sources: Central Statistics Office, Census SAPS file 2002; Northern Ireland Statistics and Research Agency, Census files; Ordnance Survey Ireland

These contrasts are brought out more clearly in Table 4.5, which shows the density of urban centres at the level of the NUTS 3 and NUTS 2 regions that form the basis for EU regional funding. The greater urban density in Northern Ireland is evident, and this is especially marked for the larger (10,000+) centres of population. The dominance of the capital city regions is also clearly revealed: the Dublin and Belfast regions have by far the highest density of urban centres, and again this is mainly due to their greater concentration of larger centres. For all urban centres and for larger centres the next highest densities are found in the adjoining regions of the East of Northern Ireland and the Mid-East. The lowest densities in both these categories are found in the four regions in the Republic that adjoin the western seaboard. Even at NUTS 2 level, the differences are pronounced, with urban densities in the Southern and Eastern region (which are significantly below those in Northern Ireland) varying between twice and 2.8 times those in the Border, Midland and Western Region. McCafferty (2002) examines the weakness of the urban system in the west of Ireland in more detail.

Table 4.5 Density of urban centres, 2001–02

| Region (NUTS 2 and NUTS 3) | Number of centres per 1,000 sq. km. | | |
	Centres over 5,000	Centres 5,000–10,000	Centres over 10,000
Republic of Ireland	0.94	0.47	0.47
Border, Midland & Western Region	*0.54*	*0.24*	*0.30*
Border	0.57	0.24	0.32
Midland	0.75	0.15	0.60
West	0.42	0.28	0.14
Southern & Eastern Region	*1.30*	*0.68*	*0.62*
Dublin	7.60	3.26	4.34
Mideast	2.64	1.32	1.32
Midwest	0.61	0.36	0.24
Southeast	1.16	0.63	0.53
Southwest	0.74	0.41	0.33
Northern Ireland (NI)	*2.33*	*0.92*	*1.41*
Belfast & Outer Belfast	6.25	2.08	4.16
East of NI	2.94	1.18	1.77
North of NI	2.49	1.24	1.24
South and West of NI	1.37	0.46	0.91

Note: Northern Ireland comprises a single region at NUTS 2 level. Because of its comparatively small area, Belfast is combined with Outer Belfast. The Northern Ireland urban system is as per definition (c) Table 4.4 and accompanying text.

According to the classical models of settlement patterns developed by Christaller (1966) and Losch (1954), in which urban centres primarily function as service centres for their rural hinterlands, contrasts in urban densities between regions are explained by variations in the rural population density. In the Republic, the regional densities of both smaller and larger places show a strong (though non-linear) relationship with rural population density.[5] Thus the comparatively low density of urban places in the West region can be attributed to the fact that this region has the lowest rural population density. However, somewhat less support for central-place theoretic principles emerges from a consideration of contrasts *within* regions in the density (or number) of centres of various sizes. On the basis of the Christaller-Losch model we would expect that the density of smaller places in any region would exceed that of larger places. However, this relationship does not hold in Northern Ireland, nor for four of the eight NUTS 3 regions in the Republic (Dublin, Mid-East, Border, Midland), in all of which the density of centres with over 10,000 population is at least as great as that of the smaller centres. In part this is due to the categories used: the smaller size category covers a relatively small range of population sizes. But in the Republic it is also a reflection of the trend noted earlier, whereby rapid growth in the formerly medium-sized places in the urban system has increased considerably the number (and hence density) of larger places.

This developmental aspect of the urban system in the Republic has been strongly focused on the hinterland of Dublin. This is illustrated by classifying centres according to the year in which they attained a population of 5,000 or 10,000 (see Figure 4.2). In total, 13 new centres of 10,000 population or more emerged between 1981 and 2002, 7 of which (Balbriggan, Celbridge, Greystones, Leixlip, Malahide, Maynooth and Naas) are located in the Greater Dublin region (Dublin plus the Mid-East). Growth in these centres, which are amongst the fastest growing in the country, is largely due to the development of new commuter estates focused on Dublin, a process that has been fuelled by the escalation of house prices in the capital. This can be illustrated by using data from the 2002 census of population to estimate median travel-to-work distances for urban residents (also see Figure 4.2). Thus, the estimated median commuting distance for workers residing in the seven towns ranges from 16.3 miles in the case of Balbriggan, to 9.9 miles in Malahide, as compared to a median of 6.0 miles for the country as a whole and 4.6 miles for all towns with over 5,000 population. The emergence of Carrigaline (median commuting distance 8.3 miles) as a commuter town for Cork is part of the same trend. By contrast, the growth of Letterkenny (2.4 miles), Castlebar (2.1 miles) and Killarney (2.3 miles) reflects the development of these towns as key locations for employment growth in their respective counties.

In summary then, while a degree of *deconcentration* of urban population has been a feature of the urban system of the Republic over the last two decades, this has not been associated to any significant extent with a spatial *decentralisation* of the system. If anything, the distribution of new entrants to the urban system, and of newly emerging towns with 10,000 or more population, suggests that the spatial imbalance of the system has actually increased. Moreover, it is easy to see that the modest and gradual decrease in the concentration measures noted earlier, may be replaced in the future by a more significant increase. This will happen if continued urban growth (and sprawl) in the Dublin area results in the future incorporation of centres such as Swords, Malahide and Portmarnock into the built-up area of the city. Such 'growth by absorption' is a well established feature of Dublin's recent development.

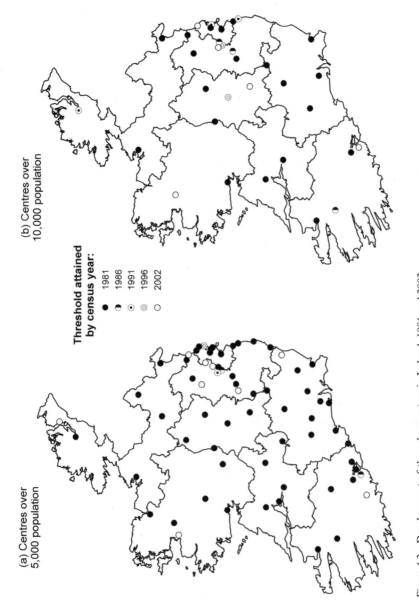

(a) Centres over
5,000 population

(b) Centres over
10,000 population

**Threshold attained
by census year:**

● 1981
◑ 1986
◉ 1991
◎ 1996
○ 2002

Figure 4.2   Development of the urban system in Ireland, 1981 and 2002

Sources: Central Statistics Office; Ordnance Survey Ireland

CONCLUSION: URBAN SYSTEMS AND PUBLIC POLICY

The pattern of urban system development in both Northern Ireland and the Republic of Ireland over the last two decades can be described in terms of a process of diffusion of growth that has both neighbourhood and hierarchical elements. The hierarchical element is evident in the diffusion of growth from the largest to the medium centres of population. The neighbourhood element is reflected in growth spreading from both large and medium centres to smaller towns and villages in their immediate hinterlands. In Northern Ireland these two elements have been blurred to some extent by virtue of a geography in which most of the large centres of population are located close to Belfast. In the 1970s these centres were the main recipients of population movement out of the capital (Poole, 1991). However, in recent years much of the overspill growth from Belfast has taken place in the smaller towns and villages of the BMA, as well as the open countryside. In the Republic of Ireland a different history of urbanisation means that there are fewer large centres close to Dublin, and as a result the overspill growth from the capital has tended to be located in what were, until recently, smaller centres of population, though many of these are now among the country's middle-ranking centres of population.

These developments have raised a number of policy issues both at the local level and at the regional/national level. At local level, the strength of the neighbourhood effect has placed severe strains on the physical planning systems of both jurisdictions. One of the biggest challenges is that resulting from the development of commuter towns and villages in the hinterlands of the capitals. In addition to economic and environmental sustainability issues associated with commuting (Horner, 1999) there is an increasing recognition of significant quality-of-life issues, as well as issues of access to services for commuters and their families. Concerns also exist for the character and identity of the small towns in which often disproportionate development of new housing has taken place (Department for Regional Development, 2001).

At the macro-spatial scale, imbalance in the spatial structure of the urban system poses significant challenges for regional development, particularly in the Republic of Ireland where peripherality is more pronounced. Since the early 1980s, industrial policy has been geared toward the encouragement of investment, both foreign-owned and indigenous, in high-technology manufacturing sectors such as electronics, pharmaceuticals and biotechnology, as well as in internationally traded services including financial services, software, shared services and e-commerce. While this policy has met with a broad measure of success, as measured in terms of both output and employment growth, most of the new investment has been located in the larger urban areas, particularly the cities. Dublin has been the major focus, and it has now developed a role as a niche city in the European and global urban systems (Breathnach, 2000a). But this urban focus, in a context where the spatial distribution of urban areas is extremely uneven, has meant that the new jobs have been unequally spread at regional level, and this has been reflected in a degree of regional divergence in the 1990s (Boyle et al. 1999; O'Leary, 2001). While the erosion of competitiveness in traditional, less urbanised, sectors means that there is little alternative to the current thrust of industrial policy, the spatial distribution of the new growth runs counter to the National Development Plan's goal of balanced regional development. This conflict between industrial policy and regional policy has been brought about because of the country's particular urban structure: solving it represents one of the most difficult dilemmas confronting policy makers at national level.

5

Urban Property Development

Andrew MacLaran and Sinéad Kelly

The urban landscape normally changes only very slowly. The enormous investment of labour power and construction materials that each building embodies is generally amortised slowly, buildings paying back that investment over a very long period of time. Thus, the physical environment appears to be relatively fixed. Nevertheless, it does undergo change: imperceptibly at times, more rapidly at others; more quickly in some districts than in others. The profusion of cranes punctuating Ireland's skyline over the past 15 years has been testimony to the rapidity with which the city has been changing in recent times. Indeed, many areas of the inner city have undergone a scale of transformation unseen since they were first developed during the city's eighteenth-century 'Golden Age'.

This chapter reviews the impact of the 'Celtic Tiger' economy of the 1990s and early 2000s on two major elements of the property development sector. First, it examines office development in Dublin and the changing geographical focus of activity. Second, it reviews the development of private sector apartments in the inner city which, in aggregate, have effected considerable transformation of the residential environment in the city centre.

PROPERTY DEVELOPMENT AND THE CREATION OF URBAN FUNCTIONAL SPACES

Buildings are developed in order to accommodate specific functions. Broadly, these relate to the underlying elements of the social system: production, distribution, exchange and the reproduction of the workforce. They include industrial and distribution space (manufacturing, warehousing and retailing), office buildings accommodating managerial functions in both the private and public sectors, together with residential areas that accommodate the workforce. To a considerable extent, these different functions tend to operate in different areas of the city and in different types of building. Thus, the city comprises a vast mosaic of different types of functional space.

It is sometimes said of property markets that, 'just as you don't buy an envelope unless you have a letter to post, so businesses don't buy or rent buildings unless they have a function to accommodate'. This is because the demand for buildings (functional spaces) is fundamentally a 'derived demand'; the demand for buildings ultimately being determined by how the economy is performing and how the population is changing: whether businesses are expanding or contracting, if overseas business are seeking a local presence or if entirely new firms are looking for accommodation in which to set up and whether there is an effective demand for the development of new or refurbished residential space. As new types of function appear and as others die out, or as functions alter their locational preferences and building requirements, these shifts in demand become reflected in changes in the built environment. The city expands geographically and adapts internally to the changing demands of those who require built space. Thus, although state policies may have a role to play, notably through planning and tax policy, urban change is largely driven by the dynamics of businesses and households, the outcomes being mediated through land and property markets.

It is precisely because the user demand for property is a derived demand dependent on the vicissitudes of the economy and changes in population growth rates and migration that property development is subject to major fluctuations in levels of output. These boom-slump cycles are particularly evident in the office, industrial and housing sectors (Beamish and MacLaran, 1985; MacLaran et al., 1987; MacLaran, 1993, 2000, 2003).

During the Irish economic boom of the late 1990s, of all Irish urban areas, it was the physical environment of Dublin which was most acutely to experience the impact of the restructuring forces of the property development sector as it responded to the increasing demands for new buildings and new locations. Although each of the major property sectors was touched by the boom, the trends in the office property sector and the construction of inner-city apartments most clearly reveal the shifts in development strategy whereby developers sought to meet rising demand.

BOOM AND BUST IN DUBLIN'S OFFICE MARKET

Until the 1990s, the inner city had adapted very slowly to the property requirements created by Ireland's 'first economic miracle' of sustained growth during the 1960s and early 1970s. It resulted in the conversion of eighteenth-century residential buildings to office functions (an 'upgrading' of land uses in property development terms) and in the development of scattered modern office blocks around Dublin 2. As economic boom gave way to slump in the wake of the oil crisis of the early 1970s, the development sector entered a period of much reduced activity.

Then, from the late 1970s, office development entered a second boom. While development activity remained focused on the office core, spilling over into Ballsbridge, a few tentative schemes were also completed in outer suburbs such as Blackrock and Dun Laoghaire. Others were developed as individual blocks in residential suburbs or became the first office buildings at locations which subsequently evolved into significant suburban office nodes, such as at Clonskeagh and Sandyford-Leopardstown. The boom culminated in 1982 when a crisis in the public finances and resultant public sector cutbacks projected the economy into a major recession. This impacted severely on the office development industry as the public sector had taken up some 60 per cent of all the post-1960 speculatively-developed office space (Malone, 1985). By mid-decade, with coincidental slumps in the office, industrial property and residential sectors, unemployment in the construction sector reached 50 per cent.

Then, during 1986, in an effort to boost employment in the ailing construction sector, the Irish government established a series of property-based urban regeneration programmes (see Chapter 2). Slowly, the stringent economic policies pursued in the mid-1980s created a basis for sustained and unprecedented high rates of economic expansion in the 1990s; the so-called 'Celtic Tiger'.

Nowhere were the consequences of economic development more sharply felt than in Dublin, its landscape becoming transformed in response to the massive increase in the demand for accommodation of all types. This new Celtic Tiger economy, together with central government tax incentives for property-based urban renewal in designated geographical areas of the city, propelled the property development sector into rising levels of activity (see MacLaran, 1993, 2003). The quiescence, which had characterised the development industry during much of the 1980s, rapidly gave way to a full-scale boom. The inner city in particular became subjected to enormous property development pressures, often creating whole new precincts and transforming historic townscapes almost beyond recognition, notably at the Custom House Docks, Temple Bar and along tracts of the quays bordering the River Liffey.

However, the impacts of this intensive scale of development activity were felt far more widely within the inner city than had been the case in previous development booms. They stretched well beyond the prime office zone and the retailing core, which had been the only inner-city districts that had received any significant private sector development during the twentieth century. In the case of the offices sector, major changes occurred in the location of development, both within the inner city and on a metropolitan-wide scale. Simultaneously, an unprecedented private sector residential development boom occurred throughout in the inner city. It is to these two sectors that the chapter now turns.

DUBLIN'S FOURTH OFFICE DEVELOPMENT BOOM

The office development boom which was generated by over a decade of economic growth after 1990 was the most intensive which the city had ever witnessed (see Figure 5.1). It had taken three decades to develop a modern office stock totalling 1,055,490 sq. m. of space by the end of 1990. Over the following 14 years, the stock more than doubled as an additional 1,345,920 sq. m. of floorspace was built.

It has already been noted that, at times of boom, development activity tends to expand into secondary areas adjacent to the core, while retrenchment into prime areas occurs during slumps. This pulsating pattern of activity typifies each of Dublin's office property booms. However, during the development boom of the 1990s considerable quantities of development became deflected away from the prime office core into the surrounding inner-city areas and towards the

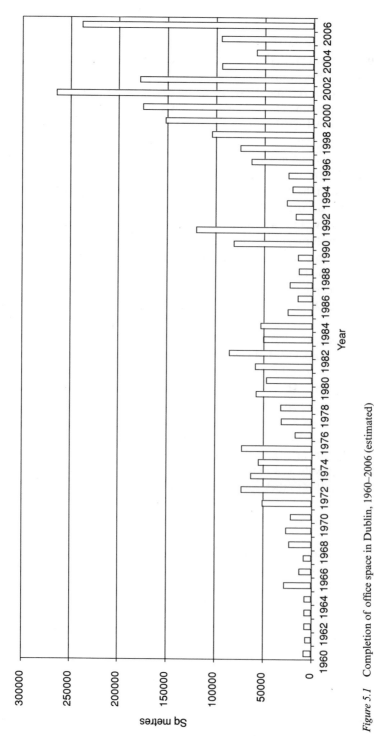

Figure 5.1 Completion of office space in Dublin, 1960–2006 (estimated)

Data sources: A. MacLaran and Hamilton Osborne King, various years

outer suburbs (MacLaran and O'Connell, 2001, 2003; Killen and MacLaran, 2002; MacLaran and Killen 2002). This can clearly be seen from Figure 5.2, inner-city areas accounting for a much reduced proportion of development in more recent years.

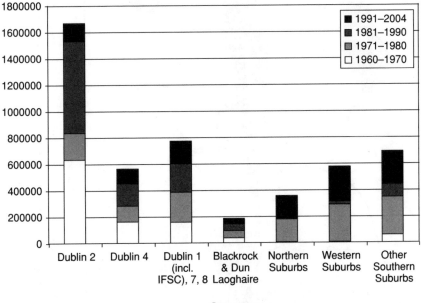

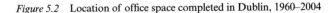

Sq. metres

Figure 5.2   Location of office space completed in Dublin, 1960–2004

Sources: A. MacLaran and Hamilton Osborne King, various years

One important underlying reason for the widening geography of development activity during the fourth office boom was the availability in certain locations of tax incentives for property-based renewal (see MacLaran, 1993, 1996a; MacLaran and O'Connell, 2001; MacLaran and Williams, 1996, 2003). These significantly altered the calculations of potential profitability from development over a large area of the city (see Figure 5.3) and at some suburban sites. These Designated Areas included a broad zone lying to the north and west of Dublin's prime office core, in the postal districts of Dublin 1 (including the Custom House Docks), Dublin 7 and 8, in addition to a small Enterprise Area on the edge of docklands on the boundary of Dublin 2 and 4. They also included an inner-suburban site at Alfie Byrne Road in the docklands of Dublin 3, together with even more peripheral metropolitan locations in central Tallaght and an area to the north of the Nangor Road, adjacent to the M50 circumferential motorway (see Figure 5.3).

The initial response of developers to the availability of such incentives after 1986 was the development of significant amounts of office space in areas of

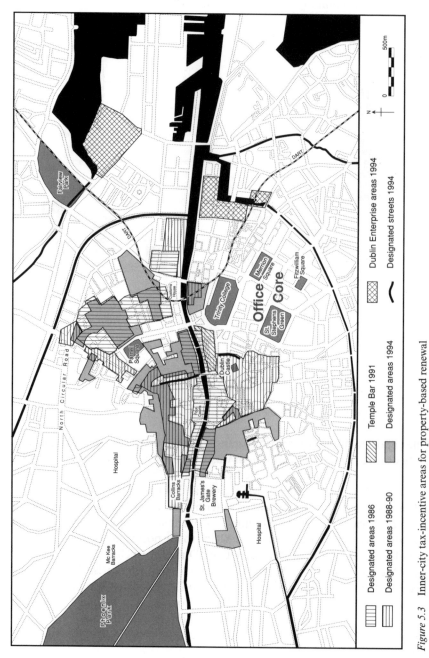

Figure 5.3 Inner-city tax-incentive areas for property-based renewal

Sources: Department of Environment, Heritage and Local Government, various years; Ordnance Survey Ireland

the inner city which had been largely neglected by private sector investment throughout the twentieth century. In addition to the large-scale redevelopment of the Custom House Docks, office schemes were developed at a number of sites along the Liffey's quays, down Winetavern Street, at High Street and in the vicinity of Stephen Street and Golden Lane. In 1993, some developments started to reach completion in Tallaght. By the end of 1995, over 135,000 sq. m.[1] of office space had been developed in the incentive areas. Over 58,520 sq. m. was located at the Custom House Docks, 65,780 sq. m. was located in the other central-city incentive areas (the original Designated Areas together with the Dublin 2/4 Enterprise Area) and 10,760 sq. m. was in Tallaght.

However, during the early 1990s, it became increasingly apparent that significant 'over-development' had taken place in the inner-city designated areas outside the Custom House Docks. Office establishments proved reluctant to locate in such areas and, by mid-1992, this had become reflected in a vacancy rate of 42 per cent in those areas. Thereafter, the focus of development activity in such inner-city locations as Dublin 1, 7 and 8 switched from offices to apartment schemes, with only a further 4,646 sq. m. being completed by the end of 2000 (see Figure 5.4).

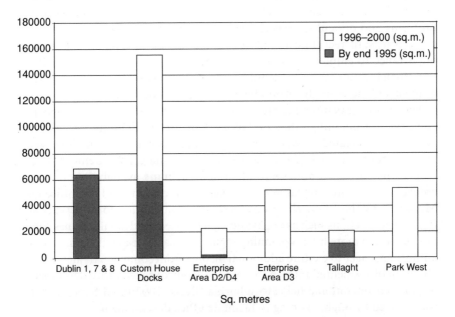

Figure 5.4 Office development in the tax-incentive areas

Sources: A. MacLaran and Hamilton Osborne King, various years

Elsewhere, in other incentive areas, office development continued apace. By the end of 2000, a further 96,506 sq. m. had been completed at the Custom House Docks, while in Tallaght, some 10,730 sq. m. was added. An additional 71,816 sq. m. was developed in the two Enterprise Areas, of which 20,160 sq. m.

was in the Dublin 2/4 Enterprise Area and 51,656 sq. m. was located at East Point (Dublin 3). Furthermore, the availability of tax incentives at Nangor Road had encouraged the development of some 53,100 sq. m. of space at a suburban location which was very poorly served by public transport (see MacLaran and Killen, 2002), an additional 16,580 sq. m. being completed in 2001.

By the end of 2000, over 377,250 sq. m. of office space – the equivalent of 166 buildings the size of Liberty Hall – had been developed in locations for which tax incentives had been available for property development, excluding local-authority offices at Wood Quay (9,575 sq. m.) and in Tallaght (6,801 sq. m.) which had not availed of the tax incentives. However, the availability of tax incentives provides only a partial explanation for the change in the geography of office development and the massive increase in suburban office development during the late 1990s.

On the user-demand side, one factor in office suburbanisation was the creation of 'call centres' engaged in tele-services operations, ranging from IT-related sales and after-sales back-up for companies such as IBM and Dell, to hotel and car-hire reservation services. Such functions possessed wide freedom of locational choice and cheap suburban sites were often favoured because large amounts of floorspace were needed. Secondly, given central Dublin's growing congestion problems and difficulties experienced by employees in gaining access to the city centre, staff recruitment and retention issues became matters of growing importance to employers in the tightening labour market of the late 1990s. Suburban locations near residential areas and with good provision of parking were viewed increasingly favourably by employers (Bertz, 2002a).

The changing planning context was also significant. The increasingly pro-conservation planning ethos of Dublin Corporation/Dublin City Council planners had created greater levels of protection for historic buildings which might, under previous planning regimes, have undergone demolition and redevelopment. Such policies resulted in a declining availability of suitable redevelopment sites for large office schemes in and around the office core. Moreover, by the 1990s, there was increasing competition for inner-city sites from other functions such as hotels and highly priced residential schemes. Simultaneously, the more liberal planning regimes of cash-strapped suburban local authorities, eager to capture additional income from commercial rates after the abolition of residential rates in the late 1970s, encouraged office developers to widen their operational fields to suburbia (Bertz, 2002b). At Sandyford, this was effected through rezoning to facilitate office development.

Furthermore, long-term investors in property, anxious to jump onto the bandwagon of rapidly inflating property prices, found that there was a shortage of prime inner-city office buildings available for purchase. Increasingly, such funds were diverted elsewhere and effectively underpinned massive investment-led development in some locations, driving development far beyond what the user-market would require.

The result was a dramatic shift in the location of office development activity during the 1990s, as can be seen from Figure 5.2. More than three-quarters of the office space that had been developed in Dublin between 1960 and the end of 1990 had been built in the prime office core (Dublin 2 and its overflow into Dublin 4), with less than 10 per cent being located in the outer suburbs. However, from 1991 to 2004, less than a quarter of new floorspace was developed in the core and some 60 per cent was located in the outer suburbs.

Sandyford

Nowhere is the development of edge city better exemplified than in the prestigious southern suburb of Sandyford-Leopardstown, some 8 km. (5 miles) south of the city centre. The suburban local authority, Dun Laoghaire Rathdown County Council, had been keen to increase its income from business rates in order to improve its budgetary position. Its local authority planners have facilitated a process of land-use upgrading by rezoning an industrial estate from industry to office-based industry. Large-scale office development was able to benefit from the availability of large development sites and to capitalise on the presence of prestigious companies such as Microsoft, ICL, Oracle, Allied Irish Bank and Trintech. It was further encouraged by a position near to the projected route of the M50 circumferential motorway and from a planned connection to the city centre by a light-rail line. By 2004, the area had undergone a major transformation.

From an initial office stock amounting to just 5,967 sq. m. in 1990, an additional 16,440 sq. m. had been developed by the end of 1995. Thereafter, growth proceeded rapidly. By the end of 2004, Sandyford had developed into a substantial suburban office node with an office stock totalling over 161,600 sq. m., equating to 50 buildings the size of Liberty Hall (see Figure 5.5). Substantial floorspace had been taken by Eircell (the major Irish mobile phones operator), First Active bank, Bank of Ireland and Barclaycard, with significant additional space being taken up by Microsoft. This office node includes some of the largest stand-alone office blocks in Dublin, with Central Park (see Figure 5.6) planned to incorporate over 160,000 sq. m. of space on completion, thus doubling available office space.

The office developments which occurred at Sandyford had involved both green-field sites and also the redevelopment of low-value industrial space. Typically, single-storey warehouses with a workforce of perhaps a dozen people might be replaced by multistorey office buildings accommodating dozens of employees. With a transportation infrastructure geared to its original numerically small employment base, severe traffic congestion has been the inevitable consequence as car-based commuters attempt to reach work.

However, by the early years of the twenty-first century it was clear that the supply of office space had considerably outpaced the scale of user demand. At the end of 2004, 32,960 sq. m. of office space lay vacant, amounting to 23.7 per cent of the available stock. Consequently, development activity was drastically curtailed and no further development was projected to reach completion during 2005.

Figure 5.5   Liberty Hall, central Dublin (Completed 1965, 3,252 sq. m.)

Source: Authors

Figure 5.6   Central Park, Sandyford-Leopardstown

Source: Authors

Park West

Park West Business Park on the Nangor Road was created in response to the availability from 1997 to 1999 of tax incentives at a time when the office market was booming. It is a good example of how tax inducements led to significant over-development. Arguably, from an infrastructural perspective, the location was ill suited to the creation of a significant office employment node as it lacked adequate public transport services (MacLaran and Killen, 2002). Designation resulted in an immediate response with 27,200 sq. m. reaching completion in 1999. A further 25,900 sq. m. was completed in 2000 and 16,580 sq. m. was developed during the following year. Within three years, almost 70,000 sq. m. had been developed at Park West Business Park, equivalent to 21 buildings the size of Liberty Hall, with a further 8,282 sq.m. having been constructed nearby on the Nangor Road at Kilcarbery Business Park and Westland Park.

However, it became increasingly apparent from rising vacancy levels that significant over-development was occurring, especially with the global economic down-turn subsequent to the attacks of 11 September 2001. Financial institutions withdrew from funding further development and no additional office space was completed after 2001. Yet, as late as January 2005, its vacancy rate remained at over 55 per cent.

Citywest

Located in Baldonnel at the western approaches to Dublin on the Naas Road, Citywest represents a more measured approach to office development in which user demand was more closely reflected in the scale of completions. The initial phase was marked by a rising intensity of activity marked by the completion of 4,877 sq. m. in 1997, rising to 5,852 sq. m. in 1998, 7,896 sq. m. in 1999, peaking at 17,114 sq. m. in 2000 and reducing to 14,581 sq. m. in 2001. Thereafter, development was curtailed as economic circumstances changed, user demand faltered and local vacancy topped 30 per cent, with 15,762 sq. m. lying unoccupied. However, much of this was taken up over the ensuing years and, by late 2004, as vacancy dropped below 5 per cent, with just 2,270 sq. m. lying vacant, development activity was renewed and 8,055 sq. m. of new space reached completion in 2005.

INNER-CITY PRIVATE SECTOR RESIDENTIAL DEVELOPMENT

The residential environment and social structure of Dublin's inner city have undergone major transformation since 1990. Tax allowances for residential landlords under Section 23 of the Finance Act 1981, renewed in the Act of 1988 under Section 27, had encouraged the construction of apartments and, in the later Act, small houses for rent. The provisions allowed the cost of acquiring properties, net of site value, or the costs of converting buildings into flats, to be deducted from landlords' rental income from all sources until the tax allowance was used up. This considerably reduced the real purchase price of such investment properties.

The bulk of apartment developments during the 1980s had been located in prestigious inner-suburban areas. However, from the late 1980s, developers began to test the marketability of new locations. In 1989, a scheme of 36 townhouses in Ringsend sold out within three hours of release. Somewhat surprisingly given its location, a quarter of the units were sold for owner occupation. At the release of the second phase in 1991, 70 of the first 85 sold were bought by young owner occupiers (MacLaran, 1996b).

In the 1992 Finance Act, tax relief for investors in rented residential accommodation became linked to Urban Renewal Initiatives and only available in areas designated under the Urban Renewal Schemes. This occurred simultaneously with the appearance of a significant over-supply of office space, particularly in the Designated Areas (see above). Consequently, developers and site owners within the inner city became increasingly willing to embrace the emerging opportunities provided by the city-centre apartment sector. This received strong support from public agencies, including Dublin City Council whose efforts to encourage residential functions in the city centre involved the sale of development sites at significantly discounted prices.

A number of demand-related factors also contributed to the 'return to the city'. Rising rates of car ownership and car-based commuting had created increasing levels of traffic congestion in the city and proximity to the central area was a strong marketing feature. The new residential units proved attractive to a younger generation possessing ideas about urban living which differed significantly from those of their parents. The lure of a central-city lifestyle more akin to that of Amsterdam, London or Paris outstripped any attractions of suburban living, bereft of amenities relevant to the urban-oriented culture of the young. This emergent culture of new city living, borrowing from and imitating the lifestyles depicted in the international media, was adopted by the advertising industry and used in marketing the new inner-city residential developments. The financial incentives, together with growing employment and rising incomes associated with the economic upturn of the 1990s, created a growing demand for inner-city dwellings based upon the enhanced spending power of the young. The schemes therefore sold well, not only to landlords but to young middle-class owner occupiers.

Table 5.1 details the geography of this development. Between 1989 and March 1996, 7,730 new private sector residential units were built in 135 developments in inner Dublin (MacLaran et al., 1994; MacLaran et al., 1995; MacLaran, 1996b; MacLaran and Floyd, 1996). Between April 1996 and December 2003, a further 8,769 residential units were constructed in 198 developments in Dublin's Inner-40 Wards (see Figure 5.7). In December 2003, an additional 2,485 units were under construction in 48 separate developments and live planning permissions existed for 95 schemes covering a further 4,962 residential units. Planning applications for 37 developments covering 2,277 residential units had also been submitted to Dublin City Council and awaited determination. Thus, since April 1996, development at various stages of activity has involved 18,493 residential units (Kelly and MacLaran, 2004a, 2004b).

Table 5.1   Location of Dublin residential units completed, 1989–2003

Arena	Built end March '96		Built April '96 –Nov. '03		On site Nov. '03		Live Nov. '03		Applics. Nov. '03	
	Units	%	Units	%	Units	%	Units	%	Units	%
Dublin 1 & 3	2,138	27.66	2,521	28.75	624	25.11	1,813	36.54	916	40.23
Dublin 2	981	12.69	2,014	22.97	29	1.17	1,324	26.68	255	11.20
Dublin 4	563	7.28	869	9.91	818	32.92	526	10.60	241	10.58
Dublin 7	1,735	22.45	1,355	15.45	661	26.60	206	4.15	189	8.30
Dublin 8	2,313	29.92	2,010	22.92	353	14.21	1,093	22.03	676	29.69
TOTAL	7,730	100.00	8,769	100.00	2,485	100.00	4,962	100.00	2,277	100.00

Sources: Centre for Urban & Regional Studies, TCD, database; Dublin City Council Planning files

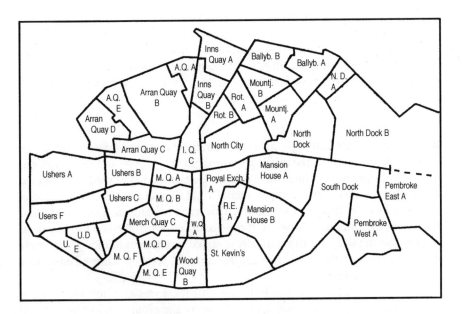

Figure 5.7   Dublin's inner-40 wards

Source: Ordnance Survey Ireland

Population

The impact on the inner city of this intensity of development during the 1990s has been considerable and has resulted in the termination of the long-run reduction in its number of residents. Indeed, Table 5.2 shows that while the population of the 40 inner-city wards rose by a total of 10,357 persons between 1991 and 1996, the population of the remainder of the County Borough actually fell by 6,892. Then, between 1996 and 2002, the population of the inner-40 wards increased even more strongly, by 17,664 persons or 18.7 per cent, while that of the remainder of the County Borough declined by 3,737 persons. Thus, between 1991 and 2002, the 40 inner-city wards increased their share of the County

Borough's residents from 17.6 percent to 22.6 per cent (Kelly and MacLaran, 2004a, 2004b).

Table 5.2   Population of the inner-40 Dublin wards and the County Borough, 1991–2002

Arena	1991		1996		2002	
	Persons	%	Persons	%	Persons	%
Inner-40 wards	84,055	17.57	94,412	19.59	112,076	22.61
Other	394,334	82.43	387,442	80.41	383,705	77.39
Dublin Co. Borough	478,389	100.00	481,854	100.00	495,781	100.00

Source: CSO Population Census, various years

The population of six inner-city wards (North City, Royal Exchange A, Ushers A, Arran Quay C, Rotunda A and Merchants' Quay B) more than doubled between 1991 and 2002 and a further nine wards each experienced an increase of over 50 per cent. In absolute terms, twelve wards each recorded an increase of more than 1,000 residents and three (North City, Royal Exchange A and Rotunda A) each increased by over 2,000 persons.

Gentrification

Research in the 1990s strongly suggested that there was a considerable difference between the occupiers of the newly developed residential units and the indigenous inner-city population, which was typically elderly, poorly skilled and suffered from a high incidence of unemployment (MacLaran et al., 1994; MacLaran et al., 1995; MacLaran and Floyd, 1996). This trend towards the gentrification of the inner city continued throughout the decade and is confirmed by the census of population 2002. It is dramatically revealed by changes in the age structure of the population, its social class composition, its level of achieved education and rates of unemployment.

Table 5.3 shows that between 1991 and 2002 there was a notable reduction in numbers of both children and the most elderly age group, while a 90 per cent increase occurred in the number of adults aged between 25 and 44 years. Table 5.4 further reveals that the number of persons in the upper social classes 1–3 increased substantially between 1991 and 2002, while the numbers in the lower social classes 4–6 registered a drop. More detailed census data relating to the social class composition of those aged 25–44 years demonstrate a considerable increase in those from social classes 1 and 2. In 1991, these two social classes had totalled 5,075 persons, comprising 21 per cent of the age cohort. In 2002, they accounted for 39 per cent of the cohort and totalled 17,578 persons. Evidence for gentrification is further supported by census data relating to levels of achieved education. In 1991, only 17.9 per cent of the adult population had undertaken tertiary-level education, with 27.6 per cent having received only a primary level of education. In 2002, 34.4 per cent of adult residents had undertaken tertiary-level education and fewer than 20 per cent had received education at primary level only.

Table 5.3   Age structure of the inner-40 Dublin wards, 1991 and 2002

Age groups	1991		2002	
	Persons	%	Persons	%
0–14	15,185	18.07	14,296	12.76
15–24	16,158	19.22	23,935	21.36
25–44	23,621	28.1	45,107	40.26
45–64	15,541	18.49	17,485	15.6
65+	13,550	16.12	11,230	10.02
Total	84,055	100.00	112,053	100.00

Source: CSO, Census of Population, 1991 and 2002

Table 5.4   Social class structure of the inner-40 Dublin wards, 1991 and 2002

Social class	1991		2002	
	Persons	%	Persons	%
1	4,194	4.99	7,302	6.52
2	7,807	9.29	21,173	18.90
3	13,801	16.42	16,637	12.17
4	13,048	15.52	11,943	10.66
5	12,408	14.76	10,039	8.96
6	12,893	15.34	7,195	6.42
7	19,904	23.68	40,755	36.37
Total	84,055	100.00	112,044	100.00

Source: CSO, Census of Population, 1991 and 2002

Property Prices and Affordability

Recent research (Kelly and MacLaran, 2004a, 2004b) has highlighted the rising real price of inner-city dwellings and declining degree of their affordability. Although by the mid-1990s the newly developed apartment stock had attracted few indigenous inner-city residents (MacLaran et al., 1994; MacLaran et al., 1995; MacLaran, 1996), the asking prices at that time were remarkably affordable when expressed in terms of the income multipliers that these prices represented. For example, a one-bedroomed apartment could be purchased at The Maltings (Watling Street) or at Temple Court (Dominick Street) for less than twice the annual level of average industrial earnings.

Between 1995 and 2002, the consumer price index rose by 25 per cent, average earnings rose nationally by 43 per cent, well above the rate of inflation, while building costs increased by 52 per cent. However, new house prices rose nationally by 181 per cent. Yet in inner Dublin, price increases were far more dramatic and by November 2003, the income multipliers required to purchase a new apartment in the inner city were staggering. No developments had one-bedroomed units available at less than *nine* times the level of annual average industrial earnings. Three-bedroomed units cost at least *fourteen* times that figure (Kelly and MacLaran, 2004a, 2004b).

Even for white-collar groups (e.g., the banking, insurance and building society sector), gaining entry to owner occupation in newly launched inner-city residential developments was highly problematic. Annual income multipliers of more than six were necessary to secure ownership of the cheapest one-bedroomed units, while three-bedroomed units demanded multipliers ranging from 11 to over 19 (Kelly and MacLaran, 2004a, 2004b).

Moreover, significant price inflation affected the earlier phase of apartments built between 1989 and 1995. Apartments completed during 1995 which returned second-hand to the market late in 2003 had recorded prices that commonly exceeded the 1995 launch price by 250 to 350 per cent. Typically, the price for a one-bedroomed apartment represented 6.7 to 9.9 times the figure for annual average industrial earnings. This outstripping of general price inflation and of earnings has resulted in a declining level of affordability of the stock of dwellings completed during the earlier phase of renewal. Indeed, such were the income multipliers required to purchase one of these dwellings second-hand in November 2003 that there is good reason to believe that a degree of second-generation gentrification is now taking place within that slightly older stock.

Within the stock of dwellings dating from the nineteenth and early twentieth centuries price inflation has also been evident. In November 2003, asking prices in the Liberties area of the south-west inner city ranged from €208,000 for a 42 sq. m. one-bedroomed cottage in Pimlico and €270,000 for a 51 sq. m. two-bedroomed cottage on Brabazon Square, to €380,000 for a two-bedroomed house on Greenville Avenue and €540,000 for a 69 sq. m. two-bedroomed house on Spencer Street. This is particularly problematic for the local community as this stock has traditionally provided a first step on the housing ladder for newly formed households of young, indigenous inner-city residents (also see Chapter 18).

CONSEQUENCES

As prices for inner-city redevelopment sites became propelled to ever higher levels as a consequence of the development booms in the office and residential sectors, unforeseen pressures were thrust onto inner-city communities. These exacerbated existing difficulties born of continuing high levels of unemployment and poverty. Within widening areas of the inner city, in docklands, the Liberties, Stoneybatter and the markets, industrial and other low-grade functions providing relevant employment to inner-city residents became displaced by offices, hotels or expensive new residential developments as developers competed vigorously for available redevelopment sites (similar processes have also been at play in Ireland's other cities) .

Simultaneously, as the inner city was undergoing its late-twentieth-century metamorphosis, development in suburbia proceeded apace. Within a period of 14 years, a major shift had taken place in the geography of the office stock and of office employment. Unwittingly, Dublin had embarked in earnest on the creation of an 'edge city', with all the problems that this would entail. Effectively, it had been transformed from a relatively compact city to a sprawling, multinodal metropolis in which clusters of industrial, retail and office employment were strung along the route of the M50 motorway, tied together in a Gordian knot of reliance on a complex patterns of car-based, inter-suburban commuting (see Killen and MacLaran, 2002). Moreover, for commuters living in towns such as Arklow, Carlow, Portlaoise, Mullingar, Navan and Dundalk, the new edge-city nodes were readily accessible, encouraging the development of an outer commuter belt which now extends some 90 km. from the city (Williams and Shiels, 2000). It is a pattern of development highly dependent on low-cost fossil fuels and one which is therefore unlikely to prove sustainable in the longer term.

6
Rural Development

John McDonagh

Rural areas, covering approximately 85 per cent in terms of territory, have a population base of some 50 per cent of the EU's 25 member state total population. Characterised by diversity in terms of landscape and geography, rural areas are increasingly being challenged by issues of agricultural restructuring, poor service provision, depopulation and counter-urbanisation, communication and infrastructural difficulties, and threats to the natural environment. Like many of its fellow EU member states the last two decades have seen a remarkable transformation of Irish rural society in terms of economic, demographic and social restructuring of its rural areas. Reduced dependency on farming and other primary industries are paralleled by local economies being more readily identified with new service industries, increased counter-urbanisation and associated commuting patterns.

Concern for rural areas and rural development still maintains considerable priority on the policy agenda of both Ireland and the EU. From an EU perspective, rural development has changed in emphasis due to restructuring of the agricultural sector and the acceptance that the viability of rural areas, while desirable, cannot be dependent on agriculture alone. EU rural development policy has changed from its initial preoccupation with agriculture to one which places greater emphasis on maintaining viable rural communities with myriad spaces of production, consumption, conservation and other uses. This change is no less apparent in Ireland and this chapter contextualizes this transformation within the varying approaches and challenges facing rural areas, and the constructs of rurality and development that mould rural development policy and practice.

WHAT IS 'RURAL' IRELAND?

It is perhaps fitting to start by suggesting that the biggest problem with 'rural' is that there is no consensus on what it is or whom it includes, whether rural space is mainly for production or whether it is now a space more suited to consumption (as places to live and pursue leisure activities). Consequently developing a theoretical insight into rural development is difficult and requires interpretation of the different constructs of rurality. Such constructs are made up of a whole set of meanings (political and socio-cultural), of lived experiences rather than just physical space (see Murdoch and Pratt, 1993; Cloke, 1995).

Conceptually, discourses of the rural in Ireland have been much more comfortable in dealing with statistics, hard numeric facts and 'policy-relevant' information (on farm size, or farm outputs for example) than on any attempt to heighten awareness of the social and cultural marginalisation and experiences of rural lifestyles (McInerney, 1995). The slow conceptual shift away from this mechanistic and reductionist view gives way to the need to interpret different constructs of rurality in Ireland. However, a continued weakness in Irish rural discourse has been the interchangeable use of 'rural' with 'agricultural'. While this is problematic, there is a change in thinking; the paradox being that the current over-insistence on separating agriculture from rural development is leading to a lack of evaluation of how such things as farm structure, efficiency, land use management are affecting rural areas (see Boylan, 1992) and consequently a lack of a holistic view of rural development.

RURAL CLASSIFICATIONS

In trying to make some further contribution to dispelling this lack of clarity it is useful to explore the different rural classifications that have been employed in recent times. There have been a number of attempts, using a variety of criteria, to 'classify' rural areas. The OECD classification, for example, uses population indicators in order to provide international comparisons. The OECD classification is determined at a NUTS 5 (Nomenclature des Unités Territoriales Statistiques) community level which identifies rural areas as communities with a population density below 150 inhabitants/km^2. At a regional level (NUTS 3) the definition draws on the share of population living in rural communities – namely predominantly rural regions (over 50 per cent of the population living in rural communities); significantly rural (15 per cent to 50 per cent); and predominantly urban regions (less than 15 per cent). The Eurostat approach uses the degree of urbanisation. The system developed in this instance refers to densely populated zones (groups or contiguous municipalities with population densities superior to 500 inhabitants/km^2 and a total for the zone of at least 50,000); intermediate zones (groups of municipalities with population densities superior to 100 inhabitants/km^2 not belonging to a densely populated zone); and sparsely populated zones (groups of municipalities not classified as either densely populated or intermediate). The Council of Europe, in its European Charter for Rural Areas, defines rural areas as 'a stretch of inland or coastal countryside, including small towns and villages, where the main part of the area is used for agriculture, forestry, aquaculture and fisheries; economic and cultural activities of country-dwellers; non-urban recreation and leisure areas and other purposes such as housing'.

The key recommendation of the Third Report on Economic and Social Cohesion (February 2004) was that people should not be disadvantaged by wherever they happen to live or work in the EU. The recognition that many of the problems of rural areas were territorial in character, and that to ensure equity, citizens should have access to essential services, basic infrastructure and knowledge, led to the Cohesion Report identifying three types of rural areas largely contextualized by the extent of their integration into the broader economy and larger urban centres. These types are: areas integrated into the global economy which are experiencing economic growth and have increasing population; intermediate rural areas which are relatively far from urban centres but with good transport links and a reasonably well developed infrastructure; and isolated rural areas (European Commission, 2004).

In Ireland classifications and divisions are often used in a more fluid way, and more often than not as a prelude to obtaining funds from Europe. Indeed, for the most part, much of the country outside of the main urban centres of Dublin, Galway, Limerick, Cork and Sligo is thought of as rural. This is reinforced by the White Paper on Rural Development (1999) which describes its remit as one of developing policies that 'are directed towards improving the physical, economic and social conditions of people living in the open countryside, in coastal areas, towns and villages and in smaller urban centres outside of the five major urban areas' (Department of Agriculture and Food, 1999, p. vi). McHugh and Walsh (2001) have also attempted to grapple with this fluidity by identifying six types of rural areas: peri-urban; very strong rural; highly diversified areas; strong agricultural areas; structurally weak; and marginal areas (see Figure 6.1). In terms of other divisions, Ireland has emerged from an all-encompassing Objective 1 region to its current position of Objective 1 region in the Border, Midlands and West of Ireland (BMW) region and an Objective 1 in transition region in the South and East (S&E) region of the country.

What is apparent from these examples is that creating some kind of objective, all-encompassing definition of rural is difficult, if not impossible. What it also suggests is that there is a tendency to over-generalise about rural areas. Such generalisations indicate that rural areas are in some way homogeneous, and not the complex entities that we think they are. However, it is easily argued that within an area of decline there may also be pockets of growth, and vice versa.

THE NARRATIVE OF IRISH RURAL
DEVELOPMENT POLICY AND PRACTICE

Rural development has a long history in Ireland from the Congested Districts Board at the end of the nineteenth century through contrasting pictures of small farming self-sufficiency in the 1940s to rural 'crisis' in more recent decades. In all these cases, it is clear that rural development policy and practice has a determining role in Ireland's social, cultural, economic and political make-up. What has been central to much of the debate is the continued disparity between the east and west of the country and the necessity for successive governments to introduce specific policies (in the form of growth centres, industrial dispersion and special regional packages – the Western Package in the 1980s, for example) to alleviate this disadvantage. In taking an initial starting point in the Irish rural debate it is perhaps the contribution of American anthropologists Arensberg and Kimball (1940) that still holds significance. Focusing on a study of small

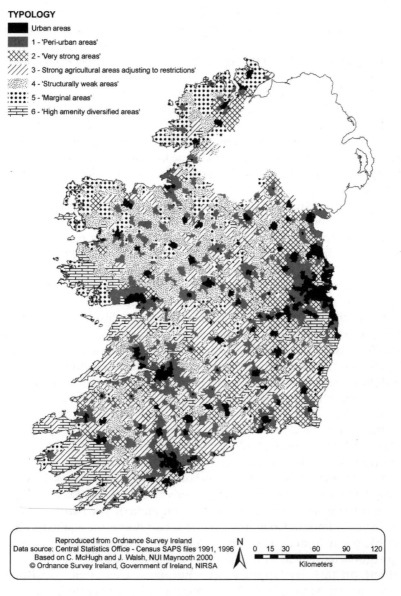

TYPOLOGY

Urban areas
1 - 'Peri-urban areas'
2 - 'Very strong areas'
3 - Strong agricultural areas adjusting to restrictions'
4 - 'Structurally weak areas'
5 - 'Marginal areas'
6 - 'High amenity diversified areas'

Reproduced from Ordnance Survey Ireland
Data source: Central Statistics Office - Census SAPS files 1991, 1996
Based on C. McHugh and J. Walsh, NUI Maynooth 2000
© Ordnance Survey Ireland, Government of Ireland, NIRSA

N

0   15   30   60   90   120
Kilometers

Figure 6.1   Rural typology of Ireland, 2001

Sources: McHugh and Walsh (2001); Ordnance Survey Ireland

farming in County Clare in the 1930s, this research emphasised the familial nature of the local form of farming as the basis for understanding the rural social system. Though it was much criticised for its suggestion that 'the rural' in the West of Ireland at that time could be generalised to the whole of Irish rural society (Tovey, 1992), Arensberg and Kimball's generalised equation of the rural with farming has been typical of Irish rural development down through the years. As such, whatever difficulties arise in defining the rural today, for much of the previous century, the Irish definition seemed to take for granted that 'rural' meant agricultural, and for any interpretation of the rural, explorations of farming had to come first.

From the 1980s profound changes in all aspects of rural Ireland were evident and a new agenda began to emerge. This new agenda attempted to reinterpret the very concepts of community, rurality and development which Irish society had, prior to this, accepted almost unquestioningly. These changes included the declining overall importance of agriculture in rural areas and, in the areas where agriculture still played a dominant role, its recognition more as a business than a 'way of life'.

In terms of tracing Ireland's rural development evolution, it is perhaps most easily done by taking a chronological route through EU and, by extension, Irish rural development policy. The main rural development policy strategy in Ireland of the late 1970s and early 1980s appears to have been defined by its absence, apart from that suggested by Lee (1989) of making the greatest short-term gains in the fastest way possible. With the introduction of the CAP (Common Agricultural Policy) with its price supports and its agenda of increasing farming productions and incomes there was 'a direct positive impact on all rural areas through raising product prices to farmers and thus raising their incomes' (Cuddy, 1991, pp. 30–1). However, it also became apparent that the CAP shielded farmers from the realities of market pressures and to an extent widened the prosperity gap between the larger and smaller producers. Indeed for much of this initial period of the CAP, rural development in Ireland was placed on the back-burner, perhaps due to the assumption that the CAP and the EC Regional Fund would cure domestic rural problems.

By the mid-1980s there emerged a new-found interest in rural development, particularly in response to the added recognition given to rural areas by the EU. The growing realisation that the CAP was not reducing regional disparities and that many communities were experiencing a crisis brought about by conventional top-down development thinking led to the publication of *The Future of Rural Society* by the European Commission (1988). This document marked a clear shift in EU policy from a top-down approach to the recognition of the need for a grassroots movement with respect to rural development.

Building on this new approach the European Conference on Rural Development which took place in Cork from 7 to 9 November 1996 (the Cork Declaration) heralded a new start in rural development policy. Its principal call was for sustainable rural development to be put at the top of the agenda of the EU; that rural development would be multidisciplinary in concept, multisectoral in application with a clear territorial dimension, and that there was a need to preserve and improve the quality of the rural environment and to make rural areas more attractive to people to live and work in.

Following on from this, rural development was given a new status in Agenda 2000. This action programme, agreed by heads of government of EU member states in Berlin in March 1999, combines reforms and the modernisation of key policies while also providing the framework for the challenges of enlargement over the period 2000–06 and onwards. In terms of this strengthening of the EU, the Commission's demands focused on the need for greater equality of opportunity; quality of life issues; protection of the natural environment; access to high-quality foodstuffs; a farming population guaranteed reasonable incomes; and responsible and efficient management of the Union's finances. In terms of Agenda 2000 and rural development, the importance of agriculture to the rural economy was recognised, but more significantly, it was viewed in terms of its multifunctional nature and the realisation that to safeguard the vitality of rural communities as regards jobs and growth, agriculture could not do this alone. Consequently while each member state would set up its own programme for rural development and choose rural development measures (for example, investments in farm businesses; human resources; less favoured areas and agri-environmental measures) that best suited their rural needs, they also had to adhere to a set of guiding principles.[1]

As part of the process of developing rural development policy post-2006, the Commission held an EU Conference in Salzburg, Austria from 12 to 14 November 2003. This was essentially a follow-up to the Cork Declaration and for the most part presented nothing very new or radical. Instead it was framed as an opportunity for reflection on the experience of rural development programmes, what had worked well (LEADER for example, see below) and a time to draw lessons for the post-2006 period. At the conference the continued importance of rural areas to sustainable economic, social and environmental development was stressed. The key outcomes of the conference included reinforcing the principle that a living countryside was not only important for rural society but for society as a whole; the growing importance of multifunctional agriculture; that agriculture is still important although undergoing deep reaching changes; the importance of a partnership approach to rural development policy, and that the need for significant simplification of EU rural development policy was both necessary and urgent.

While these milestone policies were being developed at EU level, the Irish government was also attempting to develop its own complementary rural strategy. This culminated in the production of the White Paper on Rural Development, *Ensuring the Future – A Strategy for Rural Development in Ireland* (Department of Agriculture and Food, 1999). While rural development in Ireland has always been a prominent theme of public policy, no coherent set of policy responses has ever been formulated. In 1999, the publication of the White Paper sought to change this by providing an 'over-arching strategy' which would establish a coherent plan that would inform future government policies, and governmental response to the issues of concern in rural Ireland. The White Paper stated that its key objective was to provide a 'coherent strategy for rural development ... [that] ... identify[ied] the policy responses at national, regional and local levels which will most effectively address the issues of economic and social underdevelopment in rural areas' (1999, p. 1). Dealing with issues such as employment opportunities in rural areas, counter-migration, depopulation, and public service delivery, these policies were to facilitate balanced and sustainable regional development while tackling the issues of poverty and social inclusion. The commitments were to be financed by the National Development Plan 2000–06 with the added concept of 'rural-proofing' introduced.

While the sentiment of the White Paper is laudable there are many shortcomings in terms of its proposed objectives. For example, there would appear to be variance between the government policies of 'rural-proofing' and 'eco-auditing'. The emphasis on environmental protection rivals the emphasis on increasing industry in rural areas. There is also a conflict of interest between environmental protection and the emphasis on increasing competitiveness in agriculture, increasing and intensifying the number of inland fisheries, and increasing the area of ground under conifer plantation. Further, although the advantages of connecting rural areas to the fibre-optic network are discussed, no concrete plans for the roll-out of broadband services were mentioned. Also recognised was the role a good public transport system has to play in reducing marginalisation. However, other than a mention of various pilot programmes operating under the aegis of the local partnership body, Area Development Management (ADM) Ltd, there was practically no discussion on how to design or implement an adequate public transport system that would be beneficial to rural areas. These conflicts between 'rural-proofing', 'eco-auditing' and indeed 'poverty-proofing' exist because by their very nature, they strive for very different and contrasting results.

If the policy framework described in the White Paper was to be successfully applied then a stronger co-ordination between different levels of government was necessary. What resulted however was a maintaining of the status quo in the vertical and sectoral policy structures, contrary to the desire of creating a 'multisectoral, integrated and well co-ordinated policy framework which addresses public policy issues which do not fall within the remit of any one particular department' (Department of Agriculture and Food, 1999, p. 24). Despite the government's description of the White Paper as being a 'comprehensive and cohesive approach' for rural Ireland and the White Paper's many noteworthy strategies, the lack of concerted proposals made it extremely lightweight in terms of its impact on rural Ireland.

The other major driver of rural policy in Ireland is that of the National Development Plans (NDPs). Up to 1993, the NDP was largely confined to efforts at local area-based approaches to rural problems. The most prominent of these was the Integrated Rural Development Plan (1988–90), and the Programme for Economic and Social Progress (1991) which were 'committed to establish(ing) a national programme for integrated rural development which would draw upon the experience of pilot programmes and other initiatives' (Commins and Keane, 1994, p. 116). Their major weakness was, however, their over-identification of rural development with agricultural issues and, consequently, a very narrow view of rural development.

The NDP 2000–06, on the other hand, emerged from a very different economic environment to that of its predecessor, namely a resurgent economy. This NDP has:

- three Inter-regional Operational Programmes: Economic and Social Infrastructure, Employment and Human Resources, and the Productive Sector;
- two Regional Operational Programmes: the BMW Operational Programme and the S&E Operational Programme;
- a separate Operational Programme for the PEACE Programme which operates in the border counties and in Northern Ireland.

Although the Regional Operational Programmes will have the most immediate and visible effect on rural Ireland, the Inter-regional Operational Programmes also contain elements that are of great importance to rural areas, with investment in physical infrastructure having a positive effect on rural areas by making it more attractive for industry to locate away from larger urban areas, while improved public transport services would make it easier for rural people to commute.

The Employment and Human Resources Operational Programme (total provision of just under €13 billion) places a strong emphasis on social inclusion measures in the education sector and labour market integration, while one of the main aspects, the productive sector, including agriculture and fisheries, was to support Foreign Direct Investment (FDI) in the BMW region. A separate programme is implemented for measures accompanying the CAP rural development programme with a total of approximately €4.3 billion to be spent on the:

- Rural Environment Protection Scheme;
- Early Retirement Scheme;
- Compensatory Allowances;
- Forestry Measures.

The culmination of these EU and national policies has brought about a shift from sectoral support, largely centred on agriculture, to a more territorial approach. Consequently Irish rural development, somewhat belatedly, is moving to a more holistic view of rural areas and the challenges for rural development. This move is certainly more in line with the desire for economic efficiency, equity and the need to care for the environment. The Rural Development Programme 2000–06 forms part of this overall strategy aimed at 'promoting more competitive agriculture, fostering environmentally sustainable production systems, diversifying activities on- and off-farm to generate alternative sources of incomes for farmers and promoting rural development at a local level' (European Commission, 2000). Within this context a new Rural Development Regulation has laid the foundations to promote rural development as the second pillar of the CAP, with rural development in Agenda 2000 linked to two types of interventions: the Rural Development Council Regulation (1257/1999) providing for farm investment and human resources, less favoured areas, REPS, forestry, processing and marketing of agricultural produce and development of rural areas; and the LEADER + Community Initiative which succeeded LEADER I and II.[2]

The manifestation of this 'new' approach to rural development encapsulated in such programmes as LEADER and the Rural Environmental Protection Scheme will be explored in more detail in the remainder of the chapter.

LEADER IN IRELAND

Since the initial pilot programme of LEADER I launched by the EC DGVI in 1991, there has been LEADER II (1995) and LEADER + (2000). From its inception, LEADER has promoted the notion of local participation in the designing and implementation of rural development projects in specific territorial areas. In Ireland, LEADER is seen to have been very influential in rural development policy, so much so that it has been held up as the best example of local community participation in local development (Jouen, 1999; see also Chapter 13). Initially 17 groups (two were later amalgamated) were selected in Ireland on the basis of their business plans. Although there had been a gradual growth in the setting up of community groups prior to LEADER I, many of the groups (almost 75 per cent) were established specifically for the purpose of attracting and administering LEADER funds (see Walsh, 1998). Each Local Action Group (LAG) entered into a formal contract with the intermediary body that set out the terms and conditions (terms for payment, reporting arrangements, etc.) under which they would operate. The areas targeted were predominantly rural, suffering from population decline, a dependency on agriculture and peripheral disadvantage. The dominant areas of activity were rural tourism, small enterprises and natural resources, with the allocations of funding being in the region of 44 per cent, 11 per cent and 15 per cent respectively (Kearney et al., 1994).

LEADER II was to be the consolidation of the achievements of LEADER I. This programme was seen as a continuation of the earlier programme and involved double the number of community groups. LEADER II was established for the period 1994–99. The Operational Programme for the implementation of LEADER II was prepared when Ireland was still an Objective 1 region and subsequently all rural areas could apply/benefit to/from this programme. The objective of LEADER II was to 'stimulate innovative measures by those, whether public or private, engaged at local level, in all sectors of rural activity; to make known the results of these experiments throughout the Community; to assist rural operators in different Member States who wish to profit from the lessons learnt elsewhere, and, to work jointly on some projects' (Kearney & Associates, 2000, p. 2). This programme was to be administered by local rural groups pursuing medium and long-term developmental projects for their own areas. The role of animation and capacity-building within the developmental phase was viewed as the foundation of the LEADER II initiative. Further, issues of innovation, transnational co-operation and transfer of know-how/best practice were promoted as desired goals.

The most recent addition to this strategy is LEADER +. The aim of LEADER + is 'to encourage and help rural actors to think about the longer-term potential of their area' (European Commission, 2000, p. 3). This, as a concept or objective, indicates nothing new, springing directly from LEADER I and II and their objectives of improving the lot of rural communities. Further, the timescale over which LEADER + is to operate is not significantly longer than that of its predecessors. Jointly funded by member states and the European Community, LEADER + is intended to support pilot strategies (yet again) and to develop the indigenous potential of rural areas. All rural areas are eligible under LEADER +, but member states may limit its application to certain rural areas (European Commission, 2000). This initiative seeks to encourage the implementation of integrated, high-quality, original strategies for sustainable development designed to encourage experimenting with new ways of enhancing the natural and cultural heritage; reinforcing the economic environment, in order to contribute to job creation; and improving the organisational abilities of their community (European Commission, 2000).

Overall, the LEADER initiative would appear to have been successful thus far. Under LEADER I, projects receiving assistance created almost 1,445 jobs, with close to 50 per cent of those employed being previously unemployed. Kearney & Associates (2000) suggested that a large majority of those involved in the LAGs perceived the initiative as providing an opportunity for local people to initiate development by harnessing local resources and generally in 'empowering' local groups to adopt a multisectoral approach to development. Some also perceived the initiative as the related concept of the 'bottom-up' approach, while a small minority considered it in the first instance, as a source of funds for local development and as a means of generating employment and value-added to the areas concerned (this relating to the original understanding of LEADER rather than its mode of operation) (McDonagh, 2001). Some of the weaknesses of the initiative include the selective nature of the groups; requirement of matching funds; short time frames; lack of flexibility and perceived shift in responsibility from government to community (McDonagh, 2001). Overall, it would appear that while there have been positive outcomes to the LEADER initiatives thus far in terms of successfully promoting the idea of local participation (and perhaps it is still too early to judge), the longevity of these outcomes is questionable.

THE RURAL ENVIRONMENTAL PROTECTION SCHEME (REPS)

In a parallel stream, the introduction of the REPS can be viewed as an equally significant development in terms of defining the future of rural development in Ireland. The REPS scheme was introduced in June 1994 by the Department of Agriculture and Food as the Irish government's response to regulation (EEC) 2078/92. The key objectives included the establishment of farming practices which reflect due concern for conservation; landscape protection and wider environmental problems; the protection of wildlife habitats, and the promotion of quality food production (Department of Agriculture and

Food, 2004). Essentially the REPS saw a restructuring of agriculture away from intensive 'modern' set-ups to a more extensive and sustainable use of resources. Open to all areas of rural Ireland, the REPS is characterised by its voluntary nature, its environmental ethos, and how it acts as an income support measure with payments designed to act both as an incentive to participate and as compensation for participating. Adoption of the REPS was initially slow with only 527 farmers being involved (19,020 ha) (Emerson and Gilmore, 1999), while the most recent figures (following introduction of REPS II) report 42,861 farmers at the end of 2004 with a payment level of €1.05 billion (Department of Agriculture and Food, 2004).

While the success of the REPS is undoubted in terms of controlling nitrates, use of fertiliser, maintaining and protecting habitats, and initiating nutrient management plans, what has also emerged is that the REPS does not attract the larger, more intensive farmer in terms of participation. Over 50 per cent of the 'area farmed throughout most of the western districts in Galway, Mayo and Donegal is included in the REPS programme, compared to less than one-sixth throughout much of the east and south' (Lafferty et al., 1999, p. 128). Consequently, while the REPS is a useful environmental measure and indeed is a useful income support to the smaller farmer, its depiction as an agri-environmental measure is somewhat stretched in that it is taken up almost exclusively by the smaller, older and less intensive farmers, largely based in the west and north-west of the country, who by the very nature of the farming they carry out are less polluting, and therefore less threatening, to the environment. As a result, a number of questions can be asked about the introduction of such a scheme, its objectives and more significantly, its likely contribution to the future sustainability of farming in many parts of rural Ireland and to the concept of a 'living countryside' as promoted in many current EU and Irish policy documents.

CONCLUSION

The latter two examples (LEADER and REPS) are illustrative of the changing emphasis of rural development not only in Ireland but also in the broader EU. What they also show is that rural areas are perhaps facing their greatest challenges in the coming decades: challenges that will determine how we live, work and engage with rural spaces and the activities, both production and consumption, that take place within these spaces. The idealised view of rural Ireland (see Greer and Murray, 1993) and the preconceived notion that 'rural' should be essentially equated with all things 'agricultural', with little evaluation of the wider rural economy, is coming to be increasingly challenged. 'Rural' is now being viewed as a construction made up of a whole set of meanings (see McDonagh, 2001). From the late 1980s and early 1990s we have witnessed the emergence of rural development onto the European policy stage in a much stronger capacity. There is currently a desire to focus more on bottom-up development in contrast to previous top-down strategies. From the development of the CAP and addressing the structural problems of the farming community, rural development has evolved to address the multiple roles of farming and the wider rural population. The changing conceptions of rural development as it has moved through the 1990s have begun to stress the importance of local capacity building, empowerment of rural communities, and the combining of the 'agricultural structure measures of the CAP with the partnership approaches to rural development employed in the Structural Funds' (Baldock et al., 2001, p. 7). Embedded within this broader rural development concept has been the overall objective of maintaining viable rural communities. For this to be realised there is still a lot of work to be done. What seems to be emerging from current debates is that there is a need for a more simplified and integrated approach to rural development policy and practice. The broadening-out of national and EU policy to integrate the concerns of rural people (in terms of jobs, quality of life, access to services, etc.) is a further necessary step. What also seems clear from the Irish rural experience is that many opportunities exist within our rural areas and that what is now required is the access to knowledge and the development of capacity to grasp such opportunities.

7

Transport

James E. Killen

The issues and challenges currently facing Ireland's transport sector need to be viewed against the background of the country's evolving geography and within the context of recent global and local trends. Ireland is a small country by world standards. Internal trips are relatively short. The island location emphasises the strategic importance of the country's ports and airports.

In 1901, Ireland's population was 3.22 million of which 18.6 per cent lived in urban settlements of over 10,000 persons. The country's extensive road and railway infrastructure had evolved to serve what was primarily a dispersed, rural society. In 2002, Ireland's population was 3.92 million of which 48.2 per cent lived in urban settlements of over 10,000 persons. While the overall increase in population in the twentieth century is notable, the redistribution of population from rural to urban areas is even more striking. As Ireland's urban centres have grown, they have spread out rapidly. The hinterlands from which Irish towns and cities and most notably Dublin are drawing commuters have expanded considerably (Horner, 1988).

The foregoing trends have led to two quite different sets of transport issues. First, there are problems associated with the larger urban centres and on the routes between them that have seen massive increases in traffic. Second, many rural areas have undergone depopulation and decline, which has raised such issues as the cost of maintaining a relatively under-used roads infrastructure and how (if at all) public transport should be provided.

This chapter reviews the foregoing themes. The country's road system and the challenges facing it are examined first. The provision of public transport is then examined, paying particular attention to the evolving role of the national railway system. Then rural transport is considered, after which urban transport issues and problems are reviewed with particular reference to Dublin. Finally, the evolving role of the country's ports and airports is examined.

Other chapters in this volume detail the recent rapid growth of the Irish economy. This period of expansion has placed considerable pressures on Ireland's transport infrastructure, so much so that it has appeared at times that such infrastructure improvements as have occurred have not even been sufficient to cope with increasing demand. The availability of a good transport infrastructure has been cited as a necessary prerequisite for on-going social and economic development (Government of Ireland, 1994b, 2000a).

While few would argue that additional investment in the country's transport infrastructure is desirable, the nature of major transport infrastructure projects needs to be underlined. Major transport schemes, for example the construction of a new motorway, require large amounts of capital. They are usually time-consuming to execute. Very often, considerable disruption occurs during construction. Many transport infrastructure proposals raise serious environmental concerns.

In Ireland, transport infrastructure and services have been provided traditionally by the public sector. A recurring theme in this chapter is the increasing role of the private sector, both as a provider of finance for major projects and as a provider of services. As will be seen, the increasing role of the private sector reflects, at least in part, the declining availability of finance from European Union (EU) sources.

THE IRISH ROAD SYSTEM

Ireland is served by c. 92,100 route-kilometres of roads. The road network carries 96 per cent of passenger traffic and 90 per cent of freight traffic. The corresponding figures for the EU as a whole are 88 per cent for passenger traffic and 72 per cent for freight traffic (Government of Ireland, 2000a, p. 18).

Traditionally, Ireland's road system has been maintained by the local authorities using monies raised through rates on property and through grants from central government. In 1970 and in recognition of their strategic importance, responsibility for the upkeep and improvement of the main roads, which are now referred to as National Primary and National Secondary roads, passed to central government. The National Roads Authority was set up in 1993 to oversee the maintenance and development of these roads. The National roads comprise 5,431 route-kilometres, i.e., just 6 per cent of the total network, but carry 38 per cent of total road traffic. The bulk of investment in Irish roads over the past 20 years has been directed towards improving these links.

While the National Roads Authority has overseen the completion of many projects since its inception, a National Roads Needs Study completed in 1998 suggested that the standard of the Irish national road network was still seriously deficient (National Roads Authority, 1998). In 2003, only 3.2 per cent of the national roads were of motorway standard with a further 4.5 per cent constituting dual carriageways (National Roads Authority, 2003a). One reason for the continuing inadequacy of the Irish national road network is the rapid rise in vehicle ownership (see Table 7.1). Yet levels of vehicle ownership in Ireland are still low by European standards. This suggests that further increases in vehicle numbers are likely, especially within a context of on-going economic development. It is predicted, for example, that heavy goods vehicle traffic on Irish roads will increase between 2002 and 2040 by a factor of 1.50 on the non-national routes and by a factor of 2.25 and 2.07 on the National Primary and National Secondary routes respectively (National Roads Authority, 2003b).

Table 7.1   Population of the Republic of Ireland and number of vehicles, 1961–1996

Year	Population (000s)	Number of cars (000s)	Number of goods vehicles (000s)	Cars per 1,000 persons
1961	2,818.3	186.3	43.8	66.1
1971	2,973.2	414.4	45	139.3
1981	3,443.4	775.9	67.4	225.3
1986	3,540.6	711.1	101.5	200.8
1991	3,525.7	836.6	148.3	237.3
1996	3,626.1	1,057.4	146.6	291.6

Sources: *Statistical Abstract* (Dublin: Stationery Office); *Statistical Yearbook of Ireland* (Dublin: Stationery Office); *Irish Bulletin of Vehicle and Driver Statistics* (Dublin: Department of the Environment and Local Government)

In these circumstances, it is not surprising that the current National Plan calls for greatly increased investment in the national roads network (Government of Ireland, 2000a). The plan emphasises in particular the need to improve further the standard of the National Primary routes between Dublin and the other major cities, most notably Belfast, Galway, Limerick and Cork. The Transport 21 Plan announced by government in November 2005 also emphasises the importance of developing the national roads system and includes a proposal to develop an Atlantic Corridor route that would run from Letterkenny to Cork and Waterford (Government of Ireland, 2005). An important point to note within the context of investment in Irish roads (and Irish transport infrastructure generally) is that EU funds are not as readily available to Ireland as in the past. The Operational Programme for Transport 1994–99 called for an investment of €1.85 billion in the Irish national road system, of which 61 per cent was to come from EU sources and the remainder from the national exchequer (Government of Ireland, 1994b). The current plan calls for an investment of €5.59 billion between 2000 and 2006, a greatly increased sum. Of this total, just 14 per cent is expected to come from EU sources and 63 per cent from the national exchequer (Government of Ireland, 2000a). The remaining 25 per cent is to be raised from private sources and to be financed by placing tolls on the newly constructed roads. The involvement of the private sector in Irish road projects represents a significant departure from former practice.

THE NATIONAL RAILWAY SYSTEM

The first railway in Ireland opened in 1834 and ran from Dublin to Kingstown, now Dun Laoghaire. Throughout the second half of the nineteenth century, the railway network developed rapidly. By 1900, the railway had reached the remotest parts of the country (Killen, 1997). By the 1930s, the economics underlying Irish railway operations were causing concern and legislation was passed with a view to protecting the railway from competition from privately owned freight vehicles and buses. This legislation did not have the desired effect. Instead, the railway network shrank steadily as small rural stations and secondary routes were closed. By 1970, the Irish railway system comprised essentially a series of routes radiating from Dublin and serving the major urban centres only (see Figure 7.1).

Figure 7.1   Rail and air transport infrastructure

Source: Ordnance Survey Ireland

Figures for railway traffic since 1980 reveal different trends in the freight and passenger sectors (see Table 7.2). Despite the rapid economic development in recent times, freight traffic carryings have declined to a point where the main role of the railway is now restricted to carrying certain types of freight only, most notably sugar beet, timber and cement. Various factors explain this decline. For journeys within Ireland, haulage distances are short and can be undertaken more conveniently by road hauliers where a door-to-door service can be provided. In the case of international traffic (other than that to/from Northern Ireland), the Irish railway system has always been constrained by the fact that the track gauge in Ireland is wider thereby precluding the use of train ferries. Road transport generally offers a more convenient alternative, especially since the development of roll-on, roll-off (RO-RO) vessels.

Table 7.2   Railway traffic, 1980–2003

Year	Passengers (000s)	Freight (000s tonnes)
1980	7,671	3,571
1985	6,730	3,379
1990	7,787	3,278
1995	8,312	3,179
2000	9,625	2,707
2003	11,256	2,251

Note: The passenger figures exclude those carried on the Dublin suburban services.
Sources: *Statistical Abstract* (Dublin: Stationery Office); *Statistical Yearbook of Ireland* (Dublin: Stationery Office).

The trend in passenger carryings on the Irish railway system in recent decades is in contrast to that for freight (see Table 7.2). Three factors in particular explain the steady increase in passenger numbers. The first is the redistribution of population referred to earlier; although the railway network has shrunk, it still serves the larger urban centres where an increasing proportion of the population resides. It is estimated that between 60 and 70 per cent of Ireland's population now lives within a 20-minute drive of a railway station (Booz Allen Hamilton, 2003). A second important factor has been the increased congestion on Irish roads which has meant that the travel times offered by the railway have become more attractive. Finally, the increasing spread of the major urban centres, especially Dublin, has meant that the railway is playing an increasing role as the preferred mode for commuting, especially long distance commuting.

Looking to the future, the primary role of Ireland's railway for the foreseeable future would appear to be as a passenger carrier. The most recent proposals call for hourly services to be introduced between Dublin and Belfast, Cork and Limerick with a two hour frequency on most of the other routes radiating from the capital (Booz Allen Hamilton, 2003). It is noted that the railway will have a key role to play in the transport of commuters, especially long-distance commuters and especially within the Greater Dublin[1] area. It is suggested that the future role of the railway as a freight carrier should be confined to 'niche' traffics which are either commercially viable, or attract a subsidy for carrying the traffic concerned, or can be justified in cost–benefit terms.

The era of railway closures appears to be at an end; indeed, the reopening of certain lines is likely (see Figure 7.1). A scheme to reconnect Midleton, County Cork to the railway network and to provide services for commuters travelling to and from Cork City has been announced. The Century 21 Transport Plan announced by government in November 2005 approves the upgrading of a series of lightly used and disused railway routes to form a Western Rail Corridor connecting Claremorris (and later Sligo) to Galway and Limerick (Government of Ireland, 2005). A rail link to Shannon Airport has been mooted (see Figure 7.1).

RURAL TRANSPORT PROVISION

As mentioned previously, legislation was passed in the 1930s with the aim of protecting the position of the railway. As part of this legislation, Irish bus services were effectively nationalised. By the 1950s, the railways together with the bulk of Irish rural bus services were being operated by a single semi-state concern, Coras Iompair Eireann (CIE). One administrative convenience of this was that as railway services were withdrawn, parallel substitute bus services could be introduced. Thus for example, the extent of CIE's rural stage-carriage bus route network increased by 13.4 per cent between 1962 and 1972, mainly as a result of the introduction of new bus routes to locations previously served by the railway (Moynes, 2001). In many cases, the bus services replacing withdrawn railway services lasted only for a short period.

Over the past 30 years, the manner in which public transport is provided in rural areas in Ireland has changed considerably. One major innovation has been the development since the early 1970s of a network of express bus routes. Initially, and in keeping with the philosophy of the time, the express bus routes did not parallel the railway. The most important early routes ran from Dublin to the northwest of the country, an area that had lost all of its railway services, and also connected the western regional centres of Donegal, Sligo, Galway and Limerick.

In 1987, the main businesses of CIE were separated into three semi-independent companies, Iarnrod Eireann (Irish Rail), Bus Eireann (Irish Bus) and Bus Atha Cliath (Dublin Bus). Bus Eireann lost no time in developing potentially profitable express bus routes, most notably those linking the capital to the other major urban centres. In many instances, these routes ran parallel to the railway.

The development of a nation-wide network of express bus routes had an important implication for transport provision in rural areas. In many instances, the new services were introduced as a replacement for pre-existing stage-carriage services, that is buses that stopped anywhere along the route to receive and discharge passengers. While the new express services offered faster journey times, they generally called at the larger urban centres only. Those living in rural locations through which the services passed were no longer served directly.

The second major innovation in the provision of public transport in rural areas relates to schools transport. Free secondary school education was made available to most students in Ireland in 1967. It was realised that in order for the policy of free secondary education to be effective, it would be desirable to offer free school transport services to the approximately 57,000 students living in excess of three miles from their local school (Moynes, 2001). While the contract for the management and operation of the free school transport scheme was given to CIE, 60 per cent of the bus services were subcontracted out to private operators. Most of these operators had heretofore engaged in the private hire business only.

The introduction of the free schools transport scheme gave a fillip to the private bus operators who, in time, were able to purchase new vehicles and expand their fleets. By the late 1970s, a number of these operators had commenced operating scheduled routes. For legal purposes, those availing of these services were technically members of travel clubs that existed to provide the services.

To summarise, two major trends underlie the provision of bus services in rural Ireland in recent decades. The first has been the increasing role of competition between the railway and the bus services of Bus Eireann and the private sector operators. The second has been the effective withdrawal of bus services from many rural areas. As has been the case in other countries, this latter trend has led to calls for alternative types of public transport provision in such areas. Such alternative types of rural transport include demand-responsive buses, where customers telephone their requirements for transport in advance; community buses, where a small vehicle owned and managed by a committee of local volunteers provides services; post buses, where postal vehicles carry passengers; car pooling, and allowing fare-paying passengers access to school bus services.

Initially, the development of alternative forms of rural public transport in Ireland was hesitant. One reason for this was that CIE and later Bus Eireann did not consider the provision of such services to be part of their remit; nor did the relevant government departments take an initiating role. In the absence of any 'top-down' approach, such developments as occurred tended to do so in a piecemeal fashion.

The foregoing situation changed in 2001 with the introduction of the Rural Transport Initiative (RTI). This provides financial support to bodies attempting to introduce rural transport services and has given rise to a number of schemes offering both fixed-route and demand-responsive services. The first such scheme began in January 2002 and 34 schemes provided 514,000 trips in 2004 (Area Development Management, 2005). At least one RTI service is currently operating in each county except County Louth. The largest RTI, Kerry Community Transport, now serves 85 towns and villages. Geographical coverage is likely to increase in the future.

Recent trends in rural public transport provision in Ireland mirror those that have occurred in other countries. The model whereby rural transport needs are met by a single semi-state monopolistic operator via co-ordinated railway and bus services has been replaced. Now, the major role of the conventional public transport modes is to provide inter-urban transport which passes through but does not necessarily serve rural areas and to connect major urban centres to their hinterlands, especially for journeys to work and school. What can be thought of as truly rural transport needs are being met, albeit somewhat falteringly so far in the case of Ireland, by new types of transport. In terms of organisation, the recent changes in rural transport provision have meant an increased role for the private sector and for locally based initiatives.

URBAN TRANSPORT PROBLEMS AND ISSUES

The outcomes of urban transport problems are clear to all. Many Irish towns suffer from severe traffic congestion. The transport sector is now the single greatest contributor to Ireland's greenhouse gas emissions (Environmental Protection Agency, 2004). For urban and suburban residents, the most common source of noise pollution is transport.

The primary causes of Ireland's urban transport problems have been referred to already. They include an increasingly urban-based population and increased trip making that has been encouraged by increasing vehicle ownership. Urban transport problems have been compounded in Ireland by the way in which Irish urban centres themselves have been developing. Traditionally, the majority of workplaces, shops and services existed near the core of relatively compact urban centres with residences surrounding these. This geography of land uses created a pattern of trip making with relatively large flows of traffic along a limited number of radial routes that could be served efficiently by public transport. The bulk of suburban bus routes serving Irish towns and cities operate along radial routes.

In recent decades, Irish urban centres have spread out. At the same time, workplaces and services have become increasingly dispersed away from central areas towards the periphery. Suburban business parks and out-of-town shopping centres are now a feature of most Irish cities and towns. These recent land-use trends have had major repercussions for the evolving geography of urban transport patterns: average trip lengths have increased while the overall pattern of travel has become more diffuse. A much larger proportion of work trips now occurs between suburban areas. Some inner-city residents now travel to work on the periphery. A more diffuse pattern of trip making is one where public transport is less well positioned to play a significant role. It can be argued that increased car availability has permitted urban centres to spread out and services to disperse. Trip patterns have become more complex and less easily served by public transport; yet increasing car use has led to increased traffic congestion and ever increasing difficulties of movement for all.

The case of Dublin is worth considering in more detail. Like most other urban centres, the population of the Greater Dublin region[2] increased rapidly in recent decades but vehicle ownership increased even more rapidly (see Table 7.3). With increasing city spread and with greater numbers having to travel further to work, the amount of trip making has increased dramatically; it is estimated that the number of trips taking place in the Greater Dublin region during the morning peak hour increased from 172,000 in 1991 to 283,000 in 1999 (Dublin

Transportation Office, 2001). In contrast, the number of passengers carried by the main bus operator, Dublin Bus, increased at a more modest rate (see Table 7.3). As stated already, the declining role of the bus in relative terms reflects the increases in vehicle ownership and also the manner in which the geography of land uses and therefore of trip making has evolved.

Table 7.3   Greater Dublin region: population, car ownership and public transport trends, 1961–2002

Year	Population (000s)	Number of cars (000s)	Cars per 1,000 persons	Passenger journeys (millions)	
				Bus	**Railway**
1961	906.6	68.8	75.9	229.8	Not available
1971	1,062.2	159.8	150.4	196.7	4.9
1981	1,290.1	284.4	220.4	158.0	8.0
1986	1,336.1	258.6	193.6	165.2	17.2
1991	1,350.6	391.7	236.3	173.0	19.1
1996	1,405.7	406.4	289.1	185.5	19.5
2002	1,535.4	558.5	363.7	196.8 (2001)	24.1

Sources: *Statistical Abstract* (Dublin: Stationery Office); *Statistical Yearbook of Ireland* (Dublin: Stationery Office)

One of the difficulties faced by the bus as a public transport provider is that in most instances, buses must compete with other vehicles for road space. No matter how far average private vehicle speeds decline, journeys by bus that involve multiple stops take longer. In the long run, therefore, even more trip makers transfer to private transport.

Unlike the bus, the rail-based modes generally run on their own right of way and thus are less prone to traffic congestion. In common with most other cities, the number of passengers using Dublin's suburban railway in recent years has increased (see Table 7.3). These increases have led to service enhancements that have caused further increases in carryings. The improvements in Dublin have included the introduction of suburban train services to Maynooth in 1981, the commissioning of the Dublin Area Rapid Transit (DART) scheme in 1984 and the introduction of suburban train services to Kildare in 1994. More recently, DART has been extended to Greystones and Malahide while the outer-suburban train services to such destinations as Dundalk, Longford and Gorey have been improved. The most recent rail-based development has been the opening under the Luas brand name of light rail transit (LRT) routes between the city centre and Dundrum and Tallaght respectively. The Transport 21 proposals announced by government in November 2005 propose the reinstatement of the railway route from Dublin to Dunboyne and Navan (see Figure 7.1); the construction of a metro system in Dublin; the opening of further LRT routes including one from the city centre to Lucan, and the development of the railway infrastructure within the city centre area to cater for the increased number of services that are predicted to converge there (Government of Ireland, 2005).

The foregoing renaissance of the suburban railway system suggests that where high-quality and reliable public transport services are provided, they will be used. The introduction in Dublin of Quality Bus Corridors (QBCs), that is, road lanes that may be used by public transport vehicles only, represents another attempt to improve the quality of public transport. The most successful QBC in Dublin, along the N11 route to Stillorgan and Foxrock, was carrying 243 per cent more passengers in 2001 after the QBC was complete than in 1995 (Coras Iompair Eireann, 2002).

The increased role of the private sector as an operator of bus services passing through rural areas has been referred to earlier. Within the Irish urban context, virtually all bus services are currently provided by the semi-state sector in the form of Dublin Bus (in the case of Dublin) and Bus Eireann (outside Dublin). As has occurred in the United Kingdom, there is currently debate as to whether a proportion of urban bus routes should be franchised out to private sector operators; indeed the newly opened Luas LRT system operates in this manner. Experience elsewhere, most notably in the United Kingdom, suggests that serious questions need to be asked about this process. While in theory the privatisation of urban bus services leads to greater competition and customer benefits, the outcome has often been that in the medium term, a single semi-state operator has been replaced by a small number of semi-monopolistic private operators over whom less control can be exercised.

Looking to the future, the transport problems that face Dublin and other Irish urban areas are unlikely to ameliorate significantly within the foreseeable future. The current planning guidelines have finally recognised the desirability of directing new development to locations that are (or can be) well served by public transport and the desirability of allowing higher development densities that can be served more readily by public transport (Brady Shipman Martin et al., 1999). In the longer term, implementation of these policies is likely to lead to improvements, at least locally. That said, the fundamental issues referred to here are likely to remain for the foreseeable future.

PORTS AND AIRPORTS

As was mentioned at the outset, Ireland's island location underlines the strategic importance of the country's ports and airports. This importance is emphasised by the crucial role that international trade plays within Irish economic activity. The expansion of the Irish economy during the 1990s has placed increased demands on the country's ports and airports and these are now handling vastly increased traffic (see Table 7.4).

The greatest proportion of Ireland's port traffic is handled by a relatively small number of ports (see Figure 7.1). In 2003, 36.1 per cent of freight tonnage handled passed through Dublin followed by Foynes/Shannon (21.9 per cent) and Cork (19.8 per cent) (Central Statistics Office, 2004). Dun Laoghaire and Rosslare, together with Dublin and Cork, handle significant volumes of RO-RO traffic. Waterford and Drogheda, together with Dublin and Cork, handle significant volumes of lift-on, lift-off (LO-LO) traffic.

Table 7.4 Airport and port traffic, 1980–2003

Year	Airport passengers (000s)	Goods handled by ports (000s tonnes)
1980	3,227	20,278
1985	3,264	23,372
1990	6,607	26,152
1995	9,560	32,380
2000	16,384	45,273
2003	19,340	46,165

Note: The airport passenger figures refer to inbound plus outbound passengers but exclude those in transit; the port figures refer to inbound plus outbound traffic.

Source: *Statistical Bulletin* (Dublin: Stationery Office)

Unlike, for example, the national road network and the railway, Ireland's major ports are not controlled by a single body but rather by a number of port authorities and companies, each within the semi-state sector. The different ports operate according to a variety of models. Dublin, for example, is operated by the Dublin Port Company but many port services, for example cargo handling, are provided by private operators. In other cases, port services are provided directly by the company operating the port. Rosslare Harbour is operated by Iarnrod Eireann; this is because the port was developed originally by railway company interests.

Looking to the future, it is predicted that freight traffic through Irish ports will increase significantly. The *Transport Corridors in Europe* report that was completed as part of the National Spatial Strategy (Department of the Environment, Heritage and Local Government, 2002) suggests that by 2012, RO-RO traffic will have risen by 80 per cent. It is predicted that in the case of Dublin, demand will exceed capacity for RO-RO traffic by 2007 and for LO-LO traffic soon after 2010. The construction of a new port on the east coast to the south of Drogheda has been mooted as one way of relieving the pressure on Dublin port.

A recent governmental review of Irish ports (Department of Communications, Marine and Natural Resources, 2003) suggests that individual port authorities cannot expect in the future to receive significant public monies to finance their expansion plans. It is therefore likely that public–private partnerships will have a greater role to play in this regard and that a greater proportion of port services will be offered by private companies. The review suggests also that the amalgamation of port companies operating at adjacent locations might be considered, for example Cork and Bantry, and Dublin and Dun Laoghaire. The review suggests that the opening up of port companies to private sector ownership should not be pursued at present.

Ireland possesses three national airports and six regional airports (see Figure 7.1). Until recently the national airports were run by the semi-state company, Aer Rianta. Each of the regional airports is operated by a separate company. The regional airports have met with varying degrees of success. The increases in traffic passing through the national airports have been dramatic in recent times (see Table 7.4) and have placed considerable pressure on airport infrastructure. The *Transport Corridors in Europe* report predicts that Dublin Airport will be handling in excess of 25 million passengers per annum by 2012. Current plans call for expanded terminal facilities and the construction of a new runway. Significant terminal developments are under way at Cork.

As with the country's ports, it is obvious that the national airports will require considerable investments in infrastructure over the next decade in order to cope with the increased demands that will be placed upon them. Once again, a key question concerns the extent to which this investment will come from public as against from private sources. Recently enacted legislation has placed control of the three national airports under three independent authorities. This means that to a greater extent than before, they will be in competition with each other.

CONCLUSION

Transport is fundamental to day-to-day life as we know it. It sustains social well-being and economic development. Even when at rest, we are assailed by the noise of transport. Transport affects the quality of the air that we breathe. Many of the phenomena described in other chapters of this book would not exist, at least in their current forms, without the various means of transport that are so often taken for granted.

This chapter has shown that transport operates in a variety of environments, each with its own problems and opportunities. Yet, it is important to stress that the various facets of the transport sector are interlinked. Problems of how best to provide public transport in rural areas may seem to have little to do with the efficient functioning of the country's ports; yet, the fuel to run the vehicles that will provide rural access and indeed the vehicles themselves must be imported through the ports.

This chapter has shown also that the transport sector in Ireland has changed rapidly in recent times. Burgeoning vehicle ownership and increasing urbanisation have given rise to significant problems that have demanded an urgent rethinking concerning, for example, the most appropriate design and layout for our evolving urban and suburban areas. Transport and sustainability considerations lie at the core of the types of solution that are currently being suggested.

Traditionally, the state has been the main agent in the supply of transport infrastructure and many transport services. As has been shown in this chapter, the private sector is now becoming increasingly involved, in part because the state cannot on its own provide the significant resources that are required for major transport projects. Yet unlike the state, the private sector operates on a 'for profit' basis. At the same time, the fact that transport is a service suggests that government will continue to be involved in the transport sector on an on-going basis. The evolving relationship between the public and private sectors within transport will have a significant impact on the future social and economic well-being of the country as a whole.

8

Strategic Spatial Planning in Northern Ireland

Michael R. Murray and Brendan Murtagh

On 17 September 2001 the Minister for Regional Development, Mr Gregory Campbell, introduced a motion to the Northern Ireland Assembly that called for agreement by the Assembly on the content of the proposed regional development strategy – *Shaping Our Future*. A two-hour debate concluded with a resolution endorsing the strategy thus bringing to an end a strategic spatial planning process that had commenced in June 1997. This journey of inquiry was marked by a number of prominent milestones:

- the publication of a discussion paper in November 1997;
- a draft proposals document in December 1998;
- a public examination of proposals in the autumn of 1999;
- the publication of the report of the public examination panel in February 2000;
- the publication of a response to the panel's report by the Department for Regional Development in April 2000; and
- the submission of final representations from interested parties by the end of May 2000.

Throughout this lengthy period there was extensive consultation and discussion. Key goals comprised the need to secure a broad consensus on the future spatial planning framework for Northern Ireland and the need for policy prescription to go beyond land use planning. Both aspirations were distinctively different from previous regional planning initiatives in Northern Ireland during the 1960s and 1970s. Intensive interaction between Members of the Legislative Assembly and public officials secured complete cross-party political support for this 25-year strategy and might suggest, therefore, that these ambitions were realised. This chapter explores these matters. The discussion commences with a short overview of the background to strategic spatial planning and its relationship with regional governance in Northern Ireland. This is followed by a description of the principal features of *Shaping Our Future*. The chapter concludes by highlighting important implementation challenges for this spatial development strategy during the years ahead.

STRATEGIC PLANNING AND REGIONAL
GOVERNANCE IN NORTHERN IRELAND

Land use planning responsibilities in Northern Ireland are currently divided between the Department for Regional Development and the Planning Service of the Department of the Environment. At the risk of being reductionist, the former deals with the formulation of high-level policy, the latter with the preparation of development plans and the operation of development control. This arrangement is rooted in the implementation of the 1998 Good Friday Agreement that led to the establishment of a power-sharing Executive and the need to allocate ministerial posts consistent with the election performance of political parties with respect to the Northern Ireland Assembly. Political context is important, therefore, in seeking to understand the emergence and character of strategic spatial planning in Northern Ireland.

Prior to the suspension of Stormont and the introduction of direct rule in 1972, Northern Ireland was administered by a legislature separate from Westminster. The region thus developed with many of the characteristics of an independent state with its own Parliament, civil service and a system of executive control of Prime Minister and Cabinet responsibilities. In 1960 the Northern Ireland Government commissioned Robert Matthew to prepare a planning report for the Belfast region. The final report was published in 1963 and recommended:

- the imposition of a stopline around the Belfast urban area in order to limit its expansion into the surrounding greenscape and hold its population to around 600,000 by 1981;
- the development of a new regional centre, subsequently to be known as Craigavon, focused on Lurgan–Portadown;
- the designation of seven towns within the eastern part of Northern Ireland as centres for major development; and
- the concentration of industry within the remainder of Northern Ireland into six key centres (see Figure 8.1).

As noted by O'Dowd (2005) Stormont was ready at that time to embrace a policy of new towns, growth centre planning, and the development of roads and industrial estates notwithstanding very considerable controversy around these locational decisions and the alleged neglect of the West of the province.

This early foray into strategic spatial planning was very much a politically driven project and contrasted with the next major effort during the 1970s when the planning governance environment was quite different. The Macrory local government reform report in 1970 had advanced an analysis whereby a suite of regional services including planning, roads, water and sewerage should be vested in a central Ministry of Development. This would be headed by a Minister who would be accountable to the Northern Ireland Parliament. A total of not more than 26 district councils was recommended as a replacement for two county boroughs, six county councils, 34 borough and urban district

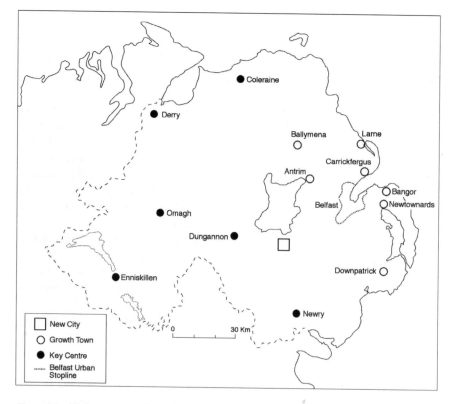

Figure 8.1   Six key centres of growth identified by the Matthew Report (1963)

Source: Matthew Report (1963)

councils and 31 rural district councils (Murray, 1991). New local government would have responsibility for a range of ceremonial, consultative, representative and much reduced executive functions. These recommendations were accepted by government and were supported by legislation in 1972. In the interim, however, escalating violence and political instability in Northern Ireland generated deep concern in Westminster and, as stated above, the Stormont-based government and Parliament was suspended in March of that year. Local government elections followed in 1973 and established a single-tier structure of 26 district councils. Planning functions were absorbed into the Northern Ireland Civil Service, within which it was appreciated that the preparation of development plans could not go ahead without an up-to-date regional planning framework.

   In 1975 the Department of Housing, Local Government and Planning published a discussion paper with spatial options related to a regional development framework for Northern Ireland. These options were configured along a concentration-dispersal continuum and a preference for a district towns strategy was indicated. This would result in the targeting of growth to 23 towns in the region, while providing for managed growth in Belfast. The strategy closely followed the distribution of new local government headquarters and, not surprisingly, received district council acclaim. The Regional Physical Development Strategy 1975–95 was issued in final form in 1977 (see Figure 8.2) and represented a second significant milestone in the history of strategic spatial planning in Northern Ireland. Greer and Jess (1987) have commented that, in theory at least, a more equitable distribution of growth points had been established across the region and that the Matthew Plan, constructed around solutions for the Belfast city region, had been abandoned. Expressed more prosaically, the routines of a civil service planning bureaucracy wedded to impartiality, efficiency and effectiveness had secured a more balanced spread of urban-driven development opportunity between a predominantly unionist East and nationalist West in Northern Ireland. But, perhaps not surprisingly in the context of the time, the strategy said little about the deep sectarian divisions and social inequalities within the region, preferring instead to hide behind a methodology of statistical inquiry and evaluation techniques. This was a strategy dealing with population, housing, retailing and employment forecasts and produced by planners for planners.

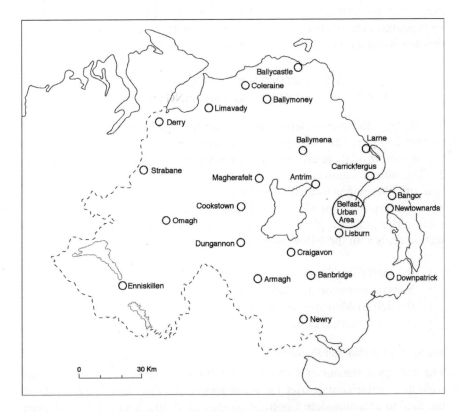

Figure 8.2 Regional Physical Development Strategy (1977) growth centres

Source: Regional Physical Development Strategy

Thirty years on from that era, the obligations of governance in Northern Ireland are substantially different and as Neill and Gordon (2001) have argued, 'difference and division can no longer be so easily ignored in official planning exercises' (p. 34). Political progress, related to a constitutional settlement, the ending of IRA terrorism, arms decommissioning, and equality safeguards, now sits alongside the maturing of a large and expressive civil society. It may seem a cliché, but a new start has warranted a new plan and in that regard the commitment in the 1998 Good Friday Agreement to produce a regional planning strategy for Northern Ireland is very significant. But just as the Agreement itself is the product of dialogue and is watermarked by inclusiveness, it is perhaps stating the obvious that similar values should be invoked to underpin the process and content of that planning strategy. From the outset the themes identified for this strategy were about 'valuing people', 'bridging the divided community', 'celebrating distinctiveness', 'targeting social need', and 'improving educational attainment', all of which go well beyond traditional land use planning (Neill and Gordon, 2001). However, while the consultative and participatory arrangements put in place for the formulation of the spatial strategy were nothing less than exhaustive, as evidenced by the fact that the initial completion date of December 1998 proved impossible to meet, it is questionable whether the challenges of this new dawn have been met by the authors of Shaping Our Future.

THE NORTHERN IRELAND REGIONAL DEVELOPMENT STRATEGY: SHAPING OUR FUTURE

The strategy document (Department for Regional Development, 2001a) runs to over 200 pages and comprises six sections made up of 13 chapters and appendices. In all there are some 43 strategic planning guidelines supported by 23 diagrams, in themselves evidence of the complex policy arena within which land use planning is located. The document guarantees a long read to those who persevere but, embedded within the language of inclusiveness, there are some very significant planning policy directions for the future. This chapter section deals with the following themes:

- the spatial development framework;
- housing provision and land supply;
- the Belfast Metropolitan Area;
- rural Northern Ireland.

The Spatial Development Framework

The strategy at the outset is careful to set out some parameters indicating the scale of possible change over the planning period. Thus mention is made of the need to accommodate a population growth of 105,000 by 2015 and some 150,000 by 2025. The dwellings requirement is estimated at 160,000 by 2015 and 250,000 by 2025, which will be capable of providing for a future population level of 1.835 million. The employment need is set at approximately 100,000 additional jobs by 2015. The number of vehicles on Northern Ireland roads is anticipated to double over the period to 2025.

In working through the implications of these headline data, the strategy adopts 'the promotion of a balanced and equitable pattern of sustainable development across the Region' as an overarching set of values. The text emphasises the complementarity of cities, towns and rural areas and underlines the need to optimise the distinctive contributions of these component areas of Northern Ireland in order to maximise the potential of the region as a whole. The spatial framework is thus constructed around an interconnected suite of elements comprising the regional gateways of Belfast and Londonderry, urban hubs comprising the regional towns, and link transport corridors of roads and railway as 'the skeletal framework' for future physical development (see Figure 8.3).

It is, perhaps, not surprising that this spatial framework should broadly mirror the earlier 1975–95 Regional Physical Development Strategy in relation to the prominent role of the cities and regional towns. The relegation of Magherafelt, Ballymoney and Ballycastle to second-tier status in the urban hierarchy is, however, a departure from the previous framework when, having regard to the then newly constituted district council areas, it was perceived as only proper that each administrative area should have a designated district town within a single tier of regional growth centres. A further similarity with the previous spatial framework is the prominent recognition given to the strategic natural resource endowment of rural areas and which, when conjoined with an extensive green belt for the Belfast Metropolitan Area, sends a strong signal of environmental protection intent. But fundamentally Figure 8.3 captures an enduring tension within Northern Ireland on the merits of concentration versus dispersal. Indeed that debate has been on-going since the publication of the Belfast Regional Survey and Plan (the Matthew Plan) in 1963 which, as noted above, sought to contain the outward growth of the city through the imposition of a stopline and link this with the selective expansion of a number of urban centres. A key paragraph in the new strategy resonates loudly with the advocacy of that earlier prescription. Thus Shaping Our Future argues:

The key to achieving an optimum balance between over-concentration around the Belfast Metropolitan Area and excessive dispersal is to sustain a reinforced network of strong urban hubs, linked by an upgraded strategic transport network. This will provide accessible counter-magnet development opportunities to the metropolitan core, thus helping to ease development and transport pressures in and around Belfast. (p. 46)

The earlier Matthew Plan, by way of comparison, states:

The prime object of the plan in this respect is, to a modest extent, simultaneously to demagnetize the centre and reinvigorate the many small towns in the region. This is a highly complex conception; both aspects (limitation and growth) must be complementary, not only on paper, but in fact in time and in balance. It implies a technique of planning and execution appropriate to administration at its highest levels. (p. 18) ... The network of main roadways as now planned and partly under construction will in general link the growth centres to Belfast, but some modifications, mainly in the form of spurs will be necessary. (p. 24)

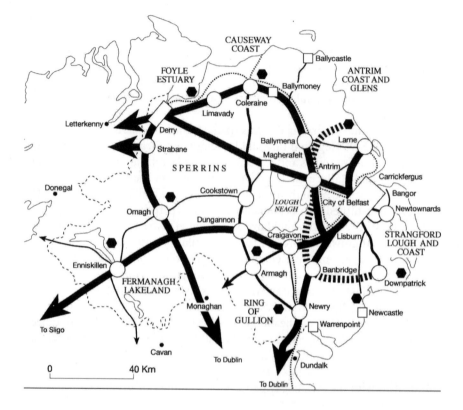

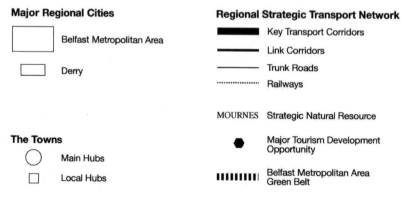

Figure 8.3 Regional Development Strategy, 2001

Source: Department for Regional Development (2001)

Housing Provision and Land Supply

At the public examination into the Draft Regional Strategic Framework considerable time was taken to work through and refine the housing need forecasts for Northern Ireland. The panel's report set out a suggested allocation between the Belfast Metropolitan Area with its hinterland and the rest of Northern Ireland. This division is retained within the adopted strategy which allocates 77,500 new dwellings to the former and 82,500 to the latter through to the year 2015. The strategy also identifies a set of district housing indicators that range from 1,400 additional residential units in Moyle District by 2015 to 51,000 units in the six districts of the Belfast Metropolitan Area. In the draft strategy the preliminary housing targets were further disaggregated to regional town and rural community components, but this task has now been left to the follow-on Area Plan process.

The strategy, however, provides a number of very strong policy steers on how the interpretation of these indicators is to be worked through:

- primacy is to be given to main towns in order to support the achievement of 'critical mass'. The optimal housing balance between towns, villages and dispersed small settlements is predicated on ensuring that the growth potential of the principal urban centres for employment and services is not undermined;
- more use is to be made of recycled land and buildings thus reducing the need for greenfield development land. The strategy sets a regional target of 60 per cent of future residential development and associated job provision within existing urban limits through to the year 2010, which contrasts with the level of achievement during the 1990s of not more than 30 per cent;
- large-scale development proposals for the expansion of an existing settlement with a population of under 5,000, or for the creation of a 'new settlement' must be 'exceptional' in their intention to meet specific housing needs in the East of the region. Important criteria are set out in the document against which such proposals will be assessed and which shift the conventional developer-led interpretation of this scale of development more towards self-sufficiency of social and physical infrastructure, along with convenience to a commuter rail network.

The implementation of this regional-scale allocative model of housing provision has, however, considerably tested the durability of the new political and technical planning consensus, especially at local level in the matter of Area Plan preparation. Simply put, the search by planners for the closest possible fit between district housing allocations and the zoning of lands in development plans has resulted in unacceptable and very constrained provision for new housing in many towns and villages across Northern Ireland. District council political pressure prompted the publication in 2005 of a review by the Department for Regional Development of the housing growth indicators. This review, the subject of a public examination in February 2006, suggested raising the overall regional housing requirement to 200,000 out to 2015. At district council level the resulting uplifts have been as high as 50 per cent above the initial allocation in Shaping Our Future.

Belfast Metropolitan Area

The Belfast Metropolitan Area (BMA) currently has a population of around 600,000 people and takes in the administrative area of Belfast City Council along with the adjacent urban parts of the district council areas of Carrickfergus, Castlereagh, Lisburn, Newtownabbey and North Down. Over 1 million people live within a 30-miles radius of Belfast city centre. The strategy notes that over the past three decades the inner city has experienced decline followed by an on-going process of renewal. This has been matched over the same period by suburban expansion and over-spill to Bangor, Carrickfergus and Lisburn. Given the seriousness of the congestion pressures on the city and the ready availability of appropriate investment locations in nearby centres, it is proposed firstly to enhance the development of Antrim, Banbridge, Craigavon, Downpatrick, Larne and Newtownards as counter-magnets to the BMA.

The second pillar of the urban strategy will be to secure the expansion of seven small towns around the BMA to help meet housing need generated by the latter. Thus Ballyclare, Ballynahinch, Carryduff, Comber, Crumlin, Dromore and Moira have been designated on the basis of their location on key transport corridors and infrastructure availability as an additional ring of over-spill settlements. And finally, for the BMA itself the thrust of policy will continue to be urban revitalisation.

What emerges for this core part of Northern Ireland, therefore, is a complex set of spatial interdependencies characterised by multidimensional patterns of living, working, shopping, education and recreation. Nevertheless, some 42,000 additional dwellings were initially estimated as representing the housing need within the BMA urban area. Notwithstanding the commitment, as noted above, to brownfield recycling, it is inevitable that peripheral land release on greenfield sites will be required over the years ahead thus widening the development footprint of Belfast. Green belt protection interest groups, such as the Belfast Metropolitan Residents Group, have emerged to strongly contest these land releases, not least in connection with the draft Belfast Metropolitan Area Plan published in November 2004 and the revised regional housing growth indicators published in January 2005.

Transportation is the glue that will hold together this emergent city-region geography. Within the new strategy emphasis is placed on the creation of a metropolitan transport corridor network radiating out from Belfast city centre and characterised by improved public transit services. The great danger, however, is that the disconnection between land use development and transportation solutions will deepen. There is every likelihood that the certainty of private sector-led new housing in accordance with the wider locational preferences of this strategy will generate increased car travel into and within the BMA. An uncertain and expenditure-constrained public sector thus faces immediate and longer-term challenges in responding adequately to these congestion realities. The strategy document is short on commitments to the contrary.

Rural Northern Ireland

In accordance with a recommendation from the Public Examination Panel, the Shaping Our Future strategy contains a separate chapter on rural Northern Ireland. At the draft proposals stage the 'rural community' was defined as comprising the distinctive elements of small towns under 10,000 people, villages and small settlements, and open countryside that in 1996 collectively totalled some 652,000 persons. In the 2001 document, in contrast, the geography of rural Northern Ireland is described as consisting of main towns, small towns and villages, and open countryside with a total population of 1.012 million in 1998. The inclusion of main towns in this definition of rurality is significant and recognises the strong degree of functional interdependence that exists across the settlement hierarchy throughout Northern Ireland. Using this broader definition of the rural, the regional development strategy estimates that just under 70,000 dwellings will be required in small towns, villages and open countryside through to 2015, with up to 40,000 dwellings located in the main towns. In short, some 44 per cent of new housing will be targeted outside the cities and main towns of Northern Ireland which is broadly in line with the 41 per cent share of the existing Northern Ireland population within this territory.

The future distribution between small towns, villages and open countryside is footnoted in the strategy as a matter to be decided at the district level through the development plan process. Nevertheless, some insights into future policy practices can be gleaned from the text of Shaping Our Future. In the first instance there is recognition of contrasting development pressures between the Belfast travel-to-work area and the rest of the region which, in turn, require a differentiation of planning response. This translates to a raft of policies that are supportive of revitalisation in declining settlements, as opposed to careful growth management in those small towns and villages that have been rapidly expanding. At least the tone of these measures goes well beyond the sphere of land use planning. However, the muted response by other government bodies to the regional strategy, linked to their unease about the degree to which the document is over-arching and binding, must cast doubt on delivery capacity. Secondly, while there is positive policy expression to create and sustain a living countryside with a high quality of life for all its residents, concerns are equally noted about the perceived cumulative visual impact of inappropriate single-house development. The strategy states:

> These growing pressures present a threat to the open countryside which is a vital resource for sustaining the genuine rural community. The cumulative impacts of this development include: loss of agricultural land and habitats; fields being sold off to house townspeople; increased traffic on rural roads; the risk of pollution from growing numbers of septic tanks; the increased visual impact of more structures in the landscape; unnecessary extension of infrastructure and services; and a weakening of towns and villages. (p. 89)

The strategy suggests that where adverse cumulative impacts are identified within rural Northern Ireland it will be necessary to take 'difficult decisions at the local level in relation to the control of individual properties' (p. 105). The publication of a Regional Planning Policy Statement on the Countryside is promised by the strategy, and was expected during the first quarter of 2006, to help refine a set of regulations connected to the implementation of the strategy in relation to rural Northern Ireland. While the regional strategy has been careful to avoid detailed policy prescription on this issue, it remains the case that single-house development in the countryside will continue to run as a deeply contested feature of the planning policy arena. The evidence from the Department for Regional Development is that the number of new single dwellings being approved in the Northern Ireland countryside increased from 1,790 in 1991/92 to 5,628 by 2002/03. Nonetheless, the possibility of stricter controls in the face of that scale of development pressure will almost certainly be energetically resisted by local authority elected representatives and a well organised coalition of over 500 rural community groups.

SPATIAL PLANNING CHALLENGES

Strategic spatial planning frameworks on the national and regional scales are much in vogue. They have been formulated for Ireland, Scotland and Wales and are emerging in England as regional spatial strategies under the provisions of the Planning and Compulsory Purchase Act 2004. Other parts of Europe also show evidence of this approach to spatial policy (see Albrechts et al., 2003). This type of strategy at a generic level can perform a number of uses, which Harrison and Todes (2001) summarise as comprising:

- guidance for public sector investment in infrastructure and services;
- the spatial allocation of public sector support to reduce spatial inequalities;
- indicative guidance for private sector investment;
- public/private collaboration in development;
- rationalised resource allocations across space and within government policies and programmes;
- a level of certainty and consistency in decision making within and across sectors;
- spatial guidance for land use management, including the content of development plans and related development control decision making.

In other words, strategic frameworks should seek to represent the visible expression of the much vaunted phrase 'joined-up government'. Their visionary ambition should be matched by a depth of possibilities which acknowledge that contemporary governance is worked out through multiple stakeholders operating with horizontal breadth and on different spatial scales. Spatial strategies should deal comprehensively with the spatial implications of all public policy domains, and give clear guidance for all investment and development.

However, the history of regional planning in Northern Ireland is dominated by devotion to the use of authoritarian and allocative housing models, and, as noted above, the content of Shaping Our Future continues this tradition in relation to the prominence given to housing growth indicators. Moreover, in the wake of an unprecedented and welcome participatory effort to engage with multiple stakeholders outside government (Murray and Greer, 2002), it is somewhat ironic that the final form of Shaping Our Future demonstrates the reality of civil service turf-protection politics by being light on interdepartmental commitment. A hard-won public administration consensus, either to support or at best not to openly contest the spatial development strategy, has been purchased on the basis of selective content, generality and policy ambiguity. For example, health and education are scarcely mentioned, the implications for public expenditure are sidelined, and there is no loudly stated and unequivocal commitment to rural development. The view of the present is overwhelmingly a view of a normal and decent society, rather than a society painfully emerging from bitter conflict. The perception of the future is that contested identities do not matter.

Part of the explanation must rest with the fact that planning and development in Northern Ireland has long had to deal with a suite of wicked dialectics which surface, for example, as the Northern Ireland and the island of Ireland relationship, west of the River Bann versus east of the River Bann, countryside development versus landscape protection, rural versus urban, and top-down bureaucratic prescription versus bottom-up citizen-led involvement in the policy process. The deeper issues that these represent are about the persistence of seemingly intractable ethno-religious divisions, spatial and social equity, how the rural is perceived, and the relative weight to be given to new alignments of participatory and representative democracy.

In the final analysis, however, it could be argued that much of the success of Shaping Our Future is its sophisticated combination of planning process and, at times, vague language, that have produced a statement with a power to appeal to multiple interests. There is something for everyone, but everyone does not get everything that they have argued for. Nonetheless, in its all too frequent retreat to development plan-related land use management in general, and development control in particular, Shaping Our Future runs the danger of falling short of providing the necessary leadership for the spatial transformation of Northern Ireland. The strategy looks out to a time horizon of 2025 but its relevance and acceptability in Northern Ireland political and civil society will unquestionably fracture much earlier if implementation is dominated by quite narrow regulatory concerns related to the moulding of Planning Policy Statements, the preparation of Area Plans and the determination of planning applications. Promoting a genuine shift to transformative spatial planning in Northern Ireland that can engage the entire governance arena remains a pressing challenge for policy makers.

Part II
Economy

Introduction

It is widely acknowledged that the key driver in the economic and social transformations that have occurred in Ireland during the past 15 years or so has been the so-called 'Celtic Tiger' phenomenon. From an economy that was struggling in the 1980s flowered a vibrant, high-wealth-generating economy in the 1990s that was the envy of nations around the globe. As we have discussed in Chapter 1 there are many reasons for this economic turnaround, and the chapters in this section provide further explanation and in-depth empirical material to illustrate the changes that occurred. They also detail that while the economy as a whole was resurgent the fortunes of particular sectors have not been so favourable – for example agriculture, once the backbone of the Irish economy. Even industries that were key to kick-starting the economic boom, such as computer manufacturing, have gone into decline to be replaced by other industries. Importantly, the replacement of some industries by others has generally worked in Ireland's favour with low-skill industries such as some manufacturing and call centres being replaced by higher-skilled, better paid work, in areas such as, for example, high-end manufacturing, marketing, accounting, research and development, and so on.

The chapters also reveal the uneven spatial variation of different sectors, highlighting that the Celtic Tiger phenomenon has not affected all places equally. They demonstrate that some areas of the country have especially benefited from foreign inward investment and domestic, indigenous growth, notably the principal cities of Dublin, Cork, Limerick and Galway, whereas others have stagnated such as the rural areas of the Northwest. In other words, the chapters reveal a complex economic landscape that varies across and within sectors (primary, manufacturing and services) and across the country depending on the location of different industries.

In the opening chapter in the section, Chris van Egeraat and Proinnsias Breathnach discuss the evolution of manufacturing industry in Ireland and its various sectors, focusing in particular on developments during the 1990s. They note that the manufacturing sector from the 1960s onwards has been dominated by foreign-owned plants that increasingly account for a large proportion of product exports. The nature and location of these firms has been changing, though, with the low-end branch plants sited outside of the Dublin region being replaced by high-tech plants employing highly skilled labour increasingly located near to Dublin and the other principal cities. These firms are attracted by low taxes, skilled labour and other incentives. Given the benefits of clustering and their supply nature, indigenous firms tend to locate near to foreign-owned business. The authors note that manufacturing in other parts of the country has steadily declined due to the lack of large pools of suitable labour thus increasing their economic peripheralisation. They illustrate their argument by providing two case studies of the computer-building and pharmaceutical sectors. Both sectors have undergone the transformation from low-skill to high-skill labour and have gravitated to sites near to large cities.

In the following chapter, Proinnsias Breathnach notes similar processes at work in relation to service industries, presently the most important part of Ireland's economy in terms of overall employed labour and GDP generated. Indeed, he notes that services accounted for almost four-fifths of employment growth over the period 1991–2002, and that this growth was important for attracting women into the workforce. During this time all service sectors grew, but some expanded more rapidly, notably wholesale and retail and other business services. And while many service sector jobs are relatively low-skilled, Ireland has been successful at attracting higher-skill jobs that have enabled a knowledge economy to develop. He provides useful overviews of both producer services such as finance and banking, software development and back-officing, and of consumer services such as shopping and entertainment.

Agriculture and food production have long been an important aspect of the Irish economy. In 1926, over 50 per cent of workers were employed in agriculture alone. As Jim Walsh observes in the next chapter, the situation is now markedly different. Agriculture and the food industry together now account for 8 per cent of employment and 10 per cent of GDP, although the food industry accounts for more than half of total exports by Irish-owned manufacturing. Agriculture, in particular, is under threat given its reliance on EU and Irish government subsidies, both of which are presently being refocused and reorganised, especially the Common Agricultural Policy. The result is that farmers are ever more reliant on off-farm sources of income to survive or are simply giving up farming. Walsh notes, however, that the changes have differential effects depending upon type of farming and size of farms, creating an array of responses to different problems. In some cases, farmers who adapt well are caught on a technological treadmill to maintain their position; those who do not adapt become more disadvantaged.

Tourism, as Catherine Kelly highlights, is seen by many to be a small, but relatively important, part of the economy. The number of visitors to the country and the amount that they spend grew steadily throughout the 1990s. However, the nature of tourist visits has been changing with an increase in city-breaks and niche-based holidays, while domestic tourists are increasingly going overseas for their holiday breaks. What this has meant is a rethinking about how to market Ireland as a tourist destination and an upgrading of the product supplied. One aspect of this, as Kelly notes in detail, is the heritage industry, one that often has an uneasy alliance with tourism. Ireland's heritage has the potential to offer one means of attracting both domestic and foreign tourists. Overall, she notes that an integrated approach to tourism is necessary to build upon recent growth and to sustain tourism in the long term.

Taken together the chapters provide an overview of how the economy has developed across sectors and place. Other important parts of the economy such as construction and property development are discussed elsewhere in the book (see Chapters 5, 7, and 18). While forecasts seem to be universally positive for the Irish economy in the short to medium term (up to 2015–20), the contributors to this section also offer some important caveats. Ireland has managed to sustain its growth by constantly being proactive in its economic strategy rather than reactive; it has constantly sought to adapt and attract higher-skilled jobs rather than to rely on the first waves of investment. That said, Ireland's reliance on foreign direct investment still potentially leaves the economy open to the flight of capital as firms seek cheaper labour and infrastructure in other locales to reduce their costs and increase their profits. The strategic response has been to try and embed companies into networks and relationships that would be difficult to replicate elsewhere, and to encourage the siting of high-skill functions in Ireland that require labour that other cheaper locales could not provide. How long this can be maintained is where analysts disagree, with some fearing that the Celtic Tiger could end sooner rather than later. Moreover, some sections of the economy, notably agriculture, look set for continued decline, and tourism seems less assured especially given the rising costs of visiting Ireland and the switch to short breaks. With new investment flocking to the cities, including tourist visits, certain areas of the country, especially those dependent on the rural economy, face serious challenge to their long-term sustainability. As explored in the previous part of the book, the cities face problems concerning infrastructure and services given sustained population growth and new property developments. As a result, the spatial unevenness of investment and development pose a number of often quite different and sometimes contradictory concerns to policy makers and those charged with implementing the strategies adopted to ensure that the economy continues to grow while regional inequalities are not exacerbated. For us, and the authors writing in this section, this necessitates that the recommendations of the National Spatial Strategy be fully implemented and that spatial planning be a central feature of the next and future National Development Plans.

9

The Manufacturing Sector

Chris van Egeraat and Proinnsias Breathnach

Manufacturing industry is a crucial ingredient in national economic development. This is because of the value which is added to natural resources and intermediate products through industrial processing. Where this value is retained in an economy, its circulation can sustain many more jobs than are created directly in manufacturing itself. Even in so-called 'post-industrial economies', rising industrial output continues to be a key source of wealth creation despite rapidly contracting employment in manufacturing industry per se. The extraordinarily high rate of economic growth which Ireland experienced in the 1990s was largely driven by rapid expansion of its manufacturing sector, arising principally from a surge of inward investment by transnational firms which began around 1993. This chapter outlines the historical background to this recent phase of strong industrial growth, before examining in some depth the key dimensions of this crucial feature of the so-called 'Celtic Tiger' economy. The chapter concludes with an assessment of the long-term developmental implications of the form recent industrial development has taken, particularly in the light of certain weaknesses in the industrial structure which have become apparent in the early 2000s. Case studies of the microcomputer and pharmaceutical sectors are presented to illustrate key themes raised in the main text. The spatial dimensions associated with successive industrial development phases are also described and analysed.

HISTORICAL BACKGROUND:
FROM PROTECTIONISM TO EXPORT-ORIENTED INDUSTRIALISATION

Upon its establishment in 1922, the Irish Free State inherited a small and underdeveloped manufacturing sector, employing only 4.3 per cent of the labour force in 1926 (O'Malley, 1989). The situation changed little during the first ten years of independence during which economic policy remained largely focused on the promotion of agricultural exports. A change in government in the early 1930s led to the introduction of a policy of protectionism which lasted until the late 1950s. This produced the desired results in the form of a spurt of industrial growth in the 1930s which continued in the immediate aftermath of World War II. In spatial terms most of the new industrial enterprises were located in the main cities, and particularly in the Dublin region which constituted the main market, the main port for imported equipment and materials, and the hub of

128

the national transport system (Breathnach and Walsh, 1994). However, the policy of economic autarky was inevitably doomed to failure. The small size of Ireland's economy ensured that the newly created industrial firms would be too small to expand into export markets once the modest needs of the domestic market were satisfied. The need for these firms to import most of their materials and production equipment created chronic balance-of-trade and payments problems for the government. By the early 1950s, industrial growth had ground to a halt and it was clear that radical measures were required to rescue the economic situation.

During the 1950s a rethink of industrial policy led to a shift to an export-oriented industrialisation strategy. The restrictions on foreign control of industry were gradually relaxed. The Industrial Development Agency (IDA) was assigned the task of promoting Ireland as a location for mobile foreign investment. In addition to the availability of cheap labour, the incentives offered to attract outside investment included substantial capital grants and, in particular, the exemption from taxation of all profits derived from exports. Tariffs on imports were also gradually reduced during the 1960s and 1970s.

The attractiveness of this package was reflected in a substantial build-up of inward investment in the two decades after 1960, boosted in particular by Ireland's accession to the European Economic Community (EEC) in 1973. Between 1961 and 1981, employment in foreign manufacturing firms grew almost fourfold.[1] The USA became by far the most important foreign investment source in this period, accounting for over 40 per cent of employment in foreign manufacturing firms in 1981. On the downside, the generally inefficient indigenous industry, now exposed to external competition, experienced considerable contraction. As a result the foreign sector accounted for all of the growth of 33 per cent in manufacturing employment over the period 1961–81, during which period its share of the total rose from about 10 to 38 per cent (O'Malley, 1989).

Foreign investment in this period was mainly concentrated in the metals and engineering and (from the 1970s) chemicals and pharmaceuticals sectors. In terms of engineering, a key new growth subsector in the 1970s was electronics assembly, reflecting the contemporary growth of this sector in the USA. Foreign firms therefore were contributing both to a sectoral diversification and technological upgrading of the industry structure. Thus, the share of total manufacturing employment taken by the metals and engineering sector jumped from 16 per cent in 1960 to 30 per cent in 1981. Because of its capital-intensive nature, the impact of foreign investment in the chemicals sector was felt more in terms of industrial output and exports than of employment. The sector's share of total industrial output doubled to 17 per cent over the period 1973–84.

No simple stereotypes can be applied to the manner in which Ireland was incorporated into the international economy in the 1960s and 1970s. As will be illustrated in the two case studies at the end of this chapter, different sectors, and different firms within sectors, were drawn to Ireland for different reasons and operated in different ways. Having said that, Ireland had acquired some characteristics of a dependent, peripheral branch-plant economy as conceived in the model of the 'new international division of labour' (Fröbel et al., 1980).

While the surge in US investment in the 1970s was mainly concentrated in high-tech sectors, the actual work which most of the plants provided was largely unskilled (assembly and packaging) and involved a disproportionately high share of women workers (Breathnach, 1993). Their inputs mainly came from affiliate firms located abroad and their outputs were almost entirely exported (McAleese, 1977). In essence, Ireland was being used as a low-cost base for supplying the European market.

One of the key features of this branch-plant industrialisation was a strong tendency to locate in smaller urban centres which dramatically reversed the pattern of concentration in the main cities during the protectionist period. And, with the indigenous industry created during the latter period experiencing substantial contraction in the 1970s, a profound regional restructuring of manufacturing employment occurred, involving strong relative growth of the more rural regions, and especially those in the west of the country (Breathnach, 1985). During the 1960s and 1970s a major element of government industrial policy was to encourage a greater dispersal of development throughout the country by steering new manufacturing activities away from the main urban centres, and especially Dublin (Drudy, 1991). The industrial dispersal policy was to be implemented by the IDA, notably through the provision of selective grants and ready-built factories. This policy was facilitated by the low-skill requirements of foreign branch-plants and their preference for the lower costs and more docile labour available in the rural areas (Breathnach, 1982, 1985).

THE 1980s: INDUSTRIAL CRISIS AND POLICY REAPPRAISAL

The vulnerability of peripheral branch-plant industrialisation became starkly apparent in the early 1980s. As a consequence of a severe international economic recession, levels of overseas investment by transnational companies contracted. During this period, Ireland witnessed a shake-out in foreign sector employment, while indigenous industry contracted even more rapidly. There was something of a recovery of inward investment towards the end of the 1980s, so that by 1990 employment in foreign firms had regained the level of 1981 but had further risen as a proportion of total manufacturing employment to 43 per cent.

In this decade, there was growing criticism of the reliance on foreign investment as the key driver of industrialisation and economic growth. In the early 1980s the report by the Telesis Consultancy Group (1982) had already identified the drawbacks of the foreign manufacturing plants in Ireland – notably the fact that they did not embody the key competitive activities of the businesses in which they were engaged, their limited number of skilled workers, and their lack of integration with subsupply industries in Ireland. Telesis recommended a major shift towards the cultivation of indigenous industry. This recommendation was reiterated in the report by the government-commissioned Industrial Policy Review Group (1992), popularly known as the Culliton Report. This report further argued that the best way to develop indigenous industry would be via the cultivation of integrated industrial clusters along the lines advocated by Porter (1990). Such clusters would incorporate end-product firms, supporting

and supplying firms and appropriate institutional and infrastructural suppo[
While these clusters would largely be built around Irish-based firms, the primary
role of future inward investment should be to contribute to the functioning of
these clusters rather than acting as stand-alone production operations.

In spatial terms, the 1980s saw a continuation of the relative shift of
manufacturing employment away from the main cities. While overall employment
in the sector fell by 8 per cent over the decade, most of this was concentrated
in County Louth and in Dublin, Cork and Limerick cities, whereas most
other counties either held their own, in relative terms, or actually experienced
significant growth, with the western counties of Donegal, Galway and Clare
leading the way in this respect. Partly in response to this, the 1970s policy of
industrial dispersal and encouragement of a shift of manufacturing employment
away from Dublin became progressively relaxed in the 1980s (White, 2000b).

THE 1990s: THE 'CELTIC TIGER' ECONOMY

In 1992 nobody foresaw the very strong economic growth that would characterise
the rest of the decade and which saw Ireland being dubbed the 'Celtic Tiger'.
Between 1991 and 2000 manufacturing employment grew by 30 per cent. More
importantly in terms of its overall impact on the economy, manufacturing
gross output grew almost threefold in real terms in this period (see Table 9.1).
The electrical and optical equipment sector accounted for almost two-thirds
of the overall growth in manufacturing employment while the chemicals and
paper and printing sectors also displayed above-average growth. Growth in the
latter sector mainly reflected the expansion of software reproduction activity
(dominated by Microsoft).

In terms of growth of gross output (distorted to an extent by transfer-price
manipulation by some of the major firms involved), the chemicals sector actually
outperformed electrical and optical equipment, and saw its share of total output
double to over one-quarter in the period, although, with a one-third share,
electrical and optical equipment was still in first place. Despite a good growth
record of its own, the food, drink and tobacco sector – traditionally Ireland's
foremost industry – fell from a clear first place in output terms in 1991 to a poor
third in 2000. The textile and leather products sector, once a major sector in the
Irish industrial economy, was the only one to experience negative growth in the
1990s and had been reduced to a position of virtual irrelevance by 2000.

These developments therefore meant a significant shift in the sectoral
composition of the manufacturing sector away from more traditional (and
less productive) sectors to more modern 'high-tech' sectors. This shift was
intimately associated with a surge of inward investment which began around
1993 and which has been recognised as the main driving force behind the high
economic growth rates which characterised the Celtic Tiger (OECD, 1999a).
Employment in foreign-owned manufacturing plants grew by over 40 per cent
over the period 1991–2000 (see Table 9.2), thereby raising their share of total
manufacturing employment from 44 to 48 per cent, despite a strong recovery
in indigenous manufacturing employment in the same period (O'Malley, 1998).

Table 9.1 Sectoral composition of manufacturing, 1991 and 2000

Sector	Employment (000s %)					Gross output (€m, 2000 prices)				
	1991	%	2000	%	Change	1991	%	2000	%	Change
Food, beverages, tobacco	44.7	22.7	48.1	18.9	+7.6	12,172	37.4	20,188	17.2	+65.9
Textile and leather products	22.3	11.3	11.0	4.3	-50.7	1,260	3.9	1,078	0.9	-14.4
Paper and printing	16.8	8.5	23.8	9.3	+41.7	2,564	7.9	12,655	10.8	+393.6
Chemicals	14.7	7.5	23.2	9.1	+57.8	4,186	12.8	30,828	26.3	+636.5
Metal and metal products	12.9	6.6	16.3	6.4	+26.4	1,355	4.2	2,588	2.2	+91.0
Machinery and transport equipment	21.3	10.8	24.0	9.4	+12.7	1,773	5.4	3,604	3.1	+103.3
Electrical and optical equipment	32.5	16.5	69.0	27.1	+112.3	5,999	18.4	39,624	33.8	+550.5
Other	31.7	16.1	39.6	15.5	+24.9	3,271	10.0	6,768	5.8	+106.9
All manufacturing industries	196.9	100	255.0	100	+29.5	32,580	100	117,333	100	+260.1

Source: Census of Industrial Production

Table 9.2 Employment, gross output and exports in manufacturing by nationality

Nationality	Employment (000)			Gross output (€m, 2000 prices)			Exports as % Gross output	
	1991	2000	Change %	1991	2000	Change %	1991	2000
Irish	110.0	132.6	+20.5	15,176	20,136	+32.7	34.8	33.2
Foreign	86.9	123.0	+41.5	17,413	72,226	+314.8	86.0	91.7
of which German	10.5	10.3	-1.9	928	1,912	+106.0	91.9	91.3
of which UK	13.0	11.2	-13.8	2,220	3,261	+46.9	42.8	51.6
of which US	39.0	77.1	+97.7	10,136	59,216	+484.2	96.3	94.7
Total	196.9	255.6	+29.8	32,589	92,361	+183.4	62.2	79.0

Source: Census of Industrial Production

More significantly, the output of these plants almost trebled in real terms in the same period, with a corresponding rise in their share of the total from 53 to 78 per cent. The USA was by far the main source of inward investment in the 1990s, during which its share of foreign manufacturing employment rose from 45 to 63 per cent and its share of foreign manufacturing output from 58 to 82 per cent. With the shares of the other main sources of inward investment (the UK and Germany) falling away, the foreign manufacturing sector is now predominantly an American sector.

A combination of factors was responsible for the 1990s surge in foreign manufacturing investment in Ireland, their relative importance varying from sector to sector. The old reliables such as low corporation tax, access to the EU market and an abundant supply of relatively cheap labour (at least during the first half of the decade) continued to prove major attractions. These were the main factors behind the arrival of a large number of relatively low-value-added new assembly-type operations in the electronics and other sectors. However, an additional factor of growing importance has been the availability of a significant reservoir of technically skilled workers due to rising education levels among the growing numbers of young people entering the labour force following a baby boom in the 1970s. Due to the increasing sophistication of manufacturing production processes, demand for such workers has grown among many of the transnational firms in the sectors targeted by the IDA (Breathnach, 1998). A notable example of such a skill-intensive operation is Intel's cluster of wafer fabrication plants in County Kildare.

The 1990s growth in inward investment meant that the thrust towards a shift in policy emphasis to the indigenous sector was effectively sidelined. While employment in indigenous manufacturing did increase by 20 per cent between 1991 and 2000, much of this growth was a spin-off from the foreign sector, in the form of growing demands for certain inputs and the rising consumer demands generated by an increasing, and increasingly well paid, foreign manufacturing workforce. As a result, the export orientation of indigenous industry actually declined from its already low level during the 1990s (see Table 9.2).

In line with the recommendations of the Culliton Report, considerable effort has been undertaken to increase the supply linkages between foreign companies and indigenous industry. In spite of these efforts, between 1991 and 2000 the proportion of materials and services sourced by foreign firms in Ireland fell substantially, from 38 to 27 per cent. There has been little progress in the direction of the kind of Porterian competitive, indigenous, sectoral clusters envisaged in the Culliton Report. Arguably, such clusters would have been difficult to develop in any case since Ireland had few competitive indigenous industries around which such clusters could have been built (O'Malley and van Egeraat, 2000). Nevertheless, research suggests that, even in the absence of fully developed clusters, there generally are appreciable benefits for the competitive advantage of Irish industries arising from the presence in Ireland of some form of groupings of connected or related companies, which may consist of foreign companies (Clancy et al., 2001).

In spatial terms, the relative shift of manufacturing employment away from the main cities that had characterised the previous three decades was reversed. During the 1990s, the main urban areas increased their share of manufacturing employment. While Dublin finally reversed its long established downward trend, spectacular growth in the adjoining County Kildare meant that growth in the overall East region exceeded the national average of 26.2 per cent for 1991–2000.[2] While County Cork also experienced above-average growth, the really powerful performers were counties Limerick and Galway, which both experienced growth of over 60 per cent.

By contrast, four rural counties (Carlow and Laois in the Midlands and Donegal and Leitrim in the West) experienced absolute employment decline and many others had below-average growth, especially those in the Border region and Kerry in the Southwest. Donegal was particularly badly hit by the collapse of the Fruit of the Loom clothing operations, which in the mid-1990s employed 2,500 workers in four locations in the county. An important factor in the improved performance of the main urban areas was the growing demand for skilled workers among foreign firms and the large size of a number of major investments in this period, including IBM in Dublin, Intel and Hewlett-Packard in Kildare, Dell in Limerick and Boston Scientific (a medical devices firm) in Galway. The changing fortunes of Dublin were also facilitated by the progressive relaxation of the industrial dispersal policy that had thwarted the city in the 1970s and part of the 1980s.

EVALUATION OF THE RECENT
INDUSTRIAL DEVELOPMENT EXPERIENCE

The continuous growth in manufacturing employment which Ireland had experienced since 1993 peaked in the first quarter of 2001, following which it went into sharp reverse. Initially it was thought that this was a short-term response to the collapse of the 'dot.com' bubble in early 2001, but as decline continued into 2005, it became clear that more long-term processes were at work. Of the overall fall of 33,500 (13.2 per cent) between March 2001 and June 2005, 70 per cent was accounted for by just two sectors – textiles/textile products and electrical/optical equipment (consisting mainly of the production of electrical and electronic hardware). By contrast, the medical, precision and optical instruments sector continued its strong growth while the chemicals sector held steady in employment terms. This selective decline in manufacturing employment was reflected in output trends: while total manufacturing output in 2005 was one-quarter higher (in real terms) than in 2000, textiles output fell by one-third and office machinery/equipment hardly grew at all. At the same time, pharmaceuticals output more than doubled, with reproduction of recorded media and medical instruments growing by 82 and 70 per cent, respectively.

While the decline in textiles continued a long-term trend, the sharp fall in electronics employment, and particularly in the office machinery and computers subsector (down 36.6 per cent), appeared to be a major new development affecting what had become one of the hallmark industries of the Celtic Tiger economy. However, as Egeraat and Jacobson (2004) have pointed out, there was already a well established pattern of contractions and closures in this sector which was masked by the overall growth of employment in the sector. In essence, what has been happening here is that the more routine forms of electrical/electronic assembly, in which skill levels are low and labour costs an important component of total costs, have been finding it difficult to withstand Ireland's rapidly growing wage levels, especially since Ireland's tax advantages have been eroded by intense competition which has been cutting into profit margins in this sector. Accordingly, there has been a growing trend for this type of production to relocate to cheap-labour locations overseas, with a rising proportion shifting to the new EU member states of Eastern Europe (Barry and Egeraat, 2005).

The loss of low-skill jobs has meant an increasing concentration of employment in high-productivity and high-skill sectors which are likely to prove more stable in the long run. In addition, the IDA's growing emphasis on the attraction of inward investment in such areas as financial services, software and shared services (see Chapter 10) has also generally meant jobs of higher quality than in traditional manufacturing. Overall, the Irish economy still experiences strong employment growth. With unemployment at low levels, the IDA's traditional remit of job creation has been substantially replaced by a new emphasis on retaining and upgrading existing industrial projects and a growing concern with achieving a better regional spread of new investments. As regards the first of these objectives, the IDA is seeking to encourage foreign production plants to add on additional functions, such as research and development (R&D) and financial and administrative services, and to forge deeper links with local research institutes and input suppliers. The idea here is that by enhancing the status of the Irish operations within the global production systems of the firms in question, and increasing their level of linkage with the local economy, these operations will become more 'embedded' in Ireland and therefore less vulnerable to future relocation.

The strategy has been a success in that a substantial number of foreign companies have upgraded their Irish operations by adding additional functions, notably R&D, technical support and financial services. However, these actions can actually mask a reduction in manufacturing employment. In some cases, additional service functions have largely or entirely supplanted the original manufacturing functions. Thus, the Ericsson and former Digital (now Hewlett-Packard) facilities in Athlone and Galway, respectively, have seen routine manufacturing being entirely replaced by software development (Barry and Egeraat, 2005).

Meanwhile, the IDA's efforts towards achieving a better regional spread of inward investment are guided by the National Spatial Strategy (NSS) launched by the Irish government in 2002 (Department of the Environment and Local Government, 2002). The NSS seeks to develop a more balanced urban system in Ireland through the selective promotion of development in and around a set of regional urban centres. Planned improvement of the social, cultural, technological and commercial infrastructures of these centres, it is hoped, will allow them to act as 'gateways' for the attraction of productive investment into the centres themselves or their surrounding hinterlands.

The IDA has taken the lead in implementing this policy through the formulation of a policy which seeks to promote particular industrial specialisms in the gateway centres (Breathnach, 1999). If local higher education institutions focus on the production of graduates in these specialisms, the resulting supply of skilled workers can act as an important magnet for firms in the industries concerned. The resultant localised concentrations of firms in particular sectors in turn can further stimulate local centres of research excellence focused on the technological needs of the respective sectoral clusters and might create greater supply opportunities for locally-based input suppliers. Already there is some evidence of the emergence of such clusters in some centres. Thus, in 2002, County Galway accounted for 5.6 per cent of national manufacturing employment but 22.8 per cent of employment in the medical, precision and optical instruments sector. Such a policy, therefore, if successful, would see foreign firms playing the crucial anchor role in the creation of Porterian-type industrial clusters with a relatively high degree of stability, although the level of vertical material supply linkages will probably remain limited.

CASE STUDIES

The Microcomputer Sector: Rise and Demise

The microcomputer hardware sector is defined as the sector producing personal computers, workstations and entry-level servers, and includes system assembly plants and computer component plants. The basis of the microcomputer hardware industry in Ireland was laid in the early 1970s, when the decision by Digital Equipment Corporation to set up a large minicomputer manufacturing plant in Galway in 1971 was quickly followed by the attraction of five other minicomputer assemblers. The economic crisis of the early 1980s and the increasing popularity of the microcomputer led to the closure of some of these plants but employment losses were offset by the arrival of the first microcomputer assemblers (notably Apple Computers). The early 1990s were characterised by a further spate of closures in the sector, mainly related to the changing competitive position of individual companies. However, there was a simultaneous surge in investment by other microcomputer assemblers which led to strong employment growth in the sector during the rest of the decade (see Figure 9.1).

In 1998, the microcomputer assembly sector reached a peak in employment terms, when, according to the Irish Economy Expenditure (IEE) Survey, five branded computer makers and one contract electronic manufacturer employed over 6,700 permanent staff. A different study, drawing on company interviews, suggests that the assemblers employed just under 10,000 (Egeraat and Jacobson, 2004). Manufacturing activities in most of the companies in question were restricted to the final assembly and test of PCs and low-end servers. During the 1990s most of the firms in question acquired non-manufacturing functions

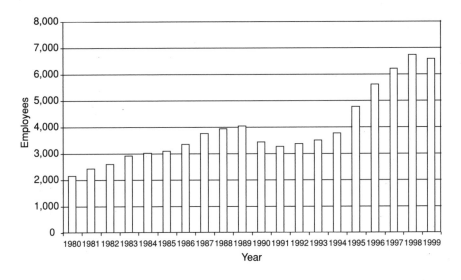

Figure 9.1   Employment in computer assembly plants, 1980–99

Source: Based on IDA/Forfás Irish Economy Expenditure Surveys

such as sales and technical support call centres and European logistics centres, but few or no R&D functions. Due mainly to their large size, these plants were generally located in the larger urban centres (see Figure 9.2).

Between 1998 and 2002, the Irish microcomputer assembly sector experienced serious job losses and plant closures. Of the six microcomputer companies in operation in 1998, by 2002 only Dell and Apple were still assembling micro-computers (and at a much reduced level, in the case of Apple). This reversal in the fortunes of the microcomputer assembly industry clearly demonstrates the vulnerability to changing circumstances of a branch-plant economy such as Ireland's. During the 1980s and most of the 1990s Ireland offered a number of advantages to the microcomputer assembly firms. First, the microcomputer assembly firms were increasingly competing on the basis of offering a wide range of customised products and fast market response. This, in combination with the high value and bulky nature of the systems, favoured the location of assembly plants at or near the main global markets (Egeraat and Jacobson, 2005). Hence one of Ireland's attractions was its close location, and access, to the European market. Within this European market, microcomputer firms were attracted to Ireland by the fiscal and financial incentives, the relatively low labour costs and the flexibility of the labour force. Although computer assembly plants require a certain amount of skilled staff, the majority of the work is largely unskilled so that wage rates represent a relatively important location factor.

By the end of the 1990s, rising wage rates meant that the Irish computer industry was experiencing increasing competition from low-wage production locations. With respect to system assembly operations, competition from the Far East was not the biggest threat since supplying the valuable, customised

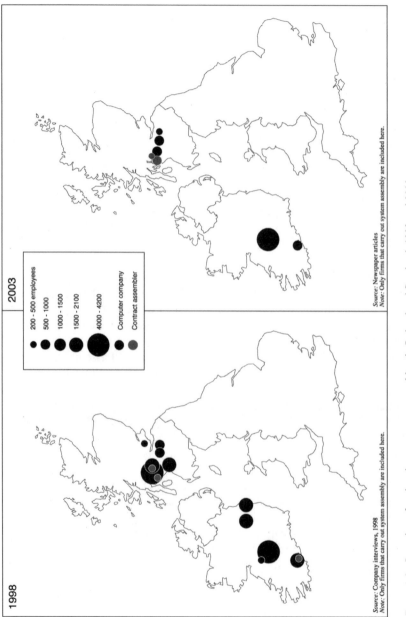

Figure 9.2 Location of main microcomputer assemblers in Ireland and Scotland, 1998 and 2003

Sources: Author interviews (1998) and collated data from newspaper articles; Ordnance Survey Ireland

systems with short lead times from the Far East would have incurred high logistics costs because of the bulky nature of the systems. However, the opening up of Eastern Europe created new production locations offering low wages and a sufficiently skilled labour force, a short distance from the EU market. It is this development, in combination with a competition-induced shake-out of individual companies (in turn partly the result of a general price decline and a global decline in microcomputer revenues in the early 2000s), which has been largely responsible for the closure of computer assembly facilities in Ireland since 1998.

The computer component sector shows a slightly different dynamic. In the early 1990s indigenous companies had begun to capture an increasing share of the local market for low-end material inputs while the IDA succeeded in attracting an increasing number of overseas medium-tech component and subassembly manufacturing plants. However, the situation started to change in the second half of the decade as rising wage rates made Ireland a relatively expensive production location, particularly compared to some of the low-wage economies in the Far East. In this case, unlike microcomputer assembly, the movement of production to these locations was not impeded by logistical considerations. Many components have a small physical volume, which makes airfreight a feasible option. In addition, the low value of many components reduces the interest costs incurred by large (in-transit) inventories. Although Ireland continued to attract a number of high-tech component manufacturing projects, between 1995 and 1998 a large number of low- and medium-tech manufacturers closed their Irish plants and shifted production abroad, mainly to the Far East. As a result, the growth in local sourcing by the computer assemblers stagnated and, by the turn of the twentieth century, they were, on average, sourcing no more than 10 per cent of their material inputs in Ireland (Egeraat and Jacobson, 2004).

The Pharmaceutical Sector: Continued Growth

The pharmaceutical sector includes a range of related activities.[3] The main subsectors in Ireland are the production of *active pharmaceutical ingredients* (API), the most important ingredients of a finished drug (i.e., responsible for its pharmacological effect), and the *formulation* of drug products (i.e., the blending of the API and other ingredients into a finished drug). In contrast to the microcomputer sector, the Irish pharmaceutical sector has been characterised by virtually continuous growth since its inception in the 1950s.

The first substantial investments by foreign pharmaceutical companies in Ireland followed promptly from the shift towards more outward-looking economic policies from the end of the 1950s. However, the sector really took off in the 1970s (see Figure 9.3) when the IDA identified fine chemicals as one of its target sectors, leading to a series of new investments, notably by US-based companies. While employment stagnated during the recessionary early 1980s, unlike other sectors, it did not fall significantly. Since the mid-1980s employment growth in pharmaceuticals has been both strong and continuous – even after 2001, when employment in most other manufacturing sectors contracted. By

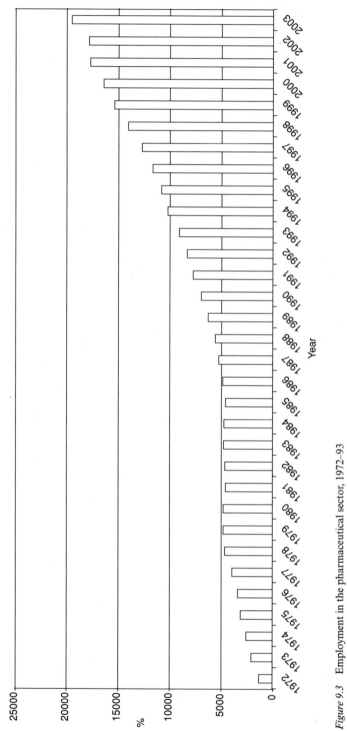

Figure 9.3   Employment in the pharmaceutical sector, 1972–93

Source: Based on IDA/Forfás Irish Economy Expenditure Surveys

2003 the pharmaceutical industry had developed into one of the main industrial sectors in Ireland, employing nearly 19,500 people in 95 operations (74 foreign operations employing 18,074 and 21 indigenous operations employing 1,401).[4] Foreign companies, accounting for 93 per cent of total employment, dominate the industry, the vast bulk of whose production is exported.

The reasons for locating in Ireland were quite different for pharmaceutical firms compared with those in other sectors. The low rate of corporation tax is particularly attractive to the highly profitable pharmaceutical firms, notably for investments in high-value-added activities such as API manufacturing. The benefit of low local corporation tax has been further exploited by extensive practice of transfer-price manipulation. To an extent the firms were also attracted by the low wage rates until the mid-1990s. Yet given their sophisticated production processes and stringent quality standards, pharmaceutical plants have always required a relatively large number of educated and technically skilled workers and firms would not have located in Ireland in the absence of such a pool. Until now, only a small number of countries offered this combination of factors for attracting API plants, notably Ireland, Singapore and Puerto Rico. Relatively free access to the European market has also been an important attraction of an Irish location, in spite of the persistence of non-tariff barriers in the industry (White, 2000a).

Some of these factors also explain the resilience of the sector in the period since 2001. High profitability means that Ireland's low-tax regime remains a key attraction. The requirement of relatively large numbers of skilled workers has made the plants more tolerant of rising wage levels. In addition, the capital-intensive nature of the API plants and the level of 'sunk costs' make the plants less 'footloose'. Yet interviews conducted at pharmaceutical plants in Ireland suggest that rising wage levels and operating costs in general are also beginning to reduce Ireland's competitiveness in this sector (Egeraat, 2006a). Rising wage costs in Ireland are increasing the relative attractiveness of its main competitors, notably Singapore. At the same time a number of new low-cost countries, notably China and India, are entering the market for certain API investment projects, particularly the more traditional chemical synthesis operations. Over the last five years Ireland has attracted relatively few new projects in this segment.

Recent investments indicate a further upgrading of the Irish pharmaceutical sector. The IDA has been successful in attracting a number of more advanced biopharmaceutical projects (notably Wyeth Biopharma in Dublin) that tend to employ even higher proportions of skilled workers. In addition, a number of companies have added non-manufacturing activities to their Irish operations, notably process development laboratories (e.g., Bristol-Meyers Squibb in Dublin).

The industry's two main subsectors portray quite different spatial configurations (see Figures 9.4 and 9.5). The formulation plants are, and have always been, widely dispersed throughout the country. The API sector, on the other hand, is strongly concentrated, notably in County Cork, which accounts for 48 per cent of total employment in the subsector, with Dublin accounting for another 26 per cent. Cork Harbour established itself as the main centre of API production

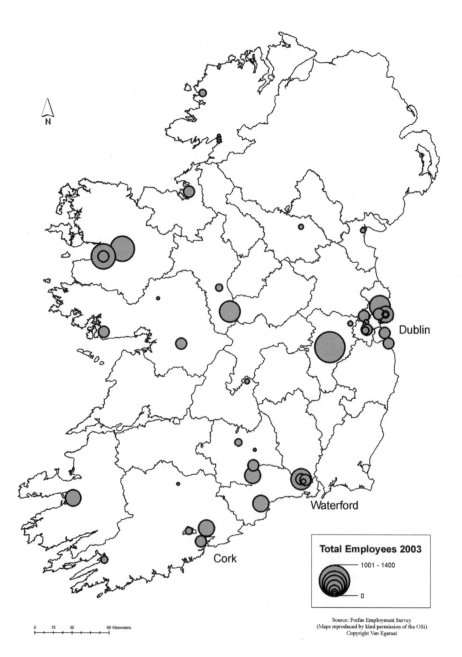

Figure 9.4   Location of drug product operations, 2003

Sources: Forfás Employment Survey (2002); Ordnance Survey Ireland

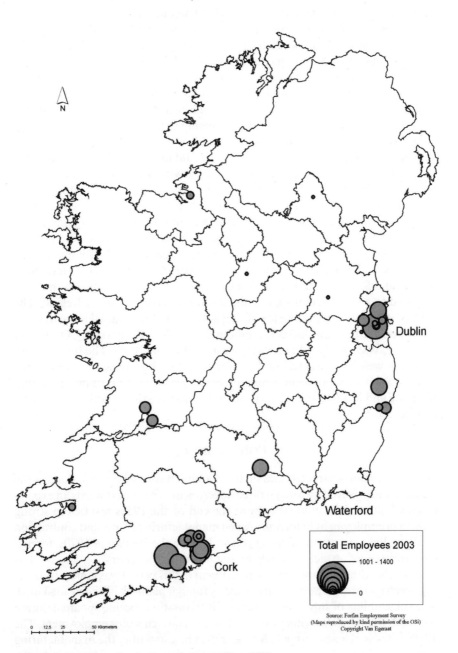

Figure 9.5   Location of active ingredient operations, 2003

Sources: Forfás Employment Survey (2002); Ordnance Survey Ireland

during the 1970s and early 1980s. The main factors responsible for this included the infrastructural requirements of the API plants, notably in relation to effluent disposal, power and fresh water supply; the government's spatial dispersal policy of the 1970s and 1980s; the related spatially selective promotional activities of the IDA; and labour requirements. During the 1970s, the IDA concentrated its limited resources and promotional activities in relation to the pharmaceutical industry in Cork Harbour which, as a result, became an obvious location for API production. The tertiary-level education facilities in Cork City provided the required stream of science and engineering graduates.

Yet some firms at the time chose to establish smaller API plants elsewhere, sometimes in small rural towns adjacent to inland rivers that were used for discharging wastewater. Increasingly strict environmental regulations from the end of the 1980s reduced the attractiveness of these sites and increased the suitability of locations in or near large urban centres where high-capacity infrastructural facilities were readily available and which could provide a pool of suitably skilled labour. This has particularly favoured both Cork Harbour and Dublin (no longer restricted by the dispersal policy of the 1970s and 1980s). Eight of the 15 new API sites established between 1987 and 2004 are located in Dublin and four in Cork Harbour. The current IDA strategy, however, might well lead to a yet different spatial distribution of API activity in Ireland. The IDA is, at present, promoting five strategic sites with the required infrastructure for large-scale biopharmaceutical production – Cork, Ringaskiddy, Oranmore (Galway), Waterford and Dundalk (see also O'Kane, 2005). The future might therefore well be characterised by a further spatial deconcentration of API activity. Such a development would further underline the importance of spatial planning and infrastructure provision in determining the spatial configuration of this sector.

CONCLUSION

One of the main characteristics of the manufacturing sector in Ireland is the dominant role played by foreign direct investment. The shift towards an export-oriented industrialisation strategy at the end of the 1950s resulted in strong growth in employment in foreign-owned manufacturing plants and contraction of the indigenous manufacturing sector. During the 1960s and 1970s, foreign companies were attracted mainly by the low rate of corporation tax and low wage levels. Although much of the investment in this period was concentrated in high-tech sectors, the actual work in many foreign plants was largely unskilled. The vulnerability of this branch-plant industrialisation became apparent during the 1980s when Ireland witnessed a shake-out in foreign sector employment. The 1990s witnessed a new surge in foreign direct investment in the manufacturing sector, again partially driven by low tax and low wages but, increasingly, by the educated and skilled labour force. The subsequent rise in wage levels is now leading to a restructuring of the foreign manufacturing sector, characterised by the loss of employment in low-tech activities and an increasing concentration of employment in high-productivity, high-skill sectors.

Despite the higher quality of the foreign operations that are currently being attracted to Ireland, the future of the manufacturing sector is far from secure. Rising wage levels are likely to further erode the suitability of Ireland as a location for many manufacturing projects. This might be the inevitable consequence of economic upgrading. The question remains whether the pursuit of inward investment, whatever its qualities, is the best long-term approach to economic development in Ireland. Such investment remains contingent on remote decision making by people whose agendas may not always correspond with Ireland's development needs. However, it might be argued that this is part and parcel of an increasingly interdependent global economy and that the real long-term challenge for Ireland is to develop a policy climate conducive to the establishment in Ireland of the highest-value-added functions in 'global production networks' (Dicken et al., 2001), including the regional and global head offices of transnational firms.

10
The Services Sector

Proinnsias Breathnach

The term 'services' refers to a disparate group of occupations which, together, comprise the so-called 'tertiary' sector of economic activity. What distinguishes service activities from those in the primary (extraction of resource from the natural environment) and secondary (transformation of natural resources into usable products) sectors is that they are not directly involved in the production of material goods. The European Union's General Industrial Classification of Economic Activities (generally known as the NACE classification), as adapted by Ireland's Central Statistics Office, subdivides services into nine broad categories: wholesale and retail trade; hotels and restaurants; transport, storage and communications; banking and financial services; real estate, renting and business activities; education; health and social work; and a residual 'other services' category. Other, more conceptual classifications distinguish, on the one hand, between consumer services (provided to the general public) and producer services (provided to businesses) and, on the other, between 'physical' services (e.g., transport, retailing, restaurants) and 'informational' services (e.g., administration, research, education, audiovisual entertainment). Indeed, so important have information-related activities become in modern advanced economies that it has been suggested that they should be allocated to a separate 'quaternary' sector of economic activity (Gottmann, 1961).

These latter divisions of services have important spatial implications. It was once widely held that services were 'parasitic' activities, supported by the circulation of the wealth created in the materially productive economic sectors. It was further thought that the spatial distribution of services was determined by the distribution of the population which in turn was determined by the spatial configuration of material production. While this is true to a certain extent (particularly in relation to consumer services), the rapid growth over the last 50 years in the importance of both producer and informational services (which themselves overlap to a considerable extent) drew increasing attention to the fact that many of the key elements of these service categories possess an independent spatial dynamic of their own (Marshall and Wood, 1995; Illeris, 1996). The implications of this in the Irish context will be discussed further below.

In the advanced economies, services today account for the great bulk of employment, following a process of 'tertiarisation' which began in earnest in most of the countries involved from the mid-twentieth century. Key factors in this tertiarisation process have been the growth of administrative bureaucracies in both the public and private sectors, in response to the growing organisational complexity of advanced economies and the increasing role of government in modern societies; the increasing demand by firms for specialised business services in response to both organisational and technological complexity; and the fact that, past a certain threshold level, additional income is increasingly spent on services rather than material goods. In addition, growing mechanisation and automation have greatly reduced the need for primary and secondary sector workers relative to the output of these sectors. Contraction of employment in these sectors, therefore, has contributed to the tertiary sector's growing share of total employment. However, the wealth generated in material production continues to be a major driver of advanced economies, a fact which tends to be overlooked by the popularisation of such ideas as that of the 'post-industrial' (Touraine, 1971; Bell, 1973) or 'informational' (Castells, 1996) society.

The remainder of this chapter is divided into three main sections. Initially, the development of services employment in Ireland is described and analysed. This is followed by an account of the sectoral and spatial development of key elements of the services sectors, divided, respectively, between producer (especially software, financial services and back-office services) and consumer (public services, shopping, entertainment) services. The chapter concludes with some observations on the future prospects of the services sector, particularly in terms of its potential for contributing to long-term economic development in Ireland.

DEVELOPMENT OF SERVICES EMPLOYMENT IN IRELAND[1]

The 1926 census of population showed that one-third of those at work in Ireland were engaged in services, compared with over one-half in agriculture. By mid-2005, the number of service workers had tripled in absolute terms and doubled in proportionate terms to two-thirds of the workforce. However, even this is still quite low by comparison with many other advanced countries such as the USA, the UK and the Scandinavian countries, where the tertiary sector's share of total employment is now well over three-quarters. This is despite the very rapid decline in the relative share of the agricultural sector (to just 6 per cent in 2005), and is mainly attributable to the unusually large current size of the construction sector and the fact that, uniquely among advanced economies, manufacturing employment actually grew strongly in Ireland in the 1990s (see Chapter 9).

Not only did the size of the services sector in Ireland grow enormously in the twentieth century, but its composition also changed dramatically. In 1926, by far the biggest services subsector was private domestic service, which accounted for over one-fifth of all service workers, was overwhelmingly female in make-up, and was generally very poorly paid. By 2002 (according to the census of population for that year), the number of workers in this category was just 2,500, compared with 85,500 in 1926. The rapid decline of this sector (and of the state's security forces) is the main reason for the very modest overall growth which occurred in services employment up to 1961. These declines were more than counter-balanced by significant growth in most other services categories, and particularly the professions (mainly teachers, but also including health and legal workers and religious). In the 1960s, accelerated economic growth and the opening up of the Irish economy were accompanied by significant new trends in services employment. Drawing on path-breaking contemporary work elsewhere in the advanced economies (Thorngren, 1970; Törnqvist, 1970; Goddard, 1975), Bannon (Bannon, 1973; Bannon et al., 1977) was to the fore in focusing attention on the major growth in office-based 'white collar' employment which was occurring in Ireland in the 1960s and 1970s. Office work, involving the 'handling' (generation, processing, storage and transmission) of information, accounted for just 6 per cent of total employment in 1946; by 1971 this had risen to 15 per cent.

While much of the growth of office employment is accounted for by the expansion of administrative bureaucracies in both the public and private sectors, an increasingly important driver of growth in this sector has been financial and business services. The contribution of this service category to the extraordinary rise in employment in Ireland since the early 1990s has been particularly spectacular. While there had been strong growth in services employment over the period 1961–91 (up 59 per cent to 663,000, representing 58 per cent of total employment), this was largely counter-balanced by declining agricultural employment, so that total employment only grew by 9 per cent. However, over the period 1991–2002, services employment grew by a further 56 per cent (or, in absolute terms, by 50 per cent more than in the previous three decades). Services accounted for almost four-fifths of the overall growth of 43 per cent in employment which occurred in this eleven-year period (construction and manufacturing accounting for the remainder). Table 10.1 allows us to identify some of the more salient features of this recent surge in services employment in Ireland.

This shows that by far the most rapid growth in services employment occurred in the 'Other business services' category: indeed, over a quarter of the overall growth in employment was accounted for by this sector. By far the single biggest contributor to this sector's spectacular expansion was the 'Computer and related activities' subcategory, which includes both software and computer services. In 1991 this category was actually included in the manufacturing sector under the heading 'Repair and maintenance of data processsing equipment'. Between it and its associate subsector 'Manufacture of data processing and office equipment', total employment in 1991 came to only 9,000. On its own, the computer services category employed 34,000 people in 2002. Other above-average growth sectors included 'Recreation, culture and sport' (albeit from a small initial base), 'Finance, insurance and real estate' and 'Health and social work', whereas 'Public administration and defence', 'Transport, storage and communications', 'Wholesaling and retailing' and 'Education' were relatively slow growth sectors. From a national economic point of view, an important finding from this table is that about two-thirds of the growth in services employment occurred in sectors (public administration, education and health, financial and business services) in which education and remuneration tend to be

Table 10.1 Change in services employment, 1991–2002

Sector	1991			2002					
	Male	Female	Total	Male	Δ%	Female	Δ%	Total	Δ%
Wholesaling & retailing	94,386	62,186	156,572	119,495	+26.6	99,670	+60.3	219,165	+40.0
Hotels, restaurants & bars	24,894	27,017	51,911	36,413	+46.6	45,005	+66.5	81,418	+56.8
Transport, storage & communications	55,422	13,975	69,397	71,316	+28.7	25,539	+82.7	96,855	+39.6
Public administration & defence	52,158	23,383	75,541	51,716	−0.8	43,030	+84.0	94,746	+25.4
Finance, insurance & real estate	23,074	24,223	47,297	33,773	+46.4	44,747	+84.7	78,520	+66.0
Other business services	22,710	19,632	42,342	81,076	+257.0	62,349	+217.6	143,425	+238.7
Education	29,094	46,020	75,114	35,478	+21.9	73,823	+60.4	109,301	+45.5
Health & social work	21,679	65,128	86,807	29,168	+43.5	114,352	+75.6	143,520	+65.3
Recreation, culture & sport	8,802	5,565	14,367	16,580	+88.4	13,065	+134.8	29,645	+106.3
Other services	18,840	24,481	43,321	11,921	−36.7	22,767	−7.0	34,688	−20.0
Total	351,059	311,610	662,669	486,936	+38.7	544,347	+74.7	1,031,283	+55.6

Note: Due to a revision of the NACE classification scheme, some minor subcategories could not be unambiguously assigned to one or other of the above categories. This will not have significantly affected the overall reliability of the categories used.

Sources: Census of Population, 1991, 2002

high, as against one-third for those sectors (wholesaling and retailing, transport and communications, and recreation) where the opposite tends to apply.

Another key feature to be drawn from Table 10.1 is the crucial role played by women workers in the recent surge of services employment growth, accounting for two-thirds of the total, despite accounting for less than half of total employment at the beginning of the period. Women now make up over one-half of all service workers. An important aspect of this growth is that the two traditional bastions of female employment – education and health – were not among the leading areas of recent growth. Apart from the small recreational services sector, the most rapid growth occurred in business and financial services and public administration (where high skills and pay prevail) as well as transport and communications. By contrast, below-average growth was experienced in wholesaling and retailing and hotels, restaurants and bars. From this, it is clear that the common image of female employment in the post-industrial informational economy being mainly confined to low-level employment categories (unskilled, part-time, casual) certainly does not apply, at least in the Irish case (Breathnach, 2002b).

Despite the fall in the overall rate of economic growth in Ireland (albeit to still quite high levels) in the early part of the twenty-first century, the strong growth in services employment has not only continued, but actually accelerated, growing by 55,000 per year (according to the National Household Survey, which is not strictly comparable to the census of population in methodology and findings) between mid-2002 and mid-2005 compared with an annual growth of 33,500 in the intercensal period 1991–2002. On this occasion, the strongest growth has occurred in the health services, followed by 'other' services and financial and business services.

RECENT DEVELOPMENTS IN PRODUCER SERVICES

The rapid expansion of the financial and business services sectors (which embrace most producer services) in the 1990s and early 2000s can be attributed to two parallel processes. On the one hand, general growth in the economy and in the public sector has generated a burgeoning demand for these services in such areas as banking, real estate, advertising and technical consultancy. On the other hand, an increasing proportion of inward investment projects secured by the Industrial Development Agency (IDA) has been in 'international' (i.e., export) services. Over the period 2000–04, just under 50 per cent of new jobs created in IDA projects were in services which, by 2004, accounted for 35 per cent of all IDA-sponsored employment.

Spatial Concentration

A key feature of recent growth in producer services employment has been its disproportionate concentration in the Dublin region. Thus, in 2002, the East region (Dublin and the adjoining counties of Meath, Kildare and Wicklow) accounted for 39 per cent of the national population and 42 per cent of the workforce, but no less than 60 per cent of all employment in financial and business services.

This tendency for business services to congregate in the main metropolitan regions can be attributed to a number of factors, the most important of which are the fact that the main customers for such services (government ministries and corporate head offices) also tend to be heavily concentrated in such areas (Daniels, 1979): the strong network linkages which exist between producer service suppliers (Bannon, 1973; Goddard, 1973), and the availability of an advanced support infrastructure for office activities (including, in particular, telecommunications infrastructure) in the world's leading cities (Sassen, 1991). Thus, in the Irish case, Bannon and Blair (1985) found that, on the basis of a range of indicators including the location of head offices and senior executives, quality of amenities and facilities and communications infrastructure, Dublin was more than five times more attractive as a location for service functions than Cork (Ireland's second city) and even more so in relation to the other main provincial centres.

Software

Foreign investors in international services have been, if anything, even more inclined to locate in the Dublin area. Investment in this area has been concentrated in three main sectors: software, financial services and back-office services. Software has been perhaps the most spectacular success story of the recent Irish development experience. American firms in this sector initially began to use Ireland in the 1980s as a cheap base for duplication of manuals and disks and subsequently for the adaptation (localisation) of American software for European markets. One consequence of this high-volume business is that, in the early 2000s, Ireland became the world's foremost exporter of software products (accounting for 10 per cent of Ireland's total exports), with Microsoft's large-scale operation in south County Dublin playing the leading role in this respect. In the 1990s the industry moved up the value chain, with existing firms evolving into, and new incoming firms engaging directly in, the more creative software development and technical support elements of the industry. Sectoral employment rose from 8,000 in 1991 to 31,500 in 2001 but then fell to 24,000 in 2004, mainly as a result of the 'dot.com' collapse in 2001.

Uniquely among the foreign business sectors operating in Ireland, the foreign software industry has helped generate a substantial indigenous counterpart (O'Gorman et al., 1997; HotOrigin, 2001). This is partly explained by the fact that, unlike most high-tech manufacturing sectors, major capital investment is not required by firms setting up in the software sector. The growth of indigenous software has been partly built on outsourcing of particular aspects of the business to indigenous suppliers, and partly on Irish employees of foreign firms setting up their own companies to exploit market niches initially identified while working in the foreign sector. An important feature of the indigenous software sector is that, rather than being heavily dependent on the foreign sector as a market outlet, it has become strongly export-oriented in its own right, with Irish firms becoming world leaders in niche sectors such as credit card security and educational software. Indigenous firms made up almost one-half of total sectoral employment in 2004 and generated over two-thirds of their revenues from exports.

In 2005, the Irish software industry employed some 32,000 people and displayed many of the characteristics of an industrial cluster of the type identified by Porter (1990) as crucial in establishing sustainable competitive advantage in the global economy. This involves a high level of interfirm linkage in terms of subsupply business, information sharing and movement of personnel. Another key characteristic of industrial clusters – their tendency to be spatially concentrated – is also apparent in the Irish software industry, in which the great majority of firms and workers are located in the Dublin region. The locational dynamics of the industry (in particular the key role of interpersonal contacts) and the declining role of routine activities indicate that this tendency to geographical concentration is unlikely to change substantially in the foreseeable future.

International Financial Services

The international financial services sector has been equally concentrated in Dublin – in this case a direct consequence of the establishment in the national capital of the International Financial Services Centre (IFSC) in 1987 (Murphy, 1998). Initially designed to both create employment and rejuvenate part of Dublin's derelict docklands, the IFSC sought to attract investment by offering the same low corporation tax rate (10 per cent) as was available to manufacturing industry. As firms seeking to avail of this concession were required to locate in the Dublin area (but not necessarily in the IFSC itself), the development of this sector of activity was entirely confined to the national metropolis. This restriction became increasingly significant as the IFSC grew in size over time, to a situation whereby in 2004 there were 443 international financial services firms operating in Dublin (Finance Dublin Yearbook, 2005) along with 700 other IFSC-licensed firms acting through third-party intermediaries. It is difficult to determine the amount of employment generated by these firms, as many also conduct other activities not related to the IFSC, while a considerable amount of spin-off employment has been created in other firms supplying services (e.g., auditing) and other inputs to the IFSC firms. However, direct employment in IFSC-licensed firms was put at 10,700 in 2005.[2] The main areas of activity engaged in by these firms tend to be in routine sectors such as fund adminis-tration, asset financing and corporate treasury management, although there is also considerable active involvement in insurance and banking. However, the original aim of establishing an active trading floor in financial instruments has not been realised.

Back-office Services

The third main sector of inward investment in services is that of back-office services. This sector originated with the attraction to Ireland in the early 1990s of a large number of international telephone call centres, created as part of a trend towards pan-European rationalisation of operations by transnational firms in the wake of the implementation of the Single European Market in

1993 (Breathnach, 2000). Eventually, some 50 (mainly American) such centres, employing 12,000 people, were set up in Ireland. These – again – were almost all located in the Dublin area, mainly due to their requirements for workers with a range of European languages. Many of these operations have since diversified into other – and generally more high-skilled, albeit still quite routine – activities such as financial and supply chain management, and sales and marketing. Simultaneously, many existing foreign firms, especially in manufacturing, have added on such 'shared services' facilities to their previous production operations. In many cases, foreign firms have set up fully fledged European operational headquarters in Ireland, leading Internet firms Yahoo, eBay and Google being important recent examples.

A Spatial Policy for Producer Services

The growth of Dublin-focused inward investment in services has been the main reason why the East region's share of employment in IDA-sponsored firms rose from one-third in 1993 to almost one-half in 2004. However, IDA attempts to promote a greater spatial spread of foreign services projects have been meeting with increasing success in recent years. They have been assisted in this process by the removal of the restriction to a Dublin location of international financial services firms, growing labour shortages (especially for skilled workers) in the Dublin region; rising living (including housing) and operating costs which are encouraging both firms and workers to seek alternative locations in which to operate and live, and growing familiarity among foreign firms with the operating environment outside Dublin. The upgrading of the telecommunications infrastructure in the regions, increasing supplies of good-quality business graduates from regional Institutes of Technology, and the creation of a network of IDA-owned business parks have also played important roles in this respect (Slattery, 2005).

Inward investors are, almost by definition, inherently mobile and open to considering a range of alternative locations. Domestic firms, by contrast, tend to be much more resistant to new locational possibilities. Furthermore, unlike the manufacturing sector (see Chapter 9), the Irish government has never formulated a specific policy designed to encourage the movement of services firms, as such, to less advantaged regions (Bannon and Lombard, 1996). Nor have past endeavours by governments in other countries been encouraging in this respect (Daniels, 1982). However, in recent years, there has been a growing trend for large firms in advanced economies to relocate routine back-office activities such as call centres and data processing to remote locations, mainly in order to avail of sharp inter-regional differences in operating costs (Wilson, 1995; Richardson and Marshall, 1996). It may be that rising costs in Dublin vis-à-vis the rest of the country may induce a similar response in Ireland, although for the moment Irish firms remain firmly committed to the long-established pattern of keeping all of their central administrative staff in a single location (and typically in a single building) even though the bulk of the work involved is routine and relatively easily relocated, especially in the context of modern information technology.

Meanwhile, the Irish government has been pursuing a fairly active policy of relocating its own civil service staff to provincial centres. Over the last 30 years some 4,000 civil servants have been relocated, and in December 2003 the government announced its most ambitious relocation programme yet, with over 10,000 staff to be moved to 53 different locations, including entire government departments. It remains to be seen whether these targets will be met, as there has been considerable opposition to the programme, especially among more senior civil servants. The programme has also been criticised for its apparent lack of cohesion with the government's National Spatial Strategy, launched in 2002, whose main focus is the development of a small number of major provincial urban centres as regional 'gateway' cities (see Chapters 2, 3 and 4). The successful implementation of this strategy could also lead to a significant level of decentralisation of private services, seeking out the new market opportunities and enhanced infrastructures which strong regional centres would offer. However, a major weakness in the spatial strategy is the absence of any reference to the devolution of administrative functions to the regional level, as a tier of regional government could play a key role in promoting the coordinated development of the gateway cities while also generating additional demands for private producer service providers (Breathnach, 2002a). The absence of any provision for such a tier of government, coupled with the nature of the government's 2003 relocation programme, does appear to indicate a lack of real commitment to the realisation of the spatial strategy.

RECENT DEVELOPMENTS IN CONSUMER SERVICES

Public Services

In the absence of a coherent national spatial strategy, the Irish government is also likely to face growing challenges in terms of the territorial arrangements for the delivery of public services such as health, education and community care. The key challenge in this respect is to achieve an acceptable balance between the popular demand for maximum access to such services and the need for efficient utilisation of scarce public funds in delivering these services. At the time of writing, for example, the whole question of the spatial arrangements for the provision of different levels of hospital service is a matter of considerable public controversy. Because of the highly centralised nature of Ireland's system of administration, a wide range of services are provided by central government which are the responsibility of subnational government in most other European countries (Breathnach, 2000b). This leads to particular problems of bureaucratic inflexibility and a lack of coordination at territorial level between various state services, including a patchwork of territorial systems within which these services are administered.

Meanwhile, even with regard to the limited range of services which *are* provided through the local government system, territorial problems arise, particularly relating to frequent cases where urban centres have expanded beyond their narrowly defined official boundaries without appropriate adjustments to these boundaries. The resulting inefficiencies have been well highlighted by the cases of Limerick and Waterford cities, where, for example, the establishment of major industries and shopping centres in suburban locations generates income streams from local taxation for adjacent county councils, while much of the infrastructural costs associated with the developments have to be borne by the cities themselves; or where the city councils have to build and maintain social housing developments in adjoining jurisdictions due to a lack of developable land within their own boundaries.

Shopping and Entertainment

While for most people shopping remains primarily a functional task, essential for human reproduction, increasingly in advanced economies it is also seen as an important form of recreation – indeed, in the USA it is now regarded as the second most popular leisure activity after watching television (Castells, 1996). Rising living standards and increased leisure time due to a shorter working week have meant that the economic importance of recreational activity has grown enormously in recent decades in advanced economies. This applies a fortiori to Ireland, where average living standards (measured in terms of per capita Gross National Disposable Income at constant prices) more than doubled over the period 1990–2004.

In terms of spatial consequences, much of the additional consumer spending has been devoted to home-based entertainment such as high-end TV, DVD and hi-fi systems, computers, playstations and broadband. Over the period 1998–2004 the number of households with a home computer almost tripled from 229,000 (19 per cent of all households) to 649,000 (46 per cent); furthermore, where only one-quarter of houses with computers in 1998 were connected to the Internet, by 2004 this proportion had risen to over 80 per cent. Much of Irish people's rising spending power has also gone into travel abroad (see Chapter 12). But perhaps the main spatial consequence of increased consumer spending has been the way it is increasingly channelled into major shopping centres which attract customers from extensive regional hinterlands (Parker, 1997). In Ireland (as elsewhere), increasing levels of car ownership, higher purchasing power and less spare time for casual shopping have meant that shopping increasingly takes the form of planned 'expeditions' to such centres. As a result, in the countryside, smaller urban centres, and in the cities, smaller neighbourhood shopping districts have been increasingly excluded from the consumption landscape as consumers travel growing distances to larger centres.

In Ireland, the first planned, purpose-built shopping centre (consisting of anchor grocery/department store and associated specialist outlets) was opened in Stillorgan in south County Dublin in 1966. Since then, there has been a proliferation of such centres in the suburban peripheries of all the main cities and towns (Parker, 1999, 2002). The inauguration of The Square shopping centre in Tallaght in south County Dublin in 1990 raised the concept of the shopping centre to a new level, and was quickly followed by similar centres in Blanchardstown and Liffey Valley near Lucan. All three of these were originally conceived as 'town centres' for their immediate suburban hinterlands, but their locations adjacent to the M50 orbital motorway and major roads leading out of Dublin have allowed them to draw custom from much further away. Key additional features of these centres have included the establishment of clusters of large-scale 'warehouse' outlets nearby and the incorporation of non-retail activities such as multiplex cinemas, restaurants, and health and fitness centres. The addition of musical performances, art exhibitions and other forms of 'spectacular' entertainment (Harvey, 1989) contributes further to the total recreational experience which such centres offer.

Urban central business districts, which in the past enjoyed a virtual monopoly on high-end shopping and cultural markets, have sought to counter the drain of customers to suburban competitors through such devices as multistorey carparks, pedestrianisation, street entertainment, spectacular enclosed shopping malls such as the St Stephen's Green and Jervis centres in Dublin, and the redevelopment of derelict precincts as new entertainment districts, such as Temple Bar in Dublin and the area just north of Patrick Street in Cork. Meanwhile, the growing demand for 'convenience' shopping outlets has been increasingly met by the incorporation of retail and catering functions into petrol filling stations (by definition highly accessible) and the proliferation of late-opening smaller 'symbol' supermarkets such as Londis, Centra and Supervalu (see Chapter 21).

CONCLUSION

With most commentators expecting Ireland's still vigorous economic growth to continue at least for the medium term, further absolute and relative expansion of the services sector seems assured. A key question in terms of Ireland's long-term development prospects centres around the extent to which services activities will themselves act as drivers of overall economic growth rather than constituting a spin-off from growth generated elsewhere. Conventional economic development theory emphasises the importance for small economies of creating an export base, the circulation of whose revenues creates an internal multiplier effect within these economies (Brookfield, 1975). Traditionally, manufacturing or the primary sector provided the foundation for successful basic sectors; however, in the case of Ireland, services are now increasingly filling this role. Although it can be notoriously difficult to monitor and quantify service exports (especially those delivered electronically), Central Statistics Office figures indicate that, in the period 1998–2004, when Ireland's merchandise exports grew by 16.5 per cent, services exports actually trebled in size. As a result, the share of total exports accounted for by services doubled, from 17 to 34 per cent, over this period. Predictably, from what has been written above, the great bulk of services exports are accounted for by software (35 per cent), financial services, including leasing and insurance (33 per cent) and other business services (26 per cent).

Clearly, therefore, Ireland has, in recent years (and mainly through the efforts of the IDA) created a strong and rapidly growing export base in international services. And with some segments of the modern manufacturing sectors recently beginning to display signs of vulnerability (see Chapter 9), the IDA is looking increasingly to the services sector as the main source of further export base growth. This, to a considerable extent, will involve continued expansion of existing areas of strength, i.e., software and financial services, and the emerging areas of shared services and administrative functions. At the same time, new areas of potential opportunity are also being opened up. These include scientific and industrial research, with existing manufacturing firms being a key target in this respect. The IDA is also seeking to build on Ireland's existing strengths in the areas of software, entertainment and culture in exploiting a range of e-business (i.e., services delivered electronically) niches, including design, operation and maintenance of websites; production of online games and other entertainment forms, and e-learning (Forfás, 2002, undated).

The success of this strategy is intimately interconnected with developments in spatial strategy. With the over-heated Dublin region portraying various forms of stress such as labour shortages, traffic congestion and high housing costs, increasingly the potential for attracting new inward investment in services will depend on the ability to offer potential investors acceptable alternative locations. Given the specific nature of the service activities concerned, with their high demand for highly educated workers (who in turn have their own demands in terms of social and cultural facilities) and office and communications services and infrastructures, it will be necessary to concentrate on the selective development of a small number of key centres where these locational requirements can be supplied to a high standard. The rudiments of such an approach have already been delineated in the National Spatial Strategy (NSS). However, for reasons already adverted to above and in Chapter 8, there are indications that the NSS are still unrealised due to a lack of political will on the part of government combined with inadequacies in implementation mechanisms. How these twin challenges are dealt with will have profound implications for national and regional economic development in Ireland in the forthcoming decades.

11
Agriculture in Transition

James A. Walsh

Despite significant reductions in its share of total employment and GDP, the agriculture and food sector remains a significant component of the Irish economy. In the 1926 census over half the working population were employed in agriculture. Direct employment in agriculture in 2005 amounted to approximately 6 percent of the total workforce. The combined agriculture and food industry accounts for 9 per cent of total employment, 8 per cent of gross exports and over 10 per cent of GDP. The food industry, based on the processing of agricultural output produced in Ireland is the largest Irish-owned manufacturing sector, accounting for 55 per cent of the total exports of Irish-owned manufacturing in 2002, which is considerably more than in most other EU countries. The significance of agriculture is particularly strong in some regions such as the Southeast, West and Border where it directly accounts for approximately 10 per cent of all employment.

Agriculture is different from all other economic sectors in the level of priority it receives in government and EU policies and the scale of financial resources allocated to supporting the sector. For example, the entire income accruing to farmers in Ireland from their agricultural activities arises from public policy transfers by the both EU and Irish tax payers and consumers (Matthews, 2005). Following decades when the dominant focus of agriculture policies was to promote further increases in output there has been since the early 1990s a broadening of the objectives and a fundamental shift in the method of supporting farmers. This chapter commences with a general outline of the principal external and internal influences on production agriculture in Ireland. This will be followed by an assessment of recent trends in the geography of agricultural production in Ireland. Then there will be a more detailed consideration of adjustments in conventional farming and of the increasing level of dependence on off-farm sources of income by the majority of farm households. The final section considers the prospects for the future. The focus is mostly on the period since the early 1990s as the adjustment experiences of previous decades have already been examined by Horner et al. (1984), Walsh (1985), Gillmor (1987), Gillmor and Walsh (1993), Walsh and Gillmor (1993) and Lafferty et al. (1999). The themes covered illustrate very clearly the interdependencies between the local, national and international domains of decision making and how these contribute to reshaping local geographies.

AGRICULTURE IN TRANSITION:
INFLUENCES ON ADJUSTMENT TRENDS

Since the mid-1980s there has been an on-going process of adjustment in agricultural production in the Western world, which includes a transition from the paradigm that encourages ever increasing levels of output from production systems that are guided primarily by policies and supports aimed at improving productivity levels of each unit of land and labour. The end-point of the transition remains somewhat unclear though there is a broad agreement that a new paradigm is required that will give greater emphasis to the environmental and social dimensions of agriculture and more generally support the multifunctional roles of the sector, and which will distinguish the European model from that applied elsewhere, most notably in north America. The timing, extent and speed of the transition that is under way varies between different classes of farmers and across regions (Bowler, 1992; Evans et al., 2002). The principal influences on the transition in the production of agriculture include a combination of, on the one hand, external drivers linked to technological progress and changes in the European and global policy environments and, on the other hand, local structural characteristics and the relative strength of the agriculture sector in the context of the total economy.

Technological Change

Technological change is a major influence on the changes in agricultural production. It includes the development of new varieties of crops and new approaches to livestock breeding and management; greater reliance upon inorganic fertilisers along with pesticides and herbicides, and also the introduction of machinery to replace labour. The overall objective of the indus-trialisation of agriculture is to increase output levels per unit of agricultural land and labour. Three aspects of this process are of interest.

Firstly, the industrialisation model relies on continuous innovation resulting in new approaches and new products that have to be diffused among the farming population. The extensive literature on innovation diffusion confirms that the process is very complex and that it is usually characterised by significant temporal and spatial lags, which affect the capacity of individual farmers in different parts of the country to adapt and improve their competitiveness. Walsh (1992) has illustrated the range of factors that influenced the pace of adoption and diffusion of mechanisation throughout Ireland in the twentieth century. In the process a strong distinction was evident between farms with a high propensity to adapt (typically larger farms on good-quality land managed by younger farmers in the east and south of Ireland) and those that are described as laggards (typically small farms on poorer-quality land managed by more conservative elderly farmers in the west and northwest).

Secondly, the industrialisation of agriculture leads to a pattern of outcomes that is unique to the sector. The costs of inputs tend to increase much more rapidly than the prices obtained by the farmers for their output. The resultant cost-price squeeze arises because the market demand for the additional levels of output achieved through more capital-intensive production systems tends to increase very slowly as it is influenced by trends in the size of the population, in the markets served by the farmers, and also by the tendency of consumers to spend a declining proportion of their incomes on food. The price-cost squeeze encourages those farmers with the capacity to further intensify their production systems to do so, which imposes even further pressure on those without the capability to adjust quickly. As the processes influencing the diffusion of innovations are likely to lead to uneven patterns of adoption, the cost-price squeeze is likely to lead to adaptive farmers becoming trapped on a technological treadmill while the majority may become further disadvantaged.

Thirdly, the industrialisation model has tended to produce a number of undesirable outcomes including unsustainable levels of surplus production of certain commodities; deepening inequalities between farmers and also between strong and weak farming areas; and a range of negative environmental impacts such as groundwater contamination, pollution of lakes and rivers, build-up of methane gases, destruction of wildlife habitats, reduction in biodiversity and losses of landscape features including archaeological remains.

Agriculture Policy

Governments in every country have for many decades attached a high priority to policies aimed at supporting agriculture. They do so for a variety of reasons including a desire to guarantee food supplies at reasonable prices for their citizens, to increase the economic efficiency of the sector, and to ensure reasonable economic returns for producers. Over recent decades governments have added to their lists of reasons for intervening the need to ensure that agriculture is practised in a way that is more environmentally sustainable and also to assure customers in relation to the quality of the food they purchase. Since the early 1970s agriculture policy in Ireland has been incorporated into or alternatively derived from the Common Agricultural Policy (CAP) of the European Union.

Throughout most of its history the CAP has supported the industrialisation model, known sometimes as the productivist approach. Supported by a dedicated fund that took up the bulk of the EU budget resources, and using a variety of instruments that included high levels of guaranteed prices for several commodities and systems of intervention buying to take care of surplus production, the CAP benefited those farmers with the capacity to modernise while at the same time leaving an enlarging cohort who became increasingly marginalised (Walsh, 1993). A combination of factors in the mid-1980s contributed to a long-drawn-out process of reforming the CAP. These included politically embarrassing levels of surplus production of several commodities (e.g., milk, beef, wine); budget pressures as the CAP budget threatened the capacity of the EU to develop and support other policies; evidence of deepening inequalities between rich and poor farmers; conflicts between the EU objectives in relation to agriculture and regional development; growing consumer concern about food quality, and increasing amounts of evidence in relation to negative environmental impacts. Towards the end of the 1980s there was the added complication that the CAP support systems were putting at risk the possibility of securing a new international trade agreement as major differences emerged between the US and the EU in relation to agriculture policy.

The first significant effort to reform the CAP was introduced by Agriculture Commissioner Ray MacSharry in 1993. The levels of guaranteed price supports for beef and cereals were significantly reduced and quotas were introduced in relation to milk production. These were particularly serious for farming in Ireland as the extent of reliance on grassland-based beef and milk production was greater than in any other EU member state, and furthermore the overall intensity of production was less than in the European regions where the industrial productivist model had been adopted earlier. The measures to curtail production were accompanied by the introduction of new agri-environment, forestry and early retirement programmes.

Further reforms were agreed in 1999 as part of the Agenda 2000 agreement in advance of the eastern enlargement of the EU. The role of direct payments to farmers (aimed at reducing the share of the CAP budget not transmitted directly to farmers) was further increased. Thus between 1992 and 2002 the contribution of EU direct payments to total farm income in Ireland increased from 22 per cent to almost 70 per cent, with their contribution exceeding 100 per cent of farm income in sectors such as beef, sheep and cereals, implying that farmers were not covering their costs, even when selling at protected EU prices (Matthews, 2005).

The most far reaching reforms of the CAP were agreed in Luxembourg in June 2003 and brought into operation in 2005. The major change was the decoupling of direct payments from production and the introduction of a single payment to each farmer. As a result, in future farmers will make their production decisions on the basis of the relative market returns from each enterprise rather than on the basis of the size of the subsidy available. Of particular interest to Ireland, especially to farmers in the southwest and northeast, is a further reduction in the support price for agriculture. The latest reforms also include a cross-compliance condition requiring farmers to keep all farmland in good agricultural and environmental condition. The latest reforms, which may be extended further after 2013 as part of a broader agreement on international trade, represent the first serious attempt to separate the public-good dimensions (environmental and social welfare aspects) of agriculture policy from its role in relation to markets, which should lead to less market distortions in the future.

Structural Characteristics of Agriculture in Ireland

Farming in Ireland is characterised by a predominance of owner-occupied units having an average farm size of 32 hectares. For climatic reasons, Ireland is better suited to grassland than arable crop production with over 90 per cent of the agricultural area devoted to grass and rough grazing. The pattern of landholding in which the majority of land transactions are within the family network has resulted in a very restricted land market which has curtailed opportunities for enlargement and therefore limited the possibilities for reaping the returns associated with economies of scale. This has been particularly the case in the regions (West and Border) with the smallest farms and where land quality is poor. In these areas for historical reasons there is a very strong attachment to the family farm, even in situations where there may no longer be a member of the family residing locally. The traditional small-farming social class has displayed a remarkable resilience and has survived by adopting a variety of coping strategies (Hannan and Commins, 1994; Commins, 1996). Beyond the small-farming areas, enlargement in many cases is dependent on renting land on short-term leases, which is not conducive to efficient use of resources (Lafferty et al., 1999).

The modernisation of both agricultural production and processing commenced later than in neighbouring countries and remains less advanced. Consequently farming in Ireland attracted proportionately less of the benefits from the CAP when prices were guaranteed at higher levels and in some sectors (especially the beef sector) it has attained a low level of competitiveness, leaving it less prepared for the transition to more open markets in the future.

Impact of the Non-agricultural Economy in Ireland

Since the early 1990s there has been a very major expansion in the Irish economy with most of the growth associated with enterprises located in or adjacent to the larger urban centres. The expansion of the labour force has provided many opportunities for farmers to reconsider their commitment to full-time farming. Increasing numbers have opted for part-time farming in order to increase their farm household income. Furthermore, large farms and agricultural contractors have found it increasingly difficult to recruit labour and many have switched from high to low labour-intensive enterprises (e.g., from dairying to beef cattle rearing). The overall relative contribution of agriculture to employment and the economy has diminished considerably and is likely to continue to do so.

RECENT TRENDS IN THE GEOGRAPHY OF AGRICULTURAL PRODUCTION IN IRELAND

The census of agriculture undertaken by the Central Statistics Office in 2000 enumerated 141,527 farms, with an average size of 31.4 hectares, compared with an average of 26.0 in 1991. The largest farms (>40 ha.) are in Dublin, Kildare, Kilkenny, Meath, Wexford, Wicklow, Waterford and South Tipperary. By contrast the smallest, (20–26 ha), are in the counties of the West and Border regions. The broad spatial division reflected in the farm size distribution is also reflected in contrasts in land-potential estimates based on climatic and soils indicators (Lafferty et al., 1999).

Grassland-based livestock enterprises are the dominant types of farming in Ireland. For example, in 2003 livestock and livestock products accounted for 72.9 per cent of total agricultural output at producer prices with arable crops accounting for the remainder. There are distinctive regional differences in the distributions of farm types (see Table 11.1) with dairying particularly strong in the Southwest, Midwest, Southeast and Border East; beef cattle farms, which represent just over half of the total, are especially prominent in the Midland,

West and Border East regions; sheep rearing is strongest in the regions with extensive uplands (e.g., Border West) along with some special lowland areas (e.g., east Galway or the Curragh); while tillage farms are important in the Mid-East and Southeast and especially in Dublin (predominantly in Fingal County). Local variations are significant in many regions which are mainly due to a combination of natural resource factors (soil conditions and climatic variables); differences in farm size which impact on opportunities to benefit from scale economies, and also historical reasons that have favoured the development of particular farm types in certain areas (e.g., dairy farming in the south).

Table 11.1 Percentage distribution of farms by farm type, 2000

Region	Tillage	Dairying	Beef Cattle	Sheep	Mixed grazing	Mixed crops	Other
Border East*	2.5	21.3	58.0	3.9	9.5	1.6	3.3
Border West	1.0	6.1	54.0	21.3	16.0	1.1	0.6
Midland	3.6	13.0	62.9	2.9	13.2	3.4	1.0
West	0.4	6.9	61.6	10.8	19.3	0.5	0.5
Dublin	24.3	7.8	28.2	10.2	14.5	4.9	10.2
Mideast	8.8	14.0	39.6	11.5	20.0	4.4	1.8
Midwest	1.1	27.8	58.4	1.3	9.5	1.0	0.8
Southeast	8.9	25.8	32.5	6.4	16.4	8.1	1.8
Southwest	4.0	36.6	36.9	7.7	10.7	2.8	1.2
State	3.4	18.6	51.0	8.6	14.6	2.6	1.2

* The Border East includes counties Louth, Monaghan and Cavan.

Source: Derived from CSO (2002), *Census of Agriculture 2000*

A selection of key attributes of the different farm types is summarised in Table 11.2. A broad distinction can be made between on the one hand tillage, dairying and mixed crops and livestock farms, and on the other hand specialist beef and sheep farms. The former category are on average larger in area and in the economic value of their output; they also tend to be managed by farmers who on average are younger, and are more likely to have farming as their sole occupation. The dairying sector is by far the most intensive when measured by the levels of economic output per hectare and per labour unit, which can be contrasted with the levels for cattle and sheep farms (see Table 11.3).

The pressures associated with the productivist model described earlier have required farmers to increase the scale of their operations by enlarging their farms and/or intensifying production. As a result the basic units of production have been steadily increasing. For example, the average number of cows per herd increased from 15.8 in 1981 to 27.1 in 1991 and 37.0 in 2000. Similarly, the average number of cattle per farm increased from 30.8 in 1980 to 45.6 in 1991 and 56.7 in 2000. The sheep sector departed from this trend in the 1990s as the total number of sheep declined, especially on low-lying farms. The average number of sheep per farm increased from 54.4 in 1981 to 162.1 in 1991, but then reverted back slightly to 157.8 in 2000. The contrasts between the two decades are mainly due to changes in the market conditions (Walsh, 1989).

Table 11.2 Summary characteristics of farms and farmers by type of farm, 2000

Type of farm	% of total 2002	Average farm size AAU* (ha.)	Average econ. size ESUs*	% aged >= 65	% with >= 1 AWU*	% sole occupation
Specialist tillage	3.4	53.9	37.9	15.4	49.9	52.3
Specialist dairying	18.6	42.8	45.8	13.6	80.9	74.7
Specialist beef cattle	51.0	24.2	9.4	22.5	47.1	49.7
Specialist sheep	8.6	31.9	10.1	20.6	44.1	48.6
Mixed livestock	14.6	33.6	17.7	20.2	56.6	56.0
Crops and livestock	2.6	50.5	32.7	16.2	64.8	62.0
Other	1.2	25.1	144.4	11.4	66.7	60.7
Total	100.0	31.4	20.7	19.8	55.3	55.7

* AAU = agricultural area used for farming; 1 ESU = €1,200 using 1996 standard gross margins; 1 AWU = 1,800 hours or more of labour input per person per annum

Source: Derived from CSO (2002) *Census of Agriculture 2000*

Table 11.3 Percentage distribution of farm types by economic size class, 2000

Econ. size (ESUs*) Type of farm	0–4	4–8	8–16	16–40	>= 40	Total
			Percentage of total farms			
Specialist tillage	1.5	2.3	3.5	4.4	6.2	3.4
Specialist dairying	1.4	2.1	7.3	33.6	64.3	18.6
Specialist beef cattle	67.7	71.7	60.8	32.6	7.6	51.0
Specialist sheep	11.4	10.9	10.5	6.5	1.5	8.6
Mixed livestock	16.2	11.1	15.0	17.4	12.0	14.6
Crops and livestock	0.7	1.5	2.3	4.5	4.8	2.6
Other	1.1	0.5	0.6	1.0	3.5	1.2
Total	25.6	18.8	20.0	21.1	14.5	100.0

* 1 ESU = €1,200 using 1996 standard gross margins

Source: Derived from CSO (2002) *Census of Agriculture 2000*

The concentration onto fewer farms was accompanied by a shift in the geographical distributions of enterprises, especially in the 1980s, with some evidence that the concentration process came to an end for most enterprises with the onset of the CAP reforms in the 1990s. For example, the share of the total dairy herd located in the eight large-farm counties[1] increased from 43.3 per cent in 1980 to 46.3 per cent in 1991 but there was only a marginal increase to 46.5 per cent in 2000. By contrast, the share in the six small-farm counties[2] declined from 11.5 per cent in 1980 to 8.7 per cent in 1991. The share in 2000 was 8.9 per cent.

ADJUSTMENTS IN CONVENTIONAL FARMING SINCE THE EARLY 1990s[3]

Rationalisation of production units through scaling up the size of farm businesses is a common mode of adjustment under modern farming conditions.

For the period 1991–2000 the size of the average farm in Ireland increased from 26.0 ha. to 31.4 ha., while the scale of business per farm, measured in European size units (ESUs), grew from 11.6 to 20.7 ESUs. Correspondingly, the number of farms declined by 17 per cent from 170,600 to 141,500. When trends by size classes (in hectares) are compared, there is a clear contrast between the lower and higher ends of the scale. The number of farms under 20 hectares declined by 46 per cent during the period 1991–2000, while those over 50 ha. increased by 23 per cent (Crowley et al., 2004). A comprehensive overview of the spatial patterns associated with adjustments in the 1990s is provided in Crowley et al. (2006).

Scaling Up and Intensification

Upscaling is related to the existing regional distribution of farm size. Consequently there is a tendency for the farm size differentiation between regions to become more accentuated. In 1991 the difference between the combined Border Midland and West region and the remaining regions in average ESUs per farm was 8.8 ESUs but this had increased to 13.8 ESUs by 2000.

Land Renting

Traditionally, scale enlargement was accomplished through farm amalgamation, by purchase or by renting. During the 1990s, however, the amount of land coming onto the market declined considerably while its price increased. By contrast, the amount of land rented-in expanded. Apart from the contraction of the land market, there were other factors responsible for this expansion. Early retirement pensions were payable to farmers on condition that, inter alia, they transferred their holdings by long-term lease to family (or non-family) members (Gillmor, 1999). There is also a rental income tax exemption for land leased out on a long-term basis which also encouraged more farmers to opt for land leasing arrangements.

Between 1991 and 2000 the amount of land rented-in increased by 51 per cent, or from 12.5 per cent to 18.7 per cent of the total stock of agricultural land. Nearly one-third of all farms rented-in some agricultural land in 2000, compared to just over one-fifth in 1991. Generally, renting-in of agricultural land is related to the larger and more commercially oriented farms in the east and south. By contrast the lowest rates of renting-in are in the poorer land-quality areas especially along the west coast (Border West, West, Midwest and Southwest). The areas with the highest percentages of farms renting land are where specialist tillage and dairying enterprises are most prominent.

Reduction in Labour Demand

The 1990s saw a continuation of the long-term trend towards the reduction of labour on farms and to a lower labour-intensive agriculture. There is little evidence of regional variation in this trend but labour intensities are somewhat lower in the more commercial farming areas where under-employment is less likely and mechanisation is more advanced. Decline is observable not only in the numbers of persons contributing labour but in the amount of labour supplied by the workers. Nationally, the number of persons declined by 17.5 per cent between 1991 and 2000, with little variation by region. Annual work units in the same period fell by 32.3 per cent, again with no major regional differences.

Farm Enterprise Change

The decline of 17 per cent in the number of farms nationally during the period 1991–2000 was not spread evenly over farms with different enterprises. The largest percentage decline (36.7 per cent) occurred among 'specialist dairying' farms, especially the smaller farms in this category. This trend is of considerable economic significance as it is on these farms that the largest gross margins are achieved. By contrast, there was a slight increase (0.5 per cent) in the number of 'specialist beef production' farms which includes farms with the smallest average gross margins. Specialist tillage farms had a relatively low rate of decline and specialist sheep farms declined at approximately the national average figure. Regionally, the switch away from dairying was most pronounced in the Western and Border regions which include those areas with the weakest tradition in dairy farming.

Reliance on Direct (Non-market) Payments

Reliance on direct payments (DPs) can be considered as a mode of adjustment in conventional farming. The influence of DPs on farm incomes increased significantly in the aftermath of the EU CAP reforms of 1993. Many aspects of the timing of the DPs are left to the discretion of the government so that they may be delayed or brought forward, with a consequent bearing on farm incomes in any particular year. In 1992, the last year before CAP reforms, DPs accounted for just over 30 per cent of average family-farm income. This had increased to 60 per cent by 1996 and to 90 per cent by 2002 (Frawley and Phelan, 2002). Their impact was strengthened by the provisions of Agenda 2000 but their proportionate contribution to family-farm income is also influenced by changing levels of producer prices. Thus in 2000, while the total value of DPs increased by 16 per cent their contribution as a percentage of family-farm income fell to 68 per cent – down from 74 per cent in 1999.

DPs can account for more than 100 per cent of family-farm income when market-based output is not sufficient to cover total costs. In 2003, on cattle and sheep farms, DPs represented 148 per cent and 120 per cent, respectively, of family-farm income. The concept of DPs as a proportion of income has not had the same relevance for dairying as for the other major systems as these payments are not used as a mechanism under CAP for supporting dairy farm incomes. Consequently DPs accounted for only 28 per cent of family-farm income in this sector in 2003 (Connolly et al., 2003). Regionally, the impact of DPs on family-farm income is highest in the Border, Midland and West regions, where they constitute more than 100 per cent of farm income. The impact is lowest in the Southwest and West due to the predominance of dairy farming.

NON-FARM EMPLOYMENT AND INCOME SOURCES
FOR FARM HOUSEHOLDS

The census of agriculture asks farm owners to state the degree of importance that farm work as an occupation holds for them. Three categories are specified: sole occupation, major occupation, or subsidiary occupation. In 2000, the distribution nationally was as follows (with corresponding figures for 1991 in brackets): sole occupation – 55.7 per cent (73.4 per cent); major – 13.9 per cent (5.7 per cent); and subsidiary – 30.4 per cent (20.8 per cent). Between 1991 and 2000 the major shift was from 'sole' to 'major' occupation status, with the distribution of non-farm employment a major influence on the extent of the transition.

Off-farm Employment

Data from the Teagasc (the Agricultural Research and Advisory Authority) annual National Farm Survey (NFS) illustrate the trend towards off-farm employment among farmers and their spouses/partners. Results for 2002 indicate that on 48 per cent of farms, either the farmer and/or spouse had another occupation. For farmers separately the figure was 35 per cent. Since the early 1990s the trend towards off-farm employment has been gradually upwards. Its extent varies significantly by system of farming, with dairy farmers being much less likely (12 per cent) and cattle rearing farmers more likely (49 per cent) to combine farm and non-farm work. Farmers with other occupations tend to have smaller farms – 27 ha. on average – with fewer livestock and lower stocking density than those without off-farm jobs. Direct (non-market) payments make up a higher percentage of their family-farm income, and they have lower incomes from farming. The incidence of part-time farming is highest in the West, Midwest, Midland and Border regions.

Non-farm Income in Farm Households

The national Household Budget Survey (HBS), conducted by the Central Statistics Office on a representative sample of private households every five to seven years, provides information on all sources of income to a household – as well as on household expenditures. The latest HBS relates to the period June 1999 to July 2000. In the HBS 'farm households' are defined as those where the head of the household is either (a) a gainfully occupied farmer, or (b) a retired farmer with at least one gainfully occupied farmer in the household. Wages and salaries accounted for 48 per cent of direct income (employment and other income but excluding state transfers) in farm households in 2000, compared to 29 per cent in 1987. The increase in this proportion between 1994 and 2000 is particularly remarkable, and coincides with the so-called 'Celtic Tiger' period of growth in the Irish economy (Commins and Walsh, 2005).

When considering income relativities across different categories of household it is more appropriate to refer to disposable household income (DHI). It is obtained by adding state income transfers to direct income (to give gross household income), and subtracting direct taxation payments. For farm households, both direct income and gross household income were close to the ɔtate average in 2002 (97 per cent and 95 per cent respectively) and higher than in the rural non-farm category. Furthermore, the operation of the national taxation system favoured farm households (because of lower personal incomes) with the result that disposable household income on farms slightly exceeded the State average and was very close to the urban average. However, as there are, on average, more economically active persons in farm households the relativities in the distributions of per capita disposable income per person at work vary more widely. The ratio (to the State average of 100) in respect of disposable income per worker for farm households drops to 73 while those for rural non-farm and urban households rises to 90 and 109 respectively (Commins and Walsh, 2005).

It would appear that over time, and with general economic growth, rural farm households have acquired more earners than other types of households. However, taking into account their low per person earnings and their low absolute levels of direct taxation, it seems that their work – whether in farming or outside it – yields relatively low incomes. Additional analyses have been undertaken comparing farm incomes with the levels of earnings outside the farm (Commins and Walsh, 2005). These show that family-farm income per family labour unit on full-time farms has, since 1987 at best, remained constantly at 20 per cent lower than average male earnings in manufacturing industries. Even in 'good farming years', farm incomes did not reach 90 per cent of industrial income. In this context and with employment levels generally approaching 'full employment' status, it is clear that workers in farming households, except on the more commercial farms, will be 'pulled' towards the non-farm labour market.

PROSPECTS FOR AGRICULTURE PRODUCTION
AND FARM HOUSEHOLDS

The future context for EU agriculture production over the medium term has been set by the Luxembourg Agreement of 2003 which came into effect in 2005. The key aspects of direct relevance to Ireland are the decoupling of direct payments from production and the lowering of intervention prices for dairy products. These policy changes will have a dramatic impact on farming in Ireland. A very significant reduction in dairy farming is anticipated which will impact mostly on smaller producers. The release of dairy quotas at more competitive prices will enable the more intensive dairy farmers to further increase the scale of their operations. This is most likely to happen in the core dairying areas in the southern regions. The decoupling of direct payments will require farmers specialising in beef and sheep enterprises to become more competitive by placing a much greater emphasis on the quality of output.

More generally, it is anticipated that there will be a further reduction in the number of full-time farms. The report of the Agri Vision 2015 Committee (2004) has forecast that the total number of farms will decline from 136,000 in 2002 to 105,000 in 2015. More significantly it anticipates that in 2015 there will be only 8,500 economically viable full-time farms which will include 5,500 dairy farms. The comparable figures for full-time farms in 2002 were 19,925 and 11,080 respectively. In addition there are likely to be 31,500 viable part-time farms which can be contrasted with 18,774 in 2002. The balance will consist of 45,000 non-viable part-time farms (43 per cent of the total) and a further 20,000 (19 per cent of total) in a transitional category. Compared to 2002 this will represent a reduction in the combined number of non-viable and transitional farms from 97,400 to 65,000.

The implications of these scenarios and others developed by the Rural Ireland 2025 Foresight Persectives Working Group (2005) will require radical responses. Detailed recommendations are contained in the Agri Vision Report (2004) and the Rural Ireland 2025 Report which can only be summarised very briefly here. For the farms that have the capacity to remain economically viable the main challenges are, firstly, to ensure that restructuring measures will be in place to facilitate long-term leases and allocation of milk quotas so that these farms can increase the scale of their enterprises and, secondly, that these farms are enabled to become more competitive. The need for enhanced competitiveness also applies to the production that will take place on part-time farms. Improving competitiveness will require a much stronger orientation towards a knowledge-based agriculture and food-processing industry which will require further investment in research, innovation and expert knowledge transfer.

The second aspect of adjustment on farms will be a greater emphasis on the Pillar 2 dimension of the CAP, especially agri-environmental and rural development initiatives. The transition to a stronger Pillar 2 orientation signifies a greater emphasis on the provision of public goods as a policy goal. Already agri-environmental programmes such as the Rural Environmental Protection Scheme (REPS) have a high level of participation in the less intensive farming regions where they also make a significant contribution to family-farm income (Emerson and Gillmor, 1999; Matthews, 2002). Rural development programmes following the model pioneered by the EU LEADER initiative will have an important role in supporting more strategic broad based local development strategies (see Chapter 6). However, these will need to be supported by stronger regional development strategies that will encompass investments in physical infrastructure, productive capital, along with more enhanced human, social and knowledge capital. Such investments are likely to be supported by specific programmes in the context of National Development Plans that will need to be organised within the spatial framework established by the National Spatial Strategy (Walsh, 2004; Commins, 2005; Commins et al., 2005). There is a need in particular for improving rural–urban linkages so that rural residents, especially farmers, can access alternative sources of employment – otherwise the prospect of developing a vibrant part-time farming economy may not be possible over the long term, which would pose a serious threat to the maintenance of settlement in the weaker farming areas.

12

Tourism and Heritage

Catherine Kelly

This chapter examines the economic and social importance of both tourism and heritage in Ireland, the policies and practices that underpin them, and their inter-relationship. Whilst tourism and heritage are distinct concepts, the Irish tourism product is often anchored around notions of heritage, and in post-modern, post-tourist societies, boundaries between culture, (travel)space and identities are increasingly blurred. Within the last 15 years, there have been significant shifts in our understandings and applications of heritage/tourism concepts and policies in modern Irish society. 'Heritage' emerged as a buzz-word in government policy in the early 1990s and has since weathered many debates within government and society as to 'what it is and what it is not'. Tourism's fate has also been renegotiated in an Ireland now facing a relatively less secure position with regard to EU funding and support given the accession of more needy new member states in 2004. In addition, the 'global terrorism' incidents of 9/11 in New York and 7/7 in London have influenced world tourism trends and patterns, the effects of which have been felt most strongly in countries such as Ireland, with high dependency levels on tourism income.

TOURISM IN IRELAND

Tourism has been defined extensively by numerous authors and organisations over the years and normally refers to journeys away from one's home at least overnight, for the purpose of business or pleasure. 'Tourism comprises the activities of persons travelling to and staying in places outside their usual environment for not more than one consecutive year for leisure, business and other purposes not related to the exercise of an activity remunerated from within the place visited' (World Tourism Organisation, 2005). Tourism can be categorised into typologies each of which involves certain types of product, visitor, marketing strategy and management issues; these include (typically, but not exclusively) urban tourism, business tourism, coastal/sun tourism, cultural tourism, ecotourism, adventure tourism, special-interest tourism, rural tourism, heritage tourism, festival and event tourism, wellness tourism and religious tourism.

Traditionally, tourism has been an important contributor to Irish national and regional development through the attraction of visitors from abroad and through their internal travel patterns within Ireland. Throughout the 1990s, both the numbers and expenditures of overseas tourists visiting Ireland grew more quickly than the global average, indicating a rising market share for Ireland. In the period 1990–2002, expenditure by overseas tourists doubled in real terms and employment generated by tourism rose by 70 per cent (Tourism Policy Review Group, 2003). Thus, despite the rapid growth of other economic sectors in this period, tourism remains a significant economic sector, accounting for 8 per cent of all employment and 4 per cent of Gross National Product in 2002. In 2004, expenditure by visitors to Ireland was estimated to be worth €4.1 billion and overseas tourists had increased by over 3 per cent (to 6.4 million) on the previous year (see Figure 12.1). However, the net contribution of foreign tourism to the Irish economy is being increasingly offset by the growth of travel abroad by Irish residents. Thus, whereas the inward flow of visitors grew more quickly than the reverse outward flow throughout the 1990s, a sharp fall in 2001 and stagnation in 2002 (associated, respectively, with the recessionary impact of the 'dot.com' collapse and the impact on international travel of the attack on the Twin Towers) led to a considerable narrowing of the gap, as the outward flow from Ireland continued to grow strongly, reflecting the rapidly rising living standards of Irish residents. From an economic point of view, of greater importance is the fact that, for the first time, foreign expenditure by Irish travellers exceeded expenditure in Ireland by foreign visitors in 2003. Prior to 2002, tourism had always made a substantial net contribution to Ireland's external balance of payments (see Figure 12.2), both directly and indirectly, in the form of the low import content of most tourism activities (accommodation, travel, catering, shopping and entertainment) compared with the manufacturing sector. The reversal of this situation is primarily attributable to the fact that Irish tourists holidaying overseas spend twice as much on their holidays as do foreign holiday makers in Ireland.

While the number of visitors to Ireland recovered strongly in 2003 and 2004 following the 2001–02 downturn, overseas tourist revenues continued to fall.

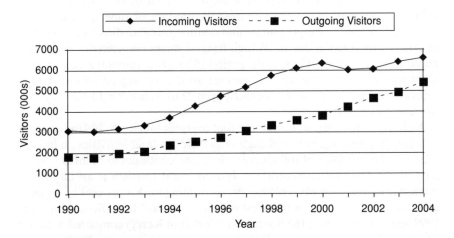

Figure 12.1   Trends in international visitor movements, 1990–2004

Sources: Central Statistics Office, Passenger Card Inquiry Survey, various years

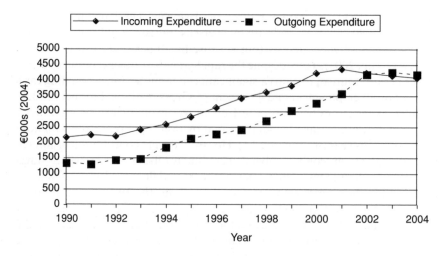

Figure 12.2   Trends in international tourism revenues, 1990–2004

Sources: Central Statistics Office, Passenger Card Inquiry Survey, various years

The fact that the average 'spend' per tourist is declining is mainly a reflection of shorter average stays in Ireland by foreign tourists. This undoubtedly is partly a response to rising costs in Ireland, but another important factor is the increasing popularity of 'short-break' holidays (especially among middle-class Europeans), facilitated greatly by the rapid fall in the cost of intra-European air travel. This, in turn, is having significant knock-on impacts on the regional distribution of tourism revenues in Ireland due, in particular, to the fact that the short-break holiday market is strongly focused on Dublin (O'Toole, 2004). This, in part, reflects the general growing relative popularity of urban tourism (Law, 1993) but, perhaps even more so, it is driven by the fact that short-break holiday makers wish to minimise the amount of time spent in transit and therefore tend to congregate around destinations with direct air links. This clearly favours Dublin due to its high level of direct connectivity with other major European cities. Thus, in the period 1990–2002, tourism expenditure in Dublin grew at twice the national average, so that the region's share of total tourism revenues also rose significantly, from 22 to 30 per cent (Tourism Policy Review Group, 2003).

An interesting contrast, however, is that overseas tourists to Ireland engaged in hiking/hill walking, golf and angling as their top three activities on holiday (Fáilte Ireland, 2004a). Rural tourism, therefore, continues to be an important part of the Irish tourism product. Indeed, rural tourism is an important economic industry for western regions, accounting for 8.3 per cent of regional gross domestic product in the West region (Galway, Mayo, Roscommon) in 1999 and 5.5 per cent in the Southwest (Cork and Kerry) compared with just 2.6 per cent in Dublin (Tansey Webster Stewart and Company, 2002).

The increased prosperity of the Irish people themselves has contributed not only to increased overseas visits but also a rise in domestic tourism and expenditure. For example, the number of domestic holidays taken in 2004 increased by 7 per cent from the previous year to 3.1 million trips, while the revenue from these trips increased by 9 per cent to €625 million (Fáilte Ireland, 2004b). Hotels were the most popular type of accommodation (29 per cent), followed by rented accommodation (23 per cent). The availability of rented-accommodation bednights and the utilisation of holiday homes has increased dramatically in the past decade in Ireland due to tax incentives born out of the European Union's early 1990s funding programmes such as the Pilot Resort Relief Scheme. This scheme gave tax incentives to those involved in coastal self-catering accommodation developments in certain resorts in Ireland (for example, Kilkee, Westport, Courtown, Achill Island). It has, however, been criticised for its environmental impacts (where scale and architectural quality have been remiss) and the knock-on economic impacts of property value increases in rural scenic areas with scarce availability of affordable homes for locals (Osbourne, 2001; McKeogh, 2004). Hotel refurbishment incentive schemes, also funded under EU operational programmes in the 1990s, have increased hotel quality and leisure facilities available in the sector, thereby encouraging greater domestic tourism participation. In terms of the preferred activities of domestic tourists, Table 12.1 indicates how 'the Irish at home' spend their time.

Table 12.1 Domestic tourist activities

Activity	%
Houses/castles	17
Gardens	13
Heritage/interpret. centres	13
Museums/art galleries	11
Monuments	9
National Parks	16
Watersports	14
Hiking/walking	14
Golf	9
Angling	4
Equestrian pursuits	3
Cycling	4

Source: Fáilte Ireland (2004b)

Interestingly, the most popular tourist activities all fall into cultural/heritage classifications, reinforcing the importance of linkages between governance, integrated policy making and interdepartmental communications for the effective management and planning of the sector's resource base. At present, the Irish tourism sector is governed through the Department of Arts, Sport and Tourism (DAST). Its associated body, Fáilte Ireland (formerly Bord Fáilte), is concerned with marketing Ireland, often on a cross-border basis, at home and abroad and implementing some of the government department's policies and procedures.

Currently, the main policy driving Irish tourism is the DAST-led New Horizons for Irish Tourism: An Agenda for Action (2003) which outlines a strategy for the sector for the period 2003–12. Its main aims include a target of increasing overseas visitor spending (to €6 billion) and to increase visitor numbers to 10 million in the same time period (DAST, 2003). Special interest tourism is targeted, encompassing business tourism, active tourism, heritage/cultural tourism, education tourism and wellness tourism as new growth areas. While there is a continuing trend for Irish tourism to concentrate on niche products, the target areas above reflect new growth areas of consumption across wider society. Business tourism is well placed for growth given the rise in leisure short-break visits to Dublin and the East coast in particular. A new Business Tourism Forum has been established to develop this sector as part of DAST/Fáilte Ireland's strategy implementation. Wellness tourism is also an emerging growth sector, focusing on holidays which help to reconcile 'body, mind and spirit' and are typically located in either upmarket hotel-spa settings, or in specifically designated retreat centres (Kelly and Smith, 2006). Ireland's brand imaging of Celtic Spirituality and the non-seasonal aspect of this tourism product allows for good potential growth, although the sector is still very much in its infancy in the Republic. In particular, the 'Horizons' strategy refers to the sector's aspirations to achieve the following objectives:

- Ireland will be a destination of choice for discerning international and domestic tourists which:
- provides a tourism experience that exceeds customer expectations in terms of friendliness, quality of environment, diversity and depth of culture;
- has a range of world-class products, widely distributed throughout all regions of the country;
- is a vibrant source of year-round earnings;
- provides attractive career opportunities in tourism;
- respects the natural and built environments and supports their conservation and enhancement;
- respects and supports Irish culture in all its diversity.

The word 'culture' appears twice in this vision, and diversity is mentioned alongside it each time. In the past 15 years, the demographic structure of Ireland has changed dramatically in terms of heterogeneity, posing new challenges for the representation of a multicultural *domestic* society, as well as meeting traditional diverse visitor needs. With economic well-being at an all-time high, fewer Irish natives are seeking employment in the tourism sector and this has led to variable responses from within and outside a sector whose foundations were firmly built on the notion of the *Irish* welcome. Eastern European nationals in particular have embraced tourism employment, but the impacts of these changes on a service-driven sector have yet to be fully assessed.

Action areas identified in the government strategy include the usual references to access, transport, information and communication technology, product development, marketing, skills and information collection. It is worth noting the huge change in the past decade in consumer tourist behaviour involving the Internet as the major source of information and holiday bookings. Old means of marketing and engaging with tourism are, in many instances, simply becoming obsolete, providing fresh challenges to Irish tourist industries. Key barriers to development centre around the issue of value for money in Ireland; physical limitations at Dublin airport; the absence of a national conference centre in Dublin; loss in shares of the British outbound markets, and inconsistencies in access rights to the Irish countryside for rural tourism (Fáilte Ireland, 2004c). It remains to be seen whether the objectives of the government's strategy will be achieved or remain aspirational.

HERITAGE IN IRELAND

An important part of Ireland's appeal to both overseas and domestic tourists has been its heritage. Heritage is therefore seen as a key part of the tourist experience and a way of sustaining and developing tourism.

Heritage has a plethora of definitions with varying emphases on buildings-centred, landscape-centred and people-centred ideologies. UNESCO (United Nations Education Scientific and Cultural Organization), with a remit for world heritage, suggests three main categories: (1) cultural heritage, (2) natural heritage and (3) intangible heritage. Cultural heritage in this instance often refers to the built environment; natural heritage to landscapes and environment; and intangible heritage to traditions, rituals, music, folklore, dance, language and other transitory or indefinable aspects of the culture of a place and its people. Ashworth (2005) is somewhat cynical about the 'delusionary' element of heritage, but acknowledges that heritage is about common values, common purpose and common interests. Lowenthal (1998) refers to heritage simply as everything we have been handed down from the past. Perhaps surprisingly it is only in recent decades that heritage has come to mean more to society than a mere legal bequest (Graham et al., 2000), for example being seen as a tourist experience.

Buildings are amongst the easiest aspects of heritage to define, classify and create policies for because they are visible, tangible and have established cultural 'value criteria' created by architects, scholars and purveyors of taste for many centuries. As a result, the built heritage is the most written-about and policy-directed aspect of Irish and many other nations' heritage. Landscape, like buildings, can perform dual heritage and utilitarian functions; a farm can simultaneously be a source of rural income and part of a Special Area of Conservation, just as a listed building can function as a working bank and so on. Conflicts arise when the balance is questioned (practically or conceptually) between the utilitarian use-values and intrinsic cultural values of such spaces. Defining people-centred heritage and events is somewhat more complex. When for example, do rituals of the current and the everyday become 'traditions'?; which cultural practices become more valued than others?; and how do we create structures and events which celebrate the contemporary as part of on-going heritage construction?

In an Irish academic context, 'Heritage Studies' has been embraced through the emergence of specific degree programmes (e.g., the Heritage Studies BA at the Galway-Mayo Institute of Technology and the MA in Cultural Heritage and Museum Studies at the University of Ulster), and the coalescence of intellectual research and writing through multidisciplinary conferences drawing scholars from the fields of geography, history, literature, archaeology, art and cultural studies. McCarthy (2005, p. 7) refers to the need 'to bridge the ill-conceived gap in Ireland between intellectual elitism and the customer-focused (and profit driven) heritage industry'. Whilst the academy and industry are usually separate in society, it is important to assess the relationships between emergent schools of thought (or the merging and renegotiation of existing ones under the umbrella of heritage) and how both the state and the industry itself define, regulate and operationalise themselves.

Governance, Policy and Practice

Given the diverse approaches to defining heritage discussed above, the task of governing and creating policy structures for heritage is no less complex. Heritage appeared for the first time in an official, named capacity in Ireland in the mid-1990s through the Department of Arts, Heritage, Gaeltacht and the Islands. There followed a period, during government reshuffles, where 'heritage' was dropped entirely from the name of any State department, again suggesting the difficulty of assigning resources and staffing to something hard to pin down. Now, State responsibility for heritage comes under the auspices of two different renamed government departments: the Department of the Environment, Heritage and Local Government (DoEHLG) and the Department of Arts, Sport and Tourism (DAST). This division reflects definitional conventions of splitting 'heritage' into tangible and intangible categorisations. Table 12.2 offers a summary of some of the main areas of responsibility for heritage in Ireland today and the related agencies associated with them. The list is not intended to be exhaustive and recognises the wide range of related private and voluntary sector organisations that could have been included.

There are obvious overlaps in many areas of heritage governance between the two departments; DoEHLG, for example, manages the country's major tourist attractions (historic houses, gardens and archaeological sites, for instance), whilst DAST's work focuses largely on private sector tourism. The work of the semi-state body, the Heritage Council, is to advise on and inform heritage policy in the built, natural and cultural aspects of heritage; it also has a remit for raising awareness of heritage, gathering data and encouraging pride in heritage values. As such, its work is multidisciplinary and interdepartmental. More acknowledgement, at least on paper, has been given to the need for collaborative work on heritage governance and policy formulation '... a need to create new partnerships and relationships that better integrate the arts/culture, sport and tourism sectors with a view to maximising forward integrated planning across the various sectoral activities' (DAST, 2005). A short-lived agency, Duchas

Table 12.2 Heritage and tourism governance structures in Ireland

Department of Arts, Sport & Tourism			Department of Environment, Heritage & Local Government		
Areas of governance	*Executive agencies*	*Policies/plans (sample)*	*Areas of governance*	*Executive agencies*	*Policies/plans (sample)*
The Arts: Music Dance Visual Arts Archives Museums Galleries Film Culture and Heritage*	The cultural institutions: National Museum of Ireland National Gallery of Ireland Irish Museum of Modern Art Chester Beatty Library National Archives Advisory Council The Arts Council Culture Ireland	Strategy statements Arts plans	Built environment: Architecture National Monuments State-managed visitor sites	Office of Public Works (OPW) The Heritage Council	Architectural Heritage Initiative National Inventory of Architectural Heritage National Heritage Plan
Tourism	Fáilte Ireland Shannon Development Tourism Ireland	New Horizons for Irish Tourism: Agenda for Action	Natural environment: National Parks Natural Heritage Areas (NHAs) Special Areas of Conservation (SACs) Special Protection Areas (SPAs)	National Parks & Wildlife Service (NPWS)	National Biodiversity Plan

('the Heritage Service') operated under the auspices of DoEHLG for a time in the 1990s and has since been disbanded with its functions dispersed into the realms of the Office of Public Works and the National Parks. Some would argue that this exacerbates the problem of profile raising for heritage in Ireland; whilst others, mainly civil servants, argue that its function was confusing and duplicative of existing structures.

At a supranational level, heritage is also subject to the wider influences of European Union and global organisations. The EU in particular has stringent regulations relating to criteria for the designation, management and conservation of National Heritage Areas (NHAs), Special Areas for Conservation (SACs) and so on. UNESCO, meanwhile, manages World Heritage Site (WHS) listings and guidance on practice and policies for global designated sites. On the island of Ireland there are three WHS's, namely Brú na Bóinne (the Newgrange Neolithic tomb site, County Meath), Skellig Michael in County Kerry, and in the North, the Giant's Causeway, County Antrim. All are high-profile visitor attractions, again emphasising the inter-relationship between heritage and tourism and the subsequent need to integrate policy and communication channels at state level.

Heritage Interpretation and Representation

Given the breadth of meaning and conceptualisation involved in the term 'heritage', the task of bringing heritage to an audience, be it domestic or overseas, is enormously challenging. Not all heritage, not all stories, and not all perspectives can be adequately displayed or told. Where heritage is engaged with in public spaces, such as heritage centres, museums and galleries, a process is undertaken by those charged with it to select, interpret and present that heritage. This process involves a commodification of the past, of objects and events, in such a way that interest is raised. In some instances, that 'interest' has related profit-driven objectives (for example, the economic viability of a local heritage site), and as such, must therefore ensure that visitors are engaged, entertained and satisfied. Ashworth and Larkham (1994) argue that in this very process, the heritage commodity becomes a product which can be *used* by consumers/visitors and therefore contains particular messages. 'These messages stem from the conscious choices of resources, products and packaging, which are performed on the basis of sets of subjective values, consciously or not, of those exercising these choices' (Ashworth and Larkham, 1994, p. 20).

The ways in which heritage objects are selected, put together, and written or spoken about have particular effects. These effects are not those of the objects per se; it is the use made of these objects and interpretive frameworks that can open up or close down historical, social and cultural possibilities (Hooper-Greenhill, 2000). The importance of insightful and inclusive repre-sentation-interpretation that acknowledges such legitimisation of difference is crucial in spaces of contested identity and multiple heritage(s). Case study research which examined the politics of contested representation at the Ulster-American Folk Park in Northern Ireland showed that visitors from different parts of the island had culturally grounded expectations of how their own heritage ought to be portrayed (Brett, 1996; Kelly and Ní Laoire, 2005). Ireland is only one space in an increasing number of global zones of conflict where concepts of 'heritage and national cultural identity' have become fragmented, blurred and often violently challenged. As tourism increasingly seeks out cultural products with the growth of cultural-heritage tourism, the politics of representation 'for-self' (local/national communities as part of identity building), versus 'for-others' (tourists, as part of entertainment/visitation) becomes much more loaded. McManus (2005) acknowledges the importance of heritage as an economic resource ripe for exploitation, but notes that it is also used to help define the meanings of culture and power, giving it a vital socio-political function. She uses case study examples of Dublin's Temple Bar area and other aspects of tourism and urban renewal in Dublin to examine links between tourism, heritage and identity.

On a micro level, the politics of representation become crucial for the practicalities of heritage site and exhibition design and layout. The process of heritage interpretation should, insists Harrison (2000), be simply about moving knowledge from specialists to the general public in a clear and effective way. What is said and what is not in complex settings becomes significant, and more importantly, *how* messages are portrayed takes on added significance. The task for curators, educators and exhibition developers is to provide experiences that invite visitors to make meaning through deploying and extending their existing interpretive strategies and repertoires, using their prior knowledge and their preferred learning styles, and testing their hypotheses against those of others, including experts (Hooper-Greenhill, 1995).

Considering the spectrum of built, natural and intangible heritage, modes of interpretation and representation in Ireland are varied. The visitor centre at Glenveagh National Park in Donegal, for example, takes a conventional chronological and descriptive approach to presenting the natural history and contemporary environmental issues of the place. The Famine Museum at Strokestown, County Roscommon is located at the site of an historic aristocratic house with a modern, attached visitor centre that engages well with the complexity of representing one of the most controversial aspects of Ireland's history. The site portrays both built heritage in terms of the architectural aspects of the historic building and the socio-cultural heritage of a difficult period in history. The gala affair that Dublin's annual St Patrick's Day parade has become is an example of the temporary portrayal of intangible heritage, not housed in a specific, fixed building, but taken to the people in the streets. Its encompassment of music, dance, language, diasporic participation and spectacle is, perhaps, more instantly consumed, by a larger audience, as 'heritage' than other less accessible forms. O'Connor (2003), Kneafsey (2003), and Quinn (2005) variously portray useful case study examples of heritage–tourism inter-relationships though Irish dance, traditional music, and the growth of festivals, respectively. The 'performance of heritage' is an integral part of popular interpretations of heritage in postmodern Irish society.

CONCLUSION

Tourism is changing rapidly in terms of its characteristic product/consumer expectations and in how it does its business; Ireland will have to keep abreast, if not one step ahead, of such challenges if it is to continue to survive successfully. As such, the tourism sector must account for changing societal and cultural changes that advocate high standards, unique experiences, cheap access and instantaneous online information, and cater for the consumer who 'wants it all – now!' in the face of increasing world competition. 'Integrated tourism' is essential – where tourism is explicitly linked to the economic, social, cultural, natural and human structures of the region in which it occurs (Gillmor, 2004). The sustained sharp growth of Irish tourism throughout the 1990s is a well documented success story. Today the sector lies at a critical point of transition. In essence, Irish tourism is now in somewhat uncharted territory as it seeks a route to sustainable and regionally balanced growth. Past remedies are certainly no guarantee of future success – and there are no quick-fix solutions (Fáilte Ireland, 2005). Heritage forms an important part of the tourist experience and is therefore a key aspect of the tourist industry in Ireland. However, heritage as a concept, sector and 'industry' has been subject to much change and confusion in Ireland over the past decade. Such confusion matters less, perhaps, than the need for integrated strategies that draw together academic, populist and decision-maker perspectives on the best way to move forward. Heritage as a form or expression of national and cultural identity is something to be nurtured and cherished, whilst the essence of such heritage forms a major part of how the tourism sector portrays Ireland and Irishness to others. Maintaining an awareness of the nuances of delicately balancing these variable objectives is crucial as we move forward and as the Celtic Tiger matures. Indeed, increased tourism mobility and the on-going march of economic and cultural globalisation forces will be interesting to assess in terms of heritage-tourism responses in Ireland.

Part III
Political Landscape

Introduction

Interestingly, the economic and social transformations that have occurred in the Republic of Ireland have been accompanied by wide-scale political change with regard to governance, government, citizenship, and the peace process. This change has had important implications in fostering economic growth and social development by providing a stable political climate that is attractive to inward investment. For example, the social partnerships developed in the mid-1980s created the conditions for good relations between employers and employees and largely heralded the end of militant union action. The need for coalition governments has created an environment in which long-term policy can be played out without the government always being on the verge of collapse, as was the case in the late 1970s through to the late 1980s, or being subject to radical change at the whim of one party. And the peace process has nullified the negative effects of 'The Troubles' and made inward investors more confident about locating in Ireland. The influence of the European Union has also driven a largely positive citizenship agenda that has sought to enhance civic engagement and combat discrimination and disadvantage. This is not to say that the political landscape is now universally positive or benign. For example, the peace process has largely been in limbo since the dissolution of the Northern Ireland Assembly in 2002; in the same year the social partners failed to come to an agreement, meaning that some partners left the process; and Ireland has failed in many cases to deliver on its citizenship agenda, most notably in relation to Travellers. In this part of the book, the authors examine these issues and their implications.

In the opening chapter, Adrian Kavanagh examines the political system operating in the Republic and the effect of its geography on its make-up. He initially details the nature of the electoral system, noting how multimember and multiparty constituencies shape the local and national political landscape. In particular, he notes that the Irish system breeds strong localism in voting and clientism in political action, especially given the weak ideological differences between the main political parties. As a result, he notes that since the political crises of the 1980s the smaller parties and independent candidates have generally held the balance of power, especially given the need for coalition governments to take office. He charts the geographical support of particular parties, how they perform within different types of election (local, national, European), and the patterns of voting in Ireland, which often differ from other European nations due to the effects of localism. Given the political and electoral landscape, it seems likely that coalition government is likely to be a consistent feature of Irish governance for some time.

In the following chapter, Joe Larragy and Brendan Bartley chart the transformation of governance through the development of the social partnership process. They detail that since the mid-1980s there has been a steady growth in governance practices within Ireland; that is, decision making by institutions that are not formally part of government, such as business and communities. While there have always been governance arrangements, the present process of widening and deepening participation started in earnest in 1987 with the Programme for National Recovery, a collaboration between government and social partners (employer, trade union and farmer organisations) that sought to stabilise industrial relations and rationalise spending by agreeing to a set plan of pay growth for ensuing years. This social partnership model has operated ever since with its partner base widening in subsequent agreements through the inclusion of community and voluntary partners. In the early 1990s, the social partnership model was broadened to include local development through the creation of local and area-based partnership 'companies' (i.e., based on the business market model) designed to drive local change. In the late 1990s, partnership companies were modified to include local government elements to make them more democratically accountable. In addition, the government itself took on some of these ideas, particularly those of New Public Management, changing its own working practices to become more dynamic, proactive, market-responsive and user-oriented. Whereas the shift to governance is often seen as a move away from government, in the Irish case central government has maintained its dominant position, carefully shepherding the governance process. Larragy and Bartley note that the Irish case blends an interesting mix of European and American influences, and that the Irish experience has itself shaped governance thinking in the EU. They point out that the social partnership agreements and new modes of governance such as area-based partnership companies have been important for the Celtic Tiger transformation by providing labour market stability and flexible modes of operation capable of reacting opportunistically to new challenges and possibilities. It is clear from their account of recent developments that orthodox government and political systems have not disappeared but have accommodated the new processes of governance that have appeared in the Irish institutional landscape.

Honor Fagan and Michael J. Murray discuss one aspect of governance, namely waste management. They discuss how Ireland's new affluence, growth in population, expansion in construction, and changing lifestyles have led to an increase in waste production and a crisis in how to manage that waste. They note that between 1995 and 1998 waste flows in Ireland increased by 89 per cent, the majority of which ended up in landfill sites. The pressure on Ireland's policy makers and implementers to cope with the waste generated and to meet

EU directives on waste management have led to political mobilisation around the issues of where to locate waste disposal sites, the costs of disposal, and forms of waste governance. Waste is now a hot topic in Ireland, and despite some changes in policy and practice, Fagan and Murray argue that the waste situation continues to deteriorate, posing a significant challenge to government and society alike. They chart the modes of governance being introduced on different scales and their likely success in tackling the waste issue.

The final chapter considers the situation in Northern Ireland, a matter of critical, political importance on the island, and examines some of the issues affecting progress and paths forward. The peace process, started by the first ceasefires in 1994, and politically cemented by the signing of the Good Friday Agreement in 1998, heralded a new era in Northern Ireland and changed the nature of the Ireland's relationship with its northern neighbour. This was quickly followed by the North South Ministerial Council, cross-border bodies, and the EU PEACE programmes' funding of reconciliation projects. While there has been real change to the lives of the Northern Irish population and those living along the border counties in Ireland, the political situation has dissolved into one largely of stalemate. Interestingly, it appears that the Irish and British governments are much closer in their thinking and ideas about how to progress the process than either government is to nationalist or unionist thinking in the North. There is also clearly a long way to go before sectarian tensions and violence become things of the past.

Brian Graham provides a detailed discussion of identity and its political constitution in Northern Ireland with a particular focus on loyalism. He argues that despite the tendency to reduce identity to binary distinctions (e.g., nationalist versus unionist), in reality identities are much more fractured and diverse. That said, loyalism is characterised by a coherent sense of betrayal and bitterness based on a sense of being marginalised in relation to the United Kingdom and the peace process. This, as Graham notes, poses a challenge and a threat to a process that seeks peace and reconciliation for all sides. To a large extent, loyalist strategy has sought to frustrate and opt out of cooperation and attempts at power sharing. And yet they are an integral part of the whole process. This clearly raises serious questions about how to maintain the peace process in the face of intransigence and victimhood, and to develop strategies that are inclusive of loyalist identity and views.

Both internally, and on a cross-border basis in relation to Northern Ireland, the political landscape on the island of Ireland has been reshaped in interesting and significant ways. It can be argued that democratic politics has been enhanced, both North and South, by widening participation, addressing issues of inclusiveness, citizenship and reconciliation, and devolving power, albeit with varying degrees of success in these political processes. While many of the processes originated in Ireland itself, the influence of the European Union, and the role of the US in the peace process, have been critical in shaping the Irish political landscape. As Ireland moves forward, all of the progressive changes that have occurred will need to be consolidated and maintained while many other issues will require serious consideration. These include, perhaps, stronger cross-border linkages and co-operation; a further decentralisation of power to regional assemblies; stronger interventionist policies around certain key issues such as health, education, transport, and regional development, and a concerted effort to address the deep social and spatial divisions in Northern Irish society.

13

Elections and Voting

Adrian Kavanagh

This chapter studies the political landscape of the Irish State, with a specific focus on analysing the geographical patterns evident in recent Irish elections, relating to patterns of support for political parties and electoral participation and the institutional and socio-structural contexts that shape these. Different electoral contests are held in the Republic of Ireland, including general, presidential, local, European, by-election and referendum electoral contests, each of which has its own specific characteristics. 'Politics is local' in Ireland and place-based concerns also matter in terms of explaining Irish electoral behaviour.

THE ELECTORAL SYSTEM AND CONSTITUENCY BOUNDARIES

The proportional representation by single transferable vote (PR-STV) electoral system, used in the Republic of Ireland, allows voters to rank-order candidates when casting their ballots, with the range of preferences limited only by the number of candidates. Another key element of the Irish electoral system is its use of multimember constituencies, with between three and five candidates elected from general election constituencies, and between three and seven candidates elected in local election contests. Sinnott (1995) argues that Irish general elections effectively amount to 40, or more, separate electoral contests, as each constituency has its own peculiar circumstances and local concerns, and the relative influence of national factors varies between different constituencies.

Electoral contests generally involve a series of counts. To be elected, candidates are required to attain a threshold proportion of the valid votes cast (quota) at any stage during these counts.

$$\text{Quota} = \frac{\text{Total number of valid votes}}{\text{Number of seats} + 1} + 1$$

The quota amounts to 25 per cent of the total number of valid votes (excluding 'spoilt' votes) cast in three-seat constituencies, 20 per cent in four-seat constituencies, and $16\frac{2}{3}$ per cent in five-seat constituencies. If a candidate exceeds the quota before the final count, their surplus – the amount by which their votes exceeds the quota – will normally be distributed between the remaining candidates, based on the proportion of the second (or subsequent) preferences awarded to these other candidates on the successful candidate's ballot papers. If no candidate reaches the quota on the first or any subsequent count, the lowest placed candidate(s) will be eliminated and their votes distributed amongst the remaining candidates, again based on second (or subsequent) preferences. The process is repeated in a number of counts until the requisite number of candidates has exceeded the quota, or all the other candidates have been eliminated. Given this complex counting process, Irish general and local elections have a particular history of 'long counts' (lasting for a number of days or even weeks). These particularly arise as very narrow margins often determine who wins the final seat, or seats, in a number of constituency contests. The strong degree of marginality associated with this system means that electoral contests in all constituencies will be competitive.

The electoral system allows for a particularly localised style of voting. Voters may express high preferences for candidates local to their area, without the risk that their votes will be 'wasted' if these candidates have little prospect of success. This links in with the phenomenon that political scientists term the 'friends and neighbours' effect, where candidates win their largest percentage of votes in areas surrounding their home base, or 'bailiwick', and their support levels decline the further one moves from this bailiwick, amounting to a distance-decay effect. Irish research has found strong 'friends and neighbours' influences on candidates' support patterns in Irish constituencies, with county boundaries being found to exacerbate this effect in two county constituencies (Cartwright et al., 2004). Parker (1982) accounts for this effect by arguing that local candidates are best placed to take advantage of local information flows, more likely to be known by local people, and also viewed as the politicians who are best able to address the concerns of that area. Political parties attempt to benefit from this effect when selecting candidates and devising canvassing strategies before elections. If a party runs more than one candidate in a constituency, they will select candidates from different areas to ensure strong support levels for the party across the constituency, benefiting from each candidate's individual 'friends and neighbours' effect. Vote management strategies generally allocate a defined area, including their home base, to each candidate for canvassing purposes and they are strongly advised against canvassing in the parts of the constituency allocated to their running mates. Even if a candidate is unlikely to be elected, they may be added to the party ticket to shore up support levels in weaker areas of a constituency and to increase the pool of transfers available to their running mates. Parties aim to have their candidates on roughly the same amount of first preference votes, so that no weaker candidate(s) is (are) eliminated early in the count, allowing their candidates to win as many vote transfers as possible from other election candidates and leaving the party in a position to maximise its number of seats.

The highly localised nature of support for candidates means that the electoral prospects of individual politicians will be adversely affected if their bailiwick is split by a new constituency boundary. Constituency size is an important factor in determining the degree to which parties will be successful in gaining representation. Each Irish general election constituency since the 1935 election has elected between three and five members, or teachtaí dála (TDs), to the Irish Parliament, Dáil Éireann. Independent candidates and relatively smaller political parties, such as the Progressive Democrats, Sinn Féin or the Green Party, have the prospect of gaining representation in their strongest areas, especially if these are located within larger four-seat or five-seat constituencies where smaller proportions of the vote are needed to secure election. Despite this, Fianna Fáil and Fine Gael usually win a higher share of the seats in general elections than their share of the national vote would warrant. Generally higher levels of support for their candidates means that they remain in contention until the latter stages of election counts and thus pick up vote transfers from less successful candidates. Three-seat constituencies generally tend to favour these parties, particularly in their stronger areas.

Constituency boundaries were directly devised by the Irish government up to 1977. Significant potential for electoral abuse existed in the form of 'gerry-mandering', a practice which involves the redrawing of constituency boundaries to maximise a particular party's representation levels. The Irish practice was generally focused on the number of seats assigned to different constituencies. In strong regions for the government party (or parties), where government support amounted to around 50 per cent of the vote, three-seat constituencies were preferred as the government would win a majority of the seats on offer (two out of three seats as it effectively had two quotas). Four-seat constituencies were preferred in regions where government support was relatively weak, as it could still win half of the seats (two) with just 40 per cent of the vote. Fianna Fáil governments generally preferred having three-seat constituencies in the west and four-seat constituencies in the east, while Fine Gael-Labour coalition governments preferred the opposite pattern. After the 1977 general election, and the spectacular failure of the outgoing coalition's 'tullymander' (so named after the Minister for Environment, James Tully, who put it in place in 1974) that actually exacerbated the coalition losses resulting from a strong swing to Fianna Fáil, responsibility for the redrawing of constituency boundaries was placed into the hands of independent boundary commissions. The most recent boundary changes were drafted by the Constituency Commission in January 2004, which made proposals to address the significant population changes within Ireland between 1996 and 2002. Fast growing commuter belt territories in Kildare, Meath and the south-western Dublin suburbs gained added representation levels, while areas that experienced relatively little population growth, or population decline, such as Cork, the Northwest region, and the north inner suburbs of Dublin City lost representation (Kavanagh, 2003: Constituency Commission, 2004).

IRISH POLITICAL PARTIES AND THEIR GEOGRAPHIES OF SUPPORT

Lipset and Rokan (1967) have proposed that contemporary European party systems are the results of past conflicts, or 'cleavages', in European states: the church versus state and centre versus periphery arising from the national revolution, and the land versus industry and workers versus employers (class) cleavages arising from the industrial revolution. They argued that European party systems were frozen exactly when the right to vote was extended to most of the population for the first time. The dominant cleavage at that time (early twentieth century) was the class cleavage, and this shaped the development of party systems dominated by strong left- and right-wing political parties (Harrop and Miller, 1987). This cleavage did not emerge as the main political division in Ireland, however. The election in which the right to vote was awarded to the majority of Irish people for the first time was the 1918 election. This was held when the Republic of Ireland was still part of the United Kingdom and was largely dominated by the nationalist question (amounting to a good example of a centre–periphery cleavage from the United Kingdom perspective). The main cleavage that would shape the Irish political system was the Irish Civil War of the early 1920s, emerging over conflicting attitudes on the Treaty that ended the War of Independence and partitioned the island of Ireland. In the wake of the Civil War, Fianna Fáil (formed from groups opposing the Treaty) and Fine Gael (comprising elements of the pro-Treaty side) emerged as the two strongest parties despite their ideological similarities (centre-right). The weakness of the class cleavage led John Whyte (1974) to view Irish politics as lacking social bases, although others argue that class factors have influenced party support patterns within the State, with their influence varying from election to election.

Fianna Fáil is the most popular party in the State, having won over 40 per cent of the vote in most elections held since it first attained power in 1932 and formed the government for much of this period. It is viewed as a 'catch-all' party, often winning the highest share of the vote both in middle-class and working-class areas, and both in rural and urban areas, as in the 2002 general election when it won the largest share of the vote in each of the 42 constituencies. In the early 1930s, for instance, Fianna Fáil emerged as the favoured party of the urban working class, who saw the party offering a more radical alternative to the then conservative Labour Party. Historically, the party tended to do best in areas with higher proportions of farmers and Irish speakers, with generally higher levels of support in rural and western constituencies. During the Haughey era of the 1980s, party support in urban middle-class areas declined and Fianna Fáil became increasingly reliant on its rural and urban working-class support base, but support levels in urban middle-class areas improved again in the late 1990s. The party has done particularly well in the Western and Midland regions, as well as the north city constituencies in Dublin in recent elections, and won over 50 per cent of the vote in Carlow-Kilkenny, Dublin North Central, Laois-Offaly and Limerick West in 2002. (It would have done so in other western constituencies but for the presence of independent candidates from the Fianna Fáil gene pool in constituencies such as Donegal North East, Galway East, Clare and Kerry South.) The party, however, experienced a significant decline in support in the 2004 local and European elections (Table 13.1), which was particularly pronounced in deprived urban areas. This suggests that Sinn Féin may now usurp its position as the strongest party in urban working-class areas.

Table 13.1   Share of national vote, 2002–04

Party	2002 General	%	2004 European	%	2004 Local	%
Fianna Fáil	770,748	41.5	524,504	29.5	578,139	31.8
Fine Gael	417,619	22.5	494,412	27.8	503,088	27.6
Labour	200,130	10.8	188,132	10.6	207,518	11.4
Progressive Democrats	73,628	4.0	–		69,056	3.8
Green Party	71,470	3.9	76,917	4.3	71,646	3.9
Sinn Féin	121,020	6.5	197,715	11.1	146,027	8.0
Independents	176,305	9.5	270,518	15.2	218,599	12.0
Total poll	1,878,609	62.6	1,841,335	58.6	1,856,570	58.6

Sources: Geary Institute/NIRSA

Fine Gael's support patterns are remarkably similar to those of Fianna Fáil, in that the party has tended to do best in the more rural and western constituencies in recent elections. While class influences on party support are hard to detect, there is some association historically with the proportion of large farmers in rural constituencies and middle-class people in urban constituencies. Fine Gael emerged as the party of the middle class in the early 1980s, but the emergence of the Progressive Democrats in the mid-1980s was to erode this support base and leave it more reliant on its rural support base as the party's fortunes in Dublin went into a marked decline. In what amounted to an 'electoral meltdown' in 2002, Fine Gael's support levels declined by 5.5 per cent nationally, and by 7.9 per cent in Dublin, leaving it with just 31 seats nationally (down from 54) and three seats in Dublin (losing three-quarters of its seats). However, the party's support levels improved significantly in the 2004 local elections.

Support for Labour has traditionally been concentrated to the south and east of a line drawn between Dundalk and Limerick, with a strong historical association with geographical concentrations of farm labourers in the large arable farming areas of southern and eastern Ireland. Familial dynasties have allowed these traditional rural support patterns to continue; for instance, the Spring family held the Kerry North seat for Labour for nearly six decades up to the loss of the seat to Sinn Féin in 2002. Indeed, rather than being class-based. much of the party's support has been 'dependent on the personal following of a diverse group of Labour incumbents' (Sinnott, 1995, pp. 137–8). Rural seats are often lost in cases where a Labour incumbent retires, or dies, and no family member emerges to take their place, as evident in the dramatic evaporation of Labour support in the west Cork constituencies in the 1980s and Laois-Offaly in 2002. Prior to the 1990s, Labour's strongest regions tended to be Munster and provincial Leinster, with party support in Dublin fluctuating dramatically, but in recent years party support in Dublin has increased relative to the other regions, especially after its amalgamation with Democratic Left in 1999. In the 2004 local elections Labour emerged as the strongest party in Dublin in terms of council seats, and as a 'catch-all' party within the region (winning relatively similar levels of support in both middle- and working-class areas).

Presently, the support level of the three small parties – the Green Party, Sinn Féin and the Progressive Democrats – stands around the 5 per cent level. The Progressive Democrats were founded in the mid-1980s and drew middle-class support away from Fianna Fáil and especially Fine Gael in subsequent elections. Party support tends to be highest in middle-class areas of Dublin and the founding members' personal bailiwicks (Limerick East and Galway West). The recruitment of high-profile candidates resulted in significant gains in Laois-Offaly and Longford-Roscommon in 2002, but these gains were not sustained in the 2004 local elections when the party did poorly in the Midland region with the exception of the eastern part of the Laois-Offaly constituency. Sinn Féin support similarly has a significant class dimension; but its supporters tend to be young, male, of a leftist ideological orientation, and concerned with Northern Ireland issues (Marsh and Mitchell, 1999). Its main areas of support are the Border region, and local authority housing areas in Dublin and other major urban centres, with north Kerry forming a significant outlier (Kavanagh, 2004, p. 78). The party made significant gains in recent elections. It won more than 15 per cent of the vote in five general election constituencies in 2002 and more than 25 per cent in five local election constituencies in 2004 in Monaghan, Carrickmacross and Clones (County Monaghan), and Finglas and Artane (Dublin City). While classed as a party of the left, the Green Party (Comhaontas Glas) consistently wins its highest levels of support from the urban, middle-class, electorate in Dublin (and, to a lesser extent, Cork and Galway). Weak support levels are found outside of the cities and the Greater Dublin area, particularly in the more rural areas, with the exception of some pockets of support in Ennis and parts of the Carlow-Kilkenny constituency. This trend was reflected in a 2002 RTE/Lansdowne exit poll, which estimated that 6.2 per cent of urban, 2.2 per cent of rural, 6.6 per cent of middle-class and 2.9 per cent of working-class voters supported the party (Gallagher et al., 2003, p. 131). The 2002 election brought unprecedented success for the party, however, as it won six seats, five of these in Dublin. This predominant focus on Dublin and its commuting hinterland was also reflected in the 2004 local elections.

The relative strength of smaller parties, as well as independent candidates, has fluctuated throughout the history of the State, with the larger parties being particularly dominant in certain periods. At present, the Dáil strength of the smaller parties and independent candidates is relatively high and this in turn is reflected in a greater propensity for coalition governments in recent decades. Single-party governments, generally involving Fianna Fáil, dominated the State for much of the period up to the late 1980s, but since 1982 coalition government has been the norm. Some have argued that this trend towards coalition government has led to a blurring of ideological differences between parties, which in turn has further acted to demobilise the Irish electorate. On the other hand, given Fianna Fáil and Fine Gael's catch-all nature and lack of a defined ideological focus, it has been argued that the junior parties in coalitions are now the ones setting the government agenda, meaning that the main policy differences in future elections may be fought out between the smaller, and more ideologically driven, political parties; the main battle may not be over who the main government party is, but who their coalition partners will be.

GEOGRAPHY OF VOTER TURN-OUT IN IRELAND

Voter turn-out is the percentage of people who turn out to vote in a given election. Ireland has one of the lowest turn-out rates for general elections in Western Europe (International IDEA, 1999) and, as with other Western democracies, turn-out levels have consistently declined over the past 25 years. Within Ireland, significant spatial variations in turn-out levels are noted, and each different type of election has its own specific geographies of turn-out. Turn-out levels tend to be higher in rural areas for general and local elections, whereas referendum turn-outs in Dublin, particularly in middle-class areas, tend to be higher than the national average (with the lowest referendum turn-outs found in County Donegal). Turn-outs may also vary considerably within individual constituencies, especially in urban constituencies for general elections and referenda, due to the greater degree of social stratification and potential for class-related turn-out variations, and in rural areas for local elections, in which candidate factors can lead to sharper differences in turn-out levels.

Lijphart (1997) views low and declining turn-outs as a concern because they weaken the legitimacy of democratic systems and will often entail class, demographic or ethnic biases that leave poorer and younger people, and ethnic minorities, significantly under-represented. Demographic factors are found to significantly influence turn-out levels, with young people the most likely to be non-voters, particularly in Ireland with its especially low turn-out rates for first-time voters in the 18–29 age category (International IDEA, 1999). Other factors, relating to demography and household structures, have an influence also, such as marital status (Crewe et al., 1992) and length of residence in a community (Caldeira et al., 1990). Turn-out levels are also shaped by socio-economic status, with lower turn-out levels observed for the unemployed and financially troubled (Rosenstone, 1982) and the educationally disadvantaged (Wolfinger and Rosenstone, 1980; Powell, 1986). Marsh (1991) found a relationship between party systems and the degree of influence class factors have on turn-out, with these particularly significant in states, such as the USA and Ireland, whose party systems are not particularly class-based. Housing tenure is found to have a bearing on turn-out propensity (Johnston et al., 2001), with home owners more likely to vote than people living in council (and also private) rented housing. In Ireland, class-related factors strongly influence turn-out levels within Dublin and other large urban areas (especially for referendum elections), but have less influence in rural areas (Kavanagh, 2002b).

Political mobilisation has a strong bearing on turn-outs, with high levels usually found in areas where political parties make strong efforts to get the vote out (Rallings and Thrasher, 1990); and the presence of local candidates in an election will also increase turn-out levels in their home areas, especially in local elections. Mobilisation efforts by Sinn Féin, and other small left-wing parties, have helped to improve turn-out levels in a number of deprived urban areas in recent elections, as evidenced in exceptional turn-out increases in 2004 in areas such as North Clondalkin, Cherry Orchard and Mulhuddart, where the numbers of voters doubled, or even trebled, relative to the 1999 levels. Candidate factors have significant influence on turn-outs, especially in local elections and especially in rural areas where voters are likely to personally know the candidates. Other factors that may influence turn-out levels include the distance to polling stations, the day of the week on which elections are held, the length of polling hours, and weather conditions on polling day. A more significant cause of concern, receiving considerable media focus recently, relates to the quality of the electoral register, with current numbers on the register believed to be considerably higher than the valid adult population, even though many thousands of people are not even on the register. Turn-out rates are expressed as a percentage of registered electors in Ireland, so over-estimated electoral registers will mean that recorded turn-out rates are significantly lower than the real level. The accuracy of the register also varies between different areas. It is significantly over-estimated in most rural and western parts areas (being over-estimated by over 13 per cent in Cavan-Monaghan and Sligo-Leitrim in 2002) and significantly under-estimated in urban and commuter-belt areas (roughly two-thirds (67 per cent) of the valid adult population in the Dublin Inner City were on the electoral register in 2002).

2002 General Election

Turn-out levels in Ireland tend to be highest for general elections, with significant turn-out variations occurring between different areas in these elections. The availability of marked register turn-out data for recent general and local elections allows for the accurate calculation of turn-out figures for smaller areas (electoral divisions, and individual townlands, housing estates, apartment blocks and streets) than used in previous studies. Marked-register analyses of turn-out levels were first carried out for a limited number of areas for the 1999 local elections (Kavanagh, 2002a and 2002b), but subsequently data were produced at the electoral division level for all of the Republic of Ireland for the 2002 general election and 2004 local, European and Citizenship Referendum elections, as part of a joint project involving the Geary Institute (UCD) and National Institute for Regional and Spatial Analysis (NUI Maynooth). The turn-out map, based on these data, produced for the 2002 general election, points to significant urban–rural variations, with low turn-out areas particularly clustered around the Dublin commuter belt and the other large cities and towns. High turn-out areas are found in rural and western areas, including the North West, Border and Southwest regions, as well as the Clew Bay areas and parts of the south Midland region (Kavanagh, Mills and Sinnott (2004) offers a more detailed discussion of these patterns).

Turn-out in 'Second-order' Elections

Significant differences are usually noted between voting behaviour in 'first-order', or general, elections and 'second-order' elections, including local, European, referenda and by-elections. Support levels for government parties generally tend to be lower in second-order elections, and turn-out levels also tend to be lower as voters feel there is less at stake in these. Horiuchi's (2005) 'turn-out twist' concept however points to situations where turn-outs are higher in lower-level elections, due to particular social and cultural contexts and the relative importance of individual votes in local elections where smaller quotas are needed to secure election, as would especially be the case in rural parts of Ireland.

Each election type has its own specific geography of turn-out. Rallings and Thrasher (1990) find that important local issues, political party campaigning, strong local identities and an influential local media will have an influence that is specific to local elections. Studying the 2004 local elections, significant turn-out variations were observed between high-turn-out rural and low-turn-out urban areas, although urban–rural differences were not as defined as in the previous contest in 1999, due to turn-out increases in the urban areas (Kavanagh, 2004). The electoral division turn-out map (see Figure 13.1) shows particularly high turn-out levels in much of Leitrim and parts of Sligo, Clare, west Donegal, west Cavan, south Monaghan, south Roscommon, north Longford, and southeast Kerry, as well as the Clew Bay and Slieve Bloom areas. The geographical extent of the low turn-out areas, encompassing the larger urban centres and the commuting hinterlands, increases significantly relative to the pattern observed for the general election. Significant clusters of low turnout are associated with the commuting hinterlands of Dublin (now extended into the east Midland region), Cork, Galway, Limerick and Waterford, while the low turn-out associated with the extension of the Derry commuter belt into eastern Donegal is readily apparent. Low turn-out levels are also associated with some provincial towns, such as Castlebar, Letterkenny, Ennis, Carlow and Newcastlewest, although candidate effects mitigate the potential for low turn-out in other towns, such as Killarney and Mountmellick. Quite significant turn-out variations also exist within counties, with such variations again largely a function of candidate effects.

Significant differences existed between turn-outs in the 1997 general election and 1999 local elections at the national level (15 per cent) and especially in Dublin (25 per cent). However a comparison between the most recent contests shows only a 4 per cent difference at the national level (Table 13.1) and 4.4 per cent difference in Dublin. In some parts of the State, local election turn-outs in 2004 were higher than those for the preceding general election, as envisaged in the turn-out twist concept. There was a particular cluster of these areas in the Northwest region, encompassing Leitrim, western Donegal and parts of Sligo and west Cavan. Higher local election turn-outs were also found in western Clare, the area surrounding the county boundary between Tipperary South and Waterford, as well as the Beara peninsula and other parts of southern and western Kerry. Higher turn-outs were also found in a number of working-class urban areas, particularly within Dublin, including North Clondalkin, Cherry Orchard, Ballyfermot, Mulhuddart, Ballymun and Darndale. Areas with higher local election turn-outs tended to be the home bases of local election candidates, or else areas that felt ignored by national government and politics and placed greater reliance on local political figures to address their concerns. Areas with substantially higher general election turn-outs (difference of greater than 10 per cent) were particularly clustered around the outer edges of the larger cities'

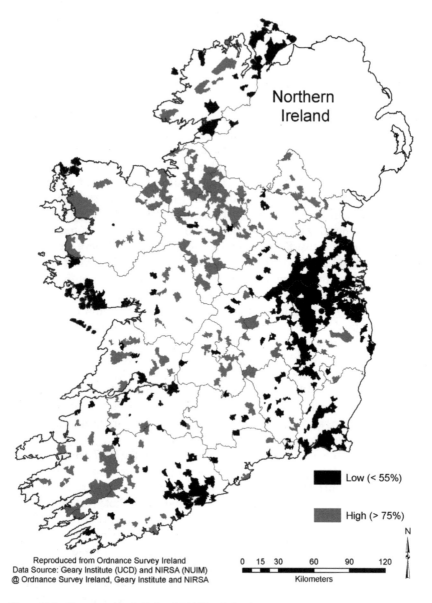

Northern
Ireland

Low (< 55%)

High (> 75%)

N

Reproduced from Ordnance Survey Ireland
Data Source: Geary Institute (UCD) and NIRSA (NUIM)
@ Ordnance Survey Ireland, Geary Institute and NIRSA

0   15 30   60   90   120

Kilometers

Figure 13.1   Voter turn-out in Ireland, 2004 local elections

Sources: Geary Institute/NIRSA; Ordnance Survey Ireland

commuter belts, suggesting that the further extension of these commuter zones
is, in turn, leading to a further extension of low turn-out areas. Alternatively,
this phenomenon might be election-specific, with local election turn-outs lower
than expected because commuter populations are less interested in contests that
mainly focus on local political figures and issues concerning which they have
little awareness or interest.

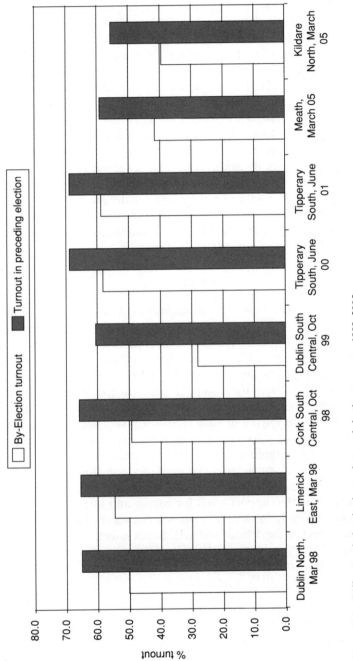

Figure 13.2 Differences in by-election and general election turn-outs, 1998–2005

Sources: Geary Institute/NIRSA; Ordnance Survey Ireland

Referendum turn-outs also generally conform to the second-order election model, and tend to be lower than those for general elections, being considerably lower in rural and western areas. Referendum–general election turn-out differences are smaller in the more urban (and middle-class) areas. In 2002, the difference in turn-outs between the general election and the second referendum on the Nice Treaty was just 6.1 per cent in Dublin and 2.5 per cent in the largely middle-class Dun Laoghaire constituency, whereas it was 17.1 per cent in the rest of the State and as high as 24.1 per cent in County Donegal. Middle-class urban electorates tend to be more interested in complex, issue-driven referendum elections than in the personality-driven local 'clientistic' issues associated with general, and especially local, elections. Rural and working-class electorates, by contrast, show greater interest in 'bread and butter' local issues and supporting local political candidates. By-election turn-outs are generally significantly lower than those for general elections, but especially when these are held in urban areas. Gallagher (1996) found an average turn-out decline of 7.0 per cent in the by-elections held over the 1921–95 period, with an especially marked decline in Dublin (16.4 per cent), and these trends have continued for by-elections held over the subsequent decade, as Figure 13.2 shows.

CONCLUSION

The Irish political landscape is a continuously evolving one, being at present defined by a propensity towards coalition governments, increased levels of support for independent candidates and smaller parties, and declining electoral participation levels, but such trends may change in time. This chapter has also shown that geographical variations exist in terms of the behaviour of Irish voters, and how this shapes the Irish political landscape; these variations may, in part, be influenced by a considerable array of socio-political structural factors. However, the impact of such factors will vary according to different geographical contexts; place matters, and a 'variety of influences emanating from a range of geographical scales' act to shape Irish electoral behaviour (Agnew, 1996, p. 130), while taking account of the 'historical specificity and uniqueness of places' (Agnew, 1987, p. 42). Socio-economic and demographic factors may shape the support levels for parties and turn-out propensity to some degree, especially in more urban areas, but more place-specific factors, such as the impact of the 'friends and neighbours' effect, also need to be taken into account. To fully understand what shapes the voting behaviour of the Irish electorate, analyses need to be geographical and rooted in local places.

14

Transformations in Governance

Joe Larragy and Brendan Bartley

In Ireland, as elsewhere in the developed world, there is a growing trend in the political sphere for traditional *government* arrangements to be supplemented by *governance* practices. Governance incorporates and extends beyond the conventional and formal institutional structures of authority and decision making associated with government – such as general elections, political parties, policy making and referenda – to focus on a wider range of institutions and actors working together on a formal and informal basis to control society and space. Governance is thus broader in scope than government and heralds a shift from centralised and bureaucratic forms of decision making to flexible and facilitative forms of collaboration (or partnership) between government and wider networks of interests across the business and community sectors on diverse spatial scales. The increased role of 'partnership' in various guises is advanced as evidence of the new form of networked governance in Ireland.

The move to governance is usually presented as taking place in two distinct contexts. First, it is an 'upward' response to emerging pressures associated with globalisation or international competition. Second, it is a 'downward' response to demands for more democracy as public agencies are confronted with new challenges to deliver more efficient services as well as improved citizen and community participation in decision-making processes. In this context, global changes are viewed as a fundamental impetus for policy and agenda change at local level. Globalisation is associated with an increasingly open arena of competition between places, which creates pressures for national governments together with their subnational constituents and partners to adopt new practices that improve their competitiveness on the global stage. As new forms of place identity emerge in response to intensifying globalisation, so new 'results-oriented' political/administrative arrangements, including single purpose agencies (QUANGOs[1]) and multi-sector partnerships, materialise as adaptive responses to competitiveness.

It has been argued that the emergence of complex modes of multilevel governance in Ireland represents an adaptive response to the challenges associated with globalisation (McGuirk, 2000; Parkinson et al., 2004; Punch et al., 2004). These commentators argue that politics has become more localised and more 'entrepreneurial' as traditional policy fields and governance have become more fluid and 'flexible'. Since the late 1980s, Ireland has become a veritable laboratory for experimentation with new governance arrangements both within and beyond government systems. In pursuit of competitive, place-based, economic development, a greater emphasis is placed on the importance of integrating increasingly complex and diffuse fields of policy without compromising competitiveness. The sphere of political action has expanded beyond the realm of traditional government politics and bureaucracy to encompass a broader range of stakeholders or interest groups. New bargaining systems and new forms of collaboration in which the role of the main stakeholders (state, market and community sector representatives) has been redefined have accompanied this trend. In particular, the traditional role and functions of the state sector have been reoriented away from bureaucratic structures and inertia towards a new managerial ethos that embraces more pro-active, market-responsive and user-oriented forms of governance.

TRANSFORMATIONS IN NATIONAL LEVEL GOVERNANCE

Coalition Governments and Social Partnership

For good reason, 1987 is considered a watershed in the evolution of governance in Ireland, as it was to mark the beginning of a new era of 'social partnership' that has continued uninterrupted since then. How a country with a predominantly liberal welfare regime succeeded in equipping itself with governance institutions more akin to continental or Scandinavian models, particularly with a close neighbour as influential historically as Britain, has prompted some comment. The context for this innovation in Irish governance might well have led to alternative political choices along the lines of the UK for example, where a decisive political departure took effect under the Conservatives from 1979. There were certainly numerous indigenous exponents of 'Thatcherism' who regarded the experience of centralised collective bargaining in the 1970s as nothing short of disastrous for economic progress, and most Irish economists viewed the prospect of such a turn with outright hostility. After all, inflation had been declining from 1983 onwards while free collective bargaining saw wages lag behind. A new party, the Progressive Democrats, gave political expression to the neo-liberal current from 1985.

Why therefore re-embark on another experiment in centralised bargaining with potentially inflationary consequences? A degree of paralysis had seized representative government from the late 1970s. Three elections had taken place in the space of 18 months in the early 1980s before a longer-duration coalition government of Fine Gael and Labour Party. This administration was faced with extraordinarily difficult challenges. Total exchequer debt doubled between 1981 and 1985 from £10.2bn (94 per cent of GNP) to £20.4bn (134 per cent of GNP) (NESC 1986, p. 303). The 1986 census saw an outflow of 75,000 people since 1981, and unemployment rose monthly despite emigration. The coalition fell apart in 1987 over attempts to implement cutbacks in public spending to curb government debt.

While in opposition during this period, 'realpolitik' informed the approach of the once-dominant, populist, nationalist Fianna Fáil party. Nonetheless, even by campaigning on the basis of rhetorical condemnation of cut-backs in health and social services, and avoiding the more difficult questions about the public finances, Fianna Fáil could only muster 81 out of 166 parliamentary seats to form a minority government in the 1987 general election. With a weak mandate and faced with a compelling case for severe fiscal correction, Fianna Fáil was under pressure to accept a post-election offer of conditional support from Fine Gael should it agree to implement the fiscal correction policies to which Fine Gael was committed.

Fianna Fáil's dilemma was how to implement such harsh public spending measures without incurring a high price in electoral support. Their solution was social partnership. An improved industrial relations atmosphere would fend off the threats of active social opposition to harsh spending cuts. And by securing the support of the trade unions, employers and farmers for a period, through a managed incomes policy, a drubbing in the next election would be averted. The Fianna Fáil leadership secured a package called the Programme for National Recovery (PNR) which was to stabilise industrial relations for a period of three years to 1990 by agreeing the terms of pay growth and offering the promise of improvements when circumstances improved.

A New Model of Centralised Negotiation

However, though extremely timely from a political perspective, the agreement was not hastily drafted. On the contrary, it was underpinned by a strategy that had been painstakingly worked out over the previous year at the National Economic and Social Council. NESC was a long-standing advisory body with an independent secretariat comprising some of the most seasoned and senior figures in the employer and trade union organisations together with farmer interests and senior civil servants. Its research focus at that time involved a sophisticated analysis of the economic predicament and fiscal crisis gripping the state. In addition, a separate series of meetings of the 'social partners' had been convened under the chairmanship of the Secretary to the Department of the Taoiseach (Prime Minister) to address the need for a unified response to the apparently intractable difficulties facing the Irish economy and society. These developments combined to provide solid foundations for a collective response centred on the NESC (1986) report *A Strategy for Development*, which was accepted as the basis for partnership agreement.

This preparatory work led to a fundamental difference between the traditional centralised wage deals of the 1970s and the new round initiated in 1987. The perspectives of employers and unions in the 1970s were far apart and mutual trust was very limited. The deals of the 1970s lasted merely 12 to 18 months at most, and were reached separately though the Employer–Labour Conference without much reference to government policy, and therefore without any attempt to achieve a coherent strategy to co-ordinate wage, tax and spending policies. Moreover, when faced with recession in the aftermath of the oil crisis of the early 1970s, governments relied on policy solutions designed to reflate the economy by stimulating spending and other demand-side measures. However, these responses only exacerbated the problem and contributed to a combination of recession and inflation, dubbed stagflation.

By 1986, therefore, much had changed. A considerable shake-out in industry pointed to the structural nature of unemployment and the need for supply-side (control) measures. The shake-out also left trade unions with reduced membership rolls at a time when multinational employers who opposed trade union representation were on the increase. Sectional bargaining in the early 1980s yielded no real wage growth and unemployment soared. Looking across the Irish Sea, Irish trade unions could see the fate of their British counterparts in the coal and other heavy industries. While the Irish unions were not very sympathetic to cut-backs they were, nevertheless, ready for a strategic alternative to industrial conflict in which the odds were stacked against them, and adopted a longer-term view of the then current crisis.

The new agreement was extremely resilient and benefited from an economic expansion in the last years of the decade. Indeed, what began in 1987 amid crisis and scepticism as an experiment in governance – involving real participation of the 'social partners' at central level – has proved to be enduring. In all, since 1987, there have been seven such agreements, each one of approximately three years' duration (see Table 14.1). The key to the success of this process is that every agreement was preceded by a period of deliberation involving the social partners and government. The talks were aimed not only at achieving agreement on pay terms but also on the key policy priorities for economic and, to a lesser extent, social policy in the medium term. There is some debate as to whether this process was purely a bargaining one. O'Leary (2002) has suggested that wage bargaining and tax reform could have achieved similar outcomes without social partnership and, moreover, that social partnership should not reach beyond this ambition. Others, however, particularly those directly involved in the process, view it very differently (National Economic and Social Forum, 1997; O'Donnell; 1998; O'Donnell and Thomas, 1998; O'Donnell and Riordan, 2000). The latter have underlined the role of social partnership in institution-alising negotiated governance – something that should be viewed as an aspect of polity as much as of the economy. This view is underpinned by a number of distinctive features, in particular role of the Department of the Taoiseach and the influence of the European Union.

The Department of the Taoiseach plays a central role in the partnership process, which gives the latter considerable flexibility. The Department chairs both the preparatory phase of deliberation at the NESC and the negotiations on wages and tax reform. It can, where necessary, broker agreement between the various social partners, between government departments (for example between Finance and Social and Family Affairs), and between government and social partners. This multirole brokerage dimension deepens the 'problem-solving' capacity of the process as a whole. The Department also plays a critical role in aligning the social partners in relation to non-wage developments, including those at the European level. In particular, the obligation to satisfy the EU criteria for Economic Monetary Union (EMU) entailed a set of rigorous membership tests for the Irish economy throughout the 1990s. While many economists were sceptical of the prospect of monetary union, Irish membership was secured and a major contribution to that success was attributed to the social partners who were committed to meeting the membership tests through their involvement in the NESC process of 'governance'.

The EU also played a directly supportive role through the allocation of structural funds under the Delors packages, supporting public capital formation in the late 1980s and funding measures to address unemployment. Again, the Department of the Taoiseach – having a 'generalist' mediating and promotional role – was gradually able to convert this into capacity building and grassroots support for social partnership at local area level. For example, in the NESC Strategy and Programme for Economic and Social Progress (Government of Ireland, 1991), a radically new idea was put into effect at local level. This was the establishment of Local Area Partnership bodies (see below) which funnelled European funding directly to targeted local areas experiencing severe long-term unemployment problems.

Expanding the Remit of Social Partnership and Widening Participation

The partnership process has displayed a flexibility and innovative exploration that were hardly anticipated in 1987. For example, when the first agreements were ratified, the emphasis was on moderation of wage growth and fiscal correction. However, under the PESP, a local level initiative on long-term unemployment was steered by central government (represented by the Department of the Taoiseach) via social partnership without any direct involvement of local government. A further development was the extension of access to the key institutions of social partnership to a variety of community and voluntary sector organisations. Collectively these are known as the Community and Voluntary Pillar.

The spending cut-backs initiated in 1987 had serious repercussions for vulnerable and marginalised groups such as the unemployed, people with disabilities, and people relying on public health care and social services, especially older people. There were cuts in home help services and hospital beds, resulting in great hardship in the form of lengthening waiting lists for elective surgery and in a rapid growth in the use of private nursing home care. In addition, while some achievements were made for those in employment, the numbers unemployed in the early 1990s increased again after a slight stabilisation. As a result, organisations of the unemployed, bodies representing local communities and religious organisations were concerned that a substantial section of society was living in conditions of poverty and deprivation. A report of the Commission on Social Welfare (CSW, 1986) recommended the introduction of minimum income thresholds to secure a baseline level of living conditions for all. However, while existing levels were clearly inadequate, the dictates of fiscal correction nonetheless took precedence over such improvements. Over the course of the early 1990s these organisations gained considerable prominence by highlighting the fact that the substantial share of the social cost of economic policies of the late 1980s had fallen on those least equipped to bear it (Allen, 2000). Some sections lobbied for the CSW-recommended minimum social welfare rates to be imposed. Others, particularly those representing the unemployed, focused on the urgency of addressing the unemployment crisis through direct intervention using imaginative new initiatives. Additional community sector groups paid particular attention to the role of EU structural funds and their potential role in generating local empowerment and wealth creation. The EU was keen to have local involvement in the utilisation of such aid.

In the early 1990s the community and voluntary sector called for, and won over, parts of the political elite to the idea of a special national forum to bring all stakeholders together to address the major questions of unemployment and social provision. The National Economic and Social Forum (NESF) was established in late 1993 and included a wide range of interests – elected political representatives, government officials, existing social partners and the community and voluntary sector. The NESF proved to be the ante-room through which the community and voluntary sector eventually gained places in the partnership process in 1996. Some NESF members were appointed to the NESC and participated in the deliberative process that preceded the new three-year agreement – Partnership 2000 – signed in December 1996. The content of that agreement reflects in some measure the influence of the community and voluntary sector. It included an envelope of social spending and a promise to implement the minimum social welfare rates recommended by the CSW within three years. It also endorsed the commitment to local area-based partnership, expanded the Community Employment (CE) scheme and other active labour market measures, and proposed a local employment service and a working group on the social economy.

The Community and Voluntary Pillar continued to participate in subsequent social partnerships and signed up to the following agreement – The Programme for Prosperity and Fairness – in 1999. However, it was divided over the terms of the 2002 agreement, Sustaining Progress, when one section of the Pillar (Community Platform) was opposed to the focus and terms of the agreement and was subsequently excluded from participation. New elements were later admitted to the process alongside the remaining original Community Pillar organisations. These developments point to the asymmetries of power in the partnership process and the terms that may be imposed on weaker parties as the price of having a seat at deliberations or negotiations. However, in spite of inevitable new pressures from a rapidly growing economy, the social partnership model has proved robust enough to retain trade union and employer support and the support of much of the community and voluntary sector.

NEW APPROACHES TO CIVIC INVOLVEMENT IN LOCAL DEVELOPMENT

A state of flux currently prevails in relation to provision for civic involvement in local development. As noted above and elsewhere in this volume, local authorities in Ireland have had an exclusive – if narrowly defined – mandate for local planning and, by extension, local development within their jurisdiction. They have also operated subject to a centralised system under the Department of the Environment, Heritage and Local Government that accords them a very limited range of powers and functions compared to their counterparts in Europe (Callanan, 2003a). The possibility of a new relationship between central and local government has emerged, however, in parallel with efforts to address neglected local development problems and to introduce new reforms designed to institute management practices in public service provision that are more business-like, competitive, responsive and open to civic involvement. A key dimension of interest here was the adoption of a local partnership company model rather than operating through the channels of the elected local authorities.

Since the early 1990s, Ireland has witnessed considerable experimentation with new participatory arrangements in the field of local development policy (Sabel, 1996; Parkinson, 1998). The earliest of the new partnerships were the LEADER companies in rural areas, which were followed in 1991 by the first of twelve Area-Based Partnership companies in designated disadvantaged areas. From 1994 the number of partnerships was expanded to 38, and these continue to operate in designated disadvantaged areas. By the end of the 1990s approximately two-thirds of the country's population fell within a partnership area. They received structural funds under the Community Support Framework (1989–93) and the Operational Programme for Local Urban and Rural Development (1994–99). These partnerships are companies limited by guarantee with representation on their boards from the local community/ voluntary sector, local State agencies, local representatives of the traditional social partners (unions, farmers, business) and local elected representatives. Originally created under the direction of the Department of the Taoiseach, more recently they have been placed under the leadership of the Department of Community, Rural Affairs and Gaeltacht. These quasi-targeted bodies were soon followed by 35 County/City Enterprise Boards (CEBs) in 1993, which are structured on a county or city basis corresponding more closely to the traditional local authority divisions. CEBs promote small enterprise in respective counties through grant aid, mentoring, training and management development. CEBs aimed to complement the activities of Enterprise Ireland at national level (O'Sullivan, 2003; Keogan, 2003).

Civic participation in local partnership structures was, therefore, endorsed as a significant element of the planning and implementation of local initiatives. The value of the new localism with its dual emphasis on local co-ordination of service provision and local socio-economic development was acknowledged (Walsh, 1999). In addition, the new local partnerships were also viewed as an extension of the national partnership model, which was perceived to have delivered successful economic prosperity and social stability to the country. Initially, local government representation was expressly excluded from these partnerships, thereby establishing tensions around questions of democratic accountability between the two separate systems of local development (Walsh, 1998). Advocates of the local government system argued that the democratic mandate accorded to local authorities by the electoral process was undermined by their exclusion from the partnerships. They resented the new functions and funding opportunities afforded to the partnerships and argued that these should be assigned to democratically elected representatives. Those who welcomed the partnerships could acknowledge the inherent democracy of the local government system but could also point to its many failings, which included (1) the inability of local authorities to respond creatively to new challenges due to perceived inefficiency and corruption, and (2) their bureaucratic distance from citizens and associated failure to engage with or satisfy the demands of local communities (Meldon et al., 2004).

Thus, the need for change in local authority structures became evident in the 1990s as their role was challenged by the emergence of local area-based development partnerships whilst their various limitations rendered them incapable of responding to the new pressures that transcended their traditional functions. The separation between local government and local partnerships came under increasing criticism as the partnerships by-passed local government. This raised concerns about the anomalous prospect that local government could deteriorate irrevocably whilst the partnerships would thrive without proper accountability or adequate co-ordination. The response to these difficulties was to seek to regularise the status of, and linkages between, the local partnerships and local authorities (Meldon et al., 2004). The thrust to normalise the relationship was given added impetus by the anticipated reduction and withdrawal of future EU funds for partnership activities as the country prospered at the end of the millennium. This raised the prospect for central government of either standing down the partnership model or providing additional direct financing for the partnerships through the Irish exchequer along with the existing funding commitments to local government. Thus, after more than a decade of operating with the partnership model in parallel with the already established structures of local government, there is presently a concerted effort to integrate local government and local development.

NEW APPROACHES TO MANAGEMENT

As part of its attempts to regularise the two types of local development and in order to consolidate and enhance the country's competitive position in the global economy and Europe, central government in Ireland introduced new governance reforms in the second half of the 1990s. These reforms sought to make state and partnership agencies more efficient, accountable and entre-preneurial. New promotional policies and new forms of management that stressed value for money, competitive practices, efficiency and accountability were applied to local authorities and partnership companies. The attempts to become more business-like, accountable and entrepreneurial in Ireland drew heavily upon New Public Management ideas introduced through the Department of the Taoiseach and the Department of Environment, Heritage and Local Government. The term 'New Public Management' (NPM) is used as a shorthand across the world for a variety of innovations introduced to address the deficiencies of the old bureaucratic model of the public sector and to replace it with a dynamic organisational model (Osborne and Gaebler, 1992). A notable feature of the NPM as applied in Ireland is that it has been introduced on a 'top down' basis. Reform of central and local government administrative structures has involved re-regulation based on tighter integration and management rather than decentralisation of control to the subordinate units. The new regulatory modus operandi is exercised by linking funding allocation to evaluation of performance, where success is based on conformity with centrally determined strategic guidelines and associated principles of accountability and efficiency.

As part of this NPM process, the area-based development policies of both local government and local partnership companies were required to acknowledge and emulate the benefits of the national partnership process by bringing the two hitherto separate development systems together. The strategic capacity of both systems was to be enhanced and directed towards more focused, targeted approaches based on competitive allocation of resources for specific improvement goals. As part of the agenda for Better Local Government of 1996, local authorities were required to replace their traditional emphasis on regulating and controlling activities within their territories with a more pro-active, results-oriented and collaborative approach to development and delivery of services. They were also assigned greater financial and decision-making autonomy in return for reorganisation of traditional management and service delivery practices. The local government reforms led initially to the introduction of partnership-style Strategic Policy Committees (SPCs) in local authorities, which brought together elected councillors with community and other sectoral representatives. This was followed by the establishment in January 2000 of City/County Development Boards (CDBs), which were assigned the key lead role of further integrating and systematising the local government and local development at county level. CDBs were also allocated the strategic tasks of producing plans for the integrated social, economic, cultural and environmental development of their city/county area over a ten-year horizon. The creation of the CDB governance structure endorsed a revitalised role for local authorities but also provided a prescribed membership structure to include representation from (a) other state agencies, (b) the local development sector, and (c) the community and voluntary sector (Meldon et al., 2004).

Local partnerships and local government have shared an uneasy co-existence since the advent of the CDBs. Local authorities house the CDBs and provide the bulk of their staff whilst local partnership boards typically contain elected members of the local authority within which they reside. At present, local government has re-emerged as the dominant local player in relation to local development. However, to achieve this status it has had to reposition itself by engaging with, and itself adopting, the participative collaboration approach which was once a key distinguishing feature of its former rivals, the partnership agencies, in the local development process. Parkinson (1998) suggests that the innovations and flexibility of partnerships, as compared with traditional local government structures, have a positive energising impact upon local authorities as they adapt to localised and partnership approaches to governance. However, the re-emergence of local government as the hegemonic stakeholder in the new governance arrangement in Ireland cements the vertical controls of central government over local development because the country continues to be a highly centralised, dual (centre and local government) state.

Central government commenced a similar process of transition to flexible and entrepreneurial governance in 1996 through the Strategic Management Initiative (SMI) which was formalised in the report *Delivering Better Government* (Department of the Taoiseach, 1998). This was one of a series of government reports – including the *Better Local Government* report (DoELG, 1996) – that drew from the New Public Management thinking in North America to recommend similar new management initiatives in Irish government. A civil service-wide group of co-ordinating Secretaries under the leadership of the Department of the Taoiseach produced the report which drew upon their experiences of the New Zealand government's management approach in order to recommend similar changes to the Irish civil service. However, the New Zealand management approach was based on New Public Management thinking emanating from the USA in the late 1980s. Hence, whilst the Irish 'entrepreneurial' approach to economic policy draws directly on American investment to provide employment, American management ideas provide much of the thinking that informs its approach to 'managing' the new governance. It is interesting to note, however, that as the North American managerial approach was being introduced in Ireland, that approach came under increasing criticism in North America and New Zealand. It has been argued that in the long term it could undermine the cultural capital of employee 'loyalty' and 'trust', which underpins successful public and private sector organisations (Bartley and Treadwell-Shine, 1999a).

The impacts on the Irish economy of direct foreign investment from America and the indirect influences of the NPM practices was counter-balanced to some extent by the simultaneous employment in Ireland of EU-style social-economy policies. Irish social policies closely mirrored EU social policies throughout the 1980s and 1990s in part because of the need to satisfy EU requirements and enable the country to maximise the call-down of potential EU structural funds. Table 14.1 illustrates the similarity between the nomenclature of the national partnership programmes in Ireland and parallel EU economic and

Table 14.1   EU and Irish policy linkages

European Union: Economic and Social Policy	Ireland: National Partnership Programmes
Single European Act [SEA] (1987)	Programme for National Recovery (1987)
Maastricht Treaty [Economic Union] (1991)	Programme for Economic & Social Progress (1991)
White Paper – Growth, Competitiveness, Employment (1993)	Programme for Competitiveness & Work (1994)
Amsterdam Treaty [Social Union] (1997)	Partnership 2000 for Inclusion, Employment and Competitiveness (1996/7)
Lisbon Summit (2000)	Programme for Prosperity and Fairness (2000)
A New Partnership for Cohesion – Convergence, Competitiveness, Co-operation (2004)	Sustaining Progress Social Partnership (2003–05)

social policies. Many of the area-based partnership approaches and the targeted initiatives developed and deployed by local partnerships in pursuit of local economic and social development also drew on the EU legacy and funding. The EU social-economy policies stressed social inclusion, common welfare provision and local community participation through social partnerships. However, the flow of influence was not unidirectional as Irish social initiatives themselves contributed to the evolution of EU social strategy. The partnership process and local development in Ireland shaped the thinking of the European Commission, which drew from the lessons generated by the Irish experiences. For example, the 1998 Treaty of Amsterdam included provisions devised by Ireland in relation to social inclusion.

CONCLUSION

It is possible to argue that the move to flexible forms of governance entails the demise of traditional state government. The transformation could be said to reflect a collapse in confidence in the role of the traditional state sector and the introduction of compensatory efforts to replace inert bureaucratic structures by more pro-active, globally responsive and user-oriented forms of governance. However, there is little evidence for a full-scale transformation to decentralised governance in Ireland. While a common trend towards reallocation of responsibilities between different organisations, including a proliferation of partnerships, can be detected in Ireland, the new arrangements have not replaced governments and cannot be equated exclusively with governance. Entrenched lines of communication between established levels of government remain intact and it is probably more accurate to say that the additional provisions constitute an accretion to the prevailing arrangements. Even where local autonomy and partnership approaches are promoted by central government, this is typically offset by countervailing trends towards the centralisation of power as new forms of managerialism enable central government to tighten its control over subnational agencies. This is in line with broader research findings on governance, which suggests that the role of the sovereign state is merely changing, rather than being superseded, as part of the move to governance. Ireland is one of many states developing new capacities and structures to exert political and economic power across space either as a response to, or a promotion of, intensified place-based international competition. While the central state may lose some powers of intervention in particular spheres of socio-economic life, it compensates by expanding or reinforcing them in others. It may, therefore, be more accurate to characterise governance changes in Ireland as a change in the *mode* of state intervention rather than a withdrawal or weakening of government.

15
Green Ireland?
The Governance of Waste

G. Honor Fagan and Michael J. Murray

At the micro level, the problem of waste is self-evident. Households are producing more waste with higher levels of packaging and toxicity. If we do not dispose of the waste we confront the instant problem of waste as a pollutant within the household. One waste official, conscious of the ever increasing individual and household output of waste, remarked once how he longed to get 30 householders together to daily dump all their waste in a closed shed, over a one-month period.[1] He claimed that for educational purposes, if they had to come to that shed, to see and smell the amount generated, and live with that amount, and take responsibility for it, and the pollution generated therein, then they would become revolutionised on the issue of waste almost overnight. In fact the 'reality check' that the civil servant wished to impose already exists for those living beside landfill sites. And yet it is also a reality that individuals and households still must dispose of their waste, the amounts and costs of which are increasing in developed countries, including Ireland. However, the problem of waste as pollutant is not being fully confronted but is instead being transferred to the local and national landscape, as well as to impoverished communities in the global landscape.

This chapter addresses the principal parameters of the problem of waste, having regard to its social context with respect to Ireland and Europe. Waste is identified in terms of the social structures and practices within which it is produced; and it is argued that unless prevailing conceptions of productivity, profit and consumerism 'build in' the waste component, it will continue to be an obscure and avoidable issue for most stakeholders in the process. The chapter also considers the international dimensions of waste governance and explores some of the policy outcomes, national and international, of the production and disposal of waste in terms of the principle of sustainability. It concludes by looking at waste alternatives and points to a potential role for Ireland in the wider, evolving green revolution that could contribute to a progressive, post-consumerist phase of globalisation.

WASTE IN ITS SOCIAL CONTEXT

Waste is part of global networks that are material, technical, social and discursive, but in simple terms it can be defined as the remnants, from production and consumption, that are deemed unproductive. It is probably best conceptualised as a global fluid (Urry, 2000, p. 5), and as a substance that is usually kept out of sight, its invisibility a marker of the success of economic growth. Strategies to hide it are constantly deployed, such as burying it underground through landfill, dumping it on seabeds, 'land filling in the air' through incineration, or exporting it from the centre to the periphery of the world economy. At the national level, waste is directed from urban rich areas to rural or poorer urban areas and at the global level it is 'hidden' through transportation from the richer countries to the poorer countries. A recent study on globalisation and the environment argues for environmental flows as always/already global:

> [t]his is particularly true for flows related to the environment: greenhouse gases, ozone threatening gases and toxic wastes move from more developed to less developed countries; raw materials and commodities, produced at huge environmental costs flow from less developed to more developed countries. (Urry, 1999)

The patterns of waste flows are particularly uneven, with waste disproportionately produced in the richer countries where there are far higher rates of production and consumption per capita, and disproportionately dumped in poorer countries. US waste generation has grown from 2.7 pounds per person in 1960 to 3.3 pounds per person in 1980 and up to 4.4 pounds per person in 1993 (Krogman, 2005, p. 266). Over 1.8 billion tonnes of waste are generated each year in Europe, equivalent to 3.5 tonnes per person. This is mainly made up of waste coming from households and a wide range of other human activities including commercial services, manufacturing industry, agriculture, construction and demolition, mining and quarrying, and energy production. With such vast quantities of waste being produced, it is of vital importance to society and to sustainable development that it is managed in such a way that it does not cause any harm to either human health or to the environment. On the basis of available evidence, it is hard to contest the claim by poor Southern nations that it is the uncontrolled consumption trends of the wealthy nations in the North that lie at the heart of the devastating health and environmental problems of the South.

One thing that has changed radically in the past 20 years (along with the massive increases in quantity and quality of waste) is that the pollution caused by its 'disposal' has now been widely recognised – keeping waste out of sight at global or local level is no longer a convenient option. Initially, the concern about waste pollution was confined to manufacturing industry and governments concerned with promoting and regulating national economic development. However, in the 1980s the ecological debate shifted from the national to the global terrain. This debate focused on the 'limits to growth', the need for production to be 'sustainable' and the curtailment of consumption. As Robin Murray puts it:

As environmental concerns came to the fore in the 1990's, all roads led to waste. From centuries of obscurity the waste industry found itself at the hub of environmental argument. (Murray, 1999, p. 20)

Waste was centre-stage in its own right as a localised pollutant, but also as a regional and global pollutant because of its link to key environmental questions such as climate change and resource depletion.

The prioritisation of economic growth by governments has led to an array of structural conditions that support production for profit regardless of the lack of sustainability of such patterns of production and consumption. In market economy systems, economic development depends on growth in consumption to increase profits. This short-term approach of always seeking to 'improve on last year's profits' does not take into account the long-term and real environmental costs or the finite stocks of many resources. Arrangements that increase production and create economic growth tend to be supported and prioritised by governments because they yield significant public sector revenues as well as private wealth. A political economy analysis is deployed in this chapter. This approach focuses on the sustainability of the waste process and aims to: (1) identify those interests that are disproportionately served by, or benefit from, current arrangements; and (2) highlight the actions needed in the political and economic systems to achieve sustainable changes.

IRELAND'S WASTE IN EU CONTEXT

Waste Generation: Type and Sector

Many EU countries use different methods to calculate waste generation so that data are not always exactly comparable. However, taking this into account, comparisons produced by the European Environmental Agency (EEA) rank Ireland as the largest per capita generator of municipal waste in the EU (EEA, 2005). The Irish Environmental Protection Agency (EPA, 2002) estimated that at the individual (micro) level, each person in Ireland in the year 2000 'produced' practically double the European average of 1 kg of municipal waste per day; an average of 600 kg of waste a year. They also calculated the average generation of household waste per person to be 398 kg per capita in 2003, an increase of 2 per cent on the 2002 figure (EPA, 2003, p. 8).

Table 15.1 summarises the amounts and proportions of waste generated by different activity sectors in Ireland in 2004. It shows that agricultural waste, at 70 per cent of the total, constitutes the largest proportion of waste, although it is decreasing from previous years. Construction and demolition waste constitutes the next biggest proportion at 12 per cent of the total. The bulk of the 15 per cent increase in total generation of waste between 2001 and 2004 is attributed to the trebling of the waste produced in this category. Municipal waste always gets a disproportionate amount of media attention, but constitutes only 4 per cent of the waste produced. However, it is also fast increasing; having risen by 1 per cent between 2001 to 2002, it rose again by 10 per cent between 2002 to 2003 when, for the first time, municipal waste exceeded 3 million tonnes (EPA, 2003,

p. 6).[2] While municipal waste increased by 4 per cent in 2004, a new statistical calculation on the part of the EPA leaves the overall figure still at just over 3 million tonnes (EPA, 2004b, p. vii).

Table 15.1   Total waste generated, 2004

Waste category	Tonnes	%
Construction and demolition waste	11,167,599	13.1
Manufacturing waste	5,044,243	5.9
Mining and quarrying waste	4,044,511	4.7
Municipal waste	3,034,566	3.6
End-of-life vehicle & scrap metal	491,860	0.6
Hazardous waste	366,291	0.4
Contaminated soil	307,340	0.4
Energy, gas and water supply waste	284,647	0.3
Dredge spoils	238,565	0.3
Drinking water sludges	59,741	0.1
Urban wastewater sludges	42,298	0.1
Sub-regional non-agricultural waste	**25,081,660**	**29.4**
Agricultural waste (total)	60,175,025	70.6
Total	**85,256,685**	**100.0**

Source: Environmental Protection Agency (2004b)

Waste Disposal and Sustainability

In all European Union countries, the quantity of waste is continuously increasing; however, in Ireland there was an above average growth rate in its production due to the economic boom of the 'Celtic Tiger'. Between 1995 and 1998, waste flows in Ireland increased by a phenomenal 89 per cent. Most of this waste (91 per cent of municipal waste and 85 per cent of industrial waste in 2000) was 'disposed' of through landfill, which is clearly the most environmentally risky option (EPA, 2002, p. 9). With the implementation of recycling policies there has been a shift in the flow and since 2001 municipal waste landfill has decreased by 8.7 per cent (EPA, 2004b, p. vii). Regardless of the policies on how to deal with waste – such as whether to divert it from landfill, recycle it, or incinerate it – the overall trend of increased waste generation remains an unresolved issue and a key matter of concern that will require concerted effort over the years to come. Sustainability is about meeting the needs of the present without compromising the ability of future generations to meet their own needs, in economic, social and environmental terms. The reality is that we are far from achieving this objective in Ireland, or elsewhere in Europe.

The main organising principle of waste is that it is 'put out' (a colloquial but significant term for placing bins outside the household for collection), where it is dealt with at regional and national level (Fagan, 2003). The growing scientific evidence, along with the environmental arguments that waste has broken down the 'sustainable limits' of natural earth and that its risk factors are multiplying, has brought communities and governments into the management-of-waste equation. This raises crucial questions about who governs, regulates and strategises waste flows in Ireland. Political economy analysis suggests that the debris of consumerism and development is managed through governance networks and that these networks require critical exploration.

WASTE GOVERNANCE IN IRELAND

The Republic has been in the grip of what has been commonly referred to as a 'waste management crisis' (Fagan et al., 2001; Fagan 2004) in the late 1990s and the early 2000s. There are two aspects to this crisis. First, there is the problem of waste in itself, and second, the interlocked problem of its management. Policies developed to manage the problem of increasing waste levels propelled local and national government into political crisis, as the public strenuously opposed proposals for both waste disposal facilities and increased costs.

Waste may be a global flow and therefore a global issue, but it is also clearly a local issue. Latour has referred to the notion of the hybridity of the global and the local. Dirlik expresses this as the concept of 'glocal': 'What it forces us to think about is a double process at work in shaping the world: the localisation of the global, and the globalisation of the local' (Dirlik, 1999, p. 158). That is to say, waste is at one and the same time global and local. It is created in someone's locality and dumped or burned in a locality, yet it also flows around globally. The political economy of waste can thus be seen as embedded in multiple and interlocking locales. When we look at waste production and its management, it is useful to think in terms of multiscalar processes, where rescaling of waste production in the era of 'glocalisation' has occurred and where its successful management relies on governance at multiple levels – global, regional, national and local (see Boyle, 2002). For this reason, the situation in Ireland has to be seen in wider context when examining its 'management practices'.

EU and National Actors

EU directives on waste have been the key driver of waste management policy in Ireland (Fagan et al., 2001). The European Economic Community (EC) Act of 1972 gave direct precedence to European Acts over domestic laws and constitutional provisions in the Republic and in Northern Ireland. The ratification of the Single European Act (1986), the Treaty of Maastricht (1992), and the Treaty of Amsterdam (1998) further ensured the supremacy of EU law over domestic law. The EU legislative programme for dealing with waste includes directives on dangerous substances, waste oils, groundwater, urban wastewater, licensing regulations, the disposal of polychlorinated biphenyls (PCBs) and polychlorinated triphenyls (PCTs), toxic waste, sewage sludge in agriculture, emissions from waste incineration plants, the disposal of animal waste, and batteries containing dangerous fluids. It also sets targets for reduction in all waste streams, and sets very specific timeframes for national governments to meet these reductions. For example, in Ireland there is a national target for recycling of 35 per cent (currently at 34 per cent) by 2013 and a household waste diversion from landfill target of 50 per cent (currently at 19 per cent) by 2013.

From Government to Governance: New Priorities

With the EU able to enforce sanctions on the nation state and the national government needing to radically change the direction and composition of waste flows, the drawing up and implementation of strategy quickly became an issue of governance at a national level. Stoker argues that governance recognises the 'blurring of boundaries and responsibilities for tackling social and economic issues' (1998, p. 21). Governance approaches patterned on consensual politics and multi-agency partnerships have replaced government by central decree over recent decades (see Chapter 13). This applies to the waste management issue, where self-governing networks were very much favoured by the Irish State. In order to reach the EU-set targets it was considered necessary to involve key players such as 'private enterprise' in partnerships. The capacity to 'get things done' did not simply rest on the power of government to command, and commands would only be invoked in a last-instance scenario.

Financial considerations were also a factor in the application and governance of the new EU criteria. In 2001 there was a need for an estimated investment of €1 billion, over a three- to five-year period, to implement the waste development plan (Forfás, 2001, p. vi) and the National Development Plan envisaged this coming mainly from the private sector. Clearly, Ireland faced a gruelling task to organise a strategy to divert waste away from landfill, to reach targets set at a fivefold increase in recycling and to find the finance for the infrastructure, especially if the objective was for the private sector to answer this call. Private capital was thus seen as a necessary 'node' in the governance of waste management (Fagan, 2004). In particular, the government's gaze focused on the private sector and on the waste industry's multinational giants, and sustainability concerns became secondary to costs. Waste governance, from this perspective, could not be resolved at its most radical level – that of sustainability. The plans relied heavily on the treatment of waste through 'thermal treatment plants' and on recycling to be funded primarily through private enterprise.

While governance necessitated a consultation process and the introduction of key players into the process, the unequal balance of power in the consultations and the fact that some partners were 'more equal than others' resulted in outright contestation of the plans. Environmentalists and local communities threatened by incineration plans in Ireland were deeply critical of what they perceived as the 'façade' of consultation that had been put in place (Fagan et al., 2001, p. 18). There was a widespread perception at the community level that government 'consultations' (often dictated by EU regulations) on the development of incinerators were simply empty rhetorical exercises for communities to 'let off steam' and were not designed to change decisions already taken on technical grounds (Fagan et al., 2001, p. 19).

Ignoring Resistance

Environmentalists and environmental scientists who contested waste management plans were worried about the growing influence of commercial interests, specifically waste companies coming into the Irish globalised waste market. The key concern from the environmentalists' point of view was the

role of 'big business' (i.e., incineration companies) in the implementation of
the plan. They argued that there had been aggressive attempts by incinerator
companies to lobby the government and to lead strategy (Fagan et al., 2001,
p. 17). This concurs with O'Brien's observations at a global level, where he
comments on waste industrialists:

> This is a market whose rational economic actors are begging, cajoling,
> threatening and coercing the states of Europe to intervene politically into
> the circulation of wastes precisely because the 'spontaneous' emergence of
> markets does not generate the values they want out of the rubbish heap.
> (O'Brien, 1999, p. 292)

Environmentalists' concerns about local authorities acquiring and mismanaging
landfill sites (i.e., the so-called 'planning' of 'dumping'), therefore, were
supplemented by concerns about private sector pressures to build incinerators.
They believed that in both cases the government was 'being wooed by, or was
wooing' large international companies and taking little responsibility for
negative impacts on localised communities (Fagan et al., 2001, pp. 16–17). Those
in opposition to the plans felt that they failed to contextualise waste in anything
other than a framework for industrial 'competitiveness' and profitability.

By-passing Resistance

Rising opposition to the proposed location of incineration plants drove the
waste management strategy into political crisis in 2000–01 as local communities,
through their locally elected representatives, blocked the subregional plans. In
order to by-pass the political blockage mechanism at local government level, the
Minister for the Environment and Local Government removed local councillors
from the decision-making process by assigning the decision-making powers to
the county managers who, as State employees, were obliged to implement State
policy and law. Thus, in response to challenge from 'below', a central decree
(government as opposed to governance) was used to achieve the localising or
embedding of waste management. However, the State did not move entirely back
to traditional government nor reject the principle of consensus politics and fail
to involve itself in multi-agency partnership. Instead, it removed the locality
from involvement in the decision-making process. The Minister stated quite
openly that the planning process on waste management was 'over-democratised'
and that he did not believe it was 'adding anything to it by having so many layers
involved' (*Irish Times*, 12 August 2002, p. 1). The so-called 'fast-tracking' for
waste management plans was to be implemented, and An Board Pleánala (The
Planning Appeals Board) becoming a 'one-stop shop' for assessing all plans
for new waste management facilities. The Minister insisted that he was not
removing from any groups or individual the rights to express their views: 'That
is sacrosanct, but I don't see a need for these views to be expressed at so many
different levels' (*Irish Times*, 12 August 2002, p. 1). In other words, a repeat of
oppositional views at multiple levels in a multilayered process of governance
was a source of irritation for government (Murray, 2003).

Complex Interactions: Discernible Outcomes

The account of the new initiatives and resistance outlined above illustrates the multifaceted and shifting dynamic of actors in the governance process, in which some gain more power and others lose it in a complex political process. That local communities were important players in the dynamic is without question, but there were ebbs and flows in their political power. Historically, the only social groups who had problems with waste were local communities living beside landfills. Alerting government to issues of pollution arising from industry had been an uphill struggle and local concerns received very limited acknowledgment from the state. It had taken the intervention of EU Directives in the 1980s to resolve conflicts between communities and local government authorities on 'waste disposal'. The fact that national government had not previously been responsive to local pollution was remembered well by communities when it came to the later disputes over waste plans (Fagan, 2004).

In terms of governance, the EU is a key player in that it regulates waste and sets the scene for its regulation at national level. However, EU policy emerges from a network of actors and competing agendas and is translated into national policy through a similar network. While we can clearly see the European agenda informed by sustainable environment concerns we can equally see the market-driven notions of development being played out when it comes to its implementation at national level. Waste legislation clearly takes cognisance of networked green politics, but at the implementation stage the contradiction between the concepts of development (market-driven in its capitalist form) and sustainability (the earth as limited resource) are in constant contention with each other.

EFFECTIVENESS OF POLICIES IN EUROPE AND IRELAND

The Failure of EU Policy

One way to measure the effectiveness of a policy is to compare its outcomes with its intended aims. On this basis, it is fair to say that the waste situation is deteriorating in the EU and that its policies for waste disposal are ineffective. The cornerstones of European policy on waste were established as hierarchically organised objectives:

- prevent waste in the first place;
- recycle waste;
- turn waste into a 'greenhouse-neutral' energy source;
- optimise the final disposal of waste, including its transport.

But despite these objectives and targets set by the EU, its Environmental Agency by the year 1999 presented a chaotic scenario unfolding:

The expected waste trends during the outlook period [up to 2005] suggest that existing policies, although providing some degree of success, will not be sufficient to stabilize waste arising, meet policy objectives, or progress towards sustainability. (EEA, 1999, p. 215)

Thus, EU waste policies were seen to be clearly failing by the end of 1999. Moreover, the environment action programmes were unable to stem the generation of waste and thus were failing to meet their foremost objective – the prevention of waste in the first place. The sheer material quantity of waste in circulation was extraordinary. The EEA statistics on the European Union for 1999 showed that 2,000 million tonnes of waste were being generated per year and that the amount had increased by 10 per cent per annum over the previous six years. It was estimated that *all* waste streams would continue to increase steadily (EEA, 1999, p. 215). Essentially waste generation was spiralling out of control. Waste disposal methods were not coping with the increased loads. Efforts to respond to the increases in waste could not keep pace with increased rates of production and consumption. Many countries had adopted increased recycling initiatives, but according to the Environmental Agency, this development 'has been only a partial success, because the total amount of waste paper and waste glass (container glass) generation has also increased in the same period' (EEA, 1999, p. 203). Landfilling, the least favoured option from an environmental perspective, remained the most common treatment for waste (EEA, 2005, p. 32).

In the light of the failure of previous policies a further phase of policy making began in the early 2000s. Most importantly, it was officially recognised that waste generation was strongly linked to economic activity, meaning that, if Europe's economy grew, so too would the waste problem. It was also established that there was a particularly close link between economic growth and waste from the construction industry (EEA, 2000). While the waste hierarchy was not removed as a general solution, further emphasis was placed on the first point, the prevention of waste and the sustainability principle of decoupling (breaking the link between) economic activity and waste production became the focus of further policy. Thus, the EU's sixth Environment Action Programme called for 'absolute decoupling', that is an overall reduction in the volumes of waste generated. Decoupling occurs if the growth rate of waste amounts is less than the growth rate of the economic driving force over a certain period of time. Relative decoupling occurs when waste amounts continue to grow, although at a slower rate than the underlying economic driver. Absolute decoupling is when environmental pressure is decreasing during a period of economic growth. (EEA, 2005, p. 27). Projections drawn up for the years 2000 to 2020 on the basis of current policy in place indicate that in the EU, most waste streams are expected to decouple relatively, but not significantly, from GDP by 2020 (EEA, 2005). None are expected to decouple absolutely and it appears that the further waste target of absolute decoupling will not to be met in the foreseeable future (EEA, 2005). This review of EU policy and its 'application' suggests that current trends in waste management are recognised as being unsustainable but that increases are not being counter-acted effectively. In short, waste policy is failing to achieve its principal objectives.

Sustainability and Effectiveness in Ireland

There are disastrous eco-social consequences arising from recent economic development trends when we view those trends from a perspective of environmental sustainability. Have real achievements been secured by the policy adopted for Ireland in response to the spiralling increase in waste production and the increased pressures from the EU to regulate waste? Table 15.2 provides major waste indicators figures for the latest waste produced, recovered, and disposed of in landfill for those years during which waste management policy has been implemented. While the figures highlight huge efforts to manage waste, particularly at the three lower levels of the waste hierarchy, it is nevertheless evident that these efforts are not effectively counter-acting waste increases. In summary, Irish policies and EU regulations are failing to stem the increasing flows of waste.

Table 15.2   Waste indicators, 2001–03

Indicator	2001	2002	2003
Municipal waste			
Municipal waste collected/person	0.59 tonnes	0.61 tonnes	0.65 tonnes
Municipal waste arising/person	0.69 tonnes	0.69 tonnes	0.77 tonnes
Disposal rate for household and commercial waste collected	86.7%	79.3%	71.6%
Recovery rate for household and commercial waste collected	13.3%	20.7%	28.4%
Number landfills accepting municipal waste	48	39	35
Number of bring banks	1,436	1,636	1,692
Household waste			
Household waste collected/person	0.34 tonnes	0.36 tonnes	0.36 tonnes
Household waste arising/person	0.37 tonnes	0.39 tonnes	0.41 tonnes
Disposal rate for household waste	94.4%	90.7%	86.9%
Recovery rate for household waste	5.6%	9.3%	13.1%
Commercial waste			
Commercial waste collected/person	0.25 tonnes	0.25 tonnes	0.29 tonnes
Disposal rate for commercial waste collected	76.2%	62.5%	52.7%
Recovery rate for commercial waste collected	23.8%	37.5%	47.4%
Packaging waste			
Best estimate of total quantity arising	872,917 tonnes	899,125 tonnes	1,006,287 tonnes
Packaging waste arising/person	0.223 tonnes	0.229 tonnes	0.257 tonnes
Best estimate of packaging waste recovery	221,226 tonnes	296,389 tonnes	419,600 tonnes
Packaging waste recovered/person	0.056 tonnes	0.076 tonnes	0.107 tonnes
National recovery rate	25.3%	33%	41.7%
Hazardous waste			
Quantity of hazardous waste exported	275,309 tonnes	249,439 tonnes	275,309 tonnes
	226,904 recovery	203,156 recovery	224,749 recovery
	47,929 disposal	42,419 disposal	162,821 disposal
	476 unspecified	3,864 unspecified	1,629 unspecified

Source: Environmental Protection Agency (2004b)

In addition to this policy failure, there has been in Ireland considerable illegal waste activity recorded since the introduction of the Waste Management Act in 1996. Large-scale dumping occurred in Wicklow from 1997 to 2002, and in 2005 there were still 25 unauthorised landfills and 15 unauthorised waste handling facilities (EPA, 2005, p. 1). There has also been considerable cross-border illegal movement of waste, and fly-tipping is a growing problem as new charges are introduced for waste disposal. In view of this propensity in Ireland for illegal activity, the EPA strongly advocates enforcement as key to progress on waste management (EPA, 2005, p. 2).

FUTURE DIRECTIONS

Ireland is at a turning point in relation to waste management. Efforts to manage waste, with or without enforcement, are no longer seen as sufficient unless integrated with processes of production and consumption. Discussing waste amounts and striving for the waste management hierarchy of more recycling and less disposal is still a necessity. However, there is also need for a more integrated approach that would examine:

• where and from what mechanisms the waste comes;
• what types of waste should not be produced;
• what resources go into the waste stream; and
• what resources can successfully be lifted out of the stream altogether.

An evidence-based understanding of waste flows can help to shape better waste regulation; but informed legislation still needs to be integrated into the wider debate on production and consumption patterns and resource management. This approach to waste, according to Murray, 'promises to be, along with the information and knowledge revolution, one of the defining features of the post-industrial era' (Murray, 2004, p. 17).

Structural conditions encourage wasteful consumption and unsustainable patterns of production that lead to waste. Sustainable production and consumption are the only viable long-term options for society, but we have a long way to go to get there. Factoring in the production of waste to economic growth, and providing a waste-costing system where the allocation of waste costs to producers and consumers would be conducted fairly, would provide part of a structural solution. Scientific innovation is also a necessary component of the switch to sustainability. Building on resource productivity is one of the key ways the scientific community can transform structural conditions. Of relevance here is the new 'materials revolution' being proposed by environmental engineers and scientists, some of whom argue that materials productivity as opposed to labour productivity will form the basis of the post-industrial era (Weizsaker et al., 1998).

While natural scientists and politicians have a role to play in regard to environmental sustainability, the role of the social sciences and humanities is also vital. Changing the social practices around consumerism should be part of developing sustainable consumerism. A social-practice approach would address lifestyles in relation to wasting, and could be used to work towards a waste future where attention is focused on the changing patterns of behaviour around consumerism. The environmental pressures of consumption are generally lower than those of production, but are expected to grow significantly. Consumption patterns around eating, housing, travel and tourism are, as in the recent past, growing significantly and this marks a shift in the environmental burden away from production to consumption. Given this shift, it is necessary to develop innovative governance strategies for dealing with sharply rising patterns of consumption. The development of appropriate governance strategies would be designed by citizens and governments together, inspired by the critical need to organise sustainable patterns of consumption. Shifts in lifestyles and societal preferences can make a huge difference in a world organised around consumerism (Spaargaren et al., 2000). Restructuring various consumption patterns can be crucial in the future, and it is possible to organise if the focus is on the intersection of the structure of production with the lifestyle of the citizen/consumer, and not on the individual or the structure alone. The artists and the literary scholars, likewise, have their role to play in creating the imagery that will inspire innovative generation of green environments and repulsion by the environmental destruction that currently confronts us.

To return to the present and the micro-level, where this chapter began, citizens are actively engaged in relating to a social process and social relations of 'wasting' through their patterns of consumption. Customers purchase what has been produced in the format in which it is being produced. Citizens have some choice in this area as some ways of consuming, and some forms of consumption, are more environmentally 'friendly' than others. However, at present, consumerism is generally organised along lines concerned with profitability rather than with a sustainable environment. Can the individual consumer be interpellated as an environmentally concerned consumer and can some or all markets respond to this trend? (see Luke, 1977). On average the number of waste bins continue to grow, there is more in them, and there are things in them that are worse for the environment that ever before. While the individual may not be producing the hair-spray canister, the plastic tractor or the so-called 'disposable' nappies (a misnomer for something that takes years to decompose), they are playing a role in their wasting. In other words, the consumption pattern of the individual results in the waste bin, acknowledging that this could be a very different waste bin if the forces of production were regulated into producing less wasteful and environmentally damaging commodities. It could, in the future, be a bin of good waste. By that we mean it could be full of recyclable materials – particularly if bad waste has been phased out of production. Currently, however, our purchasing and consuming need to be informed by a recasting of an old opposition, one presented to us by the environmentalists: 'Where we used to think of good things and bad waste, we need think of good waste and bad things' (Murray, 2004, p. 19).

CONCLUSION

In conclusion, in Ireland waste is generated at a series of spatial levels or scales, both in the long term and the short-term consistent with the recent accelerated growth of the Celtic Tiger economy. While benefiting greatly from globalisation, there have been environmental downsides to Ireland's economic success. To deal with this issue and reinvent the 'Green Ireland' of song and tourist board nostalgia, a genuine conceptual paradigm shift is called for in relation to the waste process. This will entail a multiplex response in terms of the structures of production, governance, consumption patterns, scientific advances, national mindset and personal attitudes. The challenge is to plan and implement a waste future where Ireland takes up a leading position in the wider evolving green revolution. Its future depends on the ability of its politicians, citizens, scientists and business leaders to plan a more progressive Irish role in the green revolution. It would be a shame if the globally renowned cultural and social capital that has contributed to Ireland's success story was not now turned towards innovation for environmental sustainability in the approaching post-consumerist phase of globalisation.

16
The Meaning of Northern Ireland

Brian Graham

One of the enduring illusions held about Northern Ireland is that its society can be defined through a binary distinction between Catholic and Protestant, nationalist and unionist. It is readily apparent, however, that these broad domains are themselves fractured and diverse and that self-identification is often as much a process of divisions within as without the tribes. This chapter focuses on recent processes of identity transformation from the perspective of loyalism but it is worth emphasising that the traditional nationalist discourse is also fractured if not quite so profoundly. Northern Ireland can thus be viewed as a laboratory for identity formation as unionists and loyalists strive to reconcile with or, conversely, distance themselves from, the fundamental political changes that have followed in the wake of the paramilitary cease-fires of the mid-1990s and the 1998 Good Friday (or Belfast) Agreement.

Although the differences are not absolute, loyalists differ from unionists in that their primary identity association is with Ulster (as a culturally and historically vested synonym for the political aridity of 'Northern Ireland'), while loyalty to Britain and the union is very much a secondary and highly ambivalent relationship (Ruane and Todd, 1996). Loyalism itself is by no means a coherent ideology, a fragmentation that reflects the broader fragility of the unionist discourse in Northern Ireland (Graham, 1998), undermined as it is by the British government's alignment with that of the Republic of Ireland in the peace process. Even worse, however, that sense of betrayal and alienation is internal to unionism itself, where it is compounded by class conflict and the creation of micro-scale community identities shaped by social exclusion. After decades of use and abuse by their own politicians, working-class Protestants see themselves as 'puppets no more'. They are far less interested in notions and symbols of reconciliation than in establishing a place for themselves, a place that demands its own past and claim to that past. Before cross-community negotiation comes self-understanding and acquiring the confidence that stems from a secure identity vested in historical narratives set firmly in place.

In some ways, these processes of loyalist identity formation can be likened to the debate on revisionism (in the sense of the meaning of Ireland, its history and Irishness), which has been the dominant theme in Irish historiography for the past several decades. Having failed, the union apart, to develop a coherent cultural identity of their own, unionists have no effective riposte to revisionist ideas of a more diverse and hybrid Ireland. After partition, it was always easy for unionists

221

to depict traditional Gaelic, Catholic, rural nationalism, which excluded them anyway, as other. Once unionist political control disappeared in 1972, however, when Stormont was prorogued, the inadequacies of a cultural identity defined largely by political Britishness meant an eventual surrender of the moral high ground to a republicanism bolstered by a secure if oppressively dreary and Anglophobic cultural identity. Moreover, while failing to respond to the more recent reshaping of ideas of Irishness in a newly confident and Europeanising Republic of Ireland, unionism has also been singularly unsuccessful in coming to terms with a devolving multicultural United Kingdom, often maintaining, instead, some sort of time-warped fealty to Queen and country. Thus the 'revision' of Ulster historiography as an identity resource is very different to the renegotiation of Ireland and Irishness. It is generally informed by the zero-sum characteristics of ethnic nationalism, while the Protestant and Catholic middle classes, who may espouse a British or Irish cultural identity, have opted out to share a similar consumerist lifestyle (Graham and Shirlow, 1998). 'Revisionism' in Ulster is generally beyond the union and emanates, not from the academy or chattering classes (as in the Republic) but from below, from the people.

Within its discussion of this people's history and the ways in which it informs loyalist identity transformation, this chapter has three specific objectives. First, Ulster 'revisionism' is placed within a conceptual context that links three closely related ideas: resistance; subalternity; and Thirdspace. Second, the implications of these ideas for the renegotiation of loyalist identities are explored, before, third, the chapter concludes with an examination of the heritage that constitutes the resources for those identities.

ULSTER LOYALIST REVISIONISM

Resistance, subalternity, and Thirdspace are concepts generally harnessed to the debate on progressive, multicultural, hybrid societies and thus to the deconstruction of identities created by reductionist ethno-nationalism. Here, however, they can be used in a diametrically opposed way.

Resistance

This is a diverse concept but one that often includes notions of opposition to domination or oppression. Thus implicit within it is the idea of resistant subjects shaping their identities outside or beyond the realm of hegemonic groups. This may occur spatially and it does seem clear that one response to the emergence of neo-liberal globalised capitalism has been a shift in identity location from the scale of the nation state to more local scales. The literature on resistance, however, often elides sexist, racist and, as in this case, violent groups (Shirlow, 2000). Ulster loyalism is largely united only by its resistance to the pluralist political settlement and accommodationism. Even then, some loyalists still support the Good Friday Agreement, which is vested in widely accepted consociational principles of an open civic, plural society that gives parity of esteem to other people's cultural identities.

As Bell (2003, p. 1144) argues, however, the 'Agreement was fashioned so as to avoid the need for a societal narrative'. It contains 'no mechanism for dealing with past abuses, or "truth-telling"' (Bell, 2003, p. 1097). Again, a significant if unforeseen result of the Good Friday Agreement has been a 'depoliticalisation of society' matched by an escalating stress on identity and culture:

> ... at the expense of the old contesting politics of national sovereignty, self-determination and independence. As the constitutional question arising from these contests has diminished, the focus has shifted to the problem of sectarianism. (Tonge, 2005, p. 7)

Although the 'politics of national sovereignty' are obviously about competing models of cultural nationalism and their expression through the nation state, presenting the problem of Northern Ireland as sectarianism, rather than the legitimacy of the state, reductively locates the source of conflict in religious differences alone. Sectarianism, which can be defined as 'religious bigotry, the promotion of one's religion or religious background at the expense of the alternative' (Tonge, 2005, p. 192), is a common defining characteristic of ethnic states. Nevertheless, religion, while marginalised in other contexts, remains 'an accepted and sometimes overpowering agent' (Little, 2004, p. 76). In Northern Ireland it has always overlapped with secular forms of conflict more accurately defined as ethnic or nationalist (Coulter, 1999) to encourage 'separatism, intolerance and chauvinism, patriarchalism and authoritarianism' (Fraser, 2000, p. 108). Most loyalists – and republicans – resist the idea of a society based on consocation and cross-community consensus. They also reject the idea of ambiguous 'soft-edged' territorial boundaries (Glover, 1999), opting instead for micro-scale versions of the zero-sum trap of the ethnic nation state and the further trap, in Glover's terms, of the territorial vendetta from which the only escape is an awareness of how the stories on both sides were constructed.

Therefore, in loyalist Ulster, resistances go beyond the hegemonic/counter-hegemonic interface to create landscapes of fear marked by the brutish iconography of absolute territoriality and inviolate edges. But these are not contiguous swathes of loyalism (or republicanism) but micro-communities often of no more that a few streets and juxtaposed with each other across hard lines on the ground (described by the ludicrous euphemism of 'peace lines'). Thus loyalist resistance is both conceptual and violent. It is, as Shirlow (2000) observes, fundamental to an identity linked to unwavering communal devotion, perceptions of ethnic purity, self-reflexive interpretations of power, and narratives of violence. One qualification, however, concerns the relational or situated nature of resistances, which ensures that the content of loyalist identity is not the same everywhere in unionist Ulster.

Subalternity

Loyalists are also involved through the authoring of their identity in challenging the republican claim to the hegemony of victimhood. This chimes with the concept of subalternity, which derives from Gramsci (1971) but has its widest currency in colonial and post-colonial studies. The idea, however, that official or state-sponsored historical narratives erase various oppressed and/or marginalised groups has a powerful resonance for working-class Ulster loyalists. Seen by the world beyond as oppressors themselves, their self-imaging, in contrast, centres on the neglected memory of the Ulster working class, its interests suppressed by those of the Stormont unionist government. Fundamental to the transformation of their identities is the idea of 'people's history', directly analogous to E. P. Thompson's 'history from below' and its drive to recover the collective agency of exploited, marginalised and oppressed groups. Loyalists have a firm belief in the reality and objectivity of history and memory, and among their resistances is the rejection of representation and the symbolic, subjective connotations of historical narratives. This is a discourse of betrayal and alienation, of being 'sold out' as oppressed victims of unionism and the world opinion that bought the Sinn Féin message. It is this subalternity which legitimates the 'right' to resist the imposition of a pluralist consensus.

Thirdspace

This concept evolves from the work of Bhabha (1994) and Soja (1996, 2000) and refers to the spaces beyond the forms of knowledge (including sectarian constructions of Irish history) that divide the world into binary oppositions. Thus Thirdspace is the space where new identities emerge. For Peet (1998, pp. 224–5), Soja 'wants to set aside either/or choices and contemplate the possibility of a "both/and also" logic which effectively combines postmodernist with modernist perspectives', the aim being to build on 'a Firstspace perspective focused on the "real" material world, and a Secondspace perspective that interprets this reality through imaging representations, to reach a Thirdspace of multiple real-and-imagined places'. In Thirdspace, new things happen that disrupt old and dominant ways of thinking and doing. Soja is thinking of more progressive contexts than what can often be ethno-fascist Ulster loyalism. Yet the idea of Thirdspace still seems clearly relevant to regressive, reductionist interpretations of identity and place. Those are places defined through the rejection of notions of hybridity and diversity and created as loci of resistance through the overt glorification of subaltern status. The message is: 'keep out'. But these places do combine material and representational space and new – if often regrettable – ways of thinking about identity in Ulster.

THE IMPLICATIONS OF THE RENEGOTIATION
OF LOYALIST IDENTITIES

The interconnections within this triad of resistance, subalternity and Thirdspace establish three dimensions to loyalist identities. The intersection of resistance and 'history from below' creates new identities defined as much by their opposition to traditional unionism as to republicanism. The relationship between resistance and Thirdspace elicits new real and imagined places, while that between 'history from below' and Thirdspace produces subaltern ways of thought and action consciously constructed to disrupt and perhaps deconstruct the formerly hegemonic unionism. These interconnections further intersect with two other dimensions to the emergence of loyalist identities. These are the role of territory and symbolic landscapes, and the nature of those identities themselves. As already observed, loyalism has a very strong spatial consciousness. This is indicated, for example, by the importance of territorial markers at interfaces between loyalist and republican areas. Most obvious in the urban context, these include an array of flags, emblems, wall murals and graffiti. However, the same battery of markers is used to demonstrate territories within loyalist areas, most obviously those held by the rival paramilitary organisations. This has often as much to do with drug pushing, racketeering and prostitution as with ideological discourse. Whichever, the important point lies in the localisation of territory; spatially, the claims are very finely grained and the iconography is often inner-directed to those micro-communities, as much as in opposition to republicanism. The scale of Northern Ireland – itself a relatively small space, albeit with very large physic distances – is remote and, in many ways, the wider claim to Ulster is to an imaginary place.

Thus territory is defined by its exclusivity but also by micro-communities that image themselves through representations of oppression and self-sufficiency. Their territories powerfully symbolise overlapping axes of exclusion – economic, social as well as cultural – and consequently epitomise the cult of victimhood. In many ways, loyalism can be a Protestant form of Sinn Féinism in its literal sense of being 'ourselves alone'. The sense of exclusion and alienation is further heightened by the irrelevance to the loyalist working class of globalising neo-liberalism and its technology- and knowledge-driven economies. The traditional industries of modernisation, which created the Protestant working class, are no more. Northern Ireland, therefore, has its vertical division along sectarian lines but also a horizontal divide between a relatively contented embourgeoised majority and a socially excluded lumpenproletariat living in marginalised, polarised housing estates festooned with ethnic territorial markers (Murtagh, 2001).

And so to identities themselves. The concepts cited in this chapter are generally linked to post-modern hybrid societies. They are informed by the work of theorists such as Bhabha (1994), who creates a powerful argument for the hybridity of identity and belonging beyond the binary distinctions of the modern and imperial world. They mesh too, with ideas such as Hall's 'multiply constructed' identities (1996), which envisage diffuse and situational constructs in which individuals simultaneously occupy a number of identity postures. But in this particular context of Ulster loyalism, the constructs can be employed in a regressive way to understand identities that are constructed in hard-edged places to contest the hegemonic claim to victimhood. There is no sense of hybridity or multiculturalism in these identities: indeed, they are overtly and violently resistant to hybridisation. Thus loyalist identities are fractured and often, if not necessarily so, opposed to the principles of social-democratic civic society. They incorporate a variety of ideologies extending from Marxism through fundamentalist Christianity to racism. They demonstrate the interconnection of cultural, economic and social exclusion and are often violent, sexist and homophobic.

Nevertheless, there is a curious positivity to certain aspects of the authority of loyalist identities because some dimensions, at least, can be read as reflections of the manifest need to deconstruct binary ethnic identities.

THE SUBJECT MATTER, CONTENT AND
RESOURCES FOR LOYALIST IDENTITIES

This second triangular relationship between resistance, territory and identity defines the three dimensions to the subject matter of loyalist self-imaging. In the first instance, when territory is added to resistance/subalternity/ Thirdspace, we see defined the claims to space and place that disrupt both the old dominant ways of thinking about Ulster – British union – but also the pluralist, consociational principles embodied in the Good Friday Agreement. The resistance/subalternity/Thirdspace–identity axis in turn defines the characteristics of those new identities, which, as we have seen, are often regressive and defiantly anti-pluralist. Finally, the interconnections between territory and identity point to the exclusivity of these relationships in local places that are geographical compounds of economic, social and cultural exclusion, 'gated communities' for the loyalist lumpenproletariat. And it is well to remember that the war (or the Troubles) was largely fought by the working classes in these working-class ghettos, both loyalist and republican. These are the actual sites of resistance and belonging.

If the reshaping of loyalist identities is indeed a form of revisionism, in this case of hegemonic British unionism, its content is startlingly dissimilar to that of revisionist Irish historiography, which seeks to redefine the meaning of oppression and render it in a far more nuanced way that was apparent in traditional narratives of Anglophobic Irish nationalism. This points to a broader issue in the study of loyalist identities. Essentially, the process – if it has a unifying theme – is a competition for the ownership of victimhood. Republicanism always played this card and it is still fundamentally important in Irish America. But as we move on to consider the subject matter of loyalist identities and their use, we return again to the darkness of the past and its meanings for a people who are close to reifying a self-image of oppression and exclusion. Thus loyalist 'revisionism' is engaged with republicanism in a competition for hegemonic control over victimhood, one in which defeat and the opprobrium of world opinion (largely pro-republican if not necessarily pro-IRA) are actually victories because they contribute to the self-image of a beleaguered people, betrayed on all sides, reliant only on their own resources.

This is a form of unionism that regards Northern Ireland as being more Ulster than it is British and certainly not Irish. (Indeed 'Irish' stands, not as a geographical adjective for the island of Ireland, but as a synonym for 'nationalist'.) It can be argued that unionists always viewed the union as highly conditional but now, underpinned by a strong sense of British betrayal, with mounting alienation from the peace process, and self-imaging as 'victim'. Elements of unionism, with their increasing stress on Northern Ireland's cultural and historical separation from the remainder of Ireland, are drifting towards the logic of 'ourselves alone'. Beyond that, even, lies loyalism, its alienation from Britain compounded by a sense of betrayal within. To a considerable extent, loyalist politics can be read as an attempt to reclaim the history and identity of the Protestant working classes from its subaltern position in the unionist state. Loyalists are less than interested in middle-class imagining of a common ground, nor are they prepared to celebrate the diversity and plurality of Northern Ireland. Rather, they seek to establish a place for themselves that demands its own past through which loyalism can achieve validation and legitimation. In line with the idea of an identity that sanctifies the status of victim, the six resources of the subject matter that defines this 'place' are indeed a 'dismal heritage'. These six resources are highlighted in the following paragraphs.

First, of course, the traditional iconography of unionism depends on blood and/or betrayal, mixed, whenever possible, with Catholic duplicity. Critically, however, as Walker argues, this traditional unionist and Orange history reduces the past to little more than a series of events that are lacking any sense of historical narrative to match the linear continuities of the Gaelic nationalist origin-myth (Walker, 1996). These disconnected moments include: the 1641 Rebellion, when Protestant settlers were massacred by Catholic rebels; the Siege of Derry in 1689; The Battle of the Boyne in 1690; the defiance of Home Rule in the years 1912–14 and the Ulster Covenant; the 1 July 1916 when the 36th (Ulster) Division was decimated on the opening day of the Battle of the Somme; the Anglo-Irish Agreement of 1985; and finally the betrayal of the 1998 Good Friday Agreement. This is the stuff of Orange banner and wall murals alike, depicting the history of the Protestant people as an endless cycle of conflict, fear of betrayal and sacrifice, 'one that appears to have stopped in its tracks at the moment of its supreme expression of collective identity, the sacrifice of the Somme' (Jarman, 1997, p. 184).

The sectarian connotations of unionist and Orange historiography mesh with a second resource, that of Protestantism as a theology. It is important not to under-estimate the role of religious belief in defining current trends in identity formation in Northern Ireland. There is much to be said for the argument put forward by John Dunlop, a former Moderator of the Presbyterian Church in Ireland, that IRA violence was based on a fundamentally flawed analysis of the Irish problem. In deciding to fight the British, the Provisionals failed to recognise that the problem was actually their dissenting neighbours (Dunlop, 1995). Thus Bruce (1994) claims that loyalism saw itself as being engaged in a religious war, which was sometimes grounded in Old Testament, fundamentalist ideas of revenge, and often informed by diasporic linkages to fundamentalist sects in the United States. These can shade into an anti-ecumenical, anti-Papist, anti-pluralist discourse, which is further antagonistic to Europe, the left, feminism and gays, and can have resonances with the racism of right-wing groups elsewhere, including the National Front in Britain and the British Israelites. But even if most Protestants would reject such extremes, it is apparent that the Troubles have heightened the Protestant perception of victimhood (Jordan, 2001).

A third, if not very powerful, heritage resource is provided by Northern Ireland's history of industrialisation and modernisation, although this too is double-edged. The traditional industries that employed the Protestant working classes – ship building, ropeworks, textiles – are largely gone, replaced (if at all) by the technology and knowledge-driven outputs of the new economy, which may have little relevance to working-class loyalists, thereby accentuating the senses of betrayal, alienation and exclusion. Industrialisation and modernisation are thus largely elided from loyalist iconography, being used instead as a catalyst for urban regeneration. The White Star liner, 'Titanic', is claimed as the most potent symbol of Northern Ireland's industrial heritage and the site of Belfast's Harland and Wolff shipyard is being reconfigured as the 'Titanic Quarter'. Development agencies seem curiously immune to the irony of relaunching Belfast on the back of the most famous shipwreck in history.

The Troubles themselves provide a fourth resource. Loyalist iconography often links the Somme with the Troubles – the defence of small nations, the remembrance of the dead, the return from war. The burgeoning commemorative landscape marking the activities of paramilitary organisations, with its gardens of remembrance, 'war memorials' and murals, is a powerful example of the role of symbolic landscapes in constructing these localised expressions of identity. Optimistically, the construction of commemorative landscapes by both loyalists and republicans is one of the most potent signs that the war is over.

As a fifth resource, commemoration of the Troubles is often conflated with the revision of the Somme mythology. In the first three days of the Somme offensive, which began on 1 July 1916, the 36th (Ulster) Division, raised from the ranks of the Ulster Volunteer Force (UVF) which had been formed to, if necessary, fight for Ulster against the imposition of Home Rule in Ireland, suffered around 5,500 casualties. Some 3,000 of these were fatalities and perhaps 2,000 Ulstermen were killed on 1 July alone. Subsequently, the Somme became the leitmotif of Ulster's blood sacrifice for the British crown and State and the debt that Britain owed. More recently, and particularly since the cease-fires, this role has changed and the Somme has now become an integral part of people's history and central to the imaginative narratives of memory, underpinning new formulations of working-class, loyalist self-identification (Graham and Shirlow, 2002).

The 'ownership' of the Somme mythology – not entirely uncontested – lies with the present UVF, a paramilitary organisation founded in 1966. For the UVF, the Somme has been reborn as an unofficial 'people's history', a part of the Ulster past that owes little to bourgeois official unionism. In symbolising the suffering and exploitation but also the pride of Ulster working-class people, the Somme bears no shame and is not tainted by Orange sectarianism. Above all, the Somme reflects the beliefs of some paramilitaries returned from the war (that is, released from prison) and firmly committed to the idea that only self-help and education can empower the working classes in the search for their own secure identity. It is key to a narrative designed to subvert previous readings of communal devotion, belonging and fealty to the British/unionist bourgeois establishment. Thus the Somme symbolism is crucial to the shaping of a robust – and inherently anti-British – sense of loyalist communal memorialisation. The Somme has become part of the process through which a fusion of real and imaginary space is being used to impose an identity, and therefore social control, on loyalist enclaves, while simultaneously being a central icon in the act of resistance that this constitutes to the ever-more fragmented realm of unionism and to the British state.

Finally, the sixth resource, the Ulster-Scots movement represents a very different form of historical revisionism and marks, perhaps, the increasingly jaundiced attitudes held by loyalists towards the union. It concerns Ulster's relations with Scotland, emigration and the rebirth or invention (depending on perspective) of the Ulster-Scots language and culture. At its most developed, the Ulster-Scots movement seeks an over-reaching sense of identity for Ulster that transcends the localism of loyalist history. It is, however, inherently anti-British and often can be profoundly anti-Irish. As with unionism in general, it is difficult to generalise because the Ulster-Scots movement is itself fragmented. It has origins, perhaps, in ideas that the boundary between England and Scotland can be extrapolated westwards to demarcate an Ulster that historically has always been separate from the remainder of Ireland. Hence, its principal cultural associations lie in what has been termed a Dalriadan Sea cultural province. Several writers, most notably Adamson, have gone so far as to extend this idea into the creation of an Ulster origin-myth linked to the tales and sagas of the Iron Age (Adamson, 1978, 1981, 1991). Gradually, the original inhabitants of Ulster were pushed back by Gaelic tribes from the south, ultimately being forced to retreat to Scotland. Consequently, the seventeenth-century Scottish Plantation of Ulster can be depicted, not as a confrontation of alien cultures, nor the oppressive colonisation of the Gaelic myth, but as a reunification and reconquest by an Ulster-Scots people once expelled from their rightful territory by the invading Gaels.

This process of identity creation or revival – depending on one's ideological viewpoint – was officially recognised in the Good Friday Agreement, which created an Ulster-Scots Agency. This is responsible for the Ulster-Scots language and for the promotion of Ulster-Scots history, heritage and culture. Arguably, in so doing the Agreement contributed to the exacerbation of other problematic elements of Northern Irish politics, most notably the reification of the hegemonic status of the 'two traditions' paradigm through using the legacy of the past to make what could be seen as an 'exemption for one group ... into a universal right that applied to all'. The equal status accorded Irish and Ulster-Scots represents the right to communicate in a language other than English but also underscores the point that there are 'alternative languages for everyone' (Little, 2004, p. 81). As Mac Pólin (1999) remarks, there can be a depressing sense of déja vu about the Ulster-Scots movement because it can be read as an analogy to traditional Irish ethno-nationalism in which the Irish language became the 'green litmus test'. Conversely, Irish and Ulster-Scots can be portrayed as elements of a complex shared culture and clearly certain emblems of Scottishness are very important in Northern Ireland. These include sport and Presbyterianism, together with the lowland Scots linguistic tradition (Ullans in Ulster). The status and integrity of that language remains controversial, with an apparently irresolvable debate as to whether it is a language or a dialect. It is this focus on the language that seems to push Ulster-Scots towards traditional reductionist ethno-nationalism. It is clearly a loyalist rather than a unionist mindset, one response to a definite sense of inferiority among Protestants based on the idea that they are elided by 'Irish' culture or even worse, rendered subservient by it. The danger is that in aping the isolationist and exclusive nature of traditional Gaelic nationalism, some in the Ulster-Scots movement are merely compounding the republican claim to an exclusive hegemony over Irishness.

CONCLUSION

If loyalists' place in Ulster can be interpreted through the concepts of resistance, subalternity and Thirdspace, and the ways in which their interconnectedness further integrates with territory and identity, it is apparent that new formulations of place and belonging are occurring that largely deny old and traditional unionist perspectives on Northern Ireland. If there is a dominant theme linking this iconography, it is that of a people alone, alienated, betrayed and reliant only on their own resources. In 1996 Ruane and Todd (p. 57) remarked that cultural differences among Protestants were much more apparent than were political variations, noting that 'there is no agreement on their construction of ethnic or natural identity'. This process seems to be accelerating as the triangular relationships between resistance, subalternity and Thirdspace combine to further deconstruct unionism and loyalism into beleaguered and regressive constructions of place.

Consequently, these overtly progressive post-modern or post-colonial ideas, resonant of hybrid and multicultural societies, can be suborned by groups who are ideologically opposed to recognising or even celebrating difference but who see the material world in terms of hard-edged and absolute conceptualisations of space. Essentially, at the micro scale of the community, these are analogous to the ethnic nation state and its underlying assumptions of cultural homogeneity or even purity. Loyalist subaltern resistance, with its themes of oppression, exclusion, betrayal and victimhood, is linked to an identity authoring that denies principles of consociation and consensus. Indeed it is shaped through depicting these as other. Soja (1996) argues that in Thirdspace, new things happen that disrupt old and dominant ways of thinking and doing. But unlike the Marxist dialectic, this cannot be assumed to be a progressive or even modernist form of synthesis. Instead, the new ideas can be profoundly reactionary and are visited back on Firstspace, the material world, in the form of absolute concep-tualisations of territory defended through violence. In replicating the zero-sum characteristics of ethnic nationalism, the logic of this subaltern 'history from below' is both anti-Irish and anti-British and, as such, is the very negation of the principles of the Good Friday Agreement.

It does seem profoundly depressing that Ulster loyalists seem intent on reinventing micro-scale versions of the zero-sum trap of the ethnic nation state more than a century after Gaelic nationalism began its evolution into the ideological basis of the post-partition and exclusivist Catholic Irish state. Nevertheless, this may be a necessary process. The failure of Northern Ireland as a political entity shows that the forces of cultural identity, and the dissonances which they create, cannot be assimilated within almost purely political structures. It also demonstrates the enduring power of place-centred identities, as well as the ways in which people continue to locate themselves in clearly demarcated territories, often marked by an iconography that portrays their resistance to hybridisation. Academics can be accused of observing such processes to their own advantage, but there is more to it than that. The engagement with what socially excluded people define as their material world is part of the process of ending the 'vendetta', of explaining, as Glover (1999) powerfully argues, that the only escape from ethnic absolutism is an awareness of how and why people construct such stories in the first place.

Part IV
Population and Social Issues

Introduction

It is no surprise that population concerns and related social issues should accompany a rapidly changing and spatially uneven economy. Societies adapt to take advantage of prevailing conditions. In the case of Ireland, the population and social transformations that have occurred have been as dramatic as the change in the economy. This in many ways is due the conditions in the late 1980s, where Ireland was deeply affected by mass out-migration, high levels of poverty, and poor social mobility. Family sizes were still large by European standards, the demographic structure was one of low dependency with over 40 per cent of people aged under 25, and only a small percentage of married women worked. The Catholic Church continued to play a dominant role in education, welfare and in regulating social issues. By 2000, all of this had been turned on its head. As the chapters in this section illustrate, by then Ireland was a country of net immigration; family sizes had fallen; women had entered the labour market in droves; household income increased dramatically, and society became increasingly secular. The chapters also highlight many of the problems of the 1980s that persist in the economic-miracle era in addition to the new problems generated by the Celtic Tiger itself. The following illustrative examples are far from being an exhaustive listing of these predicaments, which provide policy makers, government and communities with serious and on-going challenges:

- not everyone has benefited financially to the same extent, resulting in continued high rates of relative poverty;
- house prices have spiralled to record high rates, giving rise to growing local authority waiting lists for social housing as well as creating affordability and homelessness difficulties;
- queues for hospital beds and in Accident and Emergency departments of hospitals have reached crisis levels;
- development has been uneven, with population growth strongest in the cities;
- new housing and industry have placed inordinate pressures on local services;
- conspicuous consumption has become rampant;

- two-earner and time-poor households have become common;
- long-distance, time-consuming commuting has become a way of life for many; and so on.

In the first chapter, Piaras Mac Éinrí examines immigration to Ireland. He details the transition from a net-emigrant country to a net-immigrant country, charting the huge growth in the 1990s of both Irish people returning to Ireland and new immigrants to Ireland. Focusing on the latter, he first examines the flows of asylum seekers and refugees and labour migrants throughout the 1990s and into the new millennium. Next, he details the Irish State's reaction to these immigrants and the main policy interventions implemented to try and regulate immigrants. As he notes, Ireland faces huge challenges in both managing migration and achieving integration, something that has to be undertaken with respect to EU policy and the Common Travel Area arrangement with the UK. Mac Éinrí concludes that given the predictions for continued, sustained immigration over the next ten years and the knock-on consequences of population increase as regards services and housing, coherent immigration policies are vital.

Mary Corcoran, Karen Keaveney and Patrick Duffy focus their analysis on the issue of housing. They reveal how population change, migration and changing lifestyle preferences (e.g., 'back to the country' or second/holiday homes) have all placed enormous pressure on housing provision and house prices, and have led to a boom in housing developments that has often been supported by poor planning practice. Moreover, they highlight that the last 15 years has seen the housing market become more differentiated and flexible, with a range of different unit styles and sizes being built that cater for people who are at different stages of the property market, have varying lifestyles, and are buying for different reasons (e.g., as investments, retirement homes). They identify four key processes shaping housing provision: urban regeneration schemes, suburbanisation, social housing schemes, and the growth of rural living and second homes in the country. To illustrate their arguments they provide two case studies, the Fatima Mansions sink estate in inner-city Dublin and rural housing in Clew Bay, County Mayo.

In the following chapter, Trutz Haase provides a spatial overview of poverty and deprivation, noting that whilst new prosperity is leading to new housing estates in urban areas, and one-off housing and holiday homes in rural areas, places of long-term poverty remain the same, with the exception of some inner-city areas that have been gentrified with former poor residents displaced to other persistently poor places. As a result, in Ireland, as with many other countries, poverty has been tackled through area-based responses since 1991. Haase notes that area-based initiatives need to be broadened to take account of multiple forms of deprivation and neighbourhood effects. He also argues that they need to be supplemented by structural policy responses, such as tax and welfare reform, that benefit people who do not live in the identified poor areas. Haase stresses that deprivation needs to be conceptualised spatially and provides a spatial analysis of the distribution of poverty in Ireland from 1991 to 2002. In the final section of the chapter he charts the development of specific policy initiatives and outlines the changes he believes are necessary to tackle long-term, systemic poverty and deprivation.

Many analysts have noted a strong link between poverty and health, though as Frank Houghton and Dennis Pringle detail in their chapter, the relationship in Ireland is complex with, for example, Donegal having the highest life expectancy despite being the poorest county in the State. In their chapter they discuss general trends and spatial variations in health and disease in Ireland, the relationship between social capital and health, and also the structuring of the health system, an issue of on-going debate given the supposed crises in healthcare. In Ireland, as with other developed nations, non-infectious diseases such as heart disease and cancer are now the primary cause of death. Whilst medicines account for the decline in infectious disease, changing lifestyles have contributed to non-infectious rates reflecting diet and exercise rates. They note that health provision has been radically reorganised recently following the Hanly Report, but that Ireland still does not use an objective formula (i.e., based on population characteristics and need) to allocate health funding. They suggest that such a formula is needed if Ireland's health problems are to be tackled more effectively.

The changes in the health of the nation are related to changes in lifestyle and patterns of consumption. Denis Linehan examines 'the way we live today' and how cultural values and practices have altered since the start of the Celtic Tiger period. His wide-ranging analysis discusses issues of obesity, alcohol consumption, sexual freedom, identity, secularisation, pet keeping, housing lifestyles, disposable income, high debt, food consumption, declining social capital and community cohesiveness, and placelessness (the erosion of a distinctive Irish landscape to a hybrid American-European blandness). In short, he documents how Ireland has become a consumption-driven society and how RoI now stands for 'Rip-off Ireland' (rather than Republic of Ireland). Through these changes he suggests that the nature of Irishness has changed, although he notes that this is not necessarily a bad thing, but rather the inevitable response to changing contexts.

Population and social change in Ireland have been remarkable for their speed and nature. The country is almost unrecognisable to those returning immigrants who left in the 1980s. Whilst much of the change that has occurred has been positive, as these chapters highlight by no means of all of it is. Moreover, the positives and negatives are not universally distributed but are unequal and uneven in their processes and effects across the country. The challenge for the future is to sustain the positive trends, but to also work much harder at addressing the very real challenges that face people in their everyday social lives. This challenge needs to be met by government as well as individual citizens and communities and requires a commitment to continue the process of creating innovative interventions that address issues of inequality, promote sustainability and improve the quality of life for all who live on the island. Without this commitment the perception that Ireland is a highly desirable place to live will quickly tarnish.

17

Immigration: Labour Migrants, Asylum Seekers and Refugees

Piaras Mac Éinrí

AN EMIGRANT SOCIETY

Until the recent past, Ireland was an emigrant country. This was not necessarily unique, but formed part of a broader pattern of European Atlantic migration from the seventeenth century onwards. This wider pattern consisted of periphery–core movement within Europe itself, outflows connected with colonialism and imperialism, especially in the late nineteenth century, and rural to urban migration of a kind which is now a worldwide phenomenon.

From the pivotal event of the Great Famine of 1845–49 to the 1950s, Ireland had a unique demographic profile in European and even world terms. This was characterised by low marriage rates and a late age of marriage; high rates of fertility within marriage and very low rates of births outside marriage; and above all by on-going rates of emigration which were so high that they constantly outpaced the natural increase in the population, which accordingly fell steadily until 1961. This contrasts, for instance, with the post-World War II experience of other European countries, with historically high marriage rates; falling fertility rates within marriage; rising levels of births outside marriage; and the development of large-scale immigration in a number of European societies. Comparable developments did not begin to occur in Ireland until the 1990s.

The adoption at the end of the 1950s of new economic policies based on the encouragement of foreign direct investment (FDI) led to a turnaround in the decade which followed, with increased job creation and a dramatic drop in emigration. Ireland's accession to the European Economic Community (now the EU) in 1973 even led to net in-migration for a period of about five years, although this can largely be explained by the return of experienced Irish migrants, often with family members, to meet specific skill shortages in the Irish economy.

However, the need to restructure a more open economy after ten years of EU membership, together with poor economic management, led to a substantial loss of jobs in the 1980s, which also coincided with the arrival of the baby-boom generation of the 1960s onto the labour market. The result was a dramatic increase in the unemployment rate and an even more dramatic return to high emigration rates. In 1988–89 alone, 70,600 persons, or approximately 2 per cent of the population, left Ireland.

Irish fertility rates have dropped from a total fertility rate (TFR) of more than 4 in the 1960s to the present rate of about 1.98, below the replacement rate for the population. This fundamental demographic shift suggests that it is unlikely that mass emigration on the scale of the 1980s and 1950s will recur in the future.

FROM EMIGRATION TO IMMIGRATION

The 1990s saw the emergence of a very different Ireland. The introduction in 1987 of government-brokered national collective bargaining agreements, later expanded into national partnership agreements embracing government, employers, trades unions, agricultural interests and the community and voluntary sector, stabilised industrial and social relations (see Chapter 13). The investment that the State had made in education in the 1970s and 1980s resulted in a skilled labour force which, together with fiscal and other investment incentives, made Ireland a very attractive investment location, especially for sectors such as IT and pharmaceuticals (see Chapters 1, 8 and 9). The resulting growth rates in the mid- to late 1990s, at more than 8 per cent of GDP, were the highest in the OECD area, although rates have slowed somewhat since then. The latest OECD forecast of Ireland for 2006 predicts a return to growth of 5 per cent, whereas an average rate of only 2 per cent is predicted for the Eurozone as a whole (OECD, 2005).

As a result of this rapid economic growth the number employed in the workforce grew from 1.15m. in 1991 – not far above the 1986 low of 1.091m – to an estimated 1.982m. in the final quarter of 2005 (CSO, 2006) – an increase of more than 80 per cent. Recent data from the Quarterly National Household Survey indicates that in 2005 employment rose by 4.7 per cent, following average annual increases of 3 per cent in 2004, 1.9 per cent in 2003, 1.8 per cent in 2002 and 3.1 per cent in 2001 (CSO, 2006). Ireland's seasonally adjusted unemployment rate in the third quarter of 2005, at 4.3 per cent, was the lowest in the EU (Commission of the European Communities, 2006).

Prior to the 1990s, few immigrants came to Ireland who were not of either Irish or British background. Non-EU immigration was insignificant, notwithstanding the arrival of multinational companies. Although there had been some very modest inward migration of refugees (see below), substantial immigration from outside the English-speaking world is very recent. The dramatic improvement in economic growth in the 1990s that led to falling unemployment also produced increased participation by women in the paid economy, return migration (approx. 218,000 Irish people plus their families returned in the period 1995–2004) and, finally, a sharp and sustained growth in immigration (see Table 17.1). Estimated OECD net migration per 1,000 population for 2004 places Ireland (7.9) in third place, after Cyprus (10.6) and Spain (11.9), although this figure for Ireland ignores a significant part of the substantial inward migration of East and Central European migrant workers after accession in May 2004 (Netherlands Interdisciplinary Demographic Institute, 2005). This rise in immigration was partly from other EU countries, but there was a significant increase in non-EU immigrants, including workers on short-term work permits, asylum seekers and students. The result has been that in the period 1995 to 2004, 486,300 people moved to Ireland (including returning Irish) whilst 263,800 people emigrated, resulting in net immigration of 222,500 (see Table 17.1). In addition, as discussed below, 206,145 people from accession states registered for PPSNs (personal public service numbers) between May 2004 and 2006 (O'Brien, 2006), and other groups have continued to migrate to the country. Ireland has, therefore, been faced with the difficulties of constructing immigration and integration policies against a background of a rapidly changing picture, limited experience, an often less than positive attitude towards difference, and a largely mono-cultural tradition. As noted in Chapters 1 and 18, there have been other dramatic changes to demographic structure and internal migration in the last 15 years. The rest of this chapter, however, focuses on asylum seekers and refugees and new labour migrants.

Table 17.1   Emigration from and immigration to Ireland, and net migration rates, 1995–2004

	1995	1996	1997	1998	1999	2000	2001	2002	2003	2004	Total
Emigration from Ireland											
UK	13,300	14,100	12,900	8,500	11,200	7,200	7,800	7,400	6,300	4,900	93,600
EU	5,100	5,100	4,100	4,300	5,500	5,500	5,600	4,800	4,300	3,400	47,700
USA	8,200	5,200	4,100	4,300	5,300	4,000	3,400	4,800	2,500	2,800	44,600
ROW	6,600	6,800	7,900	4,100	9,500	10,000	9,500	8,500	7,600	7,400	77,900
Total	33,200	31,200	29,000	21,200	31,500	26,700	26,300	25,500	20,700	18,500	263,800
Immigration to Ireland											
Irish	17,600	17,700	20,500	23,200	26,700	24,800	26,300	27,000	17,500	16,900	218,200
UK	5,800	8,300	8,200	8,300	8,200	8,400	9,000	7,400	6,900	5,900	76,400
EU	3,200	5,000	5,500	5,800	6,900	8,200	6,500	8,100	6,900	10,600	66,700
USA	1,500	4,000	4,200	2,200	2,500	2,500	3,700	2,700	1,600	1,800	26,700
ROW	3,100	4,200	5,500	4,500	4,500	8,600	13,600	21,700	17,700	14,900	98,300
Total	31,200	39,200	43,900	44,000	48,800	52,500	59,100	66,900	50,600	50,100	486,300
Net migration											
	1995	1996	1997	1998	1999	2000	2001	2002	2003	2004	Total
	–2,000	8,000	14,900	22,800	17,300	25,800	32,800	41,400	29,900	31,600	222,500

Source CSO, 2000, 2004

ASYLUM SEEKERS AND REFUGEES

As Table 17.1 illustrates, there was a dramatic increase in migration from EU and non-EU countries between 1995 and 2004. Whilst the vast majority were returning migrants, their families, and labour migrants, a number were asylum seekers and refugees. Traditionally Ireland has a poor record of admitting asylum seekers and refugees and admission has largely been confined to small numbers of Hungarians in 1956, Chileans in 1973, Vietnamese in 1979, Iranian Baha'i in the mid-1980s, Bosnians in the early 1990s, and Kosovars at the end of the 1990s. As Table 17.2 documents, from a low of 39 applicants in 1992 the number seeking asylum grew to 11,634 in 2002. This growth in numbers led to consternation in political circles, with moral panics appearing in the media about the country being swamped with undesirable immigrants sponging on the welfare state and using Ireland as a backdoor into Europe. Capturing these sentiments, John O'Donoghue, the Minister of Justice, Equality and Law Reform, described asylum seekers as 'illegal immigrants and as exploiters of the Irish welfare system' (in Fanning, 2002, p. 103). It is arguable that Irish law puts pressure on the welfare system. Asylum seekers and those applying for refugee status are not entitled to work, regardless of their skills and needs, until their claim has been processed, and therefore are often reliant on welfare services. Concern over Ireland being swamped with asylum seekers and refugees has led to a series of policy and legislative interventions (see below) and a Citizenship Referendum in June 2004. This referendum, passed with a majority of four to one, changed the constitutional definition of citizenship so that a child born in Ireland is no longer entitled to automatic citizenship unless one of his/her parents is already an Irish citizen. The government argued that it was necessary to close a legal loophole, while critics argued that this 'ethnicised' citizenship and was contrary to human rights.

Applicant numbers fell dramatically to 4,304 in 2005. By the end of 2005, a total of 6,814 persons had been granted full refugee status since 2000; the largest communities were Nigerian and Romanian. This compares with a total of 48,632 applications processed since 20 November 2000 (Office of the Refugee Appeals Commissioner, 2006). In addition, 16,727 persons were granted leave to remain under the arrangements mentioned above for the parents of Irish-born children (O'Brien, 2006). Currently, therefore, there are at least 23,000 persons legally resident in Ireland who originally arrived as asylum seekers.

Table 17.2   Applications for asylum in the Republic of Ireland, 1992–2004

Year	No. of applications
1992	39
1993	91
1994	362
1995	424
1996	1,179
1997	3,883
1998	4,626
1999	7,724
2000	10,938
2001	10,325
2002	11,634
2003	7,900
2004	4,766

Source: Office of the Refugee Applications Commissioner, http://www.orac.ie, accessed October 2004, July 2005

EU MIGRANTS AND NON-EEA WORK PERMIT HOLDERS

Like asylum seekers and refugees, the number of people moving to Ireland to seek work has increased dramatically. Prior to 1 May 2004, all non-EU citizens required work permits to work in Ireland. These permits were issued through two different mechanisms: the Working Visa/Work Authorisation (WV/WA) programme administered by the Department of Foreign Affairs (under terms and conditions negotiated with the Department of Enterprise, Trade and Employment and the Department of Justice, Equality and Law Reform), and the work permits scheme administered by the Department of Enterprise, Trade and Employment. These schemes, while complementary, cater for people from different places with differing skills. The WV/WA programme targets high-skill, well educated workers needed for the service and high-skilled manufacturing sectors. The work permits scheme targets lower-skilled workers from outside the European Economic Area (EEA) (EU, plus Norway, Iceland, Liechtenstein and, under a separate agreement, Switzerland), needed for catering, agriculture, industry, nursing, and domestic home help (Crowley et al., 2006). Prior to 1998 work permit applications were below 5,000 per year; thereafter numbers of applicants rose steadily until 2003 (see Table 17.3).

Table 17.3   Work permits by sector, 1999–2004

Sector	1999	2000	2001	2002	2003	2004
Service	3,010	6,538	14,018	15,068	16,965	14,571
Catering	694	3,907	9,129	10,306	11,548	8,306
Agriculture/Fisheries	449	2,963	5,714	6,248	7,242	3,721
Industry	414	1,744	3,119	3,094	3,376	2,174
Medical and nursing	721	1,353	2,252	2,883	2,709	2,469
Entertainment	452	650	1,021	874	955	984
Domestic	80	195	521	788	944	772
Education	304	364	480	610	759	717
Sport	60	118	121	153	227	207
Exchange agreements		72	61	297	299	146
	6,184	17,904	36,436	40,321	45,024	34,067

Source: Department of Enterprise, Trade and Employment, www.entemp.ie/labour/workpermits/statistics.htm, accessed March 2005

With entry to the EU by the ten new (accession) states from May 2004 the work permits scheme was altered. On the one hand the government decided to allow migrant workers from the new member states unrestricted access to the Irish labour market, although, following the UK example, it introduced restrictions on access to welfare benefits by imposing a two-year 'habitual residence' rule before migrants could claim the full range of welfare benefits. On the other hand, it moved to restrict immigration from outside the EEA, by limiting the categories of work for which it was possible to apply for a work permit. The result was a decline in non-EEA workers: the 2004 figure was 34,067 (including 23,346 renewals), a drop of 28 per cent on 2003, and 27,136 for 2005 (including 18,970 renewals). The number of work permits issued has fallen further since that time. These figures do not include WV/WA permits.

Ireland was one of only three of the 'old' EU15 member states (the others being Britain and Sweden) which imposed no transitional arrangements concerning people from the accession states gaining admission to the labour market. Sweden experienced a very modest inward migration of 2,100 workers in the six months May–November 2004 (Statistics Sweden, 2005). For the period 1 May 2004 to 30 September 2005, 293,000 (annualised to 207,000) workers from the new accession states moved to the UK (Home Office, 2005). In Ireland, in the same period, 133,258 accession workers obtained PPSNs (Fitzgerald, 2006). By May 2006, 206,145 people from accession countries had obtained a PPSN (O'Brien 2006; see Table 17.4), with an annualised figure of half the UK annual average. To put this is context, the UK has 15 times more population than Ireland. To think of this in another way, the USA receives up to 1 million immigrants per annum under its various visa programmes (Migration Policy Institute, 2006) but on a pro rata basis to the Irish figure the US figure would be 6.75 million migrants. Moreover, the statistic does not include persons who migrated to Ireland from outside the EU with work permits, or work visas/authorisations; international students; workers and individuals from the other 14 'old' EU member states, and the non-economically active spouses and families of any of these categories of migrants. A final interesting comparison is with New Zealand, a country whose population is almost identical to that of Ireland but where the annual rate of immigration in 2004/05, including family reunification, was just 48,815 (New Zealand Department of Labour/Te Teri Mahi, 2005).

Table 17.4   PPSNs issued to EU accession-state workers, May 2004–May 2006

Accession state	PPSNs registered
Poland	116,206
Lithuania	35,497
Latvia	17,988
Slovakia	16,951
Czech Republic	8,885
Hungary	6,061
Estonia	4,045
Malta	295
Slovenia	165
Cyprus	52
Total	206,145

Source: *Irish Times*, 11 May 2006: 1

However (and it is a major however), it should be noted that these figures represent 'flows', not 'stocks'. We know relatively little about how many people come for a short period and leave again. In particular, the main data source available for new EU accession countries in intercensal periods is the issuing of PPSNs. Anecdotal evidence suggests that many Poles, for instance, register and work for a few months before returning home. They are somewhat similar to their Irish equivalents in the USA in the 1980s; that is, sometimes undocumented people with a good education who chose unskilled or semi-skilled work before returning to Ireland. It also appears that some migrants who obtained PPSNs never took up work in Ireland at all.

It should also be noted that immigration to Ireland on this unprecedented scale has not been trouble-free. A number of high-profile cases involving the exploitation of migrant workers have led to concerns in some quarters that cheap migrant labour, especially in unskilled sectors, may be leading to the displacement of Irish workers as well as downward pressure on wages and working conditions. Particular concern has been expressed about sectors such as domestic service, where feminisation and casualisation of the workforce are occurring in a poorly regulated environment. Unemployment rates at present do not bear out the charge of job displacement, but the effects of a cheap and relatively abundant source of labour (at least for the next several years) are likely to be a matter of controversy between employers and trades unions for some time to come.

The Irish economy is extremely exposed to global trends, because of its dependence on foreign direct investment and its extremely export-driven growth patterns. However, barring unforeseeable catastrophic events, current projections suggest that continuing strong growth is likely. A report by the Economic and Social Research Institute suggests that employment is likely to grow by a further 220,000 jobs between 2005 and 2010, generating further net immigration of at least 100,000 for the period (ESRI, 2003).

In addition, the government appears to be moving towards a regime which recognises a continuing need for some high-skilled migration from outside the EEA. The assumption seems to be that migrants from the new accession states will take the less skilled posts, which in fact appears to be happening (although many have post-secondary-level education). These patterns may change as other EU member states open their labour markets.

The effects of high levels of immigration are now visible across the geographical, economic, social, religious and cultural landscapes of Ireland. Goods and services aimed at ethnic niche markets; new revivalist churches and other faith communities; print and electronic media in various languages; the challenges of increasingly multilingual and multi-ethnic school, workplace and community environments; and the need for more effective action against racism and discrimination, are all testimony to the scale of change. For the first time, the 2006 census form was distributed in 16 languages as well as English and Irish; it also contains a new and hotly debated question on ethnicity.

POLICY CHALLENGES

Ireland faces a number of challenges, which may be divided into two key areas:

- managing migration;
- achieving integration.

Both policy areas will have to be developed within a framework which takes due account of Irish political, social and economic conditions, and the constraints of a 'special relationship' with Britain and Northern Ireland, embodied in the Common Travel Area Arrangement (see below), as well as evolving EU policy and migration trends at European and global level. New legislation, policy and institutional arrangements will be needed to address these issues.

Managing Migration

The government was probably initially caught unawares by the scale of changes in immigration to Ireland in the late 1990s. Moreover, initial attention, in political, media and public discourses, was very largely focused on the rise in asylum seekers arriving in Ireland at that time, to the extent that for several years there was little debate about labour migrants and their families.

Asylum Seekers and Refugees, and Immigration Generally

Government policy towards asylum seekers has been based on a frequently asserted belief that the majority of them do not meet the criteria set down in the 1951 Refugee Convention. The policy has sought to accommodate those awaiting a decision in reasonable conditions while expediting the procedures for processing claims, increasing the number of deportations and using a range of legislative and policy changes (e.g., carrier sanctions, or fines on transport companies) to bring about a stated aim of reducing the overall number of asylum seekers arriving in Ireland in the first place. Key developments included:

- The Refugee Act 1996, which incorporated the 1951 UN Refugee Convention into domestic law for the first time and replaced an ad hoc system with a more formal and transparent structure, although critics argued that it fell far short of best international practice.
- The establishment of the National Consultative Committee on Racism and Interculturalism (NCCRI) in 1998, after the European Year against Racism the previous year, and the Irish Human Rights Commission (IHRC) in 2001 following the 1998 Good Friday (Belfast) Agreement (Human Rights Commission Act 2000).
- The twin policies of dispersal and direct provision, implemented at the end of 1999, aimed at addressing a developing accommodation crisis in the Dublin area. Policy and practice currently oblige asylum seekers to stay in designated accommodation in various parts of Ireland, where they receive food and board and a small allowance while awaiting a decision on their case. The necessity to address the accommodation crisis was not in dispute, but there has been criticism of the manner in which the system has been operated.
- Non-binding public consultation procedures on immigration were undertaken by government. The first public consultation procedure on immigration policies took place in June 2001. The on-going social partnership process and direct submissions to, and meetings with,

ministers and politicians constitute the main mechanisms through which stakeholders can convey their views.

- A landmark Supreme Court judgment of 2003 struck down existing case law under which the parents of a child born in Ireland could usually obtain indefinite leave to remain. The government argued that this had become an incentive to asylum seekers to come to Ireland.
- The Immigration Act 2003 has as its main features carrier liability provisions and updated arrangements for the removal of 'non-nationals'[1] who are refused entry. The Act also made significant changes in the asylum system (including the 'safe country of origin' concept, allowing for the fast-tracking of applications from people not considered to be at risk if they are returned home).
- As a result of a High Court judgment in January 2004, the Immigration Act 2004 replaced the bulk of the Aliens Order 1946; it placed on a firm footing the derived ministerial authority of immigration officers when carrying out their functions.
- The citizenship referendum took place in June 2004. A scheme was subsequently introduced which in effect regularised the vast majority of parents of Irish-born children who had been left in legal limbo by the 2003 Supreme Court decision.
- The Irish Naturalisation and Immigration Service (INIS) was established in 2005 with the intention of creating a 'one-stop shop' for migrants in Ireland. Integration will obviously be part of the INIS brief, although as yet the details of its mission have not been revealed.

Labour Migration – Recent Policy Changes

With respect to labour migration, as well as developments that relate to immigration in general such as the INIS, the main developments have been as follows (Department of Justice, Equality and Law Reform, 2005a):

- The Employment Permits Act 2003, introduced by the Department of Enterprise, Trade and Employment, provided a revised legislative basis for work permits, including penalties for employers for illegal employment of non-nationals (up to then an offence only for non-national employees). It also made preparations for the implementation of free movement of workers from the new EU member states (the accession countries) in 2004.
- The 'habitual residence' requirement was introduced into social welfare legislation on 1 May 2004, to limit the access of non-nationals (including EU nationals) to many social welfare payments.
- The Employment Permits Bill 2005 will codify in legislation the current employment permits procedures, including the work permits and working visa/work authorisation schemes. The Bill provides for the application for, grant, renewal, refusal and revocation of employment permits. It provides that employment permits will be granted to the employee and that the permit will state certain rights and entitlements of the worker concerned.

The Bill prohibits recruitment-related deductions from remuneration and the retention by the employer of the employee's personal documents. However, it does not go as far as some advocates would wish in addressing in a substantive way the freedom of the migrant worker to sell his/her services on the open labour market, or the need for a path to permanence to be open to the majority of migrants.

Towards a More Efficient and Better Managed Policy

The claim has frequently been made by successive Irish governments that Ireland's migration regime is one of the most open and flexible in the EU and beyond. Insofar as it is market- and employer-driven, it has proven relatively fast and responsive and has enabled the economy to cope with a prolonged period of rapid growth. However, the piecemeal nature of policy changes, the lack of any long-term integration policy, and the public concern regarding well publicised cases of exploitation have led to a recognition that a more comprehensive and durable regime is needed. Concern has been expressed by the social partners (employers as well as trades unions) about the absence of transparent regulations in relation to such questions as family reunification and the absence of a path to permanence (other than citizenship) in Ireland's current immigration regime.

While the asylum situation is exceptional, it cannot in fairness be said that government has adopted an anti-immigrant position in general. The importance of immigration to the economy has been generally stressed and recognised, although the prevailing emphasis on high-skills migrants has not been matched by a commensurate concern for other migrants or their families. Some critics take a harsher view and argue that Ireland is operating a regime which, in de facto terms, is discriminatory as regards country of origin, skill levels and a general unwillingness to accept the 'other' in Irish society. For one prominent critic the concept of the 'racist state' is seen as structurally embedded in Ireland's immigration and asylum policies (Lentin, 2004).

In 2005 the Minister for Justice, Equality and Law Reform published a second discussion document entitled *Immigration and Residency in Ireland* (Department of Justice, Equality and Law Reform, 2005a), as a precursor to legislation intended comprehensively to update Ireland's immigration regime, which dates back to the 1935 Aliens Act and the 1946 Aliens Order. The document outlines the principal areas to be covered in new legislation, including: visas and pre-entry clearance; border controls; general principles for entry; admission for the purpose of work; self-employment and research; study; family reunification; non-economically active persons; residence status and residence permits; monitoring and compliance; removals; administration and delivery of services. Unfortunately, it contains virtually no mention of integration.

In addition to state intervention, a strong landscape of vibrant organisations has emerged in recent years. As well as NCCRI there is now a range of non-governmental organisations (NGOs), which engage in advocacy and support as well as service provision for migrants and new communities in Ireland. Migrants themselves are now organising and a strong migrant- and ethnic-led organisation (MELO) sector is emerging. Integrating Ireland, an independent network of such organisations, lists over 150 groups that have the explicit aim of 'working in mutual solidarity to promote and realise the human rights, equality and full integration in Irish society of asylum seekers, refugees and immigrants' (Integrating Ireland, 2005).

Achieving Integration

In 1999, the Department of Justice, Equality and Law Reform published *Integration: A Two-way Process* (Department of Justice, Equality and Law Reform, 1999). This report deals with the situation of refugees, rather than migrants in general, but it is the only official report to date on the subject of integration and gives an indication of official thinking in this regard. The working definition of integration adopted by the report was as follows:

> Integration means the ability to participate to the extent that a person needs and wishes in all of the major components of society, without having to relinquish his or her own cultural identity.

This is a rather weak definition and reflects the fact that the report was produced at a time when Ireland's experience of immigration was very new. It may not have been fully appreciated that there would also need to be a fundamental shift in attitudes, structures and services on the part of the host society as well the individual immigrant for successful integration to be achieved.

The government is now moving towards adopting a more wide-ranging approach to integration of all migrants, not just refugees. In the broader field of anti-racism and action against discrimination, proposals are already under way. The NCCRI has played the key role in developing the National Action Plan against Racism (NPAR), formally adopted by the Government in 2005 (Department of Justice Equality and Law Reform, 2005b). The five primary objectives underpinning the NPAR are:

- effective protection and redress against racism, including a focus on discrimination, threatening behaviour and incitement to hatred;
- economic inclusion and equality of opportunity, including a clear focus on employment, the workplace and poverty;
- accommodating diversity in service provision, including a focus on common outcomes, education, health, social services and childcare, accommodation and the administration of justice;
- recognition and awareness of diversity, including a focus on awareness raising, the media and the arts, sport and tourism;
- full participation in Irish society, including a focus on the political, the policy and the community levels.

The NAPR may be regarded as the template that will underpin a range of government initiatives in this field for the next three years. While it undoubtedly sets new benchmarks for action in the fields of racism and anti-discrimination, there has as yet been little consideration of integration in the light of debates (e.g., on language tests and citizenship examinations) taking place in a range of other EU member states, including the Netherlands, Denmark, Sweden and the UK. In particular, Ireland has not yet decided whether in the long term it wishes to embrace an explicitly multiculturalist policy along Canadian lines or whether it is likely to opt for a form of calibrated or de facto assimilation.

Finally, the EU is also proposing action on integration, through its common basic principles. It envisages an eleven-point programme which seeks to strike a balance between respect for diversity, inclusion, anti-discrimination and adherence to core rights. The legal basis for action in this field has yet to be clarified but it is likely to become a priority area in the coming years.

BROADER HORIZONS

Ireland is constrained to a very significant degree by the Common Travel Area (CTA) between the UK and Ireland, which allows for movement without passports for UK and Irish citizens between the two jurisdictions. The desire of the UK authorities to retain an autonomous immigration control regime, for instance, has meant that they have not joined the 'Schengen area', an EU-wide area of free movement and common controls. Ireland has been obliged to follow suit.

The maintenance of the CTA requires a strong element of policy alignment on immigration matters. Since the conclusion of the Amsterdam Treaty in 1997, there has been progress towards the creation of a common EU migration policy. But Ireland and Britain do not participate fully in this process and have chosen to 'opt in' on a case by case basis. The Irish position is to participate to the extent that is consistent with the maintenance of the CTA with the UK. It is possible that at some point in the future Ireland and the UK will become full participants in EU action in the field (Department of Justice, Equality and Law Reform, 2005a).

It may be asked whether Ireland's 'opt-out' is a position of principle or a pragmatic reflection of its close geographical and historical relationship with the UK. There can be no doubt that a significant and consistent element of British thinking about border control has been an unwillingness fully to accept EU policy because it would mean to some extent relinquishing control of UK borders in favour of a pooled arrangement. Britain, like Ireland, has historically monitored the movement of persons by monitoring its borders, rather than monitoring people in the places where they live. This has always been a more feasible and effective approach for island jurisdictions.

Irish and British attitudes are regarded as anomalous by other EU member states and by the European Parliament. The British attitude may evolve over time, particularly if national identity cards (something which was opposed by successive governments up to now) are introduced. As far as Ireland is concerned, there would not appear to be the same anxiety to uphold a position of principle as found in the UK case, but the government has made it clear on many occasions that the preservation of the CTA (presumably for as long as both governments deem it necessary) must take priority.

Ireland is also obliged to comply with its human rights obligations under international law, but to date (in common with its EU neighbours) has not ratified the United Nations or International Labour Organisation conventions on the rights of migrant workers.

CONCLUSION

Ireland is no longer a country where immigration can be regarded as a short-term or transient issue. The country has now definitively joined the European mainstream as a society where a population of mixed ethnic backgrounds will be the norm. A number of features concerning these immigration flows are worthy of note. First, immigration to Ireland has followed the classic two-tier pattern, with a strong demand for high-skills migrants in certain sectors such as medicine and high technology and a substantial flow of migrants into unskilled or relatively unskilled sectors. Second, initial strong flows of refugees and asylum seekers from the mid-1990s have significantly reduced, while labour migration from accession countries has increased dramatically. Third, the geographical spread of migrants in Ireland is highly dispersed, with almost all parts of the country experiencing some in-migration. Fourth, the range of source countries is highly diversified, although Central and Eastern Europe have been dominant and there has been a further significant shift towards the new accession countries since 2004. Most of the source countries have few previous close political or cultural connections with Ireland, posing an additional challenge for migrants arriving here as well as for the receiving society. Population projections, while never an exact science, suggest that sustained immigration is likely to continue for at least another two decades. By the 2020s it is likely that migrants and their descendants will number up to one-fifth of the population. Fundamental choices have yet to be made about how the process of integration should be managed.

18
Transformations in Housing

Mary P. Corcoran, Karen Keaveney and Patrick J. Duffy

CONTEXTUALISING HOUSING IN IRELAND

The evolution of housing and the housing market in Ireland reflects the dramatic transformations in economy and demography that have occurred in Ireland in recent years. In 2005, 81,000 housing units were completed, the eleventh year in a row of record house completions in the State. The rate of construction represents one of the highest per capita in the world and is unprecedented for any Western economy in the twenty-first century. Ireland is building at the fastest rate in Europe with 14.7 newly completed dwellings per 1,000 inhabitants in 2002, the highest by far in EU compared with around 3.5 units per 1,000 in the United Kingdom in the same period, for example (Gallent et al., 2003). Despite the growth in housing supply, average house prices rose by 11 per cent in 2004 for new and secondhand homes (DoEHLG, 2005a). The bulk of housing growth and provision has occurred in and around large cities and towns. The most recent census data available indicate that in 2002, just under 60 per cent of the population were located in urban settlements of 1,500 people or more (see Chapters 1 and 4).

Along with the increase in building units, there has been a significant diversification in terms of the types of units now coming onto the market. In the past, it was the convention for people to remain in the same home throughout their lives, to raise their families, and retire there. Now, ideas of flexibility and mobility have become integral to the housing and real-estate markets. Houses are built as 'starter homes', implying that they will be transient and that the owner occupiers will move on once the opportunity allows. Smaller units and higher densities, particularly in and around the city centres, are creating a market for single-person households, one of the fastest growing demographic categories across Europe. Older people are now under pressure to downsize, to release equity in their homes in order to get their children started on the property ladder. Some dwellings are built for investment purposes, allowing purchasers to gain tax benefits from investing in the housing market under tax incentive schemes. And finally, approximately 3 per cent of new-build houses are second homes for existing property holders, with up to 12 per cent often located in the most coveted parts of the Irish countryside.

Many towns and cities throughout Ireland suffered from poor planning in the 1960s and the 1970s. Rapid suburban development contributed to the decline of the inner-city residential areas, partly because most private and state investment since the 1970s has been channelled into suburban areas. Considerable profits were derived by key individuals from property development in town and city centres and from land speculation and the construction of housing estates in the sprawling suburbs. At the same time, city councils often vigorously pursued a policy of relocating inner-city residents to new social housing schemes on the city's perimeter. As a result, the social fabric and its capacity to form sustainable communities were systematically undermined, particularly in the principal cities. The erosion of inner-city communities through job loss and the disappearance of homes was paralleled by the growth of new ex-urbanised communities on the fringes of these cities, where population growth continues to increase at a dramatic rate.

The 1960s and 1970s also marked a distinctive shift in the territorial pattern of housing growth in rural areas. Until then, rural housing was almost exclusively associated with farming or related activities. Economic changes throughout the State resulted in the development of the idea of the one-off, non-farm dwelling house on a half-acre site accessible to a town. Towns and cities as growth points in the national, as well as local, economies emerged significantly from the 1960s with a shift from agriculture to industry, manufacturing, construction and services. This resulted in increased house building in localities more accessible to expanding towns and cities. Arising out of the general urbanisation of the economy and the strong traditions of owner-occupancy in rural areas, affinities with rural living in a rural 'idyll' have deepened. This has resulted in continued pressure for new houses and second homes in the countryside by ex-urbanites and family members of existing rural households commuting to urban-based employment. Over half of the current rural housing stock in Ireland was built from the 1970s onwards. Paralleling the pattern of urban housing development, the zones of most intense building in the countryside in the 1990s were mainly located in mid-Leinster districts within 50 miles of Dublin and in the commuter hinterlands of provincial centres such as Galway, Cork, Limerick, Sligo, Athlone and Killarney, and around smaller towns and holiday areas such as Mayo, Donegal, Kerry and West Galway (see Figure 18.1).

THE KEY PROCESSES UNDERPINNING HOUSING TRENDS

Urban Regeneration

The evolution of the built environment, whether in the urban core, on the edge of the city, in the suburbs or the open countryside takes place in a political and economic context. The political context is largely provided through the planning regime, which in the Irish case is provided by the local authorities working under the auspices of the Department of the Environment, Heritage and Local Government (see Chapter 2). According to Byrne (2001) the nominal objectives of planning in relation to the urban core have changed dramatically, particularly over the last 30 years, mirroring transitions that have taken place in capitalism. These changes at the level of the political have, to a great extent,

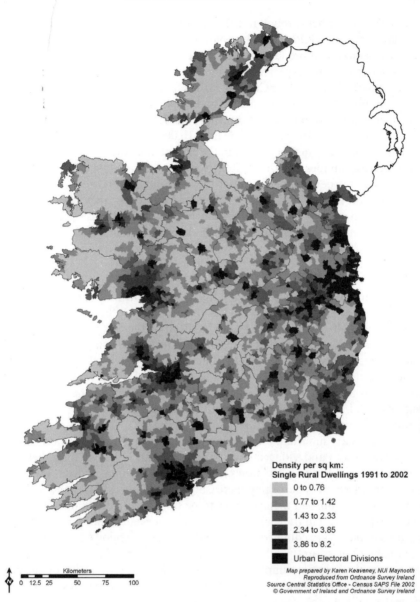

Density per sq km:
Single Rural Dwellings 1991 to 2002

- 0 to 0.76
- 0.77 to 1.42
- 1.43 to 2.33
- 2.34 to 3.85
- 3.86 to 8.2
- Urban Electoral Divisions

Kilometers
0   12.5 25   50   75   100

Map prepared by Karen Keaveney, NUI Maynooth
Reproduced from Ordnance Survey Ireland
Source Central Statistics Office - Census SAPS File 2002
© Government of Ireland and Ordnance Survey Ireland

Figure 18.1   Density per sq. km.: Single rural dwellings, 1991–2002

Sources: Central Statistics Office, Census SAPS file, 2002; Ordnance Survey Ireland

been wrought by the impact of economic global forces working themselves out on the urban landscape. In the Irish case, the impetus for change in the housing market in city and town centres was provided by the Urban Renewal Act 1986 which made available a generous package of tax-based incentives to developers, investors and home owners. The urban renewal scheme was designed to promote private investment in the built environment of designated inner-city areas either through refurbishment of existing buildings or through new developments, (KPMG et al., 1996). In response to these conditions, and given the generally more favourable prevailing economic conditions, Dublin and other Irish cities experienced a building boom in the office, residential and commercial sectors (see Chapter 5). The boom, which commenced in the 1990s, continues today. Between 2002 and 2004, for example, 42,500 flats and apartments were completed, amounting to a fifth of all new housing (*Irish Times*, 5 April 2006). In Dublin, more than 10,000 new private apartments were built in the inner city in that period. In the case of apartments that qualified for tax designation under the Urban Renewal scheme, the State effectively acted as a catalyst for development, and at the same time supported a market for what was built through additional tax incentives for occupancy of commercial buildings and private homes. More than 100,000 households – almost 9 per cent of the total number of households in the State – resided in apartments by 2002 (CSO, 2003a).

Suburbanisation

While urban regeneration is changing the nature of the housing market in the city centres, the suburb has emerged as the dominant urban form in Ireland over the last half-century. Since the foundation of the State, government has provided either direct or indirect subsidies to those purchasing private houses. This has been a key factor in Ireland's internationally high – 77 per cent – rate of home ownership. As the population has expanded, the demand for private housing has accelerated, and new estates have proliferated. The 2002 census demonstrated a pattern of high growth in the immediate hinterlands of all major cities and towns (see Figure 1.4 in Chapter 1).

In recent years suburban estates have spread to quiet rural locations, while peripheral towns and villages have grown from an influx of long-distance commuters, and the process shows no sign of weakening. Indeed, it can be argued that Ireland is becoming increasingly ex-urbanised, as many of these new forms of suburban living appear to be both post-rural and post-urban. They are post-rural in the sense that vast housing estates, shopping malls and leisure complexes are colonising more and more rural regions, threatening the sustainability of a 'rural landscape'. They are post-urban in the sense that the relocation of work, consumption and leisure facilities to the edge of the city and indeed into small and mid-sized towns reorients suburbanites away from the metropolitan core.

A recent study of four new suburban communities in the Dublin commuter belt – Leixlip, County Kildare; Esker (Lucan), County Dublin; Mullingar, County Westmeath and Ratoath, County Meath – found that, generally speaking, respondents 'electively belonged' to their communities – they felt attached to the place where they lived. People still saw the suburbs as good places to raise children. They derived sustenance from close relationship with others, particularly those who were at similar stages of family formation. Finally, the research suggests relatively modest but not negligible levels of social and civic participation (Corcoran et al., 2005). Respondents in all four localities were consistent in identifying an average of five to six people in their local social network on whom they could rely for help, support and socialising on a regular basis. However, the people who primarily constitute that network – family, neighbours and friends – vary considerably across the localities. In Ratoath, County Meath, for example, people are making a lifestyle choice to move to the countryside and express a strong attachment to place. This is in contrast to suburbanites who have moved into the new estates in Esker (Lucan) out of necessity (the affordability of the house) and who do not express as strong an attachment to place. The research also pointed to a pattern of poly-nucleated conurbation, wherein people access goods and services by commuting to different towns and villages in the hinterland rather than in the metropolitan core (Peillon, 2004). Respondents in all four localities expressed considerable concern about the problems faced locally, ranging from poor infrastructure and services (in Ratoath and Esker) to anti-social behaviour and lack of facilities for children (in Leixlip and Mullingar).

Social Housing

Despite the huge increase in house building in Ireland, almost 50,000 Irish people are currently on waiting lists for social housing. Historically, the model of social housing provision in Ireland was distinguished by three characteristics: it was primarily based on subventions from central government; policy implementation occurred through local authorities; and a standardisation (or stigmatisation) attached to house and estate design (Fahey, 1999). The latter has changed much in recent years, with local authorities pioneering good urban design in the provision of new units. However, the number of actual units built is low and far short of demand. While record numbers of private houses were completed in 2004, the number of social and affordable housing units fell from 13,000 to 12,145 (*Irish Times*, 12 July 2005). Part V of the Planning and Development Act 2000 was introduced in order to provide housing for people on the social housing list in each local authority area, to allow for the provision of 'affordable housing' (housing that requires a mortgage of approximately 3.5 times an annual salary), and to provide for the integration of all residential types in all developments of four or more dwellings. Social and affordable housing need is outlined in a housing strategy which is incorporated into all local authority development plans. In spite of the intention to make more social and affordable housing units available, figures in the *Annual Housing Statistics Bulletin 2004* show that many developers are transferring land (including serviced sites) or making financial contributions to local authorities in lieu of building houses in their own developments. The stock of social housing has also been adversely affected by the decision of local authorities such as Dublin City Council to sell considerable numbers of units, thus limiting the overall growth of the local authority rental sector. The NESC (2004) has recommended that an expanded stock of housing should be made available at a social rent to ensure an adequate safety net for vulnerable households, along with provision of adequate resources for social and affordable housing for other qualifying groups. The voluntary and co-operative housing sector has expanded considerably in recent years, providing a range of high-quality housing options in both rural and urban settings.

Given the centrality of the principle of home ownership in Irish society, social housing has generally been viewed by home owners and tenants alike as an inferior option: if private ownership is for the upwardly mobile, then social housing tenancy is for those who are going nowhere. Social housing has in the past been seen as housing for the poor, while owner occupation is now seen as the normal tenure for mainstream households. The challenge remains of how to integrate the poorest, most marginalised groups into the housing system in a problem-free way. In Dublin, as elsewhere, local authorities are seeking new ways of providing housing in the social sector that can overcome some of the problems encountered in the past. One such example is detailed in the case study of Fatima Mansions below.

Rural Housing

In spite of the growing urban population in Ireland and concentration of new housing in urban and suburban locations, demand for privately owned housing in the countryside remains high. The incidence of one-off single rural dwellings (defined as detached dwellings with individual septic tanks) throughout the countryside is a significant feature in many locations. This is overwhelmingly new-build housing which has been the favoured planning approach in Ireland, unlike in the UK where restoration of older housing stock is more stongly encouraged. Although rapid demographic expansion is characteristic of Ireland as a whole, pockets of rural areas continue to experience depopulation and demographic contraction which is reflected in an ageing population and ageing housing stock. Less accessible remoter localities, therefore, continue to experience problems of derelict housing, out-migration and social deprivation. Ironically, while average family size has fallen significantly in recent years (the average number of persons per household in rural areas was 3.72 in 1981, decreasing to 3.09 in 2002), the size of new rural housing units is increasing. Although houses with five rooms accounted for the largest proportion of rural dwellings in 2002 at over a quarter of all housing stock, the number of dwellings with eight rooms or more had the strongest growth over the period 1991 to 2002, accounting for almost a third of all new rural dwellings.

Single rural houses have normally been characterised by road-oriented locational patterns, frequently in 'ribbon developments' which sometimes negatively impact on local landscapes. In many places, the density of houses relying on septic tanks and deep bored wells, allied to the incremental addition of houses over subsequent years, has serious environmental implications for groundwater supplies.

Pressure for increased housing (planning) permissions in the countryside comes from farmers and land owners, the rural housing lobby and many local councillors, all of whom want the rural planning system relaxed to allow more rural housing in order to enhance the economic and social viability of their rural areas. Although housing growth helps to support social structures and local services, new discourses of rurality have highlighted additional, and often contradictory, aspects of change associated with the transformation of extensive countrysides. Many former landscapes of farmland, for example, now provide settings for a new consumption of landscape by incoming residents, manifested in such things as large houses, manicured lawns, decks, patios and double garages. In the comparatively treeless landscapes of west Mayo, hilltops, skylines and 'views' have been appropriated by new houses – to see and be seen. Visitors from the UK, which experiences rigid planning control in rural areas, frequently comment on the social vitality of Irish rural areas as reflected in new housing. On the other hand, there are interest groups in Ireland (heritage- and urban-focused in the main) harking back to an older eighteenth-century landscape aesthetic which values empty unpeopled views of countrysides, who want more planning controls to protect the rural landscape from being inundated with indiscriminate housing. The Heritage Council claims that inappropriate and poorly planned development is putting much landscape heritage at risk because of ineffective legislation to protect environmental and landscape heritage. The Irish Rural Dwellers' Association (IRDA) claims that legislation is too rigid and that planners (and agencies like An Taisce and the Heritage Council) are inhibiting development (IRDA, 2004). As part of the wider framework provided by the National Spatial Strategy, guidelines requiring a sustainable approach to the planning of rural housing were published in 2005 (DoEHLG, 2005b). However, the criteria for eligibility to build new dwellings in the countryside remain somewhat ambiguous at the local plan-making stage. The planning process to a large extent has kept its traditional focus on regulating planning in towns (town planning) and maintained a less stringent approach in rural areas. Rural planning practice is very heavily influenced by local clientelist politics, which has resulted in one of the most benign rural planning regimes in Europe. The notion of 'local need', for example, is poorly defined in scope and application and is open to continuing pressure from local politicians and lobbies (Gallent et al., 2003).

CASE STUDIES

Fatima Mansions, Dublin

Creation of a Sink Estate

Fatima Mansions was built between 1949 and 1951 by Dublin City Council. The development originally consisted of 15 blocks of four-storey flat units, with an average of 27 units per block. The complex is configured inwardly, which has had the effect of cutting Fatima Mansions off, both physically and symbolically, from the surrounding neighbourhood of Rialto. While there is no doubt that the flats were a vast improvement on the tenements that had preceded them, they were essentially a 'bricks and mortar' solution to the problems faced by the Dublin working class. Little thought was given to the provision of recreational facilities, or to the highly salient issues of housing density and housing allocation policy (Tobin, 1990).

In the 1970s, a confluence of factors propelled the estate into a spiral of decline. The closure and, in some cases, relocation of local industry adversely affected job opportunities in the area. The impact of unemployment was compounded when tenants were offered incentives by Dublin City Council to purchase local authority houses elsewhere. Such policy initiatives, which promoted home ownership, rewarded tenants who left Fatima Mansions. This gradually produced a residualisation effect, as less reliable tenants frequently replaced those who had moved on, undermining the social fabric that had been the basis of a strong community. Dublin City Council's services to the estate declined during the 1970s, with the removal, for example, of the uniformed caretaker officials who had informally 'policed' the area. It became more difficult for both the remaining tenants and Dublin City Council to exercise moral authority on the estate. A spiral of decline was set in motion and the estate became vulnerable to problems of social disorder – vandalism, joyriding, and later, drugs. Fatima Mansions earned the reputation of being an undesirable place to live.

Mobilisation of the Community

By the late 1990s, daily life in Fatima had become a feat of endurance. The most common motif employed by residents to characterise their daily lives was that of imprisonment. Trapped in an environment over which they had little or no control, they expressed feelings of hopelessness and despair. Their lives were dominated by two factors in particular: first, a breakdown of social order on the estate, which facilitated a drug economy and culture that continues to the present day; second, the inadequate upkeep and maintenance of the public areas of the estate. The two factors are, of course, inter-related; the degraded environment, with dimly lit stairwells and boarded-up flats, provided a safe haven for those seeking to buy and sell drugs without fear of apprehension. Residents had internalised the belief that they were perceived as 'second-class' citizens by the statutory authorities, and that the quality of service provided to them reflected their low status in society.

Alongside the simmering despair at the level of degradation into which the estate had fallen by the end of the 1990s, there was also a strong sense of an enduring social fabric. Residents relied heavily on cohesive social networks to counter the negative effects of living on a 'sink estate'. A survey carried out at the end of the 1990s found that a high proportion of people in Fatima Mansions had lived there for more than 20 years, and in some families, tenancy had passed down through a second and third generation. Social ties with neighbours and extended families were extremely strong. Significant numbers believed there was a good community spirit. Although people spoke about the horrors of daily life and child rearing in Fatima, they nevertheless displayed remarkable resilience and a sense of humour in the face of these difficulties. Clearly, the existence of associational life in the form of interactions, personal relations and institutional practices at the level of locality act as an important bulwark against total social breakdown. This resource has helped not only to sustain the community through troubled times, but has also enabled the community to begin to re-imagine itself.

The 'structural crisis' on the estate – evidenced by high rates of poverty and unemployment, low levels of educational attainment, and increased criminality and drug-related activity – are attributable at least in part to the spatial, social, and economic inequalities that characterise the city of Dublin. A structural crisis on this scale demands a structural solution. Thus, the local community came together with Dublin City Council in the late 1990s to set in motion a process of change. The local community development group, Fatima Groups United (FGU), became the driving force behind the estate's regeneration agenda and remains the key agent in the process of social change. FGU set about conceptualising and developing a set of ideas and initiatives that could be put to the statutory agencies that held a remit in Fatima Mansions. At the end of 2000, FGU produced a manifesto that was the outcome of a creative thinking exercise involving the entire community of Fatima Mansions in articulating their visions and needs for the place in which they lived. Crucially, the impetus for a plan for the regeneration came from the community, who placed themselves firmly in the driver's seat of the proposed regeneration. 'Eleven Acres: Ten Steps' comprised a brief from the community of Fatima Mansions to the planners, developers, and service providers tasked with the regeneration of the housing estate. It set out the community's vision for its future, and invited Dublin City Council to enter into a dialogue on how the area ought to be regenerated.

Development of a Regeneration Plan

In February 2001, Dublin City Council published its own plan for the regeneration, 'Regeneration/Next Generation'. This plan commits to key principles of urban regeneration, including the creation of a socially balanced neighbourhood made up of both social and private housing, with additional purpose-built community facilities. Research in Britain has demonstrated that compared with large deprived estates, socially balanced neighbourhoods are likely to be less stigmatised by outsiders (Goodchild and Cole, 2001). Central to the plan is the re-imagining of the existing housing estate, its relationship to the adjacent neighbourhood and to the wider city of Dublin. This plan seeks to create not just an integrated and sustainable community, but to devise a new template for managing the process of urban regeneration. The new vision for Fatima Mansions is underpinned by the belief that the neighbourhood is the key building block for the city and that it is at this level that democracy, participation, and integration must be achieved. This is very much in keeping with the principles that underpin the Integrated Area Planning (IAP) approach promulgated by central government and pursued by Dublin City Council in the late 1990s (see Chapter 2). Crucially, the regeneration plan maintains a dual commitment to both the physical and social needs of the area. The regeneration is guided by three aims: (1) to deliver new standards in quality of public housing and community facilities; (2) to undertake innovative actions aimed at breaking the cycle of poverty on the estate; and (3) to foster effective social integration and measures that promote and safeguard community participation in developing and sustaining the new Fatima, which will triple in size.

Application of Partnership Principles at Local Level

In tandem with the physical regeneration plan, a social regeneration programme has also been finalised by the Fatima Regeneration Board (Whyte, 2005). The social regeneration plan will be financed by Dublin City Council. The plan is the outcome of work carried out by five different subcommittees set up by the Fatima Regeneration Board and wide consultation within the community. The social regeneration plan prioritises five areas for action: anti-social behaviour, health and well-being, education and training, arts and culture, and economic development. The plan for the social, economic and cultural regeneration of the estate will work in parallel with the physical regeneration plan. The community is determined to develop an international model of 'best practice' for urban regeneration projects in deprived neighbourhoods.

The experience of the residents of Fatima Mansions in generating their estate's renewal raises many salient issues about the process of urban regeneration in Dublin, notably about how social housing should be provided, and how neighbourhoods can cope with the effects of deindustrialisation and marginalisation. In particular, there are several key lessons that can be derived from those experiences:

- If Irish cities are to be liveable and sustainable then attempts will have to be made to counteract tendencies toward social polarisation.
- Social exclusion can be addressed by adapting a principle of equity that ensures that the benefits of urban renewal are more widely distributed across the urban population.
- Urban planners must retain a sensitivity to the significance of a sense of place in the everyday life practices of city dwellers.
- Planning must proceed on the basis of a partnership approach that involves the local community as a co-equal stakeholder.

Through social movements, community development associations, and environmental advocacy groups, the urban citizenry are being engaged in a variety of re-imagining projects that attempt to specify what the nature of place-specific and place-sensitive residential development might be. In Fatima Mansions, the community activists are driving forward an imaginative programme of redevelopment that is requiring a good deal of 'thinking outside the box'. The community is confronting a history of ghettoisation and marginalisation, and envisioning a new kind of urban living that will offer a template for other cities seeking to re-imagine their deprived neighbourhoods. All interested parties, from communities to planners, developers, and politicians, must take up the challenge of identifying forms of development that are consensual across a broader spectrum of the citizenry and that are closer in design, scale, and aesthetic to the city's vernacular. In doing so, it may be possible to find a way that reaches out to the global, while simultaneously respecting the local.

Rural Housing in Clew Bay, County Mayo

The Clew Bay area of County Mayo is a popular tourist destination with attractive coastal and mountainous scenery. Proximity to the growing towns of Westport and Castlebar has driven the demand for housing either by locals or incoming commuters in accessible rural districts in the wider catchments of these towns. The highest level of new development has taken place in Westport and Castlebar towns, with significant concentrations in the accessible rural hinterlands. Just under half of the current housing stock in the Castlebar hinterland, for instance, was built in the period from 1996, with one-fifth in the Westport hinterland area. Many houses have also been built by returned overseas emigrants and up to one-tenth of the rural houses are in the holiday home category. The high-quality coastal landscapes in particular have experienced intense amounts of scattered rural housing (see Figure 18.2). In the Clew Bay area, one-fifth to one-third of the housing stock was constructed in the 1990s (see Figure 18.3). For example, in the Murrisk area of Clew Bay, to the north of Croagh Patrick, over a quarter of the total rural dwellings were built since 1991, and mostly since 1996, in what is arguably one of the most prominent sites in Mayo.

Attitudes of Residents

As in many rural locations in Ireland, there is a tension between the desire to live in the countryside and concern that continuing population growth will

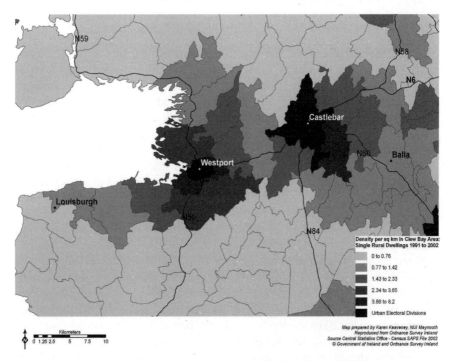

Figure 18.2   Density per sq. km. in Clew Bay Area: single rural dwellings, 1991–2002

Sources: Central Statistics Office, Census SAPS file, 2002; Ordnance Survey Ireland

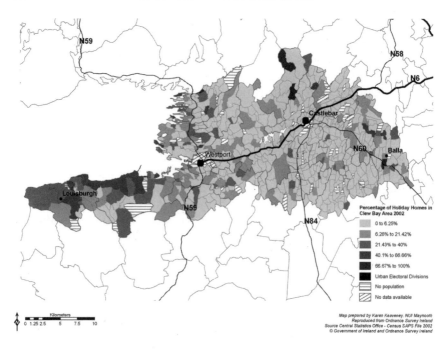

Figure 18.3   Percentage of holiday homes in Clew Bay area, 2002

Data sources: Central Statistics Office, Census SAPS file, 2002; Ordnance Survey Ireland

dissipate the attractions of moving to the countryside. In a survey of rural households in the Clew Bay area, residents articulated notions of a rural idyll when either describing their reasons for moving to the countryside or outlining the attractions of living in the countryside. Notions of community, kinship and privacy were also emphasised by residents who had returned from living in cities. In addition, the feeling of being close to nature and wildlife, being able to fully experience seasons and living in close proximity to the sea and beaches were viewed as positive features by many. The attractiveness of living in the countryside was juxtaposed with the supposed unattractiveness of living in towns. For these respondents, the rural is a peaceful place to live, with its only negative features being 'outside' factors beyond the control of local residents, such as lack of public transport, bad road maintenance and traffic speeding.

Rural landscape is a dominant consideration in assessing new housing trends for the countryside. Social issues tend to rank more highly in discourses of urban and suburban housing. Rural poverty and bad housing conditions are mainly associated with marginal, predominantly agricultural areas where demographic imbalances are linked to low levels of urbanisation and remoteness from services and employment opportunities (Pringle et al., 1999). Thus, for instance, the greatest proportions of houses built before 1919 (one-quarter to one-third) are found in the Sligo, Leitrim, and north Midland areas as well as extensive parts of south and east Munster. In the west (Mayo, Galway and Roscommon), apart from the past two decades, significant proportions of the rural houses were built between 1919 and 1940. The extensive newly populating rural zones, however, have been selected by middle-income mobile classes who have new consumption preferences (as opposed to the earlier productivist traditions of these areas). The priorities of consumption-oriented residents emphasise landscape commodities like views, nature, tranquillity and freedom from stress, as well as community and local-ness (Kaltenborn and Bjerke, 2002). The very visuality and materiality of these landscapes are particularly important in the debate on rural housing. Housing and garden design, density and location all impinge significantly on the quality of landscape habitat and heritage. The disruption/destruction of what seems an immemorial farming countryside is at issue in many places. And the west of Ireland, particularly its treeless coastal zone, is especially vulnerable to indiscriminate housing development.

However, in all of these representations of rural life, a tension between existing residents' and others' desires to live in the countryside is acknowledged. The prospect of extensive and intensive urbanisation of the countryside is regarded widely as a negative scenario. Indeed, residents' groups seeking to improve their rural areas by introducing 'urban' amenities like street lighting, footpaths and landscaped road verges have been highlighted as an example of this urbanisation or suburbanisation of landscape. There is also evidence of a tension between long-term, full-time residents and newcomers to the area. Thus, references to outsiders getting planning permission before 'locals', and developers and builders getting preference in the planning process, are often indicative of resentments against the planning regime.

Holiday Homes

Internal tensions simmer particularly around the issue of holiday homes. It has been difficult to accurately assess the number of holiday homes in Ireland due to a lack of consistent recording methods by local authorities. The 2002 census contains limited information on second-home house building. The rate of second homes as a percentage of all dwellings in the State is relatively low at 3 per cent. However, counties along the west coast have above average rates, with County Mayo having one of the higher rates at 7 per cent of total dwellings. In general it would seem that the greatest density of holiday home development is along a narrow coastal strip extending southwards from Inishowen in Donegal to west Cork and the south coast to Wexford.[1]

In 2002, one-tenth of housing in the Clew Bay study area was recorded as holiday homes, concentrated in particular localities: for example, a third of all dwellings in Louisburgh were recorded as holiday homes, dominated mainly by house clusters which are rented out on a short-term basis. The second highest rate of holiday homes is to be found in the Croagh Patrick electoral division where 27 per cent of all dwellings are holiday homes, in this case mainly one-off, privately owned houses. In the rural survey a number of respondents took issue with houses lying empty and locked up for most of the year, contributing little to the local community.

Rural Planning

Because of the often conflicting expectations of full-time residents, temporary holiday home residents and tourists, the role of the planning authorities in controlling future development in the Clew Bay area is vital. The County Development Plan (CDP) for 2003–09 preceded the national rural housing guidelines issued in 2005 by DoEHLG. CDP policy adopted for both single rural dwellings and holiday homes is brief, focusing mainly on physical planning considerations about minimum basic standards for site size and location. Eligibility criteria for planning permission in the countryside are not addressed. All planning authorities were expected to implement the DoEHLG's rural housing guidelines, which effectively superseded existing local authority policy. In addition to the Mayo CDP, draft housing design guidelines were produced in 2002.[2] In this policy document the local authority acknowledges the need to preserve both the rural community and the unique natural landscape. While rural house design and its subsequent landscape impacts are an important factor in the growth of new housing, underlying issues of the sustainability of rural housing in many countrysides need to be addressed. The notion that if one 'contributes' to the local rural area (DoEHLG, 2005b) one should be allowed to live there may be simply too flexible and open a policy. The real complexity of rural housing is not addressed in the national rural housing guidelines. The demand from non-farming, and what could be called non-rural dwellers, is without doubt having an impact on many facets of rural housing from basic site costs to community and landscape changes. The changing function of agriculture in Ireland and the growing role of the speculative developer are resulting in changing land values throughout all rural area types from urban hinterlands to scenic areas. There is a clear need to examine the contestation of housing, not as the main rural planning issue or problem, but as a manifestation of rural change in Ireland today.

CONCLUSION

Dramatic economic and demographic transformations in recent years in Ireland have greatly impacted upon the nature of housing in both rural and urban areas, creating complex demands on the housing market for both different tenure and dwelling types. Where people live and how they live are rapidly diversifying in Dublin and other major cities around Ireland. Suburbanisation is spreading and absorbing towns which function as urban centres in their own right, indicating a move toward a more poly-centric pattern of living. New centres have emerged on the edge that increasingly fulfill the functions of the city. At the same time, the metropolitan core is being strengthened in many ways through urban regeneration and gentrification. While new suburbanites express a degree of satisfaction with life in the suburbs, they nevertheless acknowledge that their communities lack basic facilities and infrastructure that are essential to quality of life. Apartment living is a relatively new phenomenon in Irish life. While a 'back to the city' movement is to be welcomed, concerns are increasingly expressed about the long-term sustainability of new apartment complexes, particularly in relation to issues of maintenance and management. The model of social housing regeneration in Fatima Mansions in Dublin is a 'good news' story and will hopefully serve as a useful template for other local authority estates undergoing regeneration. A more pressing issue however, is the overall decline in local authorities' housing stock at a time when thousands of families are in urgent need of social housing. In a trenchant critique of the housing system, Drudy and Punch (2005) have argued that housing in Ireland has for too long been treated as a commodity for trading and wealth generation rather than a social good. One of the unintended effects of the Celtic Tiger phenomenon has been the generation of both winners and losers in the housing market.

There was a territorial shift of rural house location from the 1960s onwards, with expansion of peri-urban development into the open countryside as urban-based employment became dominant. This accelerated into the 1990s when one-fifth of the current rural dwelling stock was built. In spite of the persistent decline of farming, the rural population in Ireland continues to grow. The enduring laissez-faire approach to rural planning marks Ireland out from many of its European neighbours, particularly the UK. Growing dwelling sizes, a lack of consistent design guidelines among local authorities, additional physical infrastructure such as extended street lighting and footpaths are all forces in changing the character of the rural landscape. The risk of deteriorating water quality as a result of the proliferation of septic-tank usage also highlights the need for a stronger policy for housing in the countryside. This has given rise to tension between lobbies for or against housing in the countryside. While popular notions of the rural idyll continue to fuel demand for rural housing provision, there is a growing necessity for more adequate and sustainable management strategies in rural regions. In summary, housing – urban, suburban and rural – provides significant challenges for the future, especially given projected population growth.

19

Deprivation and its Spatial Articulation

Trutz Haase

Social deprivation tends to achieve greatest prominence when it is clustered in particular locations and threatens to affect the cohesion of a society. The emergence of successive regional development programmes in Ireland during the 1920s, 1950s and 1960s was arguably a response to the emigration rates, themselves a result of widespread poverty that prevailed during these decades. The emigration issue posed a challenge to government because of its demoralising consequences, but also the threat it posed to long-term sustainability of the Irish economy and social structure, particularly in rural areas. Indeed, a long-standing tradition of research into rural decline and poverty in Ireland culminated in the acclaimed study by Curtin et al., (1997).

Since the early 1970s there has been a growing awareness that severe pockets of poverty also persist in urban areas even where overall prosperity is achieved. Until the 1990s urban poverty research in Ireland tended to be confined to specific sectoral issues such as the concentration of long-term unemployment, access to services or place-related social stigma, leaving a resultant gap in respect of significant wide-ranging studies of urban poverty. The 1990s saw a resurgence of interest in the spatial aspects of poverty (both rural and urban) amongst Irish policy makers and renewed efforts to describe and map its distribution and multidimensional complexity (see Pringle et al., 1999).

The new emphasis on the spatial aspects of poverty was in part a response to the limited effectiveness of existing traditional functional and sectoral approaches to tackling poverty. It was also driven by the opportunities provided by the newly adopted welfare policy based on localised targeting of public (especially EU-provided) resources. This approach required priority areas of need for targeted intervention to be identified so that the designated areas could be the subject of focused investment and localised partnership-based activity, including multidimensional integration and innovation. The current emphasis within spatial poverty research seeks to understand both the spatial distribution of poverty and the impacts of poverty on specific places. It looks to inform policy responses on a variety of scales by providing added value to resource usage through area-targeted initiatives and by highlighting the implications of neighbourhood and social housing effects. In summary, poverty is now recognised as being spatially diffuse but with significant and discernible variations, especially at the micro level.

WHY A GEOGRAPHICAL PERSPECTIVE MATTERS

Many of the urban-based initiatives adopted in the US during the 1970s and in the UK during the 1980s were designed as an explicit response to civil unrest and riots in the most disadvantaged urban neighbourhoods. Similarly, the housing programmes which commenced during the 1980s in Northern Ireland may best be understood as a response to the demands of the civil rights movement in preceding years. Finally, the initiatives taken in EU and OECD member countries during the 1990s are, at least in part, a response to the spatially uneven outcomes of economic restructuring following the rapid globalisation of economic development during the 1970s and 1980s. They therefore represent an attempt to maintain political cohesion in regions that have paid a high price as a result of restructuring.

As a consequence, area-based initiatives tend to be invoked in the context of 'crisis' situations, and this in itself encourages inflated expectations and an attendant risk of losing sight of what such initiatives can realistically achieve. This explains why there tends to be a cyclical element to the way in which area-based responses come into vogue for relatively short periods of time before gradually fading away. After a period of strong popular support for area-based policies to reduce the incidence of multiple deprivation in the UK during the late 1960s and 1970s, for example, many of its previously ardent supporters became disillusioned as they came to realise that the spatial distribution of poverty was highly resilient to public interventions:

An area strategy cannot be the cardinal means of dealing with poverty or 'under-privilege'. However we come to define economically or socially deprived areas, unless we include nearly half the areas in the country, there will be more poor persons or poor children living outside them than in them. (Townsend, 1979, p. 560)

In Ireland, area-based initiatives of their present form were first set up in 1991 as a response to the exceptionally high concentrations of long-term unemployed in certain predominantly urban communities. While initially being well received, a similar change in outlook occurred amongst some of their previous supporters within a decade of their implementation (Nolan et al., 1998, 1999, 2000; Watson et al., 2005). The critique is that the majority of poor people do not reside in clearly identifiable 'poor' areas, and that area-based initiatives should not therefore be the main policy instrument for combating poverty and deprivation. Instead, this requires comprehensive responses, including the restructuring of the tax and social welfare systems and equitable infrastructural and human resource programmes. However, whilst partly advancing a powerful critique, views such as these – which either treat space as an optional extra to public policy or which see spatial and non-spatial dimensions as mutually exclusive – fail to grasp the unique contribution of geography to the creation and perpetuation of cumulative disadvantage and deprivation.

Understanding Multiple Deprivation

Area-based responses should indeed not substitute for structural policy responses. The National Anti-Poverty Strategy (Government of Ireland, 1997) remains pivotal to targeting social exclusion in Ireland, and any attempt to elevate area responses to the status of 'prime mover' in the fight against social exclusion are ill advised. However, there remains a strong rationale for retaining and even broadening the remit of area-based local development initiatives. The reason for this lies with the often poorly understood cumulative effects which occur as a result of the clustering of distinct forms of deprivation amongst particular social groups and/or in specific neighbourhoods. This is frequently referred to as multiple deprivation, but it is more precise to speak of neighbourhood effects. In fact, a large body of international research has developed over the past ten to fifteen years around the conceptualisation and measurement of such effects.

'Neighbourhood effects' refer to those factors which affect the life chances of individuals over and above what could be predicted from their individual socio-economic circumstances. Two examples will suffice to highlight both their existence and immense importance. The first involves rural communities that have experienced extreme labour market disadvantage in the form of a simultaneous decline in demand for agricultural labour and an absence of alternative job opportunities. As a consequence, many of the children who grew up in marginal farming households have emigrated. Clearly, we can no longer measure the degree of deprivation in areas such as these on the basis of their unemployment level. Nevertheless, few would disagree that they are highly deprived, even though there may not be large concentrations of deprived people.

The second example comes from the educational sector, and applies mainly to deprived urban areas. It is known that children from disadvantaged family backgrounds tend to have lower educational achievements than children from more privileged backgrounds. However, children from disadvantaged backgrounds who share their school environment with other poor children have a much greater risk (up to one-and-a-half times greater) of becoming an 'educational failure' than those who study alongside children from more affluent homes (Williams, 1992). This is an example of a 'neighbourhood effect', and sophisticated statistical techniques have been developed in recent years that enable us to quantify the impact of the wider social context on individual educational outcomes. Although the study of neighbourhood effects is celebrated as a great advance in social science methodology, it is striking that only two such studies have yet been undertaken in Ireland (Smith, 1999; Haase and Pratschke, 2003).

These examples show the fundamental error that occurs when measures of spatial deprivation are based on the characteristics of poor people alone, rather than applying a wider concept of deprivation which also takes into account the structural limitations that curtail people's life chances and opportunities, including their shared environment. Local development initiatives can play an important role in countering the *additional* disadvantage encountered by people living in disadvantaged neighbourhoods.

The rest of this chapter is divided into three sections, the first of which looks at the appropriate conceptualisation of deprivation, particularly when considered in a spatial context. The second examines some empirical data for Ireland to trace the geographical distribution of affluence and deprivation over the 1991 to 2002 period. The final section discusses some of the issues surrounding government policies and institutional innovation to develop Ireland's most disadvantaged communities.

CONCEPTUALISING SPATIAL DEPRIVATION

Any attempt to describe the extent and distribution of disadvantage in Ireland, and its spatial distribution in particular, encounters the problem of appropriately defining poverty and deprivation. Within the extensive literature that has been produced on this subject over the past 20 years, the dominant approaches have built on the definition of poverty provided by Townsend, which highlights the relative character of the concept by comparing how people experience their lives relative to the community they are living in:

> People are relatively deprived if they cannot obtain, at all or sufficiently, the conditions of life – that is, the diets, amenities, standards and services – which allow them to play the roles, participate in the relationships and follow the customary behaviour which is expected of them by virtue of their membership of society. (Townsend, 1993, p. 36)

Townsend places considerable emphasis on lack of income, and income poverty is undoubtedly an essential element of deprivation. However, exclusive reliance on income poverty as a measure of deprivation is problematic for a number of reasons. Firstly, it assumes that the only unit of analysis is the individual; secondly, it assumes that deprivation should be measured solely in terms of outcomes as opposed to risks, conditions or opportunities; and thirdly, it does not consider broader aspects of the quality of life, such as, for example, health, education, environment, or access to transport and services. A definition of deprivation which is overly reliant on individual measures of income poverty unduly narrows the focus of policy and may deflect attention away from those areas where the most effective interventions towards building sustainable communities can be made.

This critical view is incorporated into the broader definition proposed by Coombes et al., (1995, p. 5) who state that:

> The fundamental implication of the term deprivation is of an absence – of essential or desirable attributes, possessions and opportunities which are considered no more than the minimum by that society.

This seems to be a preferable definition of deprivation and some of these issues are discussed briefly in the following paragraphs.

Focus on the Individual

At least in the European and North American context, the debate on poverty and social exclusion has, over the past two decades, been characterised by an increasing focus on the individual. This is not only the case in relation to the development of transfer mechanisms within the tax and social welfare systems that aim to alleviate poverty, but extends to the growing emphasis on counting the number of individuals targeted under various area-based initiatives and on 'counting the poor' in the construction of spatial deprivation indices. The argument is that one should precisely estimate the number of people suffering deprivation in a given area, before directing resources to people residing in these areas in order to minimise deprivation.

However, questions in relation to the value of 'counting the poor' have begun to emerge. As the majority of poor people are unlikely to live in designated disadvantaged areas, the principal policy instrument for targeting the poor (as individuals or households) must be the tax and social welfare system. Area-based initiatives, by contrast, are more suited to enhancing the infrastructure and services available to particular communities and should thus be based on the wider considerations of relative disadvantage.

Who Exactly Is Deprived?

This leads to the second issue, the question of who or what exactly is deprived. The question as to whether deprivation is suffered by individuals, households or communities is a difficult one. The dominant view amongst commentators has been that it is the individual who is deprived and, as such, the individual is the appropriate building-block for all definitions of deprivation, including its spatial form.

There are, however, a number of caveats associated with this assumption, particularly given that the individual's experience is also shaped by household (e.g., race and class) and neighbourhood factors as outlined in our previous section (e.g., environment and social conditions) or even regional factors (e.g., employment opportunities). In its spatial form it also leaves open the question of how an area is to be assessed which has been characterised by persistent emigration. Are remedial services to be provided at the point of emigrants' arrival or should they not be placed at the place of their departure?

Actually or Potentially Deprived

The third question, and one that is closely linked with the previous one, relates to whether our definitions should be confined to those who are 'actually deprived', or whether they should include considerations of the 'risk' of deprivation. Most commentators emphasise outcomes; that is, the actual experience of deprivation of individuals or households. However, as Coombes et al. note, in practice this distinction may not be sustainable:

> The notion of a 'cycle of deprivation' illustrates the problem: individuals who are poor are also more likely to live in unsatisfactory housing conditions and to suffer health problems, thereby endangering their employment status and

thus reinforcing their poverty. In this way, each outcome is also a condition which makes the sufferer more vulnerable to other aspects of deprivation … the tendency for individuals to thus experience more than one form of deprivation has been simplified in the term multiple deprivation. (Coombes et al., 1995, p. 7)

Summing up the points made above, definitions of deprivation, and spatial deprivation in particular, must clearly go beyond considerations of income poverty conceptualised at the individual level, to relate the experience of individuals, groups and communities to the prevailing social norms. Our definitions must reflect the fact that the socio-economic context has an impact on people's quality of life. Finally, as it becomes increasingly clear that deprivation indices are inappropriate tools for targeting poor individuals, but derive their raison d'être from their ability to inform initiatives aimed at the level of communities, they cannot be reduced to poverty outcomes alone, but must also include measures of the risk of poverty. Having thus highlighted some of the conceptual issues that underpin the study of poverty and deprivation, some measurements are now detailed.

Measuring Deprivation

It is useful to start with a discussion of the dominant approaches to the measurement of income poverty and other related measures of deprivation. Following this, the constraints of individual measures of deprivation can be examined in the context of spatial analysis, particularly at higher levels of spatial disaggregation.

The Combat Poverty Agency distinguishes between two types of poverty, absolute or consistent poverty, and relative poverty:

A person is said to be in consistent poverty when he or she has both a low income and lacks at least one of a number of specified basic necessities such as warm clothes, adequate food and heating. (CPA, 2004)

Whether someone is living in relative poverty is determined by comparing their income to a particular income threshold: if they fall below this threshold, they are deemed to be experiencing poverty. Generally, this threshold is set at either 50 per cent, 60 per cent or 70 per cent of median income. Deprivation or social exclusion are further defined as:

the process whereby certain groups are shut out from society and prevented from participating fully by virtue of their poverty, discrimination, inadequate education or lifeskills. This distances them from job, income and education opportunities as well as social and community networks and they have little access to power and decision-making bodies. (CPA, 2004)

There has been a recent trend towards using similar definitions of poverty, articulated at the individual level, in the analysis of the geographical distribution of deprivation, notably the current indices of multiple deprivation (IMD) for

England, Scotland, Wales (Noble et al., 2000) and Northern Ireland (Noble et al., 2001). However, this approach is not without its critics, as it falls short in relation to almost all of the conceptual aspects outlined in the previous sections. Above all, it assumes that the level of deprivation in an area is simply the sum of the poor individuals within it, that the risk of poverty is largely irrelevant and that there is no conceptual difference between urban and rural deprivation.

Whatever the merits of approaching spatial analysis in terms of the number of people living in (income) poverty within a given area, this approach is practically unfeasible when implemented at the level of small areas. The relative income poverty indicators utilised by the EU and by the Irish government rely on in-depth household surveys and, because of the limited sample size involved, are first and foremost geared towards providing reliable national indicators. At best, they may be able to provide reliable comparison at the regional (NUTS 2 and NUTS 3) level. County-level indicators cannot be reliably obtained from such an approach. Similarly, the IMD approach in the UK is heavily dependent upon administrative data records, many of which can only be obtained at ward level. Below this level, small-area analysis, as for example at enumeration district (ED) level, must continue to rely on the analysis of data available at that level, notably the census of population (cf. European Commission, 2003).

THE SPATIAL DISTRIBUTION OF POVERTY

In contrast to the authors of the recent British deprivation indices, the authors of the Irish index of relative affluence and deprivation (Haase and Pratschke, 2005) have consistently argued that the use of indicators from different domains should not lead us to neglect the different dimensions of deprivation, most notably its rural form. Based on a review of a large number of deprivation indices throughout OECD countries (Haase, 1998), they conclude that overall deprivation can adequately be described by three underlying dimensions: social class disadvantage, acute labour market deprivation, and demographic decline. While the social class dimension differentiates affluent and poor areas in both urban and rural locations, acute labour market deprivation, as for example measured by the prevailing unemployment rate, is a predominantly urban phenomenon. Rural areas which experience prolonged labour market difficulties, by contrast, seldom exhibit high unemployment rates. Instead, people from deprived rural areas tend to emigrate and this effectively reduces the measured unemployment rate. However, as emigration is socially selective, in as much as it is highest amongst the relatively well educated core working-age cohorts, we can measure its effects in terms of higher age-dependency rates and lower educational achievements amongst the remaining adult population.

Econometric analysis and geographical analysis both provide strong support for the close correlation between population decline and resulting population characteristics such as higher age- and economic dependency rates and lower educational attainments within the workforce. The latter has an effect not only in terms of current employment levels – and thus income-generating potential – but also in terms of the capacity of local areas to successfully attract new firms and to provide sustainable employment.

Unfortunately, it is not yet possible to fully capture the wider aspects of deprivation and well-being. To date, the only reliable data for constructing a deprivation index in Ireland derive from the census of population. To return to Coombes et al.'s (1995) definition of deprivation, we have already noted that the fundamental implication of the term 'deprivation' is of an absence of essential or desirable attributes, possessions and opportunities which are considered no more than the minimum by a given society. The census of population can provide us with some insight into population characteristics (e.g., demographic attributes, education and social class) and possessions (as measured through social class, employment and the quality of housing). However, rural areas face a particular risk of falling behind urban areas in relation to the opportunities that they offer their inhabitants, and this helps to explain the persistence, and even accentuation, of emigration during times of relative economic affluence.

Despite such limitations, the Irish Index of Relative Affluence and Deprivation does provide an extremely informative picture of the geographical distribution of deprivation throughout Ireland. Furthermore, due to the innovative approach in using confirmative factor analysis (CFA) as opposed to the more common exploratory factor analysis (EFA), the authors have produced a set of deprivation indices which measure spatial deprivation over three successive censuses while using identical structure matrices and measurement scales. It has thus been possible, for the first time, to directly compare degrees of deprivation at various points in time, which opens up the use of deprivation indices not only for the purpose of appropriate resource allocations, but also for monitoring and evaluation.

Ireland 1991–2002, a Period of Sustained Growth

The first set of maps (see Figures 19.1 and 19.2) show the level of overall affluence and deprivation in 1991 and 2002, using identical measurement scales. The scores range, in broad terms, from -50 to +50, with higher values indicating greater affluence and lower values indicating greater deprivation. The scores are not detrended; i.e., the mean for 1991 is zero, but the mean for 2002 is approximately 15, reflecting the considerable growth in the Irish economy over this eleven-year period.

The maps provide fascinating insights into the spatial distribution of this growth, most importantly its nodal character and the over-riding importance of Ireland's urban centres. The most affluent areas of the country are distributed in concentric rings around the main population centres, mainly demarcating the urban commuter belts. The maps show how rapidly these rings of affluence expanded during the 1990s as large-scale private housing development took place in the outer urban periphery, leading to high concentrations of relatively affluent young couples.

The Spatial Distribution of Deprivation over Time

The third map shows the spatial distribution of *relative* affluence and deprivation in 2002 (see Figure 19.3). The values underlying the map are derived from those used for Figure 19.2, but after deducting for each ED the underlying trend for

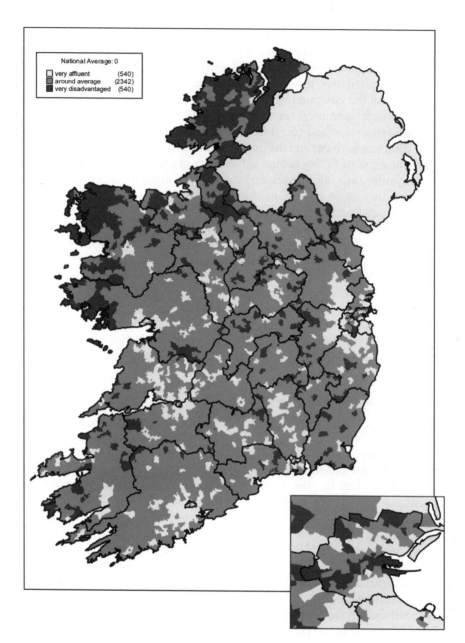

National Average: 0

☐ very affluent   (540)
▨ around average   (2342)
■ very disadvantaged   (540)

Figure 19.1   Overall affluence and deprivation, 1991

Sources: Haase and Pratschke (2005); Ordnance Survey Ireland

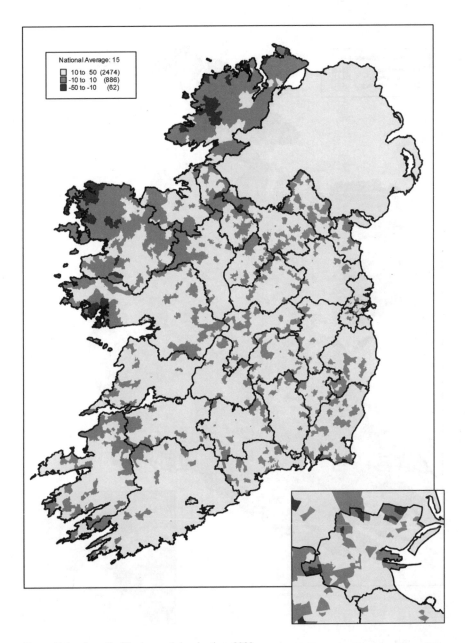

National Average: 15

☐ 10 to 50 (2474)
▨ -10 to 10   (886)
■ -50 to -10   (62)

Figure 19.2   Overall affluence and deprivation, 2002

Sources: Haase and Pratschke (2005); Ordnance Survey Ireland

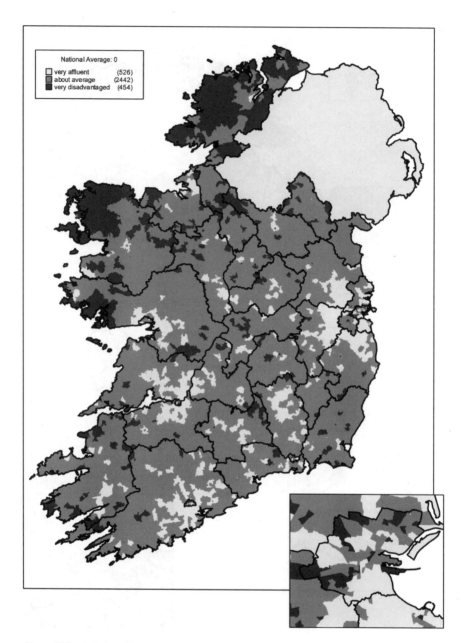

National Average: 0

☐ very affluent   (526)
▨ about average   (2442)
■ very disadvantaged (454)

Figure 19.3   Relative affluence and deprivation, 2002

Sources: Haase and Pratschke (2005); Ordnance Survey Ireland

the eleven years; i.e., the national average is again zero. The most deprived areas in 2002 were as follows:

- *Dublin*: Coolock, Darndale, Ballymun, Finglas, Cabra, Ballyfermot, Inchicore, Cherry Orchard, Clondalkin, Blanchardstown, Crumlin, Walkinstown, Tallaght, and parts of Dublin's inner city;
- *Other urban locations:* parts of Cork, Limerick, Galway and Waterford cities, as well as parts of the towns of Dundalk, Drogheda and Wexford;
- *Rural locations:* most of Donegal and Mayo, large parts of West and East Galway, significant parts of Leitrim, Cavan, Monaghan, Longford and Roscommon, North and West Kerry and Wexford.

The comparison of Figures 19.1 and 19.2 demonstrated the huge increase in the levels of affluence, as it expanded in concentric rings around Ireland's urban centres over the previous decade. A comparison of Figures 19.1 and 19.3 highlights, at the same time, the limited degree to which the relative position of local areas has changed. With the exception of Dublin's inner city, the worst affected areas in 1991 were still the worst affected ones in 2002. This is the key finding of the study. It proves what is intuitively broadly understood, particularly by those who are actively involved in the area-based initiatives: things have hugely improved in the disadvantaged areas with regard to unemployment, educational achievement etc., but at the same time nothing has changed relative to other more affluent areas which equally have improved their situation and thus maintained the differentials. This finding, whilst new in its precise measurement due to the application of a novel modelling approach, is nevertheless not unique in its generality. As is increasingly clear from analyses carried out in different countries, the spatial distribution of relative deprivation is highly stable over time. Indeed, as a recent study of England and Wales shows, the distribution of relative deprivation in these two countries has not changed dramatically over the course of a century (Gregory et al., 2001). The full report, including coloured maps for all three census years for both absolute and relative deprivation can be downloaded from the Pobal website.[1]

GOVERNMENT POLICIES AND INSTITUTIONAL INNOVATION

This final section of the chapter looks at present government policies to address spatial aspects of poverty and inequality. Looking for new ways to tackle the problem of long-term unemployment in the worst affected areas of the country, a new area-based strategy was designed during the early 1990s in order to reproduce at local level the partnership approach implemented at national level by the national agreement, the Programme for National Recovery (PNR). Area-based initiatives, in their present form, were introduced in Ireland in 1991 under the Programme for Economic and Social Progress (PESP). In the following years, the programme was gradually extended from the initial twelve partnerships to cover all disadvantaged areas throughout the country. These target areas were chosen, for the first time, on the basis of a deprivation index (Haase et al., 1996). Area-based initiatives peaked – in terms of their publicly assumed role – under the Operational Programme for Urban and Rural Development (1994–99), but continue presently under the Local Development Social Inclusion Programme (LDSIP) as well as a number of other government initiatives with a local-development dimension. As all local-development programmes have been brought under a single ministerial responsibility, the government is now committed to consolidating the multiplicity of local-development initiatives (partnerships, community groups and LEADER initiatives) into a single organisational structure. It is therefore appropriate to briefly restate some of the key considerations that underlie the rationale for area-based initiatives.

Firstly, and contrary to common belief, the most important issue is not whether area-based social inclusion initiatives represent the most appropriate way of reaching low-income households with high levels of social need. Most poor families do not live in areas that are immediately identifiable as 'poor', and it is therefore appropriate that the majority of anti-poverty measures should be aimed at individuals, families and households, and should be based on the income tax code, social welfare payments and entitlements to free state services. The budgets of area-based or local-development initiatives are thus, justifiably, small compared to the billions of euros spent on the main redistributive elements of the combined tax and social welfare regimes.

Instead, the raison d'être of area-based initiatives is that space is an important aspect of the structuring of social processes. Many people are willing to pay a premium in order to reside in affluent neighbourhoods and to pay private-school fees in order to provide their children with a superior education and a head start in their careers. The chief purpose of area-based initiatives in general, and the local development partnerships, community groups and employment pacts supported under the LDSIP in particular, is therefore to counter the *additional* or *cumulative* effects arising out of the clustering of poor households.

Examples of these include the thinning out of certain age cohorts in remote rural locations due to emigration; school-level and neighbourhood effects on educational achievements; the lack of jobs and services in disadvantaged urban and rural locations; drug and crime-related problems in areas of high unemployment, and many more. All such phenomena have an effect on those who live in disadvantaged areas, increasing the level of social exclusion that they experience in their daily lives. The key aspect of these phenomena is therefore their spatial articulation; they result from the composition of households residing in an area, but are not necessarily amenable to change through policies aimed at poor individuals and families alone.

The second issue relates to the need for the State to continuously find new and innovative solutions to the problems undergone in areas and communities which experience multiple and cumulative deprivation. Area-based partnerships were initially set up in 1991 in response to the failure of centrally administered welfare, training and job-creation programmes to offer an effective solution to the problems of unemployment and long-term unemployment in certain urban and rural communities. Over successive local-development programmes, the remit of the area-based partnerships has gradually been broadened, to the extent that it now covers a wide range of disadvantaged target groups (see Chapter 14).

Through their innovative work, area-based partnerships offer a rich 'laboratory' from which the state administration can learn how to enhance the effectiveness and efficiency of its own activities. Sabel (1996), in his evaluation of the Irish partnership experience, refers to this process as 'democratic experimentalism'. Unfortunately, this important concept is frequently misunderstood, particularly by key government departments and state agencies, so that the application of the lessons learned to the mainstream delivery of government functions remains the exception rather than the rule.

The third issue relates to the gradual changes that have occurred within the national partnership process itself over the past 15 years. Over the course of the five programmes that have been agreed since 1987, the emphasis in the national partnership negotiations has shifted from macro-economic matters to structural and supply-side policies; the range of supply-side issues under discussion has been widened to address those that are widely considered as constraints on economic growth, such as childcare and life-long learning. This change in the content of the national partnership agreements has involved a parallel change in method. While macro-economic strategy can be discussed in the context of national negotiations, complex policies that cut across different areas of society, relating to issues such as social exclusion, training, business development and childcare, cannot be devised effectively within the confines of high-level negotiations. Consequently, in order to address the growing number of supply-side issues, a wide array of working groups, 'frameworks' and 'forums' have evolved, involving representatives of the various social partners. In a few areas of policy, such as long-term unemployment, rural and urban regeneration and business development, new institutional arrangements have been created so as to involve actors on the ground.

However, despite the opportunities generated by the unprecedented boom of the 1990s, most participants in the national partnership process feel that the success rate of the partnership approach in relation to structural and supply-side issues has been lower than in relation to macro issues (O'Donnell, 2001). It seems that while we know how to do high-level bargaining, we are unsure about how to tackle multilevel problem solving, and this is further exacerbated at local level. Indeed, in most areas, the shift to multilevel and local problem solving has been limited, since the working groups are composed almost exclusively of national representatives of the social partners. It is therefore likely that at least some of the uncertainty currently evident amongst the social partners arises from the uneven development of the national social partnership system.

Once these underlying issues have been understood correctly, the uncertainties that have arisen in relation to the future role of area-based initiatives, partly as a result of the proliferation of local development structures, can be resolved more easily:

- Firstly, area-based initiatives have a fundamental and unique contribution to make to the local development process.
- Secondly, as the analysis of the spatial distribution of affluence and deprivation shows, the rising tide has lifted all boats, but, with very few exceptions, the poorest areas of the 1990s are still the poorest areas in 2002.
- Thirdly, far from it being possible to 'absorb' local development initiatives into the state administration, it is essential that such organisations maintain a semi-independent status. 'Semi-independence' thereby refers to the freedom to develop innovative solutions to the problems of multiple and cumulative disadvantage at local level, whilst simultaneously being accountable through ongoing monitoring and evaluation.
- Finally, in order to achieve this, local development organisations will have to address two serious issues: (1) they must resist the temptation to become mainstream providers of social inclusion programmes which do not contain significant innovations; and (2) a fundamental rethinking of the evaluation process is necessary in order to determine the actual impact of innovative measures and to apply the lessons learned to the state's mainstream functions.

20
Health and Disease

Frank Houghton and Dennis Pringle

Health was defined in the founding charter of the World Health Organization in 1946 as 'a state of complete physical, mental, and social well-being and not merely the absence of disease or infirmity' (Meade and Earickson, 2000, p. 2). This definition is useful because it defines health as a positive attribute to be promoted, rather than simply a neutral state found in the absence of disease. It also draws attention to the fact that health should be viewed as more than simply a state of physical well-being. The definition therefore defines the (probably unachievable) goals that, as a global society, we should work towards. However, it does not provide an easily implemented framework for the development of research instruments, so for practical research purposes health is usually defined de facto as the absence of disease (i.e., the focus tends to be on disease rather than on health per se).

It is important to retain a clear distinction between people's health (or ill health) and their access to the health (i.e., medical) services. This chapter looks briefly at some aspects of the inequalities in health in Ireland, before reviewing some of the on-going changes in the health services. The review concludes with a brief discussion of the potential role of a spatial perspective in improving disease surveillance and health service planning in Ireland.

TEMPORAL TRENDS IN HEALTH AND DISEASE

Life expectancy at birth is arguably the best single indicator of the overall health of a population, although it tends to be especially sensitive to changes in the death rate of those in the younger age groups (especially infants). Life expectancy at birth in Ireland increased markedly throughout the twentieth century from 49.3 years in 1901 to 75.1 years in 2002 for males, and from 49.6 years to 80.3 years for females (Central Statistics Office, 2004). The biggest increases were in the two decades before independence and in the period 1946–1961.

As in most economically developed countries, there was a marked change in the causes of death. Infectious diseases, although declining as a cause of death since the mid-nineteenth century, remained a major cause of death at the beginning of the twentieth century, but by the end of the millennium they had become a comparatively insignificant cause of death. This decline in deaths from infectious diseases, and the corresponding increase in life expectancy, is usually referred to as the epidemiological transition. This transition is often attributed to the introduction of effective therapeutic drugs in the 1940s and 1950s, but several commentators, most notably Thomas McKeown (1976, 1979, 1988), have noted that deaths from the major infectious diseases in other countries were in decline long before the introduction of effective drugs. Nevertheless, much of the increase in life expectancy in Ireland in the period 1946–61 was probably due to a massive decrease in deaths from tuberculosis, which in turn probably reflected the introduction of more effective medical interventions.

As infectious diseases declined as a cause of death, deaths from non-infectious diseases (sometimes referred to as degenerative diseases) increased. Deaths from non-infectious diseases, such as heart disease and cancer, are more common in developed countries, and in the developed countries they were initially more common in the more affluent social groups. They are therefore sometimes referred to as diseases of affluence. However, as the twentieth century progressed, deaths from most of the so-called diseases of 'affluence' in developed countries, including Ireland, actually became more common amongst the less affluent social groups.

One issue that continues to generate debate is whether the increase in deaths from non-infectious diseases should be viewed negatively as an 'epidemic' indicating a deteriorating situation, or (given that everyone must die from something) whether this increase should be viewed more positively as a natural outcome of the decline in the number of deaths at a younger age from infectious diseases. It might be noted, in this context, that there have been changes in recent years in the relative importance of different types of non-infectious disease, suggesting that deaths from non-infectious diseases should not be regarded simply as a residual effect. For example, ischaemic heart disease (IHD) (ICD 410–414) was the largest killer in Ireland throughout much of the twentieth century (accounting, for example, for 8,326 deaths in 1980) but, as in many countries, it has been declining as a cause of death since the 1980s and accounted for 6,589 deaths in 2000. Meanwhile, cancer (ICD 140–208), which accounted for 6,287 deaths in 1980, has increased to overtake IHD as the leading cause of death, accounting for 7,666 deaths in 2000.

When making comparisons over time it is necessary to take account of changes in the age composition of the Irish population. Using standardised rates to take account of Ireland's increasingly ageing population, it would appear that there has been comparatively little change in cancer rates over the past two or three decades. However, there has been a very substantial decline in ischaemic heart disease mortality, indicating a considerably reduced risk since the 1980s.

SPATIAL VARIATIONS IN HEALTH AND DISEASE

Information on the spatial variations in health and disease in Ireland is comparatively sparse. The main source is the Annual Report on Vital Statistics, which on occasions included maps of tuberculosis mortality, infant mortality or all-cause mortality. The reports for 1899 to 1901 included maps of deaths from tuberculosis, whilst maps of tuberculosis and infant mortality were included in 1911 to 1914. No further maps appeared until 1950, after which maps of all-cause mortality were published most years until 1990 (Houghton, 2002). However, they were based on directly standardised rates (which are sensitive to stochastic variations) and were not particularly informative. The reports since 1990 contain no maps, and since 2001 they do not even include spatially disaggregated information on the age of death for specific causes, thereby eliminating the possibility of calculating age-specific rates.

On the plus side, there would appear to be a growing awareness of the importance of the spatial dimension within health-related public bodies such as the National Cancer Registry, Health Protection Surveillance Centre, and the Institute of Public Health, each of which have produced reports containing maps in recent years (e.g., Balanda and Wilde, 2001; National Cancer Registry, 2001; Walsh et al., 2001). Likewise, the Department of Health and Children regularly produces a database called the Public Health Information System (PHIS), which contains an option to map morbidity and mortality data.

Maps of all-cause mortality and deaths from selected causes over the past 35 years generally indicate a higher death rate in the major urban areas (i.e., the county boroughs), although Galway tends to be an exception in this regard (Pringle, 1982, 1986a, 1986b; Creton and Pringle, 1991; Howell et al., 1993). Higher mortality in urban areas is consistent with the patterns found in other countries. For the 1970s the maps also indicate a regional disparity between the more prosperous south and east of the country, and the less prosperous north and west (see Figure 20.1). However, the regional disparity is the inverse of that most commonly found in other countries. Normally the areas of higher mortality are found in the less prosperous areas, but in Ireland the areas normally regarded as the economically most disadvantaged (i.e., in the north and west) actually had the lowest rates of mortality and therefore the highest life expectancy. A similar anomalous pattern was found for infant mortality for the period 1915–35 (Pringle, 1998).

This anomaly is difficult to explain. Studies of mortality at an individual level consistently show a strong association between high mortality and low socio-economic status (e.g. Nolan, 1990; O'Shea, 1997, 2003; O'Shea and Kelleher, 2001). However, the socio-economic groups with the highest death rates are predominantly found in urban areas. Given that there is a higher density of medium-sized towns in the south and east of the country, it is possible that the regional disparities in mortality may to some extent reflect regional variations in the degree of urbanisation. However, even when spatial variations in urbanisation are taken into account, the anomalous regional patterns in the 1970s persist.

More recent evidence suggests that the anomalous regional pattern of mortality found in the 1970s may be beginning to break down. Life expectancy has increased everywhere in Ireland since the 1970s, but it would appear that parts of the north and west have lost their comparative advantage. The reasons are far from clear, but one possibility is that the high levels of social capital (see below) that previously existed in such areas may have been undermined by social changes associated with the Celtic Tiger phenomenon, creating a situation that is less conducive to good health. The negative implications of the Celtic Tiger

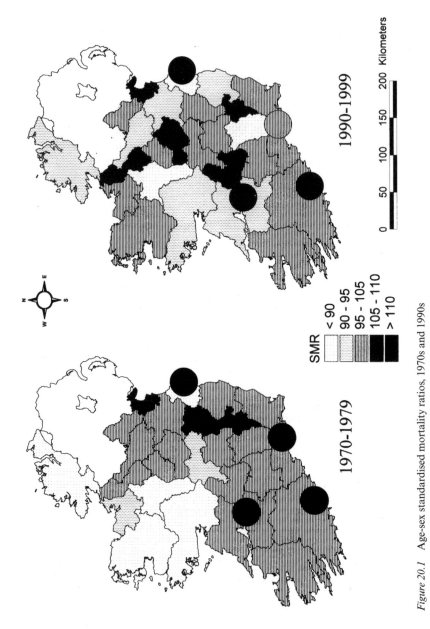

Figure 20.1   Age-sex standardised mortality ratios, 1970s and 1990s

Sources: Central Statistics Office, Census, various years; Ordnance Survey Ireland

phenomenon for health inequalities are discussed in more detail in a slightly different context by Cullen (2004).

Studies of health and mortality at an intra-urban level are few, but the existing evidence suggests that in Dublin at least there is an association at enumeration district (ED) level between higher mortality and lower levels of affluence, conforming with the pattern generally found in other countries (Pringle, 1987; Johnson and Dack, 1989; Johnson and Lyons, 1993). The patterns are not as clear-cut as one might assume, but this is probably a function of mapping rates based upon relatively small numbers of deaths.

SOCIAL CAPITAL AND HEALTH IN IRELAND

Significant attention has been focused over the last decade on the issue of social capital and its effects on health. 'Social capital' is a nebulous concept and despite a significant amount of work on this theme, there is little agreement on what exactly it is, or how it should be measured. However, common themes associated with social capital include trust, neighbourliness, civic participation and reciprocity. Much of the debate around social capital was sparked in 1996 with the publication of the seminal work *Unhealthy Societies: The Afflictions of Inequality* by Richard Wilkinson. However the subsequent publication of *Bowling Alone* by Robert Putnam (2000) has helped propel these concerns into the international limelight. In *Unhealthy Societies*, Wilkinson presented data to show that health indicators in developed countries were unrelated to the total wealth of the countries, but that countries with a less equitable distribution of wealth had poorer health outcomes than more egalitarian countries. Wilkinson argued that income inequalities were associated with lower levels of community cohesion, resulting in less civic trust and public engagement (i.e., social capital). Through these and other mechanisms, he argued, people may become more isolated, introspective and alienated from wider community life and potential social support. They were consequently more vulnerable to psycho-social stresses, which translated to individual psychological stress and negative physical health through a myriad of pathways.

Wilkinson's work draws heavily on an earlier work by Putnam et al. (1993) which contrasted the more wealthy, democratic and civic-minded Northern Italian regions with the poorer Southern Italian regions which he described as being characterised by amoral familism. The 'income inequality and health' hypothesis remains hotly contested, with what appears to be a significant volume of research equally both supporting and refuting this proposed relationship (Subramanian and Kawachi, 2004). The added importance of this hypothesis for Ireland lies in the growing level of income inequality experienced in Ireland in recent times, particularly since the beginning of the economic boom in the mid to late 1990s (Cullen, 2004).

The impact of *Bowling Alone* has been significant. A significant volume of national and international reports has investigated and explored this theme. Ireland, and the Irish, have been the subject of a number of studies examining the relationship between social capital and health. The most comprehensive of these, conducted by Balanda and Wilde (2003), reported that 'many aspects of the social environment, measured by ... social capital indicators ... play an important role in health on the island'. This study, which examined perceived health, is based on the All-Ireland Social Capital and Health Survey and included a total of 2,000 participants (1,000 in each jurisdiction). Balanda and Wilde (2003) note that a number of indicators of social capital used in their study were found to have significant independent effects on perceived health including whether or not a person is civically engaged; whether or not people trust most of their neighbours; social support networks; social contacts; views about services in the local area; and views about problems in the local area. For example exploring the issue of trust, Balanda and Wilde note that 'people who do not trust most of their neighbours are a quarter as likely than those who do to have excellent/very good general health'. They also report, with regard to social contact, that 'people who have infrequent contact with their friends are a third less likely than those who have frequent contact to have excellent/very good general health'.

HEALTH SERVICES ORGANISATION

The health services in Ireland are currently undergoing a period of intense reorganisation and restructuring. Unlike many Western economies, such as the UK and New Zealand, which have spent much of the last 25 years organising and reorganising their services, Ireland has undergone few changes in the organisation of its health services since the early 1970s when eight regional health boards were established and health care ceased to be a function of the local authorities.

On 1 January 2005 the Health Services Executive (HSE) was formally established and is now responsible for running the State's health services. This date also marked the formal dissolution of the country's health boards (and the Eastern Regional Health Authority). The details of the new health structures are still being worked out at the time of writing, but the system is moving towards having three distinct pillars. These are the National Hospitals Office (NHO), the Primary, Community and Continuing Care (PCCC) directorate, and the Shared Services pillar.

The NHO runs the country's 53 acute general hospitals, which are organised into ten local hospital networks. Much of the reorganisation of the acute hospital services in Ireland is based on the findings of the Hanly Report (National Task Force on Medical Staffing, 2003). This report, which focused on two former health board areas, outlined the need for hospital networks, the expansion of regional hospitals and the downscaling of other acute hospitals, including their Accident & Emergency (A&E) units. These proposals have already encountered significant public opposition, forcing some political backtracking on this issue. As Wren (2003, p. 176) notes, 'there are few more potent issues in Irish politics than the local hospital'.

The PCCC directorate has responsibility for primary care including general practice, community-based health and personal social services, services for older persons and children, disability services, mental health services and social inclusion. The PCCC directorate will have 32 (i.e., county-based) local health offices, designed to provide a more local orientation of health services offering greater user involvement. Currently there are severe concerns as to how health and social care services, particularly in relation to mental health, will integrate between the NHO and PCCC pillars to provide the much needed and talked about 'seamless service'.

Having dissolved the health boards the HSE has formally established four regions (Western, Southern, Dublin/North-East, Dublin/Mid-Leinster). It remains very unclear at present however what the exact role of these regional offices will be. Mr Kevin Kelly, the former interim chief executive of the HSE, conceded that the reorganisation of the health boards in Ireland into a unitary health system is part of a 'centralisation journey'. However, it is interesting to note that parallel to this centralisation journey within the health services is the somewhat contrary current strategy involving the roll-out of primary care services. The latest Irish health strategy notes that 'Primary care must become the central focus of the health system' and states that primary care 'is the appropriate setting to meet 90–95 per cent of all health and personal services needs' (Department of Health and Children, 2001a, p. 95). The reasons behind this proposed reorientation of the health services range include improved effectiveness and value for money. The strategy also states that 'a properly integrated primary care service can lead to better outcomes, better health status and better cost effectiveness'.

The essence of the primary care strategy is the formation of locally based primary care teams (PCTs). As the strategy states, 'a group of primary care providers will come together to form an inter-disciplinary team, known as the primary care team' (Department of Health and Children, 2001b, p. 22). The strategy outlines the full range of health and allied disciplines that will constitute the primary care team. It is envisaged that between 600 and 1,000 PCTs will be established across the country. Each PCT, it is suggested, will service a population of approximately 3,000–7,000 people. The variation in PCT size, it is thought, will depend upon whether the region involved is rural or urban, while the number and ratio of staff will reflect the result of a local health 'needs assessment' as well as 'location and population size' (Department of Health and Children, 2001b, p. 22). The primary care strategy also details how access to less routine health services will be organised and developed. It is envisaged that small groups of PCTs will be organised into primary care networks, which will facilitate access to more specialised services.

Few people involved in the Irish health services would challenge the need to substantially develop primary care services. A significant proportion of general practitioners (GPs) are still operating in isolation without adequate out-of-hours cover, or the assistance of practice nurses or computerisation. In relation to the roll-out of the primary care strategy it should be noted that at present only ten pilot PCT projects have been initiated throughout the country, and these have encountered not only their fair share of problems, but also concerns over future funding.

The critical, and related, issues of PCT premises and funding undoubtedly present enormous issues for the successful implementation of the primary care strategy. However, other serious challenges also beset this process. In addition to the manpower crisis afflicting most occupations within the health services, there is also the issue of trying to introduce such changes during a period of uncertainty and reorganisation within the wider health services. Additionally there is a lack of a culture of working with other disciplines among GPs, as well as the issue of a lack of trust, familiarity and knowledge between different disciplines. Further impediments include trade union intransigence; professional loyalties and boundaries; and the reality that, in the largely private system of primary care that currently operates in Ireland, some GPs see other GPs and allied health professionals as little more than economic rivals.

THE POTENTIAL ROLE OF A SPATIAL PERSPECTIVE

These changes in the health services have obvious spatial implications. There is consequently an enormous potential role to be played by spatial analysis, in helping to maximise the benefits of the changes whilst ensuring their costs, both economic and social, are minimised. Teljeur et al. (2004), for example, have examined the likely impact on access to Accident & Emergency services of the Hanly proposals, using computer mapping technology (GIS). This technology also has a major role to play in an objective assessment of the health implications of suspected hazards, such as landfills, high-voltage powerlines, and air pollution sources, as well as the surveillance of infectious diseases. However, this potential has remained largely untapped until now. Nevertheless, there are a number of reasons for cautious optimism that things might improve.

Within the health services there appears to be a slow but growing acceptance of the role of GIS and spatial analysis in examining health and healthcare provision. At present the development of GIS within the Irish health system is haphazard, uneven and unco-ordinated. It is anticipated that the new Population Health Directorate will be able to co-ordinate, streamline and progress developments in this field.

Perhaps one of the most important factors that may influence the development of the mapping of health and disease in Ireland may be that of politics. Here there are a number of distinct and potentially contrary elements. The first of these appears to be the desire of the Irish State to avoid any real discussion on the issue of inequalities, including spatial inequalities in health status and healthcare provision. The decline in the detail and usage of meaningful maps of disease in the Annual Report on Vital Statistics is mirrored by the absence of such maps in other official publications. Only those organisations with a formal link beyond the Republic of Ireland appear to be routinely using disease maps. As mentioned earlier, both the National Cancer Registry of Ireland and the Institute of Public Health in Ireland have recently produced numerous all-Ireland disease maps. It is worth questioning why these two organisations have incorporated significant numbers of such maps in the production of reports spanning both Ireland and Northern Ireland, whilst such disease maps are used so infrequently elsewhere in Ireland. It is clear that part of the reason may lie in the reality that the UK has a much stronger tradition of disease mapping and spatial epidemiology, as exemplified in the work of John Snow's pioneer investigation into the London cholera epidemic of 1849, and reinforced by critical works, such as the Black Report (Townsend and Davidson, 1982). However it seems clear that this is only part of the reason. By operating on a cross-border basis, one might surmise that these institutions have 'permission' to use such techniques, something that other official agencies in the Republic of Ireland may not feel they have. The absence of maps of health and disease in official reports, and the decline and then disappearance of disease maps from the Annual Report on Vital Statistics, are suspicious. Their decline and disappearance came at a time when computerised mapping packages and geographical information systems were becoming more common, more user-friendly, and significantly less expensive. It seems more probable that this reflects a reluctance on the part of the State to acknowledge inequalities both in health status and healthcare provision, particularly in relation to spatial inequalities (Houghton, 2005). While such debates are clearly 'out in the open' in the UK, they remain peripheral to date in Ireland.

Given the geographical basis of political representation, the potential for spatial inequalities in health status and healthcare provision to become significant political issues is huge. What undoubtedly makes this prospect more daunting for the Irish State is the absence of any objective funding formula for Irish health services, coupled with significant regional variation in funding levels. Unlike the UK, which first tackled the issue of spatial inequalities in healthcare funding with the introduction of the Resource Allocation Working Party (RAWP) formula in the mid-1970s, Ireland's funding formula appears to follow the more traditional basis of 'what you got last year, plus an allowance for growth, plus an allowance for scandals' (Maynard and Ludbrook, 1988).

Although politics may in one way hinder the development of disease mapping in Ireland, it may also advance it. The National Anti-Poverty Strategy (NAPS) and subsequent work in this field have set a number of health targets which the government is obligated to achieve within set timeframes. More importantly perhaps, this process has identified significant information gaps relating to Irish information on health and poverty/deprivation. Similarly, growing pressure from the European Union for accurate and timely information is forcing Irish government departments to improve and update their information systems. Therefore despite what may be the best efforts of the Irish State to dampen the development of a spatial analysis of health and health services provision, it appears to have a challenging and relevant future in Ireland.

CONCLUSION

The day-to-day administration of the health services in Ireland has traditionally been decentralised, either through the health boards since 1971 or, before then, at county and even subcounty level (e.g., Poor Law unions). This has inevitably resulted in regional disparities in the provision of health services. The recent creation of the Health Services Executive provides a potential framework for addressing these disparities, but there is a deficiency of spatial information currently available which could form the basis for rational evidence-based decision making. This deficiency is especially marked with regard to small-area data on health outcomes, without which it is impossible to accurately gauge service needs or to assess the effectiveness of alternative service provision strategies. It also precludes the possibility of using spatial epidemiological techniques to identify potential health risk factors and thereby develop effective preventive measures. There are some indications of an improved awareness of the importance of the need for a spatial perspective in some branches of the health services, even if it is simply to get into line with the rest of Western Europe. But there are also unfortunately many indications of a continued aspatial myopia as, for example, in the continued push towards a reorganisation of services driven by economies of scale, with seemingly little consideration given to the implications for spatial accessibility.

21
'For the Way We Live Today':
Consumption, Lifestyle and Place

Denis Linehan

In Michel Houellebecq's novel *Atomised*, the central character seeks to escape the chaos of his personal life in France by taking a new job in the west of Ireland. He expects to find a rural idyll, but he is disappointed. One of his new colleagues tells him, 'people don't go to mass as much as they used to, there's more sexual freedom, more nightclubs, more anti-depressants [and ...] Microsoft of course; every kid in the country dreams of working for Microsoft.' (Houellebecq, 2000, p. 349). These kinds of observation about the lifestyles of the contemporary Irish are increasingly commonplace. The expectations of foreigners and of the Irish themselves are ever more overturned by recent transformations. Within this commentary, reference to increased consumption often looms large. Reports about new cars, new houses, a surge in foreign holidays and crowded shopping centres contrast sharply with the traditional image of the Irish as a rural peasantry cultivated in *Ballykissangel* or *The Quiet Man*. Against a background of continuing modernisation and social and urban transformation, this chapter interrogates contemporary representations and practices of consumption in Ireland. The chapter illustrates how consumption offers insights into both questions of cultural identity and new relationships which people have to place. In so far as all social relationships write their signature into space, the chapter highlights how new patterns of consumption demonstrate the restructuring of socio-spatial relations in contemporary Ireland.

CONSUMPTION AND SOCIAL CHANGE

According to Ryan (2003), since the mid-1990s, the principal drivers of consumption in Ireland have been a long-term increase in disposable income and wealth and the short-term availability of low-interest credit. The underlying strength of the economy, notably in terms of GDP, encouraged increases in private consumption – especially in cars, property, recreation and personal services. Private consumption peaked at the height of the Celtic Tiger phenomenon in 2000 but domestic demand continues to fuel Irish economic growth. Regarded internationally as an economic success, in 2004, *The Economist* announced that Ireland had the best quality of life in the world. The index of 111 states produced by the Economist Intelligence Unit combines data on incomes, health, employment, climate, political stability, job security, gender equality as well as what it termed 'freedom, family and community life' (*The Economist*, 2005). Ireland emerged as the winner of this global lifestyle tournament because it combined 'the most desirable elements of the new with the preservation of certain cosy elements of the old, such as stable family and community life' (Bowcott, 2004). The reaction in Ireland to this news was muted. Undoubtedly the standard of living of the population has been raised in general and growth has regenerated and developed wide areas of the country. In 2005 the OECD ranked Ireland in the top group of high-income countries, along with Luxembourg, Norway, USA and Switzerland (see Table 21.1). However, whilst Ireland performs well in international league tables, examined on a national scale a number of questions about inequality and the social and environmental costs of transformation have become apparent.

Table 21.1   Consumption per capita in selected OECD countries, 2002

Country	PPP* (euro)
Poland	2,802
Hungary	3,488
Spain	9,267
Netherlands	11,900
Finland	12,544
France	12,706
Germany	13,242
Ireland	13,688
Denmark	14,435
UK	15,386
US	20,816
Switzerland	20,889

* Purchasing power parities

Source: OECD Economic Outlook, http://caliban.sourceoecd.org

In terms of the experience of working in the Celtic Tiger economy, the National Economic and Social Forum has established that the wealthiest 20 per cent of the Irish labour force earns almost 12 times as much as the poorest fifth. On this criterion, Ireland has one of the highest levels of income inequality amongst the industrialised countries of the OECD. Critically, 14 per cent of Irish households defined as being in poverty are now headed by those with a job. This means that the measurement of the 'working poor' is twice as high as the data available from 1994, before the emergence of the Celtic Tiger (National Economic and Social Forum, 2005). In addition, between 1998 and 2003, Ireland's inflation exceeded that of the EU15 countries, increasing by 17.5 per cent between December 1999 and December 2003. A 2003 report by Forfás found that Ireland is the second most expensive country in the euro zone, marginally behind Finland. This has resulted in an estimated overall consumer price level which is 12 per cent above the euro-area average (Forfás, 2003). One outcome, according to the National Competitiveness Council, is that in the four years to May 2004 the average price of Irish goods and services increased by 22 per cent relative to the country's main trading partners. The conclusion – in particular as it has been propagated in the media – is that Ireland has become a 'Rip-Off Republic' (RTE, 2005). Together with the rising cost of living, the increased pace of everyday life, and the radical transformation of place, a more uneasy sense about the quality of life is present in Ireland than what is represented in international media.

In particular, the changes in patterns of consumption and its effects on way of life have raised concerns about the social conditions of Irish society. Consumption appears to represent the contradictions of increased prosperity and the loss of community. For John Waters, commenting on the impact of the 'Rip-Off Ireland' debate, the:

> ... feeling exposed is not simply of being ripped-off. The feeling is of being part of a machine, a machine that grinds mercilessly week after week; demanding of us that we put our lives on hold, dump our children in the creche, mortgage ourselves to the hairline and run ever faster to stand still on the M50. (Waters, 2005)

Waters' response connects to a deeper sense that consumption and economic growth are driving a more substantial remaking of Irish society and lifestyle. For others consumption is a source of profound cultural dislocation. New shopping centres are represented as the new churches. The Bishop of Dublin has observed: 'I get the impression that the energy Irish people once put into achieving the salvation of their own souls – and the souls of others – has now been channelled into creating heaven on earth' (quoted in Alvarez, 2005). Evidence of conspicuous consumption seem to abound. The economist David McWilliams has wryly observed how the new commitment to consumerism in Ireland manifests itself in new spectacles of home ownership and conspicuous displays of wealth:

> Walking into 'artisan' cottages in Dublin these days is like entering Doctor Who's Tardis. You walk in through a small door and emerge into a cavernous double-height warehouse that screams good taste and glossy interiors magazines. No house is too small for a kitchen extension with the ubiquitous sloping Velux windows and ceiling-to-floor glass doors, looking out onto a smooth timber deck. No back yard is too pokey for varnished cherry wood decking, and no winter too inclement for outdoor gas heaters. We express ourselves by our slate bathrooms and laser touch taps. Ultimately, through our dinner parties, we convey who we are. (McWilliams, 2005)

For some commentators, new forms of consumption represent a fissure with the traditional organs of the state, notably the church. The decline of the established Catholic-nationalist order is a decline of identities defined around church and citizenship. Consequently, Cleary has argued that identity in Ireland is 'increasingly articulated in terms of individual capacity to participate in various modes of consumer "lifestyle"' (Cleary, 2004). Amongst public commentators, these shifts in the values of the Irish are a matter of acute anxiety. Emily O'Reilly, the government's ombudsman and information commissioner, has complained that

> ...released from the handcuff of mass religious obedience, we are Dionysian in our revelry, in our testing of what we call freedom ... hence the staggering drink consumption, the childlike showing off of helicopters and four-wheel drives and private cinemas, the fetishizing of handbags and high heels. (O'Reilly, 2004)

Such concerns were echoed by the Irish President, Mary McAleese, on her second-term inauguration in 2003 when she observed,

> ...we are busier than before, harder to please, less heedful of the traditional voices of moral guidance and almost giddy with greater freedom and choice. Our Constitution is an important ethical compass directing us to a practical patriotism, 'to promote the common good', to choose responsible citizenship over irresponsible individualism. (McAleese, 2004)

Or, as the novelist Joseph O Connor put it more pithily for the *New York Times*, 'there are some of us who worship Versace the way our grandmothers worshipped the Virgin Mary' (quoted in Alvarez, 2005).

Anxieties about the links between consumption and 'irresponsible individualism' have found expression in government inquiries into obesity and alcohol consumption. The National Taskforce on Obesity reported that obesity rates for men rose by 3 per cent from 11 per cent in 1998 to 14 per cent in 2002 and for women from 9 per cent in 1998 to 12 per cent in 2002. It has been found that Irish men are now amongst the most obese in the EU. Unsurprisingly the taskforce argued for a direct link between levels of obesity and the marketing and advertising of processed foods. However, such bio-political concerns have been most intensely articulated in relation to alcohol. Both the Report on Alcohol Misuse by Young People, issued by the Joint Committee on Health and Children (2004), and the second report of the Strategic Task Force on Alcohol (Department of Health and Children, 2004), catalogued the problems of increased alcohol consumption. They reported that between 1989 and 2001 alcohol consumption per capita in Ireland increased by 49 per cent, whilst ten other European Union member states showed a decrease during the same period. In 2001, Ireland ranked second after Luxembourg for alcohol consumption, with a weekly rate of 11.4 litres of alcohol consumed per person, compared to the EU average of 9.1 litres per person. Eurostat statistics claim that more beer is consumed in Ireland per head than in any other country on the planet (see Table 21.2). Between 1995 and 2003, the amount of personal income spent on alcohol rose from €3.3 to €6 billion per annum, representing almost €2,000 for every person over 15 years of age (Oireachtas Joint Committee on Health and Children, 2004; Strategic Task Force on Alcohol, 2004).

Table 21.2   Litres of beer consumed per person per year in selected countries, 2002

Country	Beer consumption (litres)
Ireland	155
Germany	119
Austria	106
Denmark	98
Belgium	98
UK	97
Australia	89
United States	85
Netherlands	80
Finland	79
New Zealand	78
Canada	70
Switzerland	57
Sweden	56
Norway	56
Japan	55
France	41
Italy	29
Average	76.7

Source: Eurostat, http://epp.eurostat.ec.europa.en/portal

The increased consumption of alcohol is often associated with social breakdown. According to Dr Sean Brady, Archbishop of Armagh, 'we may be witnessing another lost generation – a generation of young people who, instead of emigrating abroad, are leaving the shores of moderation, responsibility and spirituality'. Senator Jim Higgins of Fine Gael has remarked that Ireland is 'facing an alcohol problem of epidemic proportions, which in the next five or ten years will leave us on a par with the AIDS epidemic in Africa' (Higgins, 2002). Such concerns have been quickly associated with a rise in urban social problems, notably street violence, but also a decline in moral values. In what can be regarded as a concern for the moral geography of the street in July 2000, a district court judge in Galway became a focus of media attention when he refused to extend late-night opening hours for a number of nightclubs in the city. In a manner which betrayed the gendered nature of public space and discourses about consumption, he argued, 'I hear from respectable young men they can't meet nice, respectable girls in these nightclubs. The girls they meet there are dreadful, at least that is what I am told'. He continued:

What about the ordinary, respectable citizens of Galway? They are concerned about the hooliganism that goes on in the streets of Galway at the weekends. Do you want it every night of the week now? There is drink and mayhem on the streets. Not a weekend goes by but Supermac's window is broken. If people want a night out let them go out at a respectable hour. Of course, if the truth be known, you won't find respectable people out at all hours. It's uncivilised and a lot of them just won't go out. (Healy, 2000)

These concerns about alcohol reiterate the links that can be drawn between body, consumption and the city. Condemnation of drunken public behaviour on St Patrick's Day highlights this situation. One outcome of these concerns has been the increased regulation of the night-time economy, with the extension of CCTV in many Irish city centres now commonplace as the links between anti-social behaviour and alcohol consumption are affirmed in policing and other areas of social policy.

PLACING CONSUMPTION AND IRISHNESS

Concerns about Irish people's bodies and morality also sweep into representations of place, where the spaces of consumption have been increasingly portrayed as symbolic of cultural dissolution. The Liffey Valley shopping centre on the M50 on the edge of Dublin, advertised on the radio 'like a day out', has appalled cultural commentators and environmentalists alike. Anne Hourihane, the author of *She Moves Through the Boom*, is vague and ambiguous about the site; the 'Liffey Valley shopping centre is long and low and beige in colour. It could be an airport, it could be a factory, it could be a hospital' (Hourihane, 2000, p. 5). Her sense of displacement is underlined inside the shopping centre, when she encounters the 'South Beach Food Court' which attempts to simulate Miami. A loss of the sense of place and reference to non-Irish places is typical of this commentary. Mobilising an apparently ironic nationalist plea, according to the *Dublin People*, '...Liffey Valley Centre is like a transplanted Oxford Street and is practically owned by the Duke of Westminster. Is this what Pearce died for? Is it time to once again man the barricades and repulse the Saxon foe?' (Gormley, 2000). Frank MacDonald, in his book *The Construction of Dublin*, describes the area as a 'weird world – almost a parallel universe – of interchanges, slip roads, drive in eateries and colour-coded parking zones' (MacDonald, 2000, p. 173). For MacDonald, used to reading the architectural form of Dublin, the illegibility of the landscape and his sense of estrangement – the collapse of what Kevin Lynch (1960) noted as 'the mental image of the city which is held by its citizens' – is telling. In a culture where the on-going recollection of the city's urban fabric is central to both place and self-identity, registering the inability to do so is typical of the rhetoric of loss embedded in these concerns about the new spaces of consumption.

Condemnation of consumption is neither unique to Ireland nor indeed to this period in time. Miller (2001, p. 255) notes there is 'an ancient suspicion' of consumption in popular culture. In so far as they are seen to represent uprooting of tradition perspectives, social space and values, the consumption patterns of the new Indian bourgeoisie in Mumbai and nouveaux riches Muscovites draw comparable levels of rebuke. During the 1920s, the consumption behaviour of the 'modern girl' or 'the flapper' on the streets of Dublin – hair products and cosmetics, fashionable clothes and cigarettes – came to represent everything that was disorderly and morally dangerous to the strict values of the conservative elite (Ryan, 1998). The distrust of consumption can be also be understood in the context of Ireland's history as a post-famine society, and more directly as a society whose mores and values were largely forged in Catholicism, with its emphasis on self-denial and fasting, notably through the period of Lent. That said, practices of private consumption do have historical precedents in Ireland, it's just that it has been under-represented in historical research (Spiller, 2004).

Recent condemnation of consumption often mobilises an undifferentiated idea of a consumer society which represent consumers as foolish dupes and 'excess' as a universal activity. Aside from ignoring questions of inequality, where for example the State has intervened to offer school children in socially deprived areas breakfast, these perspectives show little recognition of the central role that consumption plays in the creation of self-identity. Consuming and the social world go hand in hand in a more sophisticated way than narratives of anomie and cultural decline suggest. McCracken has observed, 'without consumer goods, certain acts of self-definition and collective definition in this culture would be impossible' (in Miles and Paddison, 1998, p. 16). For example, for Irish emigrants, the consumption of food is an important way in which the transmission of cultural values and the connection to Ireland is maintained (Kneafsey and Cox, 2002). In his research on worldwide celebration of St Patrick's Day, Nagle (2005) found that soda bread, Ulster Frys, Irish Coffee, were specially prepared and eaten, in addition to the consumption of popular Irish brands like red lemonade, Kimberley biscuits, and Galtee cheese. Indeed rather than contemporary patterns of consumption denying Irishness, in terms of maintaining family obligations and gift relationships these apparent practices of 'excess' may actually express fundamental traits of being Irish. In 2004 the average household spent €1,270 on Christmas, 75 per cent more than the European average of just €725. According to Keohane and Kuhling (2005), contrary to popular belief, 'the extravagance of Irish spending at Christmas, weddings, housing, etc., represents a persistence rather than the erosion of Irish values of community and family'.

If pubic debates about consumption reveal something about contested versions of Irishness, they do not provide very good insights into the way consumption responds to shifts in the economy and intersects with the rhythms of everyday life. In fact, research shows that most forms of consumption involve the satisfaction of everyday needs (Zukin, 1998). It has long been recognised that consumer behaviour is shaped by an assembly of forces: demography (age, sex, income); geographical factors (urban and rural lifestyle, regional differences); socio-economic factors (social class, stage in family cycle); and for the individual consumer, psychological factors and taste. Amongst a number of sources which provide effective ways of tracking these factors are the Consumer Sentiment Index (CSI), the National Quarterly National Accounts (NQA) and the Household Budget Survey. These data sets offer sober overviews of consumer behaviour. Both the NQA and the CSI are particularly useful in that they illustrate how consumers in the Irish economy react in similar ways to those in other economies. Household expenditure rises and falls in relation to job losses, employment growth and sense of job security, all of which are well known to affect the size of, and predisposition to spend, personal disposable income. For example, following the slow-down of the global technology sector and 9/11, the global economy shrank and these impacts were felt tangibly in the activities of consumers in Ireland. Together with census information, the data point towards mobilising analysis to understand more thoroughly the dynamics of lifestyle change, which are not to do with 'irresponsible individualism' but shifts in the economy and new sources and patterns of demand and supply of goods and services (see Table 21.3).

Table 21.3   Key economic indicators 1997–2003, percentage volume change

Item/measure	1997	1998	1999	2000	2001	2002	2003
GNP	9.7	7.9	8.9	10.2	3.8	0.1	2.5
GDP	11.1	8.6	11.3	10.1	6.2	6.9	2.2
Personal consumption	7.2	7.3	9.6	8.5	5.5	2.7	2.4
Public consumption	5.1	5.5	7.7	7.5	11.1	9.4	4.2
Exports of goods and services	17.4	21.0	15.2	20.6	8.3	6.2	–4.0
Imports of goods and services	16.8	25.5	12.1	21.3	6.5	2.3	–6.0
Consumer Price Index (CPI) (% change)	1.5	2.4	1.6	5.6	4.9	4.6	3.5
Unemployment (% of labour force)	10.3	7.6	5.6	4.3	3.9	4.4	4.8
Employment (% change)	3.9	8.3	6.3	4.7	2.9	1.4	1.0

Source: Central Statistics Office and Department of Finance, various

CATS AND DOGS: SPACING CONSUMPTION

In Dublin, the pet population is changing. In popularity terms, cats are hanging in. But according to *Euromonitor*, the growth in apartment living and the soaring property prices in the city are putting space at a premium. The new trend is notably towards smaller animals – such as hamsters and chinchillas. Dogs are on the way out. The truth about cats and dogs in Dublin is helpful in that it highlights the effectiveness of taking into account the key socio-spatial factors that influence demand and reshape patterns of consumption. These shifts reveal deeper structural changes in the relationships between space, consumption and culture that may well be overlooked in macro-economic observations. Since the early 1970s, the population has increased by almost 1 million people. Life expectancy has increased significantly. The workforce has grown by almost three quarters of a million. Female employment has increased by over 460,000 and women now makes up 42 per cent of those at work compared to 27 per cent in 1973 (CSO, 2003b). There has been a significant growth in the number of households due to the increase in the number of people living alone and the greater frequency of second unions. In Cork for example, in 1971, 47 per cent of all households were made up of couples with children, but this group had declined to just 30 per cent by 2002. Over a quarter of all households in the city now are made up of just one person, reflecting the decline of the average size of the household in Ireland from 3.93 in 1971 to 2.93 in 2002 (Edwards and Linehan, 2004). This long-term restructuring of the internal make-up of households contributes to increases in consumer spending, principally as the costs of household goods and services are shared less. In addition, the increase in new households in real terms has also increased demand. If in 2005 there were 80,000 new house completions, it can be reasonably assumed that there will be a demand for 80,000 new cookers, fridges, beds, carpets and so on. To conclude that people are going to DIY stores in a period of unprecedented housing construction in the history of the State to worship at the temple of consumption ignores this obvious source of new demand in the marketplace. It is more likely that people are going to buy varnish for their windows, tools to put up shelves and garden furniture so they can sit in small suburban gardens that will take the average new mortgage holder 35 years to pay off. If they 'splash out' on a barbeque or a gas patio heater along the way to enjoy time with friends and family, it can be hardly represented as the decline of Irish values.

Through an analysis of the Household Budget Survey, the CSO has identified a number of changes in the structure of disposable income over time (see Table 21.4). Between 1975 and 2001 the proportion of income spent on food fell from just under one-third of total disposable household income to about one-fifth. Ireland now ranks second lowest in the EU in terms of the amount of household income spent on food and non-alcoholic beverages. A number of patterns feature here: less money spent on clothes; less on fuel and electricity; the same on alcohol and tobacco; small increases in transport; slightly larger increases in housing, and most significantly, very large increases in services. Higher incomes clearly have stimulated these demands, but so too has the changing environment. The impact of globalisation and competition in providing lower-cost clothes and cheaper holidays has had a clear impact on the distribution of household income. The CSO concludes that 'A greater proportion of disposable income [is] being spent on services such as meals out, entertainment, foreign holidays and other services'. In essence the income previously spent on food is now spent on services. However, it is not clear if the increase in meals eaten out is a result of changing ways of life or conspicuous consumption fuelled by an increased disposable income.

In addition to changes at the household level, geographical settlement and the restructuring of urban and regional time-space routines are important variables in explaining shifts in consumption. The failure of sustainable regional planning in Ireland has meant that dispersed settlement patterns, such as one-off housing and ex-urbanisation, stimulate new demand for cars and fuel and for the services and goods needed to keep these vehicles on the road. In this sense, whilst the M50 and Dublin's edge city have been depicted as un-Irish, these sites are deeply embedded in the new lifestyles and time-space routines of people working, commuting and consuming in Ireland. It is on 'the edge' – of villages, towns and the city – where the 'New Ireland' is located. Within these emerging spaces, new pressures on personal time also alter consumption patterns. The closure of the majority of Bewleys coffee houses in Dublin – a commercial event driven by rent maximisation – was also emblematic of changing experiences of time in the city. Drinking coffee is no longer a leisurely pursuit. Like the speeding up of traditional dance steps in Riverdance – what has been called 'set dancing on speed' – drinking coffee from paper cups whilst on the move, rather than sitting at a cafe table, is emblematic of the quickening of everyday life in Ireland as a whole.

Table 21.4   Household budget expenditure, (percentage share) 1975–2001

Item	1975	1982	1989	1996	2001
Food	30.3	25.0	25.8	22.9	20.8
Alcoholic drink	11.4	12.3	11.7	12.6	11.9
Tobacco	4.4	3.4	3.3	4.8	4.4
Clothes and shoes	10.7	8.1	6.7	6.1	4.9
Fuel and light	5.9	6.1	5.9	4.9	3.3
Housing	6.1	5.7	7.2	8.0	9.7
Durable household goods	4.8	5.1	4.7	3.6	3.6
Other goods	5.2	5.7	5.9	6.4	5.8
Transport	13.2	16.7	13.7	13.9	15.4
Services	8.0	11.9	15.1	16.7	20.2
	100	100	100	100	100

Source: Central Statistics Office, Household Budget Survey, various years

As the State sponsors higher productivity from Irish labour, people are leading increasingly busy lives, as working and commuting hours lengthen. It has been established that workloads are particularly high among the self-employed, employees and the parents of young children (Russell et al., 2006). As a result, consumers with less leisure time demand greater convenience, which in turn reshapes the supply of goods and services. Changes in personal mobility also have echoes in consumption. The demands of commuting place greater time pressures on individuals travelling long distances or for long periods of time compared to those that do not. Commuters appear to spend significantly more money on fast food than other households (Keelan et al., 2005). Similarly, single men in urban locations consume chilled ready meals rather than spend time preparing food at mealtimes (Reed et al., 2003). Together with the increasing auto-dependency of Irish society, these pressures on time help explain developments such as longer opening hours of shops, the success of new retail locations such as filling stations, and the inclusion of cinemas, fitness centres and restaurants in out-of-town shopping centres.

The Irish fast-food and food retail sectors have both responded to and shaped these new lifestyle changes. In these circumstances the growth of McDonald's, Supermac and other groups are clear beneficiaries. McDonald's has 68 restaurants in Ireland, 30 in the Greater Dublin area and the remainder across the country. McDonald's opened its first restaurant in Ireland in 1979 on Grafton Street. It now serves approximately 150,000 people every day. Symptomatic of a temporal shift in Irish society, around the same time in the mid-1990s that RTE 1 pushed the start time of its earlier morning news show from 8 a.m. to 7 a.m. to meet the demands of commuters, McDonald's began to serve breakfast. The entry of Tesco internationalised the distribution and sale of food and in particular promoted the sale of ready-made meals (Vignali, 2001). Outside the UK, Ireland is Tesco's largest market (Child, 2002). However, arguably the most significant shift in retail provision has been the emergence of convenience stores networks. Since the middle of the 1990s convenience stores such as Centra, Mace and Spar have become a significant part of the Irish retail trade. First developed in the Netherlands in the 1930s, in 2004 there were 547 Spar and Mace stores in Ireland. Sales during 2004 reached almost €1 billion. SuperValu and Centra are in the retail franchise division of the Musgrave Group and service 630 independently owned supermarkets and convenience stores in both the Republic and Northern Ireland. Centra had sales worth €930 million for 2004. With regard to food consumption, the outcome is an established model seen in advanced industrialised societies, namely the dominance of core retailers in the distribution of food, the emergence of ready-to-eat products and the increased individualisation and de-traditionalisation of eating styles – in particular the decline of the family meal and the growth of eating out (Beardsworth and Keal, 1997). Centra's advertising slogan, 'For the way we live today', typifies the way these new retail strategies deliberately set out to cater for emerging lifestyles. For Centra, the model offered by the company is in tune with the rhythm of contemporary Ireland. 'It's very much part of city life. We're talking about the inner city, apartments, smaller families and a move towards shopping four, five or six times per week, which takes you back to the concept of convenience' (quoted in Connolly, 1996). Spar has also recognised that

> a convenience store is really for families where both parents are working or where they can't get time to shop at weekends. Basically, it allows us to give easy access to what they want: ready meals, hot foods, deli. People have less time to cook now and they want their freedom. (Quoted in Connolly, 1996)

The conclusion one can take from these strategies is that these stores respond to a segment of Irish society that is increasingly time-poor. But there are also significant consequences for society in general. The dominance of this new retail sector is such that the turnover of the non-franchised corner shop has fallen and many have closed. Aside from niche retailers who trade on local produce, this process has led to less diversity and greater homogenisation in the food retail landscape of Irish town centre and villages. With the exception perhaps of the selection of local newspapers and postcards, a Centra in west Mayo is more or less the same as one found in Waterford city. Like the fast-food sector, through their notable employment of labour migrants, these stores also reflect further a deeper restructuring of society and economy. Centra stores now employ some 6,000 people and the company is amongst the largest employer of migrant labour in Ireland. Tesco Ireland is also a significant employer of cheaper migrant labour. The situation is one in which in some instances, the labour conditions for low-cost preparation of food have proved to be problematic (Sawicki 2005).

CONCLUSION

Teasing out the nature and consequences of new forms of consumption on the island of Ireland presents a dynamic and challenging set of research questions, which this brief chapter could only touch upon. At issue is the schizophrenic manner in which these forms of consumption have been greeted, which in turn reflects upon the problems encountered with modernisation. It may be that new found wealth and the new terrain of consumption have unravelled what Giddens has termed 'ontological security': 'the confidence most human beings have in the continuity of their self-identity and in the constancy of the surrounding social and material environments of action' (Giddens, 1990, p. 92). However, whilst moralising about consumption reveals a great deal about questions of cultural identity, attention needs to be given to the social, economic and spatial contexts in which changes in lifestyle and consumption have occurred. Shifts in patterns of consumption in Ireland are not a result of fecklessness but rather reflect the social and geographical changes, the transformation of contours of Irish identity and expectations, together with the creation of new sources of demand. It is likely that new forms of consumption and lifestyles will continue to undermine older dualities, of urban and rural, of past and present, of North and South. In this sense, the transformation of patterns of consumption in contemporary Ireland is very profound and reflects on many levels 'the way we live today'.

22

Ireland Now and in the Future

Rob Kitchin and Brendan Bartley

As the chapters in this book reveal, Ireland is a country in flux, successfully sustaining a growing economy whilst trying to cope with old and new, social, political and environmental issues. By undertaking a spatial analysis, the contributors have highlighted the complex ways that different facets of Irish life operate across space and scale, and are not uniform and homogenous. Where people live and do business, and the places in which they interact, make a difference because they are embedded in structures and policies that operate across scales – local, regional, national and international – and are affected by processes that have profound spatial implications.

Arguing that spatial analysis adds value to our understanding of Irish life might seem like an obvious point, but many analyses tend to discuss national-level trends without disaggregating them to smaller spatial scales, or discuss particular examples as if they are a representative sample for the entire nation. Examining the unemployment rate, or average house prices, or number of immigrants, or growth in the economy, or any of the other issues the contributors have examined, in such general terms masks the huge variations that exist between different locales. For example, given that the economy varies as a function of the types of employment available in different areas it is no surprise that the unemployment rate and relative prosperity follow this pattern (along with lots of other things like the demand for housing, improved infrastructure, and so on). In some places the economy is growing faster than in others, and in some agricultural areas the economy is relatively stagnant and declining.

In reviewing trends and possible trajectories we have not been confined to considering only substantive changes in relation to the economy and associated sectoral issues. The governance and policy frameworks that are supposed to guide and regulate Irish life have themselves been transformed. The period under review has witnessed a move away from a reactive-style management of the economy and other policy domains to a more proactive approach that emphasises results and, more recently, integration. Conscious efforts are now being made by Irish policy makers to navigate Ireland's future in a more rigorous way. Policy has moved away from approaches that left Ireland drifting along in the slipstream of prevailing trends with all the attended dangers of being buffeted by unexpected crises.

In addition, the spatial (planning) dimension has been allocated a key role in managing the co-ordination process. Planning for Ireland's future and following through on efforts to achieve integrated planning programmes are moving to a higher place on the agenda of politicians, public servants, the business community and other sectors of Irish society. Thus, following a protracted period of focused but ad hoc project-based development policies that began in the mid-1980s, concerted efforts are under way to move away from this piecemeal approach to a more coherent approach based on an integrated planning approach that seeks to unify and co-ordinate activities both vertically (i.e., between scales/ levels) and horizontally (at the same scale/level) across all spaces and sectors. The National Spatial Strategy (NSS) and the subordinate Regional Planning Guidelines are a clear first attempt to achieve such integration insofar as they have provided the operating levels needed for a unified and comprehensive multilevel approach to planning and policy. Their introduction has filled the gap that prevented integrated co-ordination between central government strategies and those at local level. The provision of this vertical framework for decision making can now better serve to facilitate greater co-operation and co-ordination on the horizontal scales of policy and action. In particular, local authorities are now expected to produce joined-up planning at local level (the horizontal scale) rather than go their own way regardless of cost as happened frequently in the past. In short, they are in a better position to ensure that the vertical consistency of their spatial plans with the aims of the regional and national strategies is complemented by more effective horizontal integration with those of other local authorities.

The new approach places a strong emphasis on informed anticipation and evidence-based decision making. Documenting and explaining the variations, and how they should be tackled, requires geographical analysis. Some analysis involves mapping out the differences between locales and how the conditions on the ground and policy implemented on different scales intersect in complex ways to produce particular outcomes. It requires policy interventions and capital investment such as the National Development Plan, and more specific sector-based policies, to build space and scale more rigorously into strategies and actions. This needs to be more than the rhetorical gesture of stating that balanced regional development is desirable. It requires serious engagement with spatial variation and a commitment to policies that are enacted on the ground. The current National Development Plan ends in 2006 and the next will cover the period 2007–13. The latter period is also the period of the next EU Budget and Community Support Framework (CSF). There is both scope and need to review and enhance Irish policies and governance practices for this post-2006 period with evidence drawn from research and GIS sources. In an era of 'glocalisation' – the simultaneous multilevel interactions that link global and local actions in a seamless web of mutual influences – informed and evidence-based research that spans the various spatial scales is indispensable. In Ireland the immediately obvious scales of relevance range across the local through the city/county and regional levels to national and EU scales and beyond.

This is why the National Spatial Strategy was, to us at least, an important policy statement that needs to be taken seriously and its recommendations to be acted upon. And it is also why the Irish Spatial Data Infrastructure (ISDI) initiative needs to gain momentum and support within the political system. The ISDI aims to improve the quality and quantity of spatial data (and nearly all government data are spatial – that is, they have locational information), and to ensure that data generated across different government departments and agencies can be used in mutual conjunction. At present, the majority of Irish data are poorly geo-referenced (usually to ED or county level), and it is difficult to cross-reference data (usually because they do not share a common spatial unit). This problem can be illustrated by the fact that it is almost impossible to produce all-island maps with regard to any of the issues discussed in this book. This is because data in the North and South are collected using different questions and/or different units, and/or different scales. Undertaking spatial analysis is by no means impossible, but it is not made as easy as it should be. And, as the chapters have revealed, such analysis allows us rich insights.

In the opening chapter we posed two questions: (1) what can other countries, and indeed the Irish themselves, learn from the transformations that have occurred? (2) where is Ireland heading in the future?

WHAT DOES THE IRISH EXPERIENCE TEACH US?

Ireland has captured the attention and imagination of analysts and policy makers in other countries because it seemingly holds valuable lessons that can be transferred and applied in their own settings. These analysts are particularly interested in the economy, how it is structured, and the policies that kick-started the Celtic Tiger phenomenon. To them the Irish experience demonstrates that, within a European context, a stagnant economy can be radically transformed in a very short time to one that is booming (the Asian tiger economies provided such examples earlier on). Moreover, at the same time significant progress can be made with regard to political conflict. The challenge for these analysts is to determine what factors stimulated and sustained the changes that have occurred.

This view is one we share. The Irish experience does provide valuable evidence that can be of use in understanding how economies and societies can be radically transformed. A lot can be learnt from how the State has promoted Ireland, fostered inward investment and indigenous industries, and let the free market develop; and useful lessons can be drawn from the peace process in Northern Ireland and Ireland's role in that process. The danger, however, is that we only consider those things that are seemingly successful. The Celtic Tiger, as many of the contributors have discussed, has a dark side. The review of Irish trends and many of the associated growth statistics is impressive on first reading, but closer scrutiny and critical analysis suggest that the Irish experience has been at best a qualified success. The extent to which the legacy of the Celtic Tiger has been a positive one is an open question. After more than a decade of vigorous economic growth and prosperity, Ireland has been left with some severe problems. So, while much of the transformation has been positive, it has been accompanied by a widening gap between rich and poor; rising crime rates; increased environmental pollution; a large infrastructure deficit; a housing market that excludes many; a huge growth in long-distance commuting; health and welfare systems creaking under pressure; a weakening rural economy with a decline in agricultural incomes; the continued marginalisation of Travellers; and in Northern Ireland sectarianism is still rife. All of these issues are themselves, as noted above, uneven and unequal in their manifestation and consequences across Ireland.

What is needed then are balanced assessments of what has happened in Ireland, recognising that the positive changes are nearly always accompanied by negative impacts, and that these trends vary spatially. While the government might say that all boats rise on a common tide, some rise higher and are more stable, others show only marginal lift, and others capsize. Moreover, the tide itself does not rise evenly everywhere (the tide in Dublin has been a lot higher than the tide in Donegal). There is no doubt that some of the problems faced in the new century are preferable to the deep depression of the 1980s; nonetheless, they are still significant issues for many people and they demand attention. In other words, analysts and policy makers from other countries need to do more than simply study the economy and the factors that stimulated its rapid growth. They need to examine the varied consequences of economic transformation and take heed of the negative issues and how these might develop, and in turn be tackled, within their own context. Hopefully this book has provided such a balanced assessment.

WHAT DOES THE FUTURE HOLD FOR IRELAND?

It is always a dangerous undertaking to speculate on what the future holds as any predictions are likely to come back to haunt the soothsayer. This does not seem to stop many analysts being drawn on the issue, and many agencies do try to suggest what will happen in the future for all kinds of reasons (e.g., planning and investment purposes). Two reports published in early 2006 provide useful examples in this regard. NCB Stockbrokers (2006) predicted that by 2020 the population will have grown by almost a third to reach 5.3 million; that over a million people living in Ireland will be immigrants; the number of cars will double to over 3 million; 700,000 new houses will be built, and that the economy will grow on average by over 5 per cent per year (effectively doubling over the period). In other words, the transformation of the last 15 years will continue over the next 15. The Rural Ireland 2025 Foresight Perspectives Working Group report (2006) predicts that while the economy as a whole will continue to grow, this growth will not be balanced either geographically or across sectors. The report suggests that rural areas, particularly in the Northwest and North Midlands, will lag behind other areas; there will continue to be widespread decline in the agricultural sector with many farmers going out of business; a large proportion of foreign-owned manufacturing will move to lower-cost economies; and new types of employment will not benefit rural communities outside of commuting zones.

The second report clearly suggests that if the first report's predictions are right, and the economy continues to boom, then not everyone in Ireland will be 'winners'. In fact many people in rural areas might lose out. In addition, it is likely that most of the growth is going to occur selectively in a few 'favoured' places, notably Dublin, Cork, Galway and Limerick. In other words, the kinds of spatial disparities and disadvantages that presently exist might well become exacerbated. This clearly has significant implications as regards issues of sustainability and quality of life in some areas, particularly those most highly dependent on the rural economy. If these processes are not checked through policies designed to ensure balanced regional development then there is a real danger that these disparities will become more pronounced and the spiral of decline will accelerate. The result would be large parts of the country outside of the commuting areas becoming economically stagnant and unviable. The extent to which the predictions in the two reports come to pass will become evident in time. The future may even produce a combination of different prediction outcomes.

Our predictions are much more modest. Our sense is that Ireland's economy will continue to grow in the short term, and that many of the problems we documented in the first chapter will continue, if not worsen. The dominant factor shaping both the growth and the problems is, we believe, that the government's laissez-faire policies and an unwillingness to implement strong interventionist policies with regard to most problem issues will continue for the foreseeable future. Ireland is one of the most liberal countries in the world, economically and politically, meaning that the free market is allowed to run relatively unchecked; corporate and individual tax rates are low compared to other developed countries, and state provision of services is minimised. This is clearly attractive for business, but means that social issues tend to be downgraded by being left to families, community groups, the voluntary sector and the marketplace to deal with. It is difficult to say how sustainable this trend will be in the coming years.

As for the long term, this is more difficult to predict. Ireland's economy is one that is highly dependent on foreign direct investment and is strongly connected into the global economy. As such, it is tied to the health and vibrancy of external trends and patterns. If there is a world-wide recession triggered, for example, by an oil crisis, or an economic depression in the USA, or a dramatic interest rate hikes in Europe, then Ireland's economy will be put under severe pressure and is likely to suffer, at least in line with other countries. Moreover, Ireland's success has been predicated on staying 'ahead of the curve' – moving from manufacturing to services, then up the service chain – to keep ahead of competing destinations for investment capital. If it wants to retain its leading edge position it needs to stay ahead of other countries that can offer similar services but have lower wage and infrastructure costs (such as India), to offer what they are not in position to deliver. To do that, Ireland needs to move beyond being a knowledge economy (which trades in services and information) to an innovation economy (which uses research and ideas to generate new products and services). Initiatives such as the establishment of Science Foundation Ireland are meant to help stimulate such a transfer by investing in research in areas such as bio-technology and information and communication technologies, and encouraging partnerships between the universities and industry. Time will tell whether this initiative pays dividends.

What we do feel relatively comfortable predicting is an increasing emphasis being placed, by the administrations in both jurisdictions, on cross-border co-operation and joint initiatives between the Irish Republic and Northern Ireland. It is increasingly recognised that both jurisdictions will benefit from the development of an all-island economy and from trying to address common issues collaboratively. It is already clear that there are significant amounts of cross-border flows of workers and products. Working together will increase economic efficiency, further open up each other's markets, and encourage competition that will stimulate each other's economies. What this requires is an alignment of policies around the planning of infrastructure and economic development. The substantive content of the NSS also creates new opportunities for counties in the border areas. The NSS commitments to regional balance and its identification of cross-border road linkages with the equivalent strategy for Northern Ireland, the Regional Development Strategy (RDS), provide for the first time an opportunity to significantly advance cross-border and all-island infrastructure investment projects. The scope and requirements for capitalising upon the potential and savings that can accrue to both jurisdictions through cross-border planning were set out in a recent report (Inter*Trade*Ireland, 2006). The recommendations of this report for the establishment of a collaborative planning framework for the island of Ireland were adopted in both jurisdictions as the key preliminary step towards the provision of all-island infrastructure through joined-up planning. The other main opportunity for addressing the infrastructure deficits in the border regions stems from the Irish government's commitment to promoting the peace process in Northern Ireland through increased cross-border co-operation and activity. This will provide further leverage for advocacy of new transport infrastructure in the region, based on comprehensive and viable planning proposals that have clear merit and support. Such proposals must be in a position to demonstrate a collective ability and willingness in all affected counties to pursue and deliver upon the project. This solidarity will not be evident unless there is clear evidence of integration across their respective development plans for the relevant projects.

Whatever the outcomes of the predictions presented by us, or others, one thing is certain – Ireland will continue to change and new transformations will occur. Even if the economy slows, developments in train and the new processes at play will continue to reshape the social, economic, political and environmental landscape. Whether the changes that occur will be as dramatic as those witnessed over the past 15 years remains to be seen, but hopefully the sustained growth enjoyed over this period will not be turned off as quickly as it seems to have started. Whatever the developments, we believe that Ireland will continue to provide an interesting case study for other countries, yielding information and lessons that will have relevance for countries that want to emulate its success.

IN SUMMARY

For us, and our contributors, Ireland is a fascinating place to study – a unique laboratory through which to examine a range of economic, social, political and environmental issues. It is a country that has undergone an enormous trans-formation in a relatively short timespan, and in many ways is still coming to terms with the changes that have taken place and their effects. And there is no doubt that Ireland does provide a number of pointers for countries that want to be the next tiger economy, but importantly it also has some other salutary lessons that need to be heeded.

From an Irish perspective, it seems to us that the most pressing questions for policy makers are, on the one hand, how to consolidate and sustain the growth experienced from the 1990s onwards, whilst on the other, how to address effectively long-standing issues and new problems that arise with rapid transfor-mation. Tangled up in these concerns are Northern Ireland, the peace process, and the challenges of developing co-operation and creating an all-island economy. Given the political stalemate in the North and the antipathy towards the Republic from some sections of Northern Ireland society, the process of developing working relations and trust will no doubt take time.

These questions will not be easy to address and require informed, evidence-based policy responses. As the chapters in this book have illustrated, spatial analysis provides a powerful way to investigate Irish society and economy, giving rich insights into the processes at play. However, what is clear to us after editing this book is that although there is much research completed and more under way, there is a great need for a more systematic programme of work in order to provide greater breadth and depth of analysis that will allow us to more fully understand the processes at work, and the different geographies they create. In some ways this situation is inevitable given the relatively small number of researchers employed within the universities and other institutions that take space and scale seriously. But hopefully the establishment of groups post-2000 such as the National Institute for Regional and Spatial Analysis, Urban Institute Ireland, the National Centre for Geocomputation, and the International Centre for Local and Regional Development will over the long term help in this regard.[1] We invite you to join the researchers at these centres, and the others who have written for this book, to reflect upon Ireland in the twenty-first century, to document and think through how Ireland is developing, and how it should develop in the future.

Notes

CHAPTER 1

1. http://migration.ucc.ie/irishmigrationinthe1990scharts.htm
2. For example the corporate tax rate in Luxembourg is 22.88 per cent; in Portugal 23 per cent; Germany 26.38 per cent; Sweden 28 per cent; Finland 29 per cent; Denmark 30 per cent; UK 30 per cent; Greece 32 per cent; Italy 33 per cent; France 33.33 per cent; Belgium 33.99 per cent, Netherlands 34.5 per cent; Spain 35 per cent. (Deloitte and Touche, 2005, cited in www.finfacts.com/irelandbusinessnews/publish/article_10003995.shtml).
3. www.finfacts.com/cgi-bin/irelandbusinessnews/exec/view.cgi?archive=2&num=284; http://www.forbes.com/home/global/2005/0523/024chart.html
4. www.finfacts.com/irelandbusinessnews/publish/article_10003995.shtml
5. www.finfacts.com/irelandeconomy/usmultinationalprofitsireland.htm
6. The reform of the structural funds was driven by the Single European Act of 1987 and the ensuing prospect of a Single Market, which, it was considered, would only be achieved through successful economic and social cohesion. The term 'cohesion' was used to describe the new policy orientation that sought to secure economic integration with political union, and the structure funds were similarly redesignated to become structural /cohesion funds.
7. Coherence and sustainability in a horizontal sense between policy sectors is an overall objective of the EU which increasingly emphasises the need to pursue a long-term planning and sustainability approach to all key policies and tasks. The most relevant EU documents or processes in this regard are:

   - the Lisbon Strategy for employment, economic reform and social cohesion, to which the environmental dimension was added at the European Stockholm summit (Spring 2001);
   - the Strategy for Sustainable Development which was presented at the European Council in Gothenburg in 2001 (European Council, 2001).

   The European Council in Lisbon defined a key objective for the EU to become the most dynamic and competitive knowledge-based economic area in the world. Progress towards this objective has recently been assessed by the European Council which found that it has been unsuccessful. Accordingly, a renewed Lisbon Agenda is being developed with new targets for competitiveness and cohesion tied to appropriate funding supports.
8. One of the most concrete developments in terms of harmonising strategic planning activities throughout the EU is the European Spatial Development Perspective (ESDP). It is a common frame of reference (i.e., it is not legally binding) for all the institutions that are involved in spatial planning and the development of the European territories on all scales. Subsidiarity is seen as the key to achieving its objectives. The Commission subsequently introduced territorial cohesion as a new, third dimension next to economic and social cohesion. The ESDP has three underlying objectives:

   - economic and social cohesion across the Community;
   - conservation of natural resources and cultural heritage;
   - balanced competitiveness across the EU.

   With this approach, the importance of the regional level increased, together with the significance of networks and relationships between territorial units. The ESDP is an important expression of the EU cohesion agenda. It is also a convenient tool for informing strategy and policy development, and has provided Ireland with a particularly important frame of reference in the production of its National Spatial Strategy (NSS) and associated Regional Planning Guidelines (RPGs).

9. www.northsouthministerialcouncil.org/
10. Foras na Gaeilge is responsible for the promotion of the Irish language and Tha Boord o Ulster-Scotch for promoting a greater awareness and use of Ullans and of Ulster-Scots culture.
11. www.northsouthministerialcouncil.org/
12. www.eu2004.ie/templates/standard.asp?sNavlocator=3,242,278
13. Calculated from CSO figures.
14. www.permanenttsb.ie/news/default.asp?nid=534
15 www.cso.ie/statistics/planperm1992to2004.htm

CHAPTER 4

1. In part this is due to the greater size range in this category, which allows for substantial growth of centres without causing centres to change size category.
2. It is not possible to replicate Poole's analysis with the data in Table 4.3, as the 'small town and village' category spans his urban–rural cut-off.
3. In application to urban population distributions a Gini coefficient of 1 would actually entail the rather unlikely situation of all of the population being concentrated in a single urban centre. Nevertheless, the rule is that the higher the value of the coefficient the greater the degree of concentration.
4. The settlements in question are Bangor, Carrickfergus, Carryduff, Groomsport and Crawfordsburn, Helen's Bay and Seahill. The first three of these have populations over 5,000 and therefore form independent centres when excluded from Belfast. Arguably, the settlement of Lisburn (population 71,465) should also be treated in this way, but it is amalgamated with Belfast because it is contiguous and includes Belfast suburbs such as Poleglass and Dunmurry.
5. The relationships can be described by the regression equation: $Y = a \cdot e^{bX}$ where X is the rural population density and Y is the density of urban centres. The related R^2 statistics are 0.69 for centres with 5,000–10,000 population and 0.73 for centres over 10,000 population.

CHAPTER 6

1. See www.europa.eu.int/comm./agenda2000/index_en.htm
2. See www.pobail.ie/en/RuralDevelopment/EUPresidencyPapers

CHAPTER 7

1. The Greater Dublin region is taken as comprising Dublin City, Dun Laoghaire, Rathdown, Fingal, South Dublin, Kildare, Meath and Wicklow.

CHAPTER 9

1. Unless otherwise stated, the data on investment, output and employment presented in this chapter are drawn from the annual census of industrial production, the annual surveys of employment in, and expenditures by, manufacturing firms conducted initially by the IDA and, since 1995, by Forfás (the National Policy Advisory Board for Enterprise, Trade, Science, Technology and Innovation) and other IDA and Forfás reports. Further details are available from the authors.
2. Based on census of industrial production data which include mining, quarrying, turf production and power and water supply in 'industrial employment'. These latter accounted for about 7 per cent of the total in 2000 and changed little over the 1990s.

3. In this chapter the pharmaceutical sector has been defined as comprising firms producing finished drug products, active pharmaceutical ingredients, other intermediate inputs, diagnostic reagents, and diagnostic kits containing reagents (see Egeraat, 2006b).
4. All figures in this section are based on the annual Forfás employment surveys.

CHAPTER 10

1. This chapter presents a wide array of statistical information. For the most part, this has been taken, or derived, from the websites or publications of a range of State agencies, including, in particular, the Central Statistics Office, the IDA, and Forfás (the National Policy and Advisory Board for Enterprise, Trade, Science, Technology and Innovation). In order to avoid presentational clutter, specific sources for the data presented are not given in most cases, but may be obtained from the author on request.
2. See www.ifsconline.ie

CHAPTER 11

1. The large-farm counties are Waterford, Kilkenny, Wexford, Cork, South Tipperary, Carlow, Wicklow and Dublin.
2. The small-farm counties are Galway, Mayo, Roscommon, Sligo, Leitrim and Donegal.
3. This and the next section draw heavily on Commins and Walsh (2005).

CHAPTER 14

1. Quasi-autonomous non-government agencies (QUANGOs) usually have a single-purpose remit or specific mandate.

CHAPTER 15

1. From interview data held as part of the research carried out for the publication Fagan et al. (2001).
2. The EPA cannot account for this 10 per cent increase other than to say that local authorities believe that the dramatic rise between 2002 and 2003 is likely to be because of increased quality of data as well as increased resource use and waste generation on the part of consumers and business (EPA, 2003, p. 7). In 2004 they calculate that municipal waste is at just over 3 million tonnes, although there has been a 4 per cent increase because they have produced the figures based on a new methodology.

CHAPTER 17

1. Although frequently criticised, this is the term almost universally used in the public service in Ireland.

CHAPTER 18

1. Data on second homes are based on unpublished Central Statistics Office data. Analysis of this data is part of an ongoing research project by Keaveney, K., Walsh, J. A. and Duffy, P. J.
2. The design guidelines were never formally adopted. New guidelines were due to be proposed in 2006.

CHAPTER 19

1. See www.pobal.ie/media/Deprivationanditsspatialarticulation.pdf

CHAPTER 22

1. NIRSA – www.nuim.ie/nirsa; Urban Institute Ireland – www.urbaninstitute.net; National Centre for Geocomputation – ncg.nuim.ie; International Centre for Local and Regional Development – www.iclrd.org

References

Adamson, I. (1978) *The Cruthin.* (Belfast: Donard Press)

Adamson, I. (1982) *The Identity of Ulster.* (Bangor: Pretani)

Adamson, I. (1991) *The Ulster People.* (Bangor: Pretani)

Agnew, J. (1987) *Place and Politics: The Geographical Mediation of State and Society.* (Boston, MA: Allen and Unwin)

Agnew, J. (1996) Mapping politics: how context counts in electoral geography, *Political Geography*, 15(2): 129–46.

Agri Vision 2015 Committee (2004) *Report of the Agri Vision 2015 Committee.* (Dublin: Department of Agriculture and Food) Available from www.agri-vision2015.ie

AIB Global Treasury Economic Research (2005) *Here to Stay: Non-national Workers in the Irish Economy*, www.entemp.ie/trade/marketaccess/singlemarket/06serv114.pdf

Albrechts, L, Healey, P. and Kunzmann, K. (2003) Strategic spatial planning and regional governance in Europe, *Journal of the American Planning Association*, 69(2): 113–29

Allen, K. (2000) *The Celtic Tiger: The Myth of Social Partnership in Ireland.* (Manchester: Manchester University Press)

Alvarez, L. (2005) Suddenly rich, poor old Ireland seems bewildered, *New York Times*, 2 February

Area Development Management (ADM) (2005) *Rural Transport Initiative 2004 Annual Report.* (Dublin: ADM)

Arensberg, C. and Kimball, W. J. (1940) *Family and Community in Ireland* (2nd Revised Edition 1968). (Cambridge, MA: Harvard University Press)

Ashworth, G. (2005) Plural pasts for plural places. Conference Paper presented at Contemporary Heritage Issues Conference, University of Greenwich, March 2004

Ashworth, G. J. and Larkham, P. J. (1994) *Building a New Heritage: Tourism, Culture and Identity in the New Europe.* (London: Routledge)

Aughey, A. (2005) *The Politics of Northern Ireland: Beyond the Belfast Agreement.* (London, Routledge)

Balanda, K. and Wilde, J. (2001) *Inequalities in Mortality: A Report on All-Ireland Mortality Data 1989–1998.* (Dublin: Institute of Public Health)

Balanda, K. and Wilde, J. (2003) *Inequalities in Perceived Health: A Report On The All-Ireland Social Capital And Health Survey.* (Dublin: Institute of Public Health)

Baldock, D., Dwyer, P., Lowe, J., Petersen, E. and Ward, N. (2001) *The Nature of Rural Development: Towards a Sustainable Integrated Rural Policy in Europe.* (WWF-GB Countryside Agencies (Countryside Agency, Countryside Council for Wales, English Nature and Scottish Natural Heritage)).

Bannon, M. (ed.) (1989) *Planning the Irish Experience 1920–1988.* (Dublin: Wolfhound Press)

Bannon, M. J. (1973) *Office Location in Ireland: The Role of Central Dublin.* (Dublin: An Forás Forbartha)

Bannon, M. J. and Blair, S. (1985) *Service Activities: The Information Economy and the Role of Regional Centres.* (Dublin: National Board for Science and Technology)

Bannon, M. J., Eustace, J. G. and Power, M. (1977) *Service-Type Employment and Regional Development.* (Dublin: National Economic and Social Council Report No. 28)

Bannon, M. J. and Lombard, M. (1996) Evolution of regional policy in Ireland, in Group, R. P. A. (ed.) *Regional Policy.* (Shannon: Shannon Development)

Barry, F. and Egeraat, C. van (2005) *The Eastward Shift of Computer Hardware Production: How Ireland Adjusted*, National Institute for Regional and Spatial Analysis (NIRSA) Working Paper Series, No. 27 (National University of Ireland, Maynooth)

Bartley, B. (1999) Spatial planning and poverty in North Clondalkin, in Pringle, D. G., Walsh, J. and Hennessy, M., *Poor People, Poor Places*. (Dublin: Oak Tree Press)

Bartley, B. (2000) Four models of urban regeneration in Dublin, *Construction Concepts*, May–June: 28–33

Bartley, B. and Borscheid, M. (2003) Partnership funding in a period of new governance, in Scott, C. M. and Thurston, W. E., *Collaboration in Context*, pp. 231–42 (Calgary: University of Calgary Health Promotion Research Group and Institute for Gender Research)

Bartley, B. and Saris, A. J. (1999) Social exclusion and Cherry Orchard: a hidden side of suburban Dublin, in Killen, J. and MacLaran, A. (eds) *Dublin: Contemporary Trends and Issues for the Twenty-First Century*, pp. 81–92 (Dublin: Geographical Society of Ireland)

Bartley, B. and Treadwell-Shine, K. (1999a) *Urban Redevelopment and Social Polarisation in the City (URSPIC): Governance and the Dynamics of Urban Regeneration in Dublin*. (Brussels: European Commission Targeted Economic and Social Research (TSER) SOE2-CT97–3037)

Bartley, B. and Treadwell-Shine, K. (1999b) Promoting economic and social gains – the emergence of Dublin as an adaptive entrepreneurial city, *Insite*, Autumn–Winter: 20–3

Bartley, B. and Treadwell-Shine, K. (2003) Competitive city: governance and the changing dynamics of urban regeneration in Dublin, in Swyngedouw, E., Moulaert, F. and Rodriguez, A. (eds) *Urbanising Globalisation: Urban Redevelopment and Social Polarisation in the European City*, pp. 145–66 (Oxford: Oxford University Press)

Bartley, B. and Waddington, S. (2000) Modern planning in Ireland – an overview, *Geographical Viewpoint*, 28: 5–10

Bartley, B. and Waddington, S. (2001) The emergence and evolution of urban planning in Ireland, *Geographical Viewpoint*, 29(1): 7–14

Beamish, C. and MacLaran, A. (1985) Industrial property development in Dublin, 1960–1982, *Irish Geography*, 18: 37–50

Beard, V. (2003) Learning radical planning: the power of collective action, *Planning Theory*, 2(1): 13–35

Beardsworth, A. and Keil, T. (1997) *Sociology on the Menu*. (London: Routledge)

Bell, C. (2003) Dealing with the past in Northern Ireland, *Fordham International Law Journal*, 26: 1095–1145

Bell, D. (1973) *The Coming of the Post-Industrial Society*. (New York: Basic Books)

Bennett, J. and Collins, R. (2003) *The Future of European Regional Policy – A Place for Ireland and its Regions*. (Brussels: Irish Regions Office)

Bertz, S. (2002a) The growth in office take-up in Dublin's suburbs: a product of occupiers' changing locational criteria? *Journal of Irish Urban Studies*, 1(2): 55–75

Bertz, S. (2002b) The peripheralisation of office development in the Dublin Metropolitan Area: the interrelationship between planning and development interests, *Irish Geography*, 35(2): 197–212

Bhabha, H. (1994) *The Location of Culture*. (London: Routledge)

Booz Allen Hamilton (2003) *Strategic Rail Review*. (Dublin: Booz Allen Hamilton)

Bourdieu, P. (1984) *Distinction*. (London: Routledge)

Bourne, L. S. (2002) The Canadian urban system: old structures, recent trends, and new challenges, in Davies, W. K. D. and Townshend, I. J. (eds) *Monitoring Cities: International Perspectives*. (Calgary: International Geographical Union, Urban Commission)

Bowcott, O. (2004) Ireland leads world for quality of life, *Guardian*, 18 November

Bowler, I. (1992) Sustainable agriculture as an alternative path of farm business development, in Bowler, I., Bryant, C. and Nellis, M. (eds) *Contemporary Rural Systems in Transition: Agriculture and Environment*, 1: 237–52 (CABI Publishing)

Boylan, T. (2005) From undeveloped areas to spatial strategies: reflections on Irish regional policy, in McEldowney, M., Murray, M., Murtagh, B. and Sterrett, K. (eds) *Planning in Ireland and Beyond*, pp. 91–107 (Queen's University, Belfast)

Boylan, T. A. (1992) Paradigms in rural development: from critique to coherence?, in O Cinneide, M. and Cuddy, M. (eds) *Perspectives on Rural development in Advanced Economies*, pp. 13–23 (University College, Galway: SSRC)

Boyle, G., McCarthy, T. and Walsh, J. A., (1999) Regional income differentials and the issue of regional income inequalities in Ireland, *Journal Statistical and Social Inquiry Society of Ireland*, 28(1): 155–211

Boyle, M. (2002) Cleaning up after the Celtic Tiger: scalar 'fixes' in the political ecology of tiger economies, in *Transactions of the Institute of British Geographers*, NS 27: pp. 172–94

Brady Shipman Martin et al. (1999) *Strategic Planning Guidelines for the Greater Dublin Area: Directions for Land Use and Transportation in the Dublin and Mid-East Regions for the New Millennium.* (Dublin: Brady Shipman Martin)

Brady Shipman Martin (2000) *The Irish Urban System and its Dynamics.* (Dublin: Department of the Environment and Local Government)

Breathnach, P. (1982) The demise of growth-centre policy: the case of the Republic of Ireland, in Hudson, R. and Lewis, J. R. (eds) *Regional Planning in Europe*, pp. 35–56 (London: Pion)

Breathnach, P. (1985) Rural industrialisation in the West of Ireland, in Healy, M. and Ilbery, B. (eds) *Industrialisation of the Countryside.* (Norwich: Geo Books)

Breathnach, P. (1993) Women's employment and peripheralisation: the case of Ireland's branch plant economy, *Geoforum*, 24(1).

Breathnach, P. (1998) Exploring the 'Celtic Tiger' phenomenon: causes and consequences of Ireland's economic miracle, *European Urban and Regional Studies*, 5(4): 305–16

Breathnach, P. (1999) Social polarisation in the informational society: evidence from the Celtic Tiger, paper presented to Conference on the Celtic Tiger, 20 March (Maynooth: NUI, Maynooth)

Breathnach, P. (1999) The role of inward investment in regional development in Ireland, conference Paper presented at 'Ireland 2000+: Developing the Regions', 25 August, (Dublin: Regional Studies Association (Irish Branch))

Breathnach, P. (2000a) Globalisation, information technology and the emergence of niche transnational cities: the growth of the call centre sector in Dublin, *Geoforum*, 31(4): 477–85

Breathnach, P. (2000b) 'Óráidí móra agus athruithe beaga': An Ghaeltacht mar réigiún pleanála, in Mac Mathúna, L., Mac Murchaidh, C. and Nic Eoin, M. (eds) *Teanga, Pobal agus Réigiún: Aistí ar Chultúr na Gaeltachta Inniu.* (Baile Átha Cliath: Coiscéim)

Breathnach, P. (2002a) Regional government: the missing link in the national spatial strategy?, conference paper presented at 'Ireland 2020: People, Place and Space', Regional Studies Association (Irish Branch), Bunratty, County Clare, 26 April

Breathnach, P. (2002b) Social polarisation in the post-Fordist informational economy: Ireland in international context, *Irish Journal of Sociology*, 11(1): 3–22.

Breathnach, P. and Walsh, J. A. (1994) Industrialisation and regional development in Ireland, *Acta Universitatis Carolinae Geographica (Univerzita Karlova Praha)*, XXIX: 1.

Brett, D. (1996) *The Construction of Heritage.* (Cork: Cork University Press)

Brookfield, H. (1975) *Interdependent Development.* (London: Methuen)

Bruce, S. (1994) *The Edge of the Union: The Ulster Loyalist Political Vision.* (Oxford: Oxford University Press)

Buchanan, C. (1968) *Regional Studies in Ireland.* (Dublin: An Forás Forbartha)

Burayidi, M. (2003) The multicultural city as planners' enigma, *Planning Theory and Practice*, 4(3): 259–73

Byrne, D. (2001) *Understanding the Urban.* (Basingstoke: Palgrave Macmillan)

Caldeira, G. A., Clausen, A. R. and Patterson, S. C. (1990) Partisan mobilisation and electoral participation, *Electoral Studies*, 9(3): 191–204

Callanan, M, (2003a) Local government and the European Union, in Callanan, M. and Keogan, J. F. (eds) *Local Government in Ireland: Inside Out*, pp. 404–28 (Dublin: Institute of Public Administration)

Callanan, M, (2003b) The role of local government, in Callanan, M. and Keogan, J. F. (eds) *Local Government in Ireland: Inside Out*, pp. 3–13 (Dublin: Institute of Public Administration)

Cartwright, A., Davinn, S., Dowling, J. and Golden, C. (2004) Voter turnout, candidate support and the local media in Longford-Roscommon, *Milieu*, 29: 60–4

Castells, M. (1996) *The Rise of the Network Society.* (Oxford: Blackwell Publishers)

Cawley, M. (1991) Town population change 1971–1986: patterns and distributional effects, *Irish Geography*, 24(2): 106–16

Cawley, M., Gillmor, D. and Kelly, R. (2004) Supporting and promoting integrated tourism in Europe's lagging rural regions (SPRITE Project), in *Integrated Rural Development in the West of Ireland: Learning from Tourists and Tour Organisers*, (Teagasc Online publications: www.teagasc.ie/publications/2004)

Central Statistics Office (1994) *Census of Agriculture 1991*. (Dublin: CSO)

Central Statistics Office (2002) *Census of Agriculture 2000*. (Cork: CSO)

Central Statistics Office (2003a) *Census 2002 Volume 1 Population Classified by Area*. (Dublin: The Stationery Office)

Central Statistics Office (2003b) *Census 2002 Principal Socio-economic Results*. (Dublin: The Stationery Office)

Central Statistics Office (2003c) *Ireland and the EU: 1979–2003*. (Dublin: CSO)

Central Statistics Office (2004a) *Population and Migration Estimates*. (Dublin: CSO)

Central Statistics Office (2004b) *Irish Life Tables No. 14, 2001–2003*. (Dublin and Cork: CSO)

Central Statistics Office (2004c) *Statistics of Port Traffic 2003*. (Dublin: CSO)

Central Statistics Office (2005) *Regional Population and Labour Force Projections*. (Dublin: CSO)

Central Statistics Office (2006) *Quarterly National Household Survey Quarter 4 2005*. (Dublin: CSO)

Child, P. (2002) Taking Tesco global, *Mckinsey Quarterly*, 3(2): 5–9

Christaller, W. (1966) *Central Places in Southern Germany* (translated by C. W. Baskin). (Englewood Cliffs, NJ: Prentice-Hall)

Clancy, P., O'Malley, E., O'Connell, L. and Egeraat, C. van (2001) Industry clusters in Ireland: an application of Porter's model of national competitive advantage to three sectors, *European Planning Studies*, 9(1)

Cleary J. (2004) Towards a materialist-formulation of twentieth century Irish literature, *Boundary 2*, 31(1): 209–41

Clinch, J. P. (2004) Planning and the environment, *Journal of Irish Urban Studies*, 3(1): 41–51

Cloke, P. (1995) (En)culturing political economy: a life in the day of a 'rural' geographer, in Cloke, P., Doel, M., Matless, D., Phillips, M. and Thrift, N., *Writing the Rural: Five Cultural Geographies*, pp. 19–33. (London: PCP)

Collins, N. (2001) External relations, in Collins, N. and Cradden, T. (eds) *Irish Politics Today*, 4th edition, pp. 149–58 (Manchester: Manchester University Press)

Collins, N. and O'Shea M. (2001) Political corruption in Ireland, in Collins, N. and Cradden, T. (eds) *Irish Politics Today*, 4th edition, pp. 89–107 (Manchester: Manchester University Press)

Combat Poverty Agency (2004), *Strategic Plan 2005–2007*. (Dublin: Combat Poverty Agency)

Commins, P. (1996) Agricultural production and the future of small-scale farming, in Curtin C., Haase, T. and Tovey, H. (eds) *Poverty in Rural Ireland: A Political Economy Perspective*, pp. 87–125. (Dublin: Oak Tree Press)

Commins, P. (2005) The broader rural economy, in Rural Ireland 2025 Foresight Perspectives Working Group, 2005, *Report on Rural Ireland 2025*, pp. 37–44. (NUI Maynooth, UCD and Teagasc)

Commins, P. and Keane, M. (1994) *Developing the Rural Economy: Problems, Programmes and Prospects*, Report No. 97. (Dublin: National Economic and Social Council)

Commins, P. and McDonagh, P. (2000) Rural areas and the development of a national spatial strategy, conference paper presented to The Regional Studies Association (Irish Branch) conference, Tullamore, Co. Offaly, 3 April

Commins, P. and Walsh, J. A. (2005) Adjustments and impacts of the Common Agricultural Policy and Rural Development Policy: Ireland, in Shucksmith, M., Thomson, K. and Roberts, D. (eds) *The CAP and the Regions – the Territorial Impact of the Common Agricultural Policy*, pp. 113–23. (CABI Publishing)

Commins, P., Walsh, J. A. and Meredith, D. (2005) Some spatial dimensions; population and settlement patterns, in Rural Ireland 2025 Foresight Perspectives Working Group, 2005, *Report on Rural Ireland 2025*, pp. 45–60 (NUI Maynooth, UCD and Teagasc)

Commission of the European Communities (2006) *Report on the Functioning of the Transitional Arrangements Set Out in the 2003 Accession Treaty (Period 1 May 2004–30 April 2006)*. (Brussels: Commission of the European Communities)

Commission of the European Communities, and Government of Ireland (1989) *Community Support Framework for Ireland 1989–1993*. (Dublin: Government Publications Office)

Commission of the European Communities, and Government of Ireland (1996) *Operational Programme: Local Urban and Rural Development 1994–1999*. (Dublin: Government Publications Office)

Commission on Social Welfare (1986) *Report of the Commission on Social Welfare*. (Dublin: Government Publications Office)

Community Relations Council (1998) *Into the Mainstream: Strategic Plan 1998–2001*. (Belfast: Community Relations Council)

Connolly, J. (1996) 24-hour shopping trip, *Irish Times*, 6 March

Connolly, L., Burke, T. and Roche, M., (2003) *National Farm Survey*. (Dublin: Teagasc)

Constituency Commission (2004) *Constituency Commission Report on Dáil Constituencies, 2004*. (Dublin: The Stationery Office)

Cook, S., Poole, M. A., Pringle, D. G. and Moore, A. J. (2000) *Comparative Spatial Deprivation in Ireland: A Cross Border Analysis*. (Dublin: Oak Tree Press)

Coombes, M., Raybould, S., Wong, C. and Openshaw, S. (1995) Towards an index of deprivation: a review of alternative approaches', Part 1 of *1991 Deprivation Index: A Review of Approaches and a Matrix of Results*. Department of the Environment (London: The Stationery Office)

Coras Iompair Eireann (2002) *Annual Report*. (Dublin: CIE)

Corcoran, M. P., Gray, J. and Peillon, M. P. (2005) Civic and social life in the suburbs, paper presented at the Royal Irish Academy Conference, 'Volunteering and Philanthropy-Research from Ireland, North and South', 24 November (Belfast: NICVA)

Coulter, C. (1999) *Contemporary Northern Irish Society*. (London: Pluto)

Creton, D. and Pringle, D. G. (1991) Variations régionales de la mortalité en République d'Irlande, *Espace, Populations, Sociétés*, 1991(1): 113–25

Crewe, I., Fox, T. and Alt, J. (1992) Non-voting in British general elections, 1966–October 1974, in Denver, D. and Hands, G. (eds) *Issues and Controversies in British Electoral Behaviour*, pp. 18–30 (Hemel Hempstead: Harvester Wheatsheaf)

Cronin, M. and O'Connor, B. (eds) (2003) *Irish Tourism – Image, Culture and Identity*. (Clevedon: Channel View Publications)

Crowley, C., Meredith, D. and Walsh, J. (2004) Population and agricultural change in rural Ireland 1991–2002, in Pitts, E. (ed.) *Rural Futures, Proceedings of Rural Development Conference*, pp. 17–34 (Dublin: Teagasc)

Crowley, C., Meredith, D. and Walsh, J. (2006) *Irish Agriculture at the Millennium: A Census Atlas*. (NUI Maynooth, UCD and Teagasc)

Crowley, U., Gilmartin, M. and Kitchen, R. (2006) Vote Yes for commonsense citizenship: Immigration and paradoxes at the heart of Ireland's 'Cead Mile Failte'. *NIRSA Working Papers*, 30 (NUI, Maynooth)

Crowley, U. and Kitchin, R. (2006) Paradoxical spaces of Traveller citizenship in contemporary Ireland, *NIRSA Working Papers*, 31 (NUI Maynooth)

Cuddy, M. (1991) Rural development in Ireland: an appraisal, in Varley, T., Boylan, T. and Cuddy, M. (eds) *Rural Crisis: Perspectives on Irish Rural Development*, pp. 28–47. (University College Galway: Centre for Development Studies)

Cullen, E. (2004) Unprecedented growth, but for whose benefit?, in Douthwaite, R. and Jopling, J. (eds) *Celtic Crisis*. (Dublin: FEASTA Review)

Curtin C., Haase, T. and Tovey, H. (eds) (1996) *Poverty in Rural Ireland – A Political Economy Perspective* (Dublin: Combat Poverty Agency and Oak Tree Press)

Daniels, P. W. (1979) *Spatial Patterns of Office Growth and Location*. (Chichester: Wiley)

Daniels, P. W. (1982) *Service Industries: Growth and Location*. (Cambridge: Cambridge University Press).

Department of Agriculture and Food (1999) *Ensuring the Future – A Strategy for Rural Development in Ireland – A White Paper on Rural Development*. (Dublin: Government Publications Office)

Department of Agriculture and Food (2004) Rural Environment Protection Scheme – Basics and Contacts, www.agriculture.gov.ie/index.jsp?file=areasofi/reps.xml

Department of Arts, Sport and Tourism-DAST (2003) *New Horizons for Irish Tourism: An Agenda for Action.* (Dublin: Central Statistics Office)

Department of Arts, Sport and Tourism-DAST (2005) *Statement of Strategy 2005–2007.* (Dublin: Government Publications Office)

Department of Communications, Marine and Natural Resources (2003) *High Level Review of the State Commercial Ports Operating Under the Harbours Acts 1996 and 2000.* (Dublin: Government Publications Office)

Department of Community Rural and Gaeltacht Affairs (n.d.) EU Presidency Papers (Rural Development) of the Department of Community Rural and Gaeltacht Affairs, www.pobail. ie/en/RuralDevelopment/EUPresidencyPapers

Department of the Environment and Local Government (DELG) (1994) *Urban Renewal Programme: New Life in Your Town,* (Dublin: Government Publications Office)

Department of the Environment and Local Government (1996) *Better Local Government: A Programme for Change.* (Dublin: Government Publications Office)

Department of the Environment and Local Government (1998) *Task Force on Integration of Local Government and Local Development Systems Report.* (Dublin: Government Publications Office)

Department of the Environment and Local Government (2001) *The National Spatial Strategy: Indications for the Way Ahead.* (Dublin: Government Publications Office)

Department of the Environment and Local Government (2002) *National Spatial Strategy for Ireland, 2002–2020.* (Dublin: Government Publications Office)

Department of the Environment, Heritage and Local Government (DoEHLG) (2005a) *Annual Housing Statistics Bulletin 2004.* (Dublin: Government Publications Office)

Department of the Environment, Heritage and Local Government (2005b) *Sustainable Rural Housing: Guidelines for Local Authorities.* (Dublin: Government Publications Office)

Department of the Environment, Heritage and Local Government (2005c) website. www.environ. ie.

Department of the Environment, Heritage and Local Government (2006) *The Atlantic Gateways Initiative: Building Critical Mass.* (Dublin: Government Publications Office)

Department of the Environment for Northern Ireland (1977) *Northern Ireland Regional Physical Development Strategy 1975–1995.* (Belfast: HMSO)

Department of the Environment, UK (1995) *1991 Deprivation Index: A Review of Approaches and a Matrix of Results.* (London: HMSO)

Department of Finance (1999) *National Development Plan 2000–2006.* (Dublin: Government Publications Office)

Department of Finance (2005) *Economic Review and Outlook 2005.* (Dublin: Government Publications Office)

Department of Health and Children (2001a) *Quality and Fairness: A Health System For You: Health Strategy.* (Dublin: Government Publications Office)

Department of Health and Children (2001b) *Primary Care: A New Direction.* (Dublin: Government Publications Office)

Department of Health and Children (2004) *Strategic Task Force on Alcohol, Second Report.* (Dublin: Department of Health and Children), also available at www.healthpromotion.ie/publications/ sendfile.php?irish=no&id=110

Department of Health and Children (2005) *Report of Inquiry into the Handling of Allegations of Child Sex Abuse in the Diocese of Ferns.* (Dublin: Government Publications Office

Department of Housing, Local Government and Planning (1975) *Northern Ireland Discussion Paper: Regional Physical Development Strategy 1975–1995.* (Belfast: HMSO)

Department of Justice, Equality and Law Reform (1999) *Integration: Two-way Process.* (Dublin: Government Publications Office)

Department of Justice, Equality and Law Reform (2005a) *Immigration and Residency in Ireland: Outline Policy Proposals for an Immigration and Residence Bill: A Discussion Document.* (Dublin: Government Publications Office)

Department of Justice, Equality and Law Reform (2005b) *National Action Plan Against Racism.* (Dublin: Government Publications Office)

Department for Regional Development (2001a) *Shaping Our Future: Regional Development Strategy for Northern Ireland 2025.* (Belfast: Corporate Document Services)

Department for Regional Development (2001b) *The Family of Settlements Report.* (Belfast: DRD)

Department of Social and Family Affairs (2003) *Statistical Report on Social Welfare Services 2002.* (Dublin: Government Publications Office)

Department of the Taoiseach (1998) Second Report to Government of the Co-ordinating Group of Secretaries: Delivering Better Government. *Strategic Management Initiative: A Programme of Change for the Irish Civil Service.* (Dublin: Government Publications Office)

Department of the Taoiseach (2005) Launch of the Ireland Poland Business Association, website www.taoiseach.gov.ie/index.asp?locID=440anddocID=2270

Dicken, P., Kelly, P., Olds, K. and Yeung, H. (2001) Chains and networks, territories and scales: towards a relational framework for analysing the global economy, *Global Networks*, 1(2)

Dirlik, A. (1999) Place-based imagination: globalism and the politics of place, *Review*, xxii (2)

Drudy, P. J. (1991) The regional impact of overseas industry, in Foley, A. and McAleese, D. (eds) *Overseas Industry in Ireland.* (Dublin: Gill and Macmillan).

Drudy, P. J. and Punch, M. (2005) *Out of Reach: Inequalities in the Irish Housing System.* (Dublin: New Island)

Dublin Corporation (1994) *HARP Plan.* (Dublin: Civic Offices)

Dublin Docklands Development Authority (1997) *Dublin Docklands Area Master Plan 1997.* (Dublin: Government Publications Office)

Dublin Transportation Office (2001) *A Platform for Change: Summary Report.* (Dublin: Government Publications Office)

Dunlop, J. (1995) *A Precarious Belonging: Presbyterians and Conflict in Ireland.* (Belfast: Blackstaff Press)

Economic and Social Research Institute: see under ESRI

Edwards, C. and Linehan, D. (2005) *City of Difference: Mapping Social Exclusion in Cork City.* (Cork: Cork City Council)

Egeraat, C. van (2006a) *Ireland's Changing Position in Global Production Networks in the Pharmaceutical Industry*, National Institute for Regional and Spatial Analysis (NIRSA) Working Paper Series, National University of Ireland, Maynooth

Egeraat, C. van (2006b) *Spatial Dynamics of the Pharmaceutical Industry in Ireland*, National Institute for Regional and Spatial Analysis (NIRSA) Working Paper Series, National University of Ireland, Maynooth

Egeraat, C. van and Jacobson, D. (2004) The rise and demise of the Irish and Scottish computer hardware industry, *European Planning Studies*, 12(6)

Egeraat, C. van and Jacobson, D. (2005) Geography of linkages in the Irish and Scottish computer hardware industry: the role of logistics, *Economic Geography*, 81(3)

Egeraat, C. van, Sokol, M. and Stafford, P. (2006) Greater Dublin in the Celtic Tiger economy: towards a polycentric mega-city region?, in Hall, P. and Pain, K. (eds) *The Polycentric Metropolis: Learning from Mega-City-Regions in Europe*, pp. 187–94 (London: Earthscan/James & James)

Ellis, G. (2001) Social exclusion, equality and the Good Friday Agreement: the implications for land use planning, *Policy and Politics*, 29(4): 393–411

Emerson, H. and Gilmore, D. (1999) The Rural Environmental Protection Scheme, *Land Use Policy*, 16: 235–45

Environmental Protection Agency (2002) *Environment in Focus, 2002: Key Environmental Indicators for Ireland.* (Dublin: EPA)

Environmental Protection Agency (2003) *National Waste Database 2003*, Interim Report. (Wexford: EPA)

Environmental Protection Agency (2004a) *Ireland's Environment 2004.* (Dublin: EPA)

Environmental Protection Agency (2004b) *National Waste Report 2004.* (Dublin: EPA)

Environmental Protection Agency (2005) *The Nature and Extent of Unauthorised Activity in Ireland*, press release 15 September 2005, www.epa.ie/NewsCentre/Press Release/MainBody,7789,en. html

ESRI (Economic and Social Research Institute) (2003) *Medium Term Review 2003–2010*. (Dublin: ESRI)

ESRI (Economic and Social Research Institute) (2005) *Irish Economic Overview*, www.esri.ie/content.cfm?t=Irish%20Economyandmid=4

ESRI, HIPE and NPRS (2004) *Report on Perinatal Statistics for 2000*, www.esri.ie/advsearch. cfm?t=Find%20PublicationsandmId=2anddetail=1andid=2099

Eurobarometer (2003) *Public Opinion in the European Union: Spring 2003* (Brussels: European Commission)

European Commission (1988) *The Future of Rural Society*, COM (88), 501. (Luxembourg: Office for Official Publications of the European Communities)

European Commission (1997) *Agenda 2000*, COM (97) 2000. (Luxembourg: Office for Official Publications of the European Communities)

European Commission (1999) *European Spatial Development Perspective: Towards Balanced and Sustainable Development of the Territory of the European Union*. (Luxembourg: Office for Official Publications of the European Communities)

European Commission (2000) *Guidelines for the Community Initiative for Rural Development* (LEADER +), C (2000), 946, www.europa.eu.int/

European Commission (2003) *Regional Indicators to Reflect Social Exclusion and Poverty* (VT/2003/43), http://europa.eu.int/comm/employment_social/social_inclusion/docs/region-alindicators_en.pdf

European Commission (2004) *A New Partnership for Cohesion – Third Report on Economic and Social Cohesion*. (Luxembourg Office for Official Publications of the European Communities)

European Conference on Rural Development (1996) *The Cork Declaration – A Living Countryside*. (ECRD)

European Council (2001) *Presidency Conclusions: Goteburg, 15 and 16 June 2001*. (Goteburg: European Council), also available at http://ue.eu.int/ueDocs/cms_Data/docs/pressData/en/ec/00200-r1.en1.pdf

European Environment Agency (1999) *Environment in the European Union at the Turn of the Century.* (Luxembourg: Office for Official Publications of the European Communities)

European Environment Agency (2000) *Environmental Signals*. (Luxembourg: Office for Official Publications of the European Communities)

European Environment Agency (2004) *EEA Signals 2004: A EEA Update on Selected Issues*. (Luxembourg: Office for Official Publications of the European Communities)

European Environment Agency (2005) *European Environment Outlook*, Report No. 4. (Luxembourg: Office for Official Publications of the European Communities)

Evans, N., Morris, C. and Winter, M., (2002) Conceptualising agriculture: a critique of post-productivism as the new orthodoxy, *Progress in Human Geography*, 26(3): 313–32

Eyben, K., Morrow, D. and Wilson, D. (1997) *A Worthwhile Venture? Practically Investing in Equity Diversity and Interdependence in Northern Ireland*. (Coleraine: University of Ulster)

Fagan, G. H. (2003) Sociological reflections on governing waste, *Irish Journal of Sociology*, 12(1): 67–85

Fagan, G. H. (2004) Waste management and its contestation in the Republic of Ireland, *Capitalism, Nature, Socialism*, 15(1): 83–102

Fagan, G. H., O'Hearn, D., McCann, G. and Murray, M. (2001) *Waste Management Strategy: A Cross Border Perspective*, (National Institute for Regional and Spatial Analysis), Working Paper 2, www.nuim.ie/nirsa/research/working_papers.shtml

Fahey, T. (1999) *Social Housing in Ireland: A Study of Success, Failure, and Lessons Learned*. (Dublin, Oak Tree Press in association with the Katharine Howard)

Fáilte Ireland (2004a) *Tourism Facts 2004*. (Government publication), also available at www. failteireland.ie

Fáilte Ireland (2004b) *Domestic Tourism 2004*. (Government publication), also available at www. failteireland.ie

Fáilte Ireland (2004c) *Tourism Matters Newsletter, October 2004*. (Government publication), also available at www.failteireland.ie

Fáilte Ireland (2005) *Summary of Activities 2005*. (Government publication), also available at www.failteireland.ie

Fanning, B. (2002) *Racism and Social Change in the Republic of Ireland*. (Manchester: Manchester University Press)

Ferriter, D. (2004) *The Transformation of Ireland 1900–2000*. (London: Profile)

Finance Dublin Yearbook (2005) *The Finance Dublin Yearbook of Ireland's Financial Services Sector 2005*. (Dublin: Fintel)

Fitzgerald, G. (2006) Some facts on 'displacement' of Irish workers, *Irish Times*, 14 January

Fitzpatrick Associates, Brady Shipman Martin and the International Centre for Local and Regional Development (2005) *Gateways Investment Priorities*. (Department of Environment, Heritage and Local Government and Forfás)

Forfás (1998), *Irish Economy expenditure Survey*. (Dublin: Forfás)

Forfás (2000) Enterprise 2010: *A New Strategy for the Promotion of Enterprise in Ireland in the 21st Century*. (Dublin: Forfás)

Forfás (2001) *Key Waste Management Issues in Ireland*. (Dublin: Forfás), www.forfas.ie/publications/waste_management_01/index.html

Forfás (2002) *eBusiness: Where Are We and Where Do We Go from Here?* (Dublin: Forfás)

Forfás (2003) *Consumer Pricing Report*. (Dublin: Forfás)

Forfás Employment Survey (2002) *Annual Employment Survey 2002* (Dublin: Forfás), also available at www.forfas.ie/publications/show/pub30.html

Forfás (Undated) *A Strategy for the Digital Content Industry in Ireland*. (Dublin: Forfás)

Fraser, N. (2000) Rethinking recognition, *New Left Review*, 3: 107–20

Frawley, J. and Phelan, G. (2002) Changing agriculture: impacts on rural development, in *Signposts to Rural Change: Proceedings of Rural Development Conference*, pp. 20–42 (Dublin: Teagasc)

Fröbel, F., Heinrichs, J. and Kreye, O. (1980) *The New International Division of Labour*. (Cambridge: Cambridge University Press)

Gallagher, M. (1996) By-elections to Dáil Eireann 1923–96: the anomaly that conforms, *Irish Politicial Studies*, 11:33–60

Gallagher, M., Marsh, M., and Mitchell, P. (2003) *How Ireland Voted 2002*. (Basingstoke: Palgrave Macmillan)

Gallent, N., Shucksmith, M. and Tewdwr-Jones, M. (eds) (2003) *Housing in the European Countryside: Housing Pressure and Policy in Western Europe*. (London: Routledge)

Geyer, H. S. (1995) Expanding the theoretical foundation of differential urbanization, *Tijdschrift voor Economische en Sociale Geografie*, 87(1): 44–59

Geyer, H. S. and Kontuly, T. (1993) A theoretical foundation for the concept of differential urbanization, *International Regional Science Review*, 15(12): 157–77

Giddens, A. (1990) *The Consequence of Modernity*. (Cambridge: Polity)

Gillmor, D. (1987) Concentration of enterprises and spatial changes in the agriculture of the Republic of Ireland, *Transactions of the Institute of British Geographers*, 12: 204–16

Gillmor, D. (1999) The scheme of early retirement from farming in the Republic of Ireland, *Irish Geography*, 32(2): 78–86

Gillmor, D. and Walsh, J. A. (1993) County-level variations in agricultural adjustment in Ireland in the 1980s, *Geographical Viewpoint*, 21: 25–44

Gillmor, D. A. (1985) *Economic Activities in the Republic of Ireland: A Geographical Perspective*. (Dublin: Gill and Macmillan)

Gillmor, D. A. (2004) Integrated rural development in the West of Ireland: learning from tourists and tour organisers, in *Rural Futures: Conference Proceeedings* (Teagasc online), www.teagasc.ie/publications

Glover, J. (1999) *Humanity: a Moral History of the Twentieth Century*. (London: Jonathan Cape)

Goddard, J. (1973) Office linkages and location: a study of communications and spatial patterns in central London, *Progress in Planning*, 1: 1–232

Goddard, J. (1975) *Office Location in Urban and Regional Planning*. (Oxford: Oxford University Press)

Goodchild, B. and Cole, I. (2001) Social balance and mixed neighbourhoods in Britain since 1979: a review of discourse and practice in social housing, *Environment and Planning D: Society and Space*, 19: 103–22

Gormley, N. (2000) The British are back and they're after your money. *Dublin People*, 5 May

Gottmann, J. (1961) *Megalopolis: The Urbanized Northeastern Seaboard of the United States.* (New York: Twentieth Century Fund)

Government of Ireland (1984) *White Paper on Industrial Policy.* (Dublin: The Stationery Office)

Government of Ireland (1987) *Programme for National Recovery.* (Dublin: The Stationery Office)

Government of Ireland (1991) *Programme for Economic and Social Progress.* (Dublin: The Stationery Office)

Government of Ireland (1994a) *Government of Renewal: Programme for Government.* (Dublin: Government Publications Office).

Government of Ireland (1994b) *Operational Programme for Transport 1994 to 1999.* (Dublin: Department of the Environment)

Government of Ireland (1994c) *Programme for Competitiveness and Work.* (Dublin: The Stationery Office)

Government of Ireland (1997) *National Action Plan Against Poverty and Social Exclusion 2003–2005*, www.socialinclusion.ie/publications/napincl_plan0305.pdf

Government of Ireland (1997) *Partnership 2000 for Inclusion, Employment and Competitiveness.* (Dublin: The Stationery Office)

Government of Ireland (1997) *Sharing in Progress – National Anti-Poverty Strategy.* (Dublin: Government Publications Office)

Government of Ireland (1999) *Ireland National Development Plan 2000–2006.* (Dublin: Government Publications Office)

Government of Ireland (2000a) *Ireland National Development Plan: Economic and Social Infrastructure Operational Programme 2000–2006.* (Dublin: Government Publications Office)

Government of Ireland (2000b) *Programme for Prosperity and Fairness.* (Dublin: Government Publications Office)

Government of Ireland (2002) *The National Spatial Strategy 2002–2020: People, Places and Potential.* (Dublin: Government Publications Office)

Government of Ireland (2003) *Sustaining Progress.* (Dublin: Government Publications Office)

Government of Ireland (2005) *Transport 21.* (Dublin: Government Publications Office)

Graham, B. (1998) Contested images of place among Protestants in Northern Ireland, *Political Geography*, 17: 129–44

Graham, B., Ashworth, G. and Tunbridge, J. (2000) *A Geography of Heritage: Power, Culture and Economy.* (London: Arnold)

Graham, B. and Shirlow, P. (1998) An elusive agenda: the development of a middle ground in Northern Ireland, *Area*, 30: 245–54

Graham, B. and Shirlow, P. (2002) The Battle of the Somme in Ulster memory and identity, *Political Geography*, 21: 881–904

Gramsci, A. (1971) *Selections from the Prison Notebooks of Antonio Gramsci* (edited and translated by Hoare, Q. and Nowell-Smith, G.) (London: Lawrence and Wishart)

Greer, J. and Jess, P. (1987) Town and country planning, in Buchanan, R. H. and Walker, B. M. (eds) *Province, City and People: Belfast and its Region*, pp. 101–24 (Antrim: Greystone Books)

Greer, J. and Murray, M. (1993) Rural Ireland – personality and policy context, in Murray, M. and Greer, J. (eds) *Rural Development in Ireland*, pp. 3–20 (Aldershot: Avebury)

Gregory, I. N., Dorling, D. and Southall, H.R. (2001) A century of inequality in England and Wales using standardized geographical units, *Area*, 33(3): 297–311

Grist, B. (2003) Planning, in Callanan, M. and Keogan, J. F. (eds) *Local Government in Ireland: Inside Out*, pp. 221–52 (Dublin: Institute of Public Administration)

Haase, T. (1998) 'The role of data in policies for distressed areas', in *Integrating Distressed Urban Areas*. (Paris: OECD)

Haase, T. and McKeown, K. (2003) Developing disadvantaged areas through area-based initiatives – reflections on over a decade of local development strategies. (Dublin: Pobal)

Haase, T., McKeown, K. and Rourke, S. (1996) *Local Development Strategies for Disadvantaged Areas – Evaluation of the Global Grant in Ireland (1992–1995)*. (Dublin: ADM)

Haase, T. and Pratschke, J. (2003) *Digital Divide – Analysis of Uptake of Information Technology in the Dublin Region.* (Dublin: Dublin Employment Pact)

Haase, T. and Pratschke, J. (2005) *Deprivation and its Spatial Articulation in the Republic of Ireland – New Measures of Deprivation Based on the Census of Population, 1991, 1996 and 2002.* (Dublin: Pobal) The full report is available at www.pobal.ie/media/Deprivationanditsspatialarticulation. pdf

Halfacree, K. H. (1993) Locality and social representation: space, discourse and alternative definitions of the rural, *Journal of Rural Studies*, 9(1): 23–7

Hall, P. (1999) The future of cities, *Computers, Environment and Urban Systems*, 23: 173–85

Hall, S. (1996) Introduction: who needs identity?, in Hall, S. and Du Gay, P. (eds) *Questions of Cultural Identity*, pp. 1–17 (London: Sage)

Hall, T. and Hubbard, P. (1998) The entrepreneurial city and the new urban politics, in Hall, T. and Hubbard, P. (eds) *The Entrepreneurial City: Geographies of Politics, Regime, and Representation*, pp. 1–23 (Chichester: Wiley)

Hannan, D. and Commins, P. (1994) The significance of small-scale landholders in Ireland's socio-economic transformation, in Goldthorpe, J. H. and Whelan, C. T. (eds) *The Development of Industrial Society in Ireland*, pp. 79–104 (Oxford: Oxford University Press)

Harrison, J. (2000) The process of interpretation, in Buttimer, N., Rynne, C. and Guerin, H. (eds) *The Heritage of Ireland*, pp. 385–93 (Cork: Collins)

Harrison, P. and Todes, A. (2001) The use of spatial frameworks in regional development in South Africa, *Regional Studies*, 35(1): 65–72

Harrison, R. T. and Anderson, T. J. (1980) Northern Ireland: the development of a rank-size distribution?, *Tijdschrift voor Economische En Sociale Geografie*, 71(4): 194–200

Harrop, M. and Miller, W. L. (1987) *Elections and Voters: A Comparative Introduction.* (London: Macmillan)

Harvey, D. (1989) *The Condition of Post-Modernity.* (Oxford: Blackwell)

Healy, A. (2000) Judge calls time on Galway's 'dreadful' girls, *Irish Times*, 25 July

Heikkila, E. (2001) Identity and inequality: race and space in planning, *Planning Theory and Practice*, 2(3): 261–75

Higgins J. (2002) *Senate Debates*, 11 December

Home Office (2005) *Accession Monitoring Report May 2004–September 2005.* (London: Home Office)

Hooper-Greenhill, E. (ed.) (1995) *Museum, Media, Message.* (London: Routledge)

Hooper-Greenhill, E. (2000) *Museums and Interpretation of Visual Culture.* (London: Routledge)

Horiuchi, Y. (2005) *Institutions, Incentives and Electoral Participation in Japan.* (London and New York: RoutledgeCurzon)

Horner, A. (1988) Developments in early morning public transport as an indicator of change in the Dublin City region, *Irish Geography*, 21(1): 45–7

Horner, A., Walsh, J. A. and Harrington, V. (1987) *Population in Ireland: A Census Atlas.* (Dublin: Department of Geography, UCD)

Horner, A., Walsh, J. A. and Williams, J., (1984) *Agriculture in Ireland: A Census Atlas.* (Dublin: Department of Geography, UCD)

Horner, A. A. (1999) The Tiger stirring: aspects of commuting in the Republic of Ireland 1981–1996, *Irish Geography*, 32(2): 99–111

Horner, A. A. (2000) Geographical regions in Ireland – reflections at the Millennium, *Irish Geography*, 33(2): 134–65

HotOrigin (2001) *Ireland's Emerging Software Cluster: A Hothouse of Future Stars.* (Dublin: HotOrigin Limited)

Houellebecq, M. (2000) *Atomised.* (London: Heinemann)

Houghton, F. (2002) A review of mortality maps included in the Annual Reports of Vital Statistics for Ireland 1864–1998, *Irish Geography*, 35(2): 213–15

Houghton, F. (2005) Hiding the evidence: the State and spatial inequalities in health in Ireland, *Irish Geography*, 38(1): 96–106

Hourihan, K. and Lyons, D. (1995) Service changes in a central-place system: County Tipperary, Ireland, 1966–1986, *Rural Sociology*, 60(2): 244–59

Hourihane, A. (2002) *She Moves Through the Boom*. (Dublin: Lilliput)

Howell, F., O'Mahony, M., Devlin, J., O'Reilly, O. and Buttanshaw, C. (1993) A geographical distribution of mortality and deprivation, *Irish Medical Journal*, 86(3): 96–9

Hug, C. (1999) *The Politics of Sexual Morality in Ireland*. (London: Macmillan)

Illeris, S. (1996) *The Service Economy*. (Chichester: Wiley)

Industrial Policy Review Group (1992) *A Time for Change: Industrial Policy for the 1990s*. (Dublin: The Stationery Office)

Integrating Ireland (2005) www.integratingireland.ie

International IDEA (1999) *Youth Voter Participation: Involving Today's Young in Tomorrow's Democracy*. (Stockholm: International Institute for Democracy and Electoral Assistance)

InterTradeIreland (2006) *Spatial Strategies on the Island of Ireland: Development of a Framework of Collaborative Action*. (Newry: InterTradeIreland)

Irish Rural Dwellers Association (2004) *Positive Planning for Rural Houses*. (Kilrush: Irish Rural Dwellers Association)

Jarman, N. (1997) *Material Conflicts: Parades and Visual Displays in Northern Ireland*. (Oxford: Berg)

Johnston, R. J., Pattie, C. J., Dorling, D. F. L., MacAllister, I., Tunstall, H. and Rossiter, D. J. (2001) Housing tenure, local context, scale and voting in England and Wales, 1997, *Electoral Studies*, 20(2): 195–216

Johnson, Z. and Dack, P. (1989) Small area mortality patterns, *Irish Medical Journal*, 82(3): 105–8

Johnson, Z. and Lyons, R. (1993) Socioeconomic factors and mortality in small areas, *Irish Medical Journal*, 86(2): 60–2

Joint Committee on Health and Children, House of the Oireachtas (2004) *Report on Alcohol Misuse by Young People*. (Dublin: Government Publications Office)

Jordan, G. (2001) *Not of This World? Evangelical Protestants in Northern Ireland*. (Belfast: Balckstaff)

Jouen, M. (1999) *LEADER's Contributions: An Overview of National Differences*. (Brussels: LEADER European Observatory)

Kaltenborn, B.P. and Bjerke, T. (2002) Associations between environmental value orientations and landscape preference, *Landscape and Urban Planning*, 59(1): 1–11

Kavanagh, A. (2002a) *Unequal Participation – Unequal Influence: Voter Participation and Voter Education in Dublin's South West Inner City*. (Dublin: South West Inner City Network)

Kavanagh, A. (2002b) *Social Deprivation, Political Alienation and Community Empowerment*, unpublished PhD thesis, Department of Geography, NUI, Maynooth.

Kavanagh, A. (2003) The Constituency Commission, *Irish Political Studies*, 18(2): 89–99

Kavanagh, A. (2004) The 2004 local elections in the Republic of Ireland, *Irish Politicial Studies*, 19(2): 64–84

Kavanagh, A., Mills, G. and Sinnott, R. (2004) The geography of Irish voter turnout: a case study of the 2002 General Election, *Irish Geography*, 37(2): 177–86

Kearney, B. and Associates (2000) *Operational Programme for LEADER II Community Initiative: Ex-Post Evaluation, Interim Report*, ww.leaderii.ie

Kearney, B., Boyle, G. E. and Walsh, J. A. (1994) *EU LEADER I Initiative in Ireland: Evaluations and Recommendations*. (Dublin: Department of Agriculture, Food and Forestry)

Keelan, C., Henchion, M. and Newman, C. (2005) Eating out on the Celtic Tiger, paper presented at the 97th EAAE Seminar: 'The Economics of Policy and Health', University of Reading, 21–22 April

Kelly, C. and Ní Laoire, C. (2005) Representing multiple Irish heritage(s): a case study of the Ulster-American Folk Park, *Irish Geography*, 38(1): 72–83

Kelly, C. and Smith, M. (2006) Holistic tourism: journeys of the self?, *Tourism Recreation Research*, 31(1)

Kelly, J. (2003) The Irish Pound: from origins to EMU, *Central Bank Quarterly Bulletin*, Available at www.centralbank.ie/data/site/spring8.pdf

Kelly, S. and MacLaran, A. (2004a) Incentivised gentrification in central Dublin, paper presented at the Conference of Irish Geographers, NUI, Maynooth, May 2004

Kelly, S. and MacLaran, A. (2004b) The residential transformation of inner Dublin, in Drudy, P. J. and MacLaran, A. (eds) *Dublin: Economic and Social Trends, Volume 4*, pp. 36–59 (Trinity College, Dublin: Centre for Urban and Regional Studies)

Keogan, J. F. (2003) Reform in Irish local government, in Callanan, M. and Keogan, J. F. (eds) *Local Government in Ireland: Inside Out*, pp. 82–96 (Dublin: Institute of Public Administration).

Keohane, K. and Kuhling, C. (2005) *Collision Culture: Transformations in Everyday Life in Ireland.* (Dublin: Liffey)

Killen, J. E. (1997) Communications, in, Aalen, F. H. A., Whelan, K. and Stout, M. (eds) *Atlas of the Irish Rural Landscape.* (Cork: Cork University Press)

Killen, J. and Maclaran, A. (2002) Land-use planning and sustainability issues: the case of offices in Dublin, in Convery, F. and Feehan, J. (eds) *Achievement and Challenge: Rio + 10 and Ireland*, pp. 253–63 (University College, Dublin: Environmental Institute)

Kitchin, R. and Mulcahy, F. (1999) *Disability, Access to Education, and Future Opportunities.* (Dublin: Combat Poverty Agency)

Kneafsey, M. (2003) 'If it wasn't for the tourists we wouldn't have an audience': the case of tourism and traditional music in North Mayo, in Cronin, M. and O'Connor, B. (eds) *Irish Tourism – Image, Culture and Identity*, (Clevedon: Channel View)

Kneafsey M. and Cox R. (2002) Food, gender and Irishness: how Irish women in Coventry make home, *Irish Geography*, 35(1): 6–15

Knox, P. L. and Taylor, P. J. (eds) (1995) *World Cities in a World System.* (Cambridge: Cambridge University Press)

KPMG Consultants with Murray O'Laoire Associates and Northern Ireland Economic Research Centre (1996) *Study on the Urban Renewal Schemes.* (Dublin: Government Publications Office)

Krogman, N. (2005) Bringing sociological theory into our understanding of the social context of waste, in *Waste: The Social Context Conference Proceedings, 11–14 May*, CD-Rom, pp. 265–71, Edmonton, Alberta, Canada.

Lafferty, S., Commins, P. and Walsh, J. A. (1999) *Irish Agriculture in Transition – A Census Atlas of Agriculture in the Republic of Ireland.* (Teagasc and NUI, Maynooth)

Larkham, P. J. (1995) Heritage as planned and conserved, in Herbert, D. T. (ed.) *Heritage, Tourism and Society.* (London: Mansell)

Law, C. (1993) *Urban Tourism: Attracting Visitors to Large Cities.* (London: Mansell)

LEADER Atlas of Rural Development (2000) *Ireland/Eire*, www.rural-europe.aeidl.be/rural-en/

Lee, J. J. (1989) *Ireland 1912–1985.* (Cambridge: Cambridge University Press)

Lenihan, B. (1987) *Newsweek*, 13 October

Lentin, R. (2004) From racial state to racist state: Ireland on the eve of the Citizenship Referendum, *Variant*, 2(20): 7–8

Lijphart, A. (1997) Unequal participation: democracy's unresolved dilemma, *American Political Science Review*, 91(1): 1–14.

Lipset, S. M. and Rokan, S. (1967) Party *Systems and Voter Alignments.* (New York: Free Press)

Little, A. (2004). *Democracy and Northern Ireland: Beyond the Liberal Paradigm?* (Basingstoke: Palgrave Macmillan)

Losch, A. (1954) *The Economics of Location.* (New Haven, CT: Yale University Press)

Lowenthal, D. (1998) *The Heritage Crusade and the Spoils of History.* (Cambridge: Cambridge University Press)

Luke, T. (1977) Green Consumerism: ecology and the use of recycling, in Bennett, J. and Chaloupka, W. (eds) *Ecocritique* (Minneapolis, MN: University of Minnesota Press)

Lynch, K. (1960) *The Image of the City*, (Boston, MA: MIT Press)

MacDonald, F. (2000) *The Construction of Dublin.* (Dublin: Gandon)

McDonald, F. (1985) *The Destruction of Dublin.* (Dublin: Gill and Macmillan)

MacLaran, A. (1993) *Dublin: The Shaping of a Capital.* (London: Belhaven/Wiley)

MacLaran, A. (1996a) Office development in Dublin and the tax incentive areas, *Irish Geography*, 29(2): 49–54

MacLaran, A. (1996b) Private sector residential development in central Dublin, in Drudy, P. J. and MacLaran, A. (eds) *Dublin: Economic and Social Trends, Volume 2*, pp. 20–42 (Trinity College, Dublin: Centre for Urban and Regional Studies)

MacLaran, A. (2000) On the edge of nowhere: urban placelessness, *Building Material*, 5: 4–7

MacLaran, A. (ed.) (2003) *Making Space: Property Development and Urban Planning*. (London: Edward Arnold)

MacLaran, A., Emerson, H. and Williams, B. (1995) *Residential Development in Central Dublin: A Survey of Current Occupiers*. (Trinity College, Dublin: Centre for Urban and Regional Studies)

MacLaran, A. and Floyd, D. (1996) *Recent Residential Developments in Central Dublin*. (Trinity College, Dublin: Centre for Urban and Regional Studies)

MacLaran, A. and Killen, J. (2002) The suburbanisation of office development in Dublin and its transport implications, *Journal of Irish Urban Studies*, 1(1): 21–35

MacLaran, A., MacLaran, M. and Malone, P. (1987) Property cycles in Dublin: anatomy of boom and slump in the industrial and office property sectors, *Economic and Social Review*, 18(4): 237–56

MacLaran, A., MacLaran, M. and Williams, B. (1994) *Residential Development as an Engine for Inner-city Renewal in Dublin: Commentary and Statistical Appendix*. (Trinity College, Dublin: Centre for Urban and Regional Studies)

MacLaran, A. and O'Connell, R. (2001) The changing geography of office development in Dublin, in Drudy, P. J. and MacLaran, A. (eds) *Dublin: Economic and Social Trends, Volume 3*, pp. 25–37 (Trinity College, Dublin: Centre for Urban and Regional Studies)

MacLaran, A. and O'Connell, R. (2003) Dublin's fourth office development boom, *Journal of Irish Urban Studies*, 2(2): 85–91

MacLaran, A. and Williams, B. (1996) Incentive areas for urban renewal, in Drudy P. J. and MacLaran, A. (eds) *Dublin: Economic and Social Trends, Volume II*, pp. 43–6 (Trinity College, Dublin: Centre for Urban and Regional Studies)

MacLaran, A. and Williams, B. (2003) Dublin: property development and planning in an entrepreneurial city, in MacLaran, A. (ed.) *Making Space: Property Development and Urban Planning*, pp. 148–71 (London: Edward Arnold)

Mac Póilin, A. (1999) Language, identity and politics in Northern Ireland, *Ulster Folklife*, 45: 106–32

Malone, P. (1985) *Office Development in Dublin 1960–1983: Property, Profit and Space*, unpublished PhD thesis, Department of Geography, Trinity College, Dublin

Marsh, M. (1991) Accident or design? Non-voting in Ireland, *Irish Political Studies*, 6: 1–14

Marsh, M.and Mitchell, P. (eds) (1999) *How Ireland Voted 1997*. (Dublin: PSAI)

Marshall, N. and Wood, P. (1995) *Services and Space: Key Aspects of Urban and Regional Development*. (Harlow: Longman)

Matthew, R. (1963) *Belfast Regional Survey and Plan: Recommendations and Conclusions*. (Belfast: HMSO)

Matthews, A. (2002) Has agricultural policy responded to the Rio Challenge?, in Convery, F. and Feehan, J. (eds) *Achievement and Challenge: Rio+10 and Ireland*, pp. 73–82 (University College, Dublin: Environmental Institute)

Matthews, A, (2005) Agriculture, rural development and food safety, in O'Hagan, J. W. and Newman, C. (eds) *The Economy of Ireland: National and Sectoral Policy Issues*, pp. 215–43 (Dublin: Gill and Macmillan)

Maynard, A. and Ludbrook, A. (1988) *The Funding of the National Health Service: What is the Problem and Is Social Insurance the Answer?* Discussion Paper 39. (York: Centre for Health Economics, University of York)

McAleese, D. (1977) *A Profile of Grant-Aided Industry in Ireland*. (Dublin: Industrial Development Authority)

McAleese, M. (2004) I will nurture and celebrate commitment to responsible citizenship, *Irish Times*, 12 November

McCafferty, D. (2002) Balanced regional development, polycentrism and the urban system in the West of Ireland, in McDonagh, J. (ed.) *Economy, Society and Peripherality – Experiences from the West of Ireland*, pp. 37–54 (Galway: Arlen House)

McCarthy, M. (2005) *Ireland's Heritages: Critical Perspectives on Memory and Identity.* (Aldershot: Ashgate)

McDonagh, J. (2001) *Renegotiating Rural Development in Ireland.* (Aldershot: Ashgate)

McGinnity, F. et al. (2005) *Time Use in Ireland 2005: Survey Report.* (Dublin: ESRI)

McGuirk, P. M. (1994) Economic restructuring and the realignment of the urban planning system: the case of Dublin, *Urban Studies*, 31(2): 287–308

McGuirk, P. M. (2000). Power and policy networks in urban governance: local government and property-led regeneration in Dublin, *Urban Studies*, 37(4): 651–72

McGuirk, P. M. and MacLaran, A. (2001) Changing approaches to urban planning in an 'entrepreneurial city': the case of Dublin, *European Planning Studies*, 9(4): 437–57

McHugh, C. (2001) *A Spatial Analysis of Socio-economic Adjustments in Rural Ireland 1986–1996*, unpublished PhD thesis, Department of Geography, NUI, Maynooth

McHugh, C. and Walsh, J. (2001) *Rural Area Typology.* (Dublin: Department of Environment and Local Government)

McInerney, C. (1995) Poverty in Rural Ireland, *Irish Reporter*, 17: 26–7

McKeogh, S. (2004) *Rural Housing and Sustainable Community Development in the West of Ireland*, unpublished MA thesis, Galway-Mayo Institute of Technology

McKeown, T. (1976) *The Modern Rise of Population.* (London: Edward Arnold)

McKeown, T. (1979) *The Role Of Medicine: Dream, Mirage Or Nemesis?* (Oxford: Blackwell)

McKeown, T. (1988) *The Origins Of Human Disease.* (Oxford: Blackwell)

McKittrick, D., Kelters, S., Feeney, B. and Thornton, C. (1999) *Lost Lives.* (Edinburgh: Mainstream)

McManus, R. (2005) Identity crisis? Heritage construction, tourism and place marketing in Ireland, in McCarthy, M. (ed.) *Ireland's Heritages: Critical Perspectives on Memory and Identity.* (Aldershot: Ashgate)

McWilliams, D. (2005) Pubs suffer in a DIY blitz, *Sunday Business Post*, 31 January

Meade, M. and Earickson, R. (2000) *Medical Geography*, 2nd ed. (New York: Guilford)

Meldon, J., Kenny, M, and Walsh, J. (2004) 'Local government, local development and citizen participation: lessons from Ireland', in Lovan, W. R., Murray, M. and Shaffer, R. *Participatory Governance: Planning, Mediation and Public Decision-Making in Civil Society*, pp. 39–59 (Aldershot: Ashgate)

Migration Policy Institute (2006) *United States: Inflow of Foreign-born Population by Country of Birth, 1986 to 2004.* (Washington, DC: Migration Policy Institute)

Miles, S. and Paddison, R. (1998) Urban consumption: an historiographical note, *Urban Studies*, 35(5–6): 815–24

Miller, D. (2001) The poverty of morality, *Journal of Consumer Culture*, 1(2): 255–43

Morgan, K and Nauwelaers, C. (1999) *Regional Innovation Strategies – The Challenges for Less Favoured Regions.* (London: The Stationery Office)

Morrow, D., Eyben, K, and Wilson, D. (2003) From the margin to the middle: taking equity, diversity and interdependence seriously, in Hargie, O. and Dickson, D. (eds) *Researching the Troubles: Social Science Perspectives on the Northern Ireland Conflict*, pp. 163–81 (Edinburgh: Mainstream)

Moulaert, F. (2000) *Globalization and Integrated Area Development in European Cities*, (New York: Oxford University Press)

Moynes, K. (2001) *The Evolution of Public Transport Provision in Rural Areas of the Republic of Ireland*, unpublished MSc thesis, Department of Geography, Trinity College, Dublin

Murdoch, J. and Pratt, A. (1993) Rural studies: modernism, postmodernism and the 'post-rural', *Journal of Rural Studies*, 9(4): 411–28

Murphy, L. (1998) Financial engine or glorified back office? Dublin's International Financial Services Centre going global, *Area*, 30(2)

Murray, M. (1991) *The Politics and Pragmatism of Urban Containment: Belfast Since 1940.* (Aldershot: Avebury)

Murray, M. (2003). *Waste Management in Ireland: A Case Study on the Impact of Transnationalisation on Governance*, unpublished PhD thesis, Department of Sociology, NUI, Maynooth

Murray, M. (2004) Strategic spatial planning on the island of Ireland, *Innovation: the European Journal of Social Science Research*, 17(3): 727–42

Murray, M. and Greer, J. (2002) Participatory planning as dialogue: the Northern Ireland Regional Strategic Framework and its Public Examination process, *Policy Studies*, 23(4): 283–94

Murray, M. and Murtagh, B. (2004) *Equity, Diversity and Interdependence: Reconnecting People Through Authentic Dialogue.* (Aldershot: Ashgate)

Murray, R. (1999) *Creating Wealth from Waste.* (London: Demos)

Murray, R. (2004) *Zero Waste.* (London: Greenpeace)

Murtagh, B. (2001) Partnerships and policy in Northern Ireland, *Local Economy*, 16: 50–62

Murtagh, B. (2004) Collaboration, equality and land use planning, *Planning Theory and Practice*, 5(4): 453–69

Nader, G. A. (1984) The rank-size model: a non-logarithmic calibration, *Professional Geographer*, 36(2): 221–7

Nagle, J. (2005) '*Everybody Irish on St. Paddy's'? Ambivalence and Conflict on St. Patrick's Day. A Research Report into People's Attitudes on St. Patrick's Day 2004*, www.qub.ac.uk/iis/projects/stpatricks/Nagle-report.pdf

National Cancer Registry (2001) *Cancer In Ireland, 1994–1998: Incidence, Mortality, Treatment And Survival.* (Cork: National Cancer Registry)

National Economic and Social Council (NESC) (1975) *Regional Policy in Ireland: A Review*, Report No. 4. (Dublin: NESC)

National Economic and Social Council (1982) *A Review of Industrial Policy*, Report No. 64. (Dublin: NESC)

National Economic and Social Council (1985) *Designation of Areas for Industrial Policy*, Report No. 81. (Dublin: NESC)

National Economic and Social Council (1986) *A Strategy for Development 1986–1990: Growth, Employment and Fiscal Balance*, Report No. 83. (Dublin: NESC)

National Economic and Social Council (1990) *A Strategy for the Nineties: Economic Stability and Structural Change*, Report No. 89. (Dublin: NESC)

National Economic and Social Council (1991) *The Economic and Social Implications of Emigration.* (Dublin: Stationery Office)

National Economic and Social Council (1993) *A Strategy for Competitiveness, Growth and Employment.* (Dublin: NESC)

National Economic and Social Council (1996) *Strategy into the 21st Century*, Report No. 99. (Dublin: NESC)

National Economic and Social Council (1997) *Population Distribution and Economic Development: Trends and Policy Implications.* (Dublin: NESC)

National Economic and Social Council (1999) *Opportunities, Challenges and Capacities for Change*, Report No. 105. (Dublin: NESC)

National Economic and Social Council (2002) *An Investment in Quality, Services, Inclusion and Enterprise.* (Dublin: NESC)

National Economic and Social Council (2004) *Housing in Ireland: Performance and Policy Report No. 112.* (Dublin: NESC)

National Economic and Social Council (2005) *People, Productivity and Purpose*, Report No. 114. (Dublin: NESC)

National Economic and Social Forum (1997) *A Framework for Partnership, Enriching Strategic Consensus through Participation*, Report No. 16. (Dublin: National Economic and Social Forum)

National Economic and Social Forum (2005) *Creating a More Inclusive Labour Market.* (Dublin: National Economic and Social Forum)

National Roads Authority (NRA) (1998) *National Road Needs Study, 1998.* (Dublin: NRA)

National Roads Authority (2003a) *National Route Lengths as of 31/12/2003.* (Dublin: NRA)

National Roads Authority (2003b) *Future Traffic Forecasts 2002–2040.* (Dublin: NRA)

National Task Force on Medical Staffing (2003). *Report of the National Task Force on Medical Staffing (Hanly Report)*. (Dublin: The Stationery Office)

NCB Stockbrokers (2006) 2020 *Vision: Ireland's Demographic Dividend*. (Dublin: NCB)

Neill, W. (2004) *Urban Policy and Cultural Identity*. (London, Routledge)

Neill, W. and Gordon, M. (2001) Shaping our future? The Regional Strategic Framework for Northern Ireland, *Planning Theory and Practice*, 2(1): 31–52

Netherlands Interdisciplinary Demographic Institute (2005) *First EU Demographic Estimates for 2004*. (The Hague: Netherlands Interdisciplinary Demographic Institute)

New Zealand Department of Labour/Te Teri Mahi (2005) *Migration Trends 2004/2005*. (Wellington: New Zealand Department of Labour)

Nic Giolla Choille, T. (1989) Emigration is no accident, in Mulholland, J. and Keogh, D. (eds) *Emigration, Employment and Enterprise*. (Cork: Hibernian University Press)

Noble, B. et al. (2000) *Measuring Multiple Deprivation at the Local Level: The Indices of Deprivation 2000*. (London: Department of the Environment, Transport and the Regions)

Noble B. et al. (2001) *Measures of Deprivation in Northern Ireland*. (Belfast: Northern Ireland Statistics and Research Agency)

Nolan, B. (1990) Socio-economic mortality differentials in Ireland, *Economic and Social Review*, 21(2): 193–208

Nolan, B. (1998) The changing face of Ireland's poor, in Kirby, P. and Jacobsen, D. (eds) *In the Shadow of the Tiger: New Approaches to Combating Social Exclusion*, pp. 12–17 (Dublin: DCU)

Nolan, B., O'Connell P. J. and Whelan, C. T. (eds) (2000) *Bust to Boom? The Irish Experience of Growth and Inequality*. (Dublin: Economic and Social Research Institute)

Nolan, B., and Whelan, C. T. (1999) *Loading the Dice – A Study of Cumulative Disadvantage*. (Dublin: Combat Poverty Agency)

Nolan, B., Whelan, C. T. and Williams, J. (1998) *Where Are Poor Households? The Spatial Distribution of Poverty and Deprivation in Ireland*. (Dublin: Oak Tree Press in association with Combat Poverty Agency)

Northern Ireland Statistics and Research Agency (2005) *Statistical Classification and Delineation of Settlements: Report of the Inter-Departmental Rural-Urban Definition Group*. (Belfast: National Statistics)

Oatley, N. (1998) Cities, economic competition and urban policy, in Oatley, N. (ed.) *Cities, Economic Competition and Urban Policy*, pp. 3–21 (London: Paul Chapman)

O'Brien, M. (1999) Rubbish values: reflections on the political economy of waste, *Science as Culture*, 8(3)

O'Brien, C. (2005) Residency for nearly 17,000 under new parent law, *Irish Times*, 27 December

O'Brien, C. (2006) Former EU accession state workers exceed 200,000, *Irish Times*, 11 May

O'Connor, B. (2003) Come and daunce with me in Irelande: tourism, dance and globalisation, in Cronin, M. and O'Connor, B. (eds) *Irish Tourism – Image, Culture and Identity*, pp. 122–41 (Clevedon: Channel View)

O'Donnell, R. (1998) Social partnership in Ireland: principles and interactions, in O'Donnell, R. and Larragy, J. (eds) *Negotiated Social and Economic Governance and European Integration: Proceedings of the COST A7 Workshop*, pp. 84–107 (Luxembourg Office of Official Publications of the European Communities)

O'Donnell, R. (2001) *The Future of Social Partnership in Ireland*. (Dublin: National Competitiveness Council)

O'Donnell, R. and Riordan, C. (2000) Social partnership and Ireland's economic transformation, in Fajertag, G. and Pochet, P. (eds) *Social Pacts in Europe*, (Brussels: ETUI)

O'Donnell, R. and Thomas, D. (1998) Partnership and policy-making, in Healy, S. and Reynolds, B. (eds) *Social Policy in Ireland Principles, Practice and Problems*, (Dublin: Combat Poverty Agency)

O'Donovan, G. (2000) Natural heritage, in Buttimer, N., Rynne, C. and Guerin, H. (eds) *The Heritage of Ireland*. (Cork: Collins)

O'Dowd, L. (2005) Craigavon: locality, economy and the state in a failed 'new city', in McEldowney, M., Murray, M., Murtagh, B. and Sterrett, K. (eds) *Planning in Ireland and Beyond: Multidisciplinary Essays in Honour of John V. Greer*, pp. 23–48 (Belfast: Queen's University)

O'Driscoll, S. (2006) Up to 2 million watch NY parade. *Irish Times*, 18 March www.ireland.com/newspaper/ireland/2006/0318/3842728638HM8NEWYORK.html

OECD (1999a) *Economic Surveys 1999: Ireland.* (Paris: OECD)

OECD (1999b) *International Direct Investment Statistics Yearbook 1999*, (Paris: OECD)

OECD (2001a) *OECD in Figures: Statistics on the Member Countries.* (Paris: OECD)

OECD (2001b) *Economic Surveys: Ireland 2000–2001.* (Paris: OECD).

OECD (2005) *Economic Outlook No. 78: Ireland*, (Paris: OECD)

OECD (2005) *OECD Economic Outlook No. 77, May 2005.* (Paris: OECD)

Office of the Refugee Appeals Commission (2006), www.orac.ie/pages/Stats/satistics.htm

O'Gorman, C., O'Malley, E. and Mooney, J. G. (1997) *Clusters in Ireland: The Irish Indigenous Software Industry: An Application of Porter's Cluster Analysis*, NESC Research Series, No. 3. (Dublin: National Economic and Social Council)

O'Grada, D. (2004) The real cost of servicing one off houses in the countryside, in *Conference Proceedings, Irish Planning Institute Annual Conference*, Mullingar, 22–23 April

O'Leary, E. (2001) Convergence of living standards among Irish Regions: the roles of productivity, profit outflows and demography, 1960–1996, *Regional Studies*, 35(3): 197–206

O'Leary, J. (2002) Pact should not be allowed to become an end in itself, *Irish Times*, 12 December

O'Kane, P. (2005) IDA changes tack to super sites, *Sunday Tribune*, 20 November

O'Malley, E. (1989) *Industry and Economic Development: The Challenge for the Latecomer.* (Dublin: Gill and Macmillan)

O'Malley, E. (1998) The revival of Irish indigenous industry 1987–1997, *Quarterly Economic Commentary*, Spring: 35–60 (Dublin: Economic and Social Research Institute)

O'Malley, E. and Egeraat, C. van (2000) Industry clusters and Irish indigenous manufacturing: limits of the Porter view, *Economic and Social Review*, 31(1)

O'Reilly, E. (2004) What has happened to us?, *Irish Times*, 6 November

O'Rourke, K. and Thom, R. (2000) *Irish Inflation: Appropriate Policy Responses*, www.tcd.ie/Economics/staff/orourkek/ibrwinter00.pdf

Osborne, D. and Gaebler, T. (1992) *Reinventing Government: How the Entrepreneurial Spirit is Transforming the Public Sector.* (Reading, MA: Addison-Wesley)

Osborne, R. and Shuttleworth, I. (eds) (2004) *Fair Employment in Northern Ireland a Generation On.* (Belfast: Blackstaff)

Osbourne, M. (2001) *The Pilot Resort Relief Scheme: A Case Study of Counties Mayo and Wexford*, NIRSA Internship Report. (Castlebar: Galway-Mayo Innstitute of Technology)

O'Shea, E. (1997) Male mortality differentials by socio-economic group in Ireland, *Social Science and Medicine*, 45(6): 803–9

O'Shea, E. (2003) Social gradients in years of potential life lost in Ireland, *European Journal of Public Health*, 13: 327–33

O'Shea, E. and Kelleher, C. (2001) Health inequalities in Ireland, in Cantillon, S., Corrican, C., Kirby, P. and O'Flynn, J. (eds) *Rich And Poor.* (Dublin: Oak Tree Press)

O'Sullivan, T. (2003) Local areas and structures, in Callanan, M. and Keogan, J. F. (eds) *Local Government in Ireland: Inside Out*, pp. 41–81 (Dublin: Institute of Public Administration)

O'Toole, P. (2004) Challenges tourism industry faces must be tackled, *Irish Times*, 6 September

Parker, A. (1997) The rise of the 'Celtic Tiger': retailing developments in Ireland in the mid-1990s, in Leunis, J. (ed), *Proceedings of the 9th International Conference on Research in the Distributive Trades*, pp. B7.11–7.20 (Louvain: Catholic University)

Parker, A. (1999) Retail trends and the suburbanisation of Dublin's retailing: into the twenty-first century, in Killen, J. and MacLaran, A. (eds), *Dublin: Contemporary Trends and Issues for the Twenty-First Century*, (Dublin: Geographical Society of Ireland)

Parker, A. (2002) Shopping centres and retail park development in the Republic of Ireland, *European Retail Digest*, 35: 31–4

Parker, A. J. (1982) The 'friends and neighbours' effect in the Galway West constituency, *Political Geography Quarterly*, 1(3): 243–62

Parkinson, M. (1998) *Combating Social Exclusion: Lessons from Area-based Programmes in Europe.* (London: Policy Press)

Parkinson, M., Hutchins, M., Simmie, J., Clark, G. and Verdonk, H. (2004) *Competitive European Cities: Where Do the Core Cities Stand?* (London: Office of the Deputy Prime Minister)

Peet, R. (1998) *Modern Geographical Thought.* (Oxford: Blackwell)

Peillon, M. (2004) The making of the Dublin conurbation, in Peillon, M. and Corcoran, M. P. (eds) *Place and Non-place: The Reconfiguration of Ireland.* (Dublin: Institute of Public Administration)

Poole, M. (1991) Recent urban changes in the Northern Ireland settlement system, in Bannon, M. J., Bourne, L. S. and Sinclair, R. (eds) *Urbanization and Urban Development: Recent Trends in a Global Context.* (Dublin: Service Industries Research Centre, UCD)

Porter, M. (1990) *The Competitive Advantage of Nations.* (London: Macmillan)

Porter, N. (1998) *Rethinking Unionism: An Alternative Vision for Northern Ireland.* (Belfast: Blackstaff)

Powell, G. B. (1986) American voter turnout in comparative perspective, *American Political Science Review*, 80(1): 17–43

Power, A. (2005) *Landscapes of Care: A Geographical Study of Informal Care and Care Support in Ireland Using International Comparisons*, unpublished PhD thesis, Department of Geography, NUI, Maynooth

Pringle, D. (1980) The Irish urban system: an overview, *Geographical Viewpoint*, 9: 29–48

Pringle, D. G. (1982) Regional disparities in the quantity of life: the Republic of Ireland, 1971–1977, *Irish Geography*, 15: 22–34

Pringle, D. G. (1986a) Disaggregating regional variations in mortality by cause of death: a case study of the Republic of Ireland, *Social Science and Medicine*, 23(10): 919–28

Pringle, D. G. (1986b) Premature mortality in the Republic of Ireland, 1971–1981. *Irish Geography*, 19(1): 33–40

Pringle, D. G. (1987) Health inequalities in Dublin, in Horner, A. A. and Parker, A. J. (eds) *Geographical Perspectives On The Dublin Region.* (Dublin: Geographical Society of Ireland)

Pringle, D. G. (1998) Hypothesized foetal and early life influences on adult heart disease mortality: an ecological analysis of data for the Republic Of Ireland, *Social Science and Medicine*, 46(6): 683–93

Pringle, D. G., Walsh, J. and Hennessy, M. (eds) (1999) *Poor People – Poor Places: The Geography of Poverty in Ireland*, (Dublin: Combat Poverty Agency and Oak Tree Press)

Punch, M., Redmond, D. and Kelly, S. (2004) Uneven development, city governance and urban change: unpacking the global–local nexus in Dublin's inner city, paper presented at City Futures: An International Conference on Globalism and Urban Change, Chicago, 8–10 July

Putnam, R. D. (2000) *Bowling Alone: The Collapse and Revival of American Community.* (New York: Simon and Schuster)

Putnam, R. D., Leonardi, R. and Nanetti, R. Y. (1993) *Making Democracies Work: Civic Traditions In Northern Italy.* (Princeton, NJ: Princeton University Press)

Quinn, B. (2003) Shaping tourism places: agency and interconnection in festival settings, in Cronin, M. and O'Connor, B. (eds) *Irish Tourism – Image, Culture and Identity*, pp. 61–83 (Clevedon: Channel View)

Rallings, C. and Thrasher, M. (1990) Turnout in English local elections – an aggregate analysis with electoral and contextual data, *Electoral Studies*, 9(2): 79–90

Reed Z. et al. (2003) Factors affecting consumer acceptance of chilled ready meals on the island of Ireland, *International Journal of Consumer Studies*, 27(1): 35–45

Reeves, D. (2005) *Planning for Diversity: Policy and Planning in a World of Difference.* (London, Routledge)

Reid, L. (2006) SUVs blamed for increasing greenhouse gas emissions, *Irish Times*, 3 April, www.ireland.com/newspaper/front/2006/0403/252030362HM1SUVS.html

Richardson, R. and Marshall, J. (1996) The growth of telephone call centres in peripheral areas of Britain: evidence from Tyne and Wear, *Area*, 28(3)

Robinson, D. (2005) The search for community cohesion: key themes and dominant concepts of the public policy agenda, *Urban Studies*, 42(8): 1411–27

Robson, B., Bradford, M. and Deas, I. (1994) *Relative Deprivation in Northern Ireland*. (Manchester: Centre for Urban Policy Studies, Manchester University)

Rosenstone, S. J. (1982) Economic adversity and voter turnout, *American Journal of Political Science*, 26(1): 25–46

RTE (2005) *Rip-Off-Republic*, Four-part television series broadcast August 2005

Ruane, J. and Todd, J. (1996) *The Dynamics of Conflict in Northern Ireland*. (Cambridge: Cambridge University Press)

Rural Ireland 2025 Foresight Perspectives Working Group (2005) *Report on Rural Ireland 2025*. (NUI, Maynooth, UCD and Teagasc)

Russell, H., Halpin, B., Strandh, M. and Zielfe, A. (2006) Comparing the labour market effects of childbirth in Ireland, Sweden, the UK and Germany, *Working Papers*, No. 170 (Dublin, ESRI)

Ryan, L. (1998) Negotiating modernity and tradition: newspaper on the 'modern girl' in the Irish Free State, *Journal of Gender Studies*, 7(2): 181–98

Ryan, M. (2003) Patterns and determinants of Irish consumption, *Central Bank and Financial Services of Ireland Quarterly Bulletin*, Summer: 66–8

Sabel, C. (1996) *Ireland: Local Partnerships and Social Innovation*. (Paris: OECD)

Sassen, S. (1991) *The Global City: New York, London, Tokyo*. (Princeton, NJ: Princeton University Press)

Sassen, S. (1994) *Cities in a World Economy*. (Thousand Oaks, CA: Pine Forge)

Sawicki, R. (2005) Billionaire Tesco exploits foreign workers, *Worker Solidarity*, 8 September: 3

Shirlow, P. (2000) Fundamentalist Loyalism: discourse, resistance and identity politics, in Gold, J. R. and Revill, G. (eds), *Landscapes of Defence*, pp. 85–101 (Harlow: Prentice-Hall)

Shirlow, P. and Murtagh, B. (2006) *Belfast: Segregation, Violence and the City*. (London: Pluto)

Simpson, G. R. (2005) Irish unit lets Microsoft cut taxes in U.S., *Wall Street Journal*, 17 November, www.post-gazette.com/pg/05311/602213.stm

Sinnott, R. (1995) *Irish Voters Decide: Voting Behaviour in Elections and Referendums since 1918*. (Manchester and New York: Manchester University Press)

Slattery, L. (2005) Dublin no longer a first port of call for companies, *Irish Times*, 14 January

Smith, E. (1999) *Do Schools Differ? Academic and Personal Development among Pupils in the Second Level Sector*. (Dublin: ESRI)

Soja, E. W. (1996) *Thirdspace: Journeys to Los Angeles and Other Real-and-Imagined Places*. (Malden, MA: Blackwell)

Soja, E. W. (2000), *Postmetropolis: Critical Studies of Cities and Regions*. (Oxford: Blackwell)

Song, S. and Zhang, K. H. (2002) Urbanisation and city size distribution in China, *Urban Studies*, 39(12): 2317–27

Spaargaren, G., Moll, G. and F. Buttel (eds) (2000) *Consuming Cultures: Power and Resistance*. (London: Macmillan)

Spiller, K. (2003) *A Historical Geography of the Irish Department Store: Modernity, Consumption and Fashion*, unpublished MPhil thesis, University College, Cork

Statistics Sweden (2004) No Immigration rush from new EU member states, press release, 6 December (Stockholm: Statistics Sweden)

Stoker, G. (1998) Governance as theory: five propositions, *Journal of International Social Science*, 155(1): 17–28

Subramanian, S. V. and Kawachi, I. (2004) Income inequality and health: what have we learned so far? *Epidemiologic Reviews*, 26: 78–91

Sweeney, P. (1999) *The Celtic Tiger: Explaining Ireland's Economic Miracle*, 2nd edition, (Dublin: Oak Tree Press)

Tansey Webster Stewart and Company (2002) *The Impact of Tourism on the Irish Economy*. (Dublin: Irish Tourism Industry Confederation)

Taylor, P. J. (2004) *World City Network: A Global Urban Analysis*. (London: Routledge)

Telesis Consultancy Group (1982) *A Review of Industrial Policy*, Report No. 64 (Dublin: National Economic and Social Council)

Teljeur, C., Barry, J. and Kelly, A. (2004) The potential impact on travel times of closure and redistribution of A&E units in Ireland, *Irish Medical Journal*, 97(6): 173–5

Tewdwr-Jones, M. and Allmendinger, P. (1998) Deconstructing communicative rationality: a critique of Habermasian collaborative planning, *Environment and Planning A*, 30(4): 1975–89

The Economist (2004) The luck of the Irish, 14 October, www.economist.com/printedition/displayStory.cfm?Story_id=3261071

The Economist (2005) *The World in 2005*. (London: *The Economist*)

Thorngren, B. (1970) How do contact systems affect regional development? *Environment and Planning*, 2: 409–27

Tobin, P. (1990) *Ways Ahead: A Case Study of Community Development in an Inner City Area of Dublin*. (Dublin: Barnardo's)

Tonge, J. (2005) *The New Northern Irish Politics?* (Basingstoke: Palgrave Macmillan)

Törnqvist, G. (1970) *Contact Systems and Regional Development*, Lund Studies in Geography, No. 35, Lund University

Touraine, A. (1971) *The Post-Industrial Society*. (New York: Random House)

Tourism Policy Review Group (2003) *New Horizons for Irish Tourism: An Agenda for Action*. (Dublin: The Stationery Office)

Tovey, H. (1992) Rural sociology in Ireland: a review, *Irish Journal of Sociology*, 2: 96–121

Townsend, P. (1979) *Poverty in the United Kingdom*. (Harmondsworth: Penguin)

Townsend, P. (1993) *The International Analysis of Poverty*. (London: Harvester Wheatsheaf)

Townsend, P. and Davidson, N. (1982) *Inequalities In Health: The Black Report*. (Harmondsworth: Penguin)

UNESCO (2005) *Defining Heritage*, http://portal.unesco.org/culture/

United Nations (1998) *Human Development Report*. (New York: UN)

Urry, J. (1999) *Global Citizenship and the Environment*, an ESRC-funded research project, Department of Sociology, Lancaster University, www.comp.lancs.ac.uk/sociology/jures.html

Urry, J (2000) *Time, Complexity and the Global*, Department of Sociology, Lancaster University, www.comp.lancs.ac.uk/sociology/soc057ju.html

Vignali, C. (2001) Tesco's adaptation to the Irish market, *British Food Journal*, 103(2): 146–63

Walker, B. (1996) *Dancing to History's Tune: History, Myth and Politics in Ireland*. (Belfast: Institute of Irish Studies)

Walsh, J. (1998) Local development, theory and practice: recent experience in Ireland, in Alden, J. and Bolan, P. (eds) *Regional Development Strategies*, pp. 159–77 (London: RKP)

Walsh, J. (1998) Local development and local government in Ireland: from fragmentation to integration?, *Local Economy*, February: 329–41

Walsh, J. (1999) The role of area-based policies in tackling poverty in Ireland, in Pringle, D. G., Walsh, J. and Hennessy, M. (eds) *Poor People, Poor Places: A Geography of Poverty and Deprivation in Ireland*, pp. 225–9 (Dublin: Oak Tree Press)

Walsh, J. (2005) Geographical perspectives on outputs from the 2002 census, paper presented at the Mapping Census 2002 Conference, 27 January (Maynooth: National Institute for Regional and Spatial Analysis)

Walsh, J. A. (1985) Uneven development of agriculture in Ireland, *Geographical Viewpoint*, 14: 36–65

Walsh, J. A. (1986) Agricultural change and development, in Breathnach, P. and Cawley, M. (eds) *Change and Development in Rural Ireland*, Geographical Society of Ireland, Special Publications, 1: 11–24

Walsh, J. A. (1989) Enterprise substitution in Irish agriculture: sheep in the 1990s, *Irish Geography*, 22(2): 106–9

Walsh, J. A. (1991) The turn-around of the turn-around in the population of the Republic of Ireland, *Irish Geography*, 24(2): 116–24

Walsh, J. A. (1992) Economic restructuring and labour migration in the European Union: the case of the Republic of Ireland, in O'Cinneide, M. and Grimes, S. (eds) *Planning and Development of Marginal Areas*, pp. 23–36 (Galway: Centre for Development Studies)

Walsh, J. A. (1993) Modernisation and marginalisation under the Common Agricultural Policy: Irish agriculture in transition, in Flognfeldt, T. et al. (eds) *Conditions for Development in Marginal Regions*, pp. 185–93 (Lillehammer: Oppland College)

Walsh, J. A. (2000) Dynamic regional development in the EU periphery: Ireland in the 1990s, in Shaw, D., Roberts, P. and Walsh, J. (eds) *Regional Planning and Development in Europe*, pp. 117–37 (Aldershot: Ashgate)

Walsh, J. A. (2004) Planning for regional development in a peripheral open economy: the case of Ireland, in Byron, R., Hansen, J. C. and Jenkins, T. (eds) *Regional Development on the North Atlantic Margin*, pp. 125–50 (Aldershot: Ashgate)

Walsh, J. A. (2004) Spatial planning for territorial cohesion: linking the urban and rural domains, in O'Cinneide, M. (ed.) *Territorial Cohesion: Meeting New Challenges for an Enlarged EU*, pp. 83–98 (Dublin: Department of Community, Rural and Gaeltacht Affairs)

Walsh, J. A. (2005a) Spatial planning frameworks for Ireland: critical reflections on the Dublin-Belfast corridor, in McEldowney, M., Murray, M., Murtagh, B. and Sterrett, K. (eds) *Planning in Ireland and Beyond*, pp. 125–38 (Belfast: Queen's University)

Walsh, J. A. (2005b) *Regional Population Projections: Policy Implications.* (NIRSA, NUI, Maynooth)

Walsh, J. A., Foley, R., Kavanagh, A., and McElwain, A. (2005) Origins, destinations and catchments: mapping travel to work in Ireland in 2002, paper presented to Statistical and Social Inquiry Society of Ireland, October, www.ssisi.ie/papers/2005/travel_to_work

Walsh, J. A., and Gillmor, D. (1993) Rural Ireland and the Common Agricultural Policy, in King, R. (ed.) *Ireland, Europe and the Single Market*, pp. 84–100 (Dublin: Geographical Society of Ireland)

Walsh, P. M., Comber, H. and Gavin, A. T. (2001) *All Ireland Cancer Statistics 1994–1996: A Joint Report On Incidence And Mortality For The Island Of Ireland.* (Cork and Belfast :National Cancer Registry and Northern Ireland Cancer Registry)

Waters, J. (2005) Postponing our lives for money, *Irish Times*, 12 September

Watson, D., Whelan, C. T., Williams, J. and Blackwell, S. (2005) *Mapping Poverty: National, Regional and County Patterns.* (Dublin: Combat Poverty Agency)

Weizsaker, E., Lovins, A. and Lovins, L. (1998) *Factor Four, Doubling Resources, Halving Resource Use.* (London: Earthscan)

White, P. (2000a) The IDA philosophy through the decades, in MacSharry, R. and White, P. (eds), *The Making of the Celtic Tiger.* (Cork: Mercier)

White, P. (2000b) The muscles of the Celtic Tiger: IDA's winning sectors, in MacSharry, R. and White, P. (eds), *The Making of the Celtic Tiger.* (Cork: Mercier)

Whyte, J. H. (1974) Ireland: politics without social bases, in Rose, R. (ed.) *Electoral Behaviour: A Comparative Handbook*, pp. 619–51 (New York: Free Press)

Whyte, J. (2005) *Great Expectations. A Landmark and Unique Social Regeneration Plan for Fatima Mansions.* (Dublin: Fatima Regeneration Board)

Wilkinson, R. G. (1996) *Unhealthy Societies: The Afflictions Of Inequality.* (London: Routledge)

Williams, B. and Shiels, P. (2000) Acceleration into sprawl: causes and potential policy responses, *Quarterly Economic Commentary*, June: 37–67 (Dublin: Economic and Social Research Institute)

Williams, J. D. (1992) *Monitoring School Performance – A Guide to Educators.* (Bristol: Falmer)

Wilson, M. (1995) The office farther back: business services, productivity and the offshore back office, in Harker, P. T. (ed.) *The Service Productivity and Quality Challenge.* (Dordrecht: Kluwer)

Wolfinger, R. E. and Rosenstone, S. J. (1980) *Who Votes?* (New Haven, CT: Yale University Press)

World Tourism Organisation, (2005), www.world-tourism.org

Wren, M. A. (2003) *Unhealthy State: Anatomy Of A Sick Society.* (Dublin: New Island)

Zukin S. (1998) Urban lifestyles: diversity and standardisation in spaces of consumption, *Urban Studies*, 35(5–6): 832–9

About the Contributors

Brendan Bartley is an urban geographer at the National University of Ireland, Maynooth and an Associate of the National Institute for Regional and Spatial Analysis (NIRSA) at Maynooth. He is the NIRSA project director of the International Centre for Local and Regional Development (ICLRD). His research interests focus on spatial planning, governance, regeneration and social integration.

Proinnsias Breathnach is Senior Lecturer in Geography and an Associate of the National Institute for Regional and Spatial Analysis (NIRSA) at the National University of Ireland, Maynooth. He has published extensively on the topics of transnational investment in Ireland, and Irish regional and national economic development.

Mary P. Corcoran is Senior Lecturer in Sociology and an Associate of the National Institute for Regional and Spatial Analysis (NIRSA) at the National University of Ireland, Maynooth. She has participated in a number of national and international projects focusing on urban transformation and change and has published extensively in this field.

Patrick J. Duffy is Associate Professor of Geography at the National University of Ireland, Maynooth and lectures in historical and cultural geography.

Brian Graham is Professor of Human Geography at the University of Ulster. He has authored or edited eleven books to date and has published extensively on numerous aspects of the historical and cultural geography of Ireland and Europe. His most recent research is concerned with the cultural geographies of the Irish borderlands and alternative spatialities in Northern Ireland.

G. Honor Fagan is Senior Lecturer in Sociology at the National University of Ireland, Maynooth and an Associate of the National Institute for Regional and Spatial Analysis (NIRSA) at Maynooth. She has researched women in South African townships, civil society and conflict resolution in Colombia, governance and waste policy, and is currently researching the potential for ICTs to deepen democratic political structures in Ireland.

Trutz Haase has been an independent social and economic consultant since 1995. Previously, he worked for the Northern Ireland Economic Research Centre (Belfast), the Combat Poverty Agency (Dublin) and the Educational Research Centre at St Patrick's College (Dublin). He is best known for his work on the development of an Irish Index of Relative Affluence and Deprivation.

Frank Houghton lectures at the Limerick Institute of Technology and is an Associate of the National Institute for Regional and Spatial Analysis (NIRSA) at NUI Maynooth. He previously worked in public health in both Ireland and New Zealand. His research interests focus on inequalities in health, healthcare provision and access to health services.

Adrian Kavanagh is Lecturer in the Department of Geography at the National University of Ireland, Maynooth, and an Associate of the National Institute for Regional and Spatial Analysis (NIRSA) and the National Centre for Geocomputation (NCG). His main research focus is on the geography of elections in Ireland.

Karen Keaveney is Lecturer in the School of Planning, Architecture and Civil Engineering at Queen's University, Belfast and an Associate of the National Institute of Regional and Spatial Analysis (NIRSA). Her research interests focus on the spatial analysis of rural housing change and contemporary socio-economic drivers in rural Ireland.

Catherine Kelly is Senior Lecturer in Heritage and Cultural Tourism Management at the University of Greenwich, London, where she is also Director of the Cultural Industries suite of MA programmes.

Her research interests include heritage representation and commodification, museum studies, rural tourism and wellness tourism.

Sinéad Kelly is Temporary Lecturer in the Department of Geography at the National University of Ireland, Maynooth and is currently writing up her doctoral research on urban governance in Dublin with the Department of Geography, Trinity College, Dublin. She is Co-Director of the Forum for Irish Urban Studies and Co-Editor of the working paper series, 'Progress in Irish Urban Studies'.

James Killen is Senior Lecturer in the Department of Geography at Trinity College, Dublin. He has published extensively on transport matters relating to Ireland and is also the author of the textbook *Mathematical Programming Methods for Geographers and Planners* (Croom Helm, 1983).

Rob Kitchin is Director of the National Institute of Regional and Spatial Analysis (NIRSA) at the National University of Ireland, Maynooth and a founding member of the International Centre for Local and Regional Development. He is managing editor of the journal *Social and Cultural Geography*, co-editor-in-chief of the forthcoming *International Encyclopedia of Human Geography*, and has published twelve other books to date.

Joe Larragy lectures in Social Policy at the National University of Ireland, Maynooth. Previous to that he was research officer at University College Dublin and the National Council on Ageing and Older People, social policy analyst at the National Economic and Social Council, and Newman Scholar in the Non-Profit Sector, University College, Dublin. His research interests focus on ageing, social policy, civil society and social partnership in Ireland.

Denis Linehan is a social and cultural geographer at University College Cork. He has a broad interest in areas concerned with the contemporary and historical conditions of urban life. He is the editor of the *Atlas of Cork City* and author of numerous essays in international journals.

Piaras Mac Éinrí was Director from 1997 to 2003 of the interdisciplinary Irish Centre for Migration Studies at University College Cork and is presently employed as Lecturer in the Geography Department. He is an advisor to the Immigrant Council of Ireland, was a member from 2003 to 2005 of the National Consultative Committee on Racism and Interculturalism, and is a Visiting Professor at the Institute for the Study of European Transformations, London Metropolitan University.

Andrew MacLaran is Senior Lecturer in Geography and Director of the Centre for Urban and Regional Studies, Trinity College, Dublin. Research interests include the social consequences of urban economic restructuring, urban housing, entrepreneurial urban planning and the impact on inner-city communities of commercial property development. He is editor of the *Journal of Irish Urban Studies*.

Des McCafferty is Senior Lecturer and Head of the Department of Geography at Mary Immaculate College, University of Limerick, and an associate of the National Institute for Regional and Spatial Analysis (NIRSA). His research interests and published work are in the areas of urban and regional development in Ireland, and social exclusion in urban areas.

John McDonagh is Lecturer in the Geography Department at the National University of Ireland, Galway. His main research interests are in rural geography and sustainable environments. He has published a number of articles in national and international journals and two books, *Renegotiating Rural Development in Ireland* (Ashgate, 2001) and *Economy, Society and Peripherality* (Arlen House, 2002).

Michael J. Murray is a Post-doctoral Research Fellow at the National Institute of Regional and Spatial Analysis (NIRSA), and part-time Lecturer in the Department of Sociology at the National University of Ireland, Maynooth. His research interests focus on multilevel governance, social partnership, community-based protest in the age of globalisation, and the sociology of the environment.

Michael R. Murray is Reader in Rural Spatial Planning at the Institute of Spatial and Environmental Planning, Queen's University, Belfast. His research interests include community-led rural development and multilevel strategic planning, on which he has published widely.

Brendan Murtagh is Reader in the School of Spatial Planning, Architecture and Civil Engineering (SPACE) at Queen's University, Belfast. He has researched and written widely on urban policy and ethnic segregation in Northern Ireland.

Dennis Pringle is Senior Lecturer in Geography and an Associate of the National Institute for Regional and Spatial Analysis (NIRSA) and the National Centre for Geocomputation (NCG). He has research interests and publications in medical geography, political geography and selected methodological issues.

Chris van Egeraat is Research Fellow (Irish Research Council for the Humanities and Social Sciences) at the National Institute of Regional and Spatial Analysis (NIRSA). His research and publications are concentrated in the areas of the geography of enterprise and regional development.

Jim Walsh is Vice-President for Innovation and Strategic Initiatives at the National University of Ireland, Maynooth where he was Head of the Department of Geography between 1995 and 2005. A founding member of the National Institute for Regional and Spatial Analysis (NIRSA), and the International Centre for Local and Regional Development (ICLRD), he has published extensively on topics related to regional and rural development and spatial planning in Ireland.

Index